Sanctuary Of The Gods

by Nathan Cate

Printed in Victoria, Canada

Canadian Cataloguing in Publication Data

Cate, Nathan
   Sanctuary of the gods

   Includes index.
   ISBN 1-55212-447-9

   I. Title.
PS8555.A82S36 2000   C813'.6   C00-910966-8
PR9199.3.C434S36 2000

TRAFFORD

This book was published *on-demand* in cooperation with Trafford Publishing.
On-demand publishing is a unique process and service of making a book available for retail sale to the public taking advantage of on-demand manufacturing and Internet marketing. **On-demand publishing** includes promotions, retail sales, manufacturing, order fulfilment, accounting and collecting royalties on behalf of the author.

Suite 6E, 2333 Government St., Victoria, B.C. V8T 4P4, CANADA
Phone   250-383-6864   Toll-free   1-888-232-4444 (Canada & US)
Fax   250-383-6804   E-mail   sales@trafford.com
Web site   www.trafford.com   TRAFFORD PUBLISHING IS A DIVISION OF TRAFFORD HOLDINGS LTD.
Trafford Catalogue #00-0112   www.trafford.com/robots/00-0112.html

10   9   8   7   6   5   4   3   2

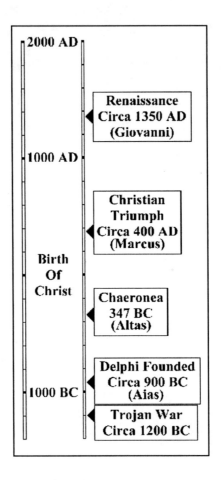

2000 AD

Renaissance
Circa 1350 AD
(Giovanni)

1000 AD

Christian
Triumph
Circa 400 AD
(Marcus)

Birth
Of
Christ

Chaeronea
347 BC
(Altas)

Delphi Founded
Circa 900 BC
(Aias)

1000 BC

Trojan War
Circa 1200 BC

Timeline For *Sanctuary of the Gods*

Sanctuary Of The Gods

Table of Contents

ix centuries ago a mystery was created. Priceless antiquities and ancient books were buried by their guardians in a cave beneath a mountain. At the same time a map describing the location of the cave and a set of clues laying bare the hidden roots of Western Civilization were cleverly encoded in a set of apparently crude illustrations, and spread across the face of Europe—later the world—by people who knew little of the role they played.

The guardian's intention was as simple as it was extraordinary: to lay the foundations of a vigorous new age—our own.

THE FLAME: HOW GIOVANNI FOUND SANCTUARY

(Lombardy and The Taro River Valley 1308 AD)

In a brilliant patch of sunlight beside an ancient oak, a young man lay on a spread-out cloak, head up, leaning on one arm. Beside him lay a crossbow, its wood weathered but well oiled, cocked and bearing a dart. The young man blew into the loosely clenched fist of his free hand, shook it several times, and let fall a pair of dice onto the roughly-woven wool. Frowning a little against the dazzle of the sunlight, he leaned forward to see how the little carved cubes had come to rest: a three and four. Straightening, his lips tightening in a wan smile, he picked up the dice and touched them briefly to the dart's iron head. "Good luck," he said under his breath. Then he awkwardly loosed the drawstrings of the coin purse on his belt with one hand and let the dice fall inside. Taking hold of the purse, he yanked it to tighten the strings around its neck and let his head fall until it rested against the crook of his arm, releasing a pent up sigh as he did so.

Though he seemed relaxed where he lay he did not close his eyes: they remained fixed on a short stretch of the road where it passed sixty or seventy paces away. A fly flew up erratically, buzzed noisily around his head several times and landed on the crossbow. It rested there a moment to wipe its antennae before flying off.

The young man's dark hair was uncombed and greasy, and cut short in the soldier's style to fit comfortably in a helmet that was nowhere to be seen. He was clean-shaven with a pale but handsome face; his chin dimpled, his blue eyes bright under a prominent brow. He was about twenty, or seemed so from a distance, but from close up the lines between his brows and around his eyes suggested too much time spent in the sun.

His soldier's tunic was tired-looking and unremarkable. His stockings were of brightly dyed wool, red, but they too carried the marks and stains of long use. They had been crudely patched many times along their length, particularly near the bottoms where they disappeared into rough-stitched leather shoes, the latter still carrying a little fresh mud from beside the brook and wet across their uppers from the dew.

Some minutes went by. From time to time a bird called out, its voice pure above the bubbling waters of the brook, or a squirrel passed, darting up the trunk of a nearby tree, leaping from branch to branch before scurrying higher up, out of sight behind the new leaves. The young man gave no sign that he noticed.

Away to the North where the road disappeared from sight a horse whinnied. Startled, the young man craned towards the sound, reaching for his bow as he did so. He stood up intently, stiffly, the weapon cradled on one arm while he listened.

There was a moment of silence. Then in the distance a man shouted something, his voice coming hollow through the trees. The young man hurriedly stooped and picked up his cloak with one hand, pushing his head through the neck-hole, and threw the bulky material back out of the way behind his shoulders. Two spare bolts were lying where they had been partially covered by the cloak, and he picked these up and tucked one of them into his belt. The sounds of many horses and men were clearly distinguishable now, just out of sight behind the trees. He hurried towards a low bush that stood between him and the road, crouching down on one knee behind it. He barely paused to jam the spare bolt into the ground beside him before setting the bow's stock up against his shoulder ready to fire.

The first to come were eleven mounted soldiers of the guard, reining in their horses to maintain a measured pace. Behind them were foot soldiers. Finally came a little group of dignitaries, among them a silver haired old man speaking quietly to the man who rode beside him, their two heads leaned close to catch one another's words.

At the sight of the gray head the young man stiffened, adjusted his aim, and after taking a deep breath and beginning its slow and measured release, loosed the first shaft.

With a shock the bolt left the bow, dipping and rising a little as it passed through the intervening air pockets before passing just in front of the startled face of the old man.

The instant he knew the shot would miss, the young man jumped up cursing, dropped the front of the bow to the ground between his feet, stepped on the braces, and heaved up the chord to set it in place before feverishly placing the spare bolt in place. He raised the bow to his shoulder and dropped back down to steady his aim, only to discover that his target had already dismounted and hidden himself from sight. Chaos was breaking out among the bodyguard, and several horses reared violently back, threatening to unseat their riders.

He began to back quickly away, towards the thick brambles that lay at the top of the incline, but not before one of the armed escort saw him and let out the alarm: "Over there! ...Jesus—it's Giovanni!"

Cover broken, the young man turned and fled up the rise, disappearing through a crawl hole in a wall of brambles even as several bowmen loosed shots hurriedly after him. The fresh-cut hole ran through the thorn bushes, ending abruptly at a clearing. Bleeding a little from countless scratches where the thorns had ripped at him, he emerged and ran across the grass, through the trees on the far side to where a horse stood saddled and ready.

Freeing the tether with a jerk, he jumped into the saddle with such force that he almost continued over it and had to fight for a moment to regain his balance. With one hand on the reins the other on his bow he dug hard with his heels even before his feet had found the stirrups. With a sudden rush, the horse set off among the trees heading south and it was all the young man could do to find the stirrups and hang on as low-lying branches whipped at him and the horse plunged and surged, traversing the rough terrain.

ithin ten minutes, Giovanni slowed the horse's pace a little and curved back to rejoin the road, relieved to find it empty. Free of the trees and brush, he pressed his horse forward at a steady canter, resisting the temptation to surrender to haste: he knew they would already be after him, but there was no sense in tiring his horse prematurely.

Mentally preparing himself for a long struggle, he rode on, feeling his mind near the breaking point. It was too late for regrets, but even so he found himself wondering what had made him think this mad scheme would succeed. Images came to him in a feverish flood as he rode, and time lost its measure so that the world moved past barely noticed.

Once, perhaps an hour into his escape, when he was looking back over his shoulder for signs of pursuit, a motion in the corner of his eye caught his attention. It was a breeze gently swaying the sunlit leaves by the roadway. It seemed so peaceful, so unrelated to recent events, that he almost surrendered to the temptation to stop and dismount. For a moment he was persuaded that he could, even now, call off the whole thing. Peace was all around him, and all he had to do was dismount and rest for it to dispel his anguish. But then his fear suddenly swelled and the reality of the situation grew clear again in his mind: he would be lucky to survive. Most terrible of all was the knowledge that he had failed, that nothing had been achieved. When, from time to time, that thought would come to him, its reality fresh and blunt, he fought hard to prevent himself from sobbing. Months of preparation and the bastard was still alive...

As the sun reached higher in the sky and then began its slow decline Giovanni rode on. Several times he took turnings in the road to throw off his pursuers until he found himself heading southwards among the foothills, into the mountains. As the hours passed his horse became exhausted from the relentless pace and he began to wonder if it would fall or go lame. He thought of slowing and almost did until, passing along the side of a steep hill, he looked back and saw his pursuers: five men on sturdy horses moving fast. Even at this distance, he could recognize a few of them from their riding styles. He realized with a shock they were barely twenty minutes behind him, and it was all he could do to prevent himself from breaking into a full gallop.

In mid-afternoon he came across a well rested, strong looking mare tethered by the road and took it, leaving his own in its place. To his relief there was no sign of the owner. Indeed, he saw few people after leaving the main road, and thankfully those were always at a distance. He rode on.

Night found him in a gently sloped mountain valley, climbing steadily, no sign of his pursuers, though for all he knew they might be close. He was hungry and tired, but fear prickled in him at the mere thought of stopping to rest. If he could put enough ground behind him before sunup, there would be little chance they would ever track him. He could hide in the mountains and plan his next move.

Well after dark, as he was crossing a knee-deep, swift-moving mountain stream, the mare stumbled and lost her footing. Somehow in the fall Giovanni's bow went missing and he spent several minutes thrashing about in the dimness of the stars' light in an unsuccessful attempt to locate it. When he realized it was hopeless, he turned his attention to the horse. As he approached her, he sensed something was wrong. He felt along her flanks, talking softly to her as he did so, and discovered she was favoring one leg. He had ridden as far as he could. From now on he would have to carry on by foot.

Cursing, Giovanni half led, half pulled the horse at a stumbling run towards a low ridge in the East, fighting through the blackness of the undergrowth and up the gentle incline. When he got there, he slapped the animal hard and listened as it crashed through the bushes, disappearing down the other side. With luck they wouldn't find it until well into the following day and by then his trail would be cold.

Giovanni made his way Westward, navigating by the stars and later by the moon when it rose. Few people lived in these parts and he saw no one. Throughout the long night he moved swiftly, never resting. A hundred times he heard low voices, the clink of armor, the sounds of horses moving fast behind him. He knew these things were only in his mind, but each time he heard them he shrank against a nearby bush or tree, unable to breath, straining to hear. It occurred to him that by the morning half the world might be looking for him: that really there was nowhere to hide. He put the thought aside.

hen Giovanni first entered the sleeping valley, no one saw him coming as he crossed the mountain from the south. A shadow in the twilight, he slipped past an abandoned farmhouse on the mountain's ridge at dawn, skirting the trees beside a woodsman's hut so silently that the owner's dog never woke from its fitful sleep, never tried with its barking to raise the alarm. As he climbed higher, clouds began to pile up on the mountain's top concealing the fading stars and the moon, hiding his advance from watchful eyes. Like a mist himself, he crept through the cold forest without a sound.

Crossing the ridge he came by sunrise to a small stream on the gentle incline north of the peak. After looking about for a moment, he walked back a little, the way he had come, and with the splashing brook out of earshot, listened carefully for the sounds of stealthy feet following his own out of the fog. This time he heard nothing but the songs of the waking birds. The minutes passed him where he waited, leaning against a tree, scarcely breathing. He knew it was unlikely his pursuers could be close, but he could not bring himself to trust in chance.

When at last he was satisfied Giovanni walked back to the stream, crossing it without stopping and moved on to explore the ground on the far side. The trees were old, and not a whisper of a breeze disturbed their leaves as the young man walked warily among them, stopping here and there to watch and listen. Beneath his feet the leaf-mold was thick and dark, the leaves of the previous fall already disintegrating into the cool damp soil. It was only after several minutes of careful investigation that he returned to the brook and lowering himself on his belly drank thirstily from its clear waters.

He did not remain there long: as soon as his thirst was slaked he moved away a little from the noise of the water, and unslinging his cloak from across his shoulder, wrapped it around himself. Stooping, he backed into the partial shelter of a small bush and settled himself there, pinching both ends of the woolen cloth together under his chin for warmth. Though spring was well advanced, up on the mountain tops the nights were still cold. For a time his eyes were watchful, moving in the direction of every sound, but at last they fell shut. A few minutes later he stirred briefly to settle himself more comfortably, and curling up under the bush, he slept.

he sun rose above the mountain tops, at first brightening the mist to a blinding white, and then burning it off by mid-morning, but the warm light never reached Giovanni under his bush, beneath the giant trees of that place. In time, the day grew hot and flies began to buzz about him, and in his sleep he responded, closing the cloak more about his face to keep them off. Throughout the long day there was no sign of men, not his pursuers, not people from those parts. He dreamed he saw his enemies giving up the chase and hurrying back to rejoin their column far away, to the northeast.

It was late afternoon by the time Giovanni at last awoke, stiffly rising and relieving himself against a tree. The events of the day before were already dim in his mind, softened in the warmth and silence that surrounded him now. Though still exhausted he resolved to go on, hoping to be off the mountain before nightfall, promising himself a full night's sleep once he was down. On unsteady feet he pushed back his cloak and set out northward again.

For a time he followed the stream, but when the ground grew too steep and tumbled, he veered to his left and began to follow a secondary ridge line downwards. Beneath his feet the stones were crumbled into angular pebbles: the whole mountain seemed to be made of crumbling rock and it was treacherous to walk on. At one point where the ridge became steeper, the trees fell away and the view opened up to reveal a small valley below him, here and there a farmer's field nestled along its base. To the Northwest the valley emptied into a larger basin, and he could see the mountains on the far side of that great span, perhaps a day's walk in the distance, pale blue in the afternoon haze. Here was a place that knew little of the world. Despite his predicament, ridiculously, he felt like singing.

He moved down the ridge cautiously until it grew less steep and the trees again covered him. Barely forty paces farther on Giovanni froze and then dropped to the ground, fear prickling the skin of his face and hands.

Not far off a thin file of men was making its way up towards him. Ready to run, he peered over a low jumble of stone and shrubs he had slid behind and studied the climbers. They did not seem to know he was there, since their energies were entirely devoted to picking their way up the ridge-line. That was the first thing he noticed. The second was very odd: every one of the figures carried a burning torch despite the warm sunshine that fell about them.

It occurred to him that perhaps he ought not to be afraid of them, that they would be no threat: surely no-one in this God forsaken place could have heard news of the assassination attempt yet. But he held back, reluctant to trust when his life was at stake, restrained by the recently acquired habit of fear. It looked as if the matter would be out of his hands soon since the men were nearly upon him.

He was just preparing to stand up and show himself, not wanting to be caught cowering when they first encountered him, but the leader of the group turned sharply and disappeared from sight, apparently following an unseen trail. Each of those behind followed in turn, until at last the ridge was empty before him. The only sound was a soft breeze stirring the leaves in the sunlight above his head.

Though he could not see it from his position, there must be some sort of a path cutting into the steep terrain of the gully that lay beside the ridge below where he hid. What were they doing? He wondered if this was some sort of local ritual of the church: he knew of no festival on this day, but then local festivals and rituals were ubiquitous throughout the towns and settlements of Europe.

Giovanni watched for a minute, and then began to pick his way cautiously downwards. He hurried, wanting to get past them lest they return and block his decent, for now that he had the opportunity to pass without being seen, he did not want to waste it. Why risk showing himself when there was no need?

When he reached the point where the men had disappeared he saw the narrow trail they had followed, sloping slightly upwards through the trees that clung to the steep terrain. He passed it and was going to continue down the mountain, but then he stopped and looked back, listening. There was no sound. It seemed as though the men had disappeared altogether. Standing there in the silent afternoon sun, he even toyed with the idea he had imagined them.

After a few moments standing quietly, he retraced his steps and entered the trail, his curiosity taking control. What were they doing? And what were the torches for? He would try to avoid being seen, but if they saw him it would not matter. After all, they would likely have food and water to offer, or directions down into the valley for a needy stranger. It seemed very unlikely they would have heard of him yet. Anyway, the truth of it was that he longed for human company even if it meant a slight element of risk. Never had he felt so lonely as the events of the past day had made him.

The trail passed through the trees and across a steep section where no plants could gain a foothold. Ten or twenty steps farther, it rounded a line of shrubs and he picked his way along it, attention focused on the cliffs he could barely make out through the foliage below. A rock he dislodged tumbled for a moment and then, out of sight, suddenly fell in silence for several seconds before he heard its impact far beneath.

When Giovanni arrived at the mouth of the cave he almost fell into it, stumbling onto the first step leading down into the darkness below. There was no one in sight as he came to a stop in astonishment, resting a hand against a low tree to steady himself. He hadn't seen the cave because the opening was small and lay around a sharp turn in the line of the cliff it lay beneath. It opened downwards, rather than straight into the rock. He could see at once that it was manmade or at least modified by the hands of men: heavy, well shaped stones framed its entrance and had been laid down to provide steps that disappeared from sight into the darkness below. The cave explained the torches, but what was a cave doing here? It might be some shrine to a saint, a hermit, perhaps, who had spent his life here in solitary contemplation of God. Now and then a faint wisp of torch-smoke curled out of the doorway, but no sound came from within.

Quietly Giovanni stepped down the steep flight of stairs, his shoulders brushing the stones of the narrow passage as he descended. Near the entrance, in a small alcove in the rock, there was a burning lamp surrounded by other unlit lamps. He considered taking one, but decided against it since he didn't really intend to stay and he wasn't sure he ought to impose on their hospitality by doing so. He was acutely conscious that he did not belong there, so aside from a brief glimpse he did not intend to investigate further.

Eight or nine steps down, the stairs ended on a flat expanse of flagstones. He stood a moment waiting for his eyes to adjust, and almost at once he made out a dim human-like shape to his left. He flinched away in surprise, but it was not moving, so it did not bring him more than a momentary flicker of anxiety. He realized it was a life sized statue. He stepped towards it, aware that the walls on either side had moved outwards somewhat from the entranceway: he was in a chamber some eight paces wide and twice again as long, with walls and vaulted ceilings lined with stone, a necessity, probably, given the unstable rock of the mountain.

The statue was cold to the touch, metallic, perhaps bronze. It was a male in the ancient style, with a cloth thrown over one shoulder and draped about the figure. Something in the way it stood with head slightly bowed in the quiet chamber made it seem unnaturally serene. When his sight grew stronger he realized the eyes had been inlaid with some lighter material and the entire piece had been painted to make it more life-like.

As he stood back and looked around, Giovanni saw there were at least a dozen statues in the chamber, presumably saints, most set back in small alcoves lining the walls. All were astonishingly lifelike, and all seemed to share in the striking serenity of the first. There were a number of females among them. Opposite the entrance stood another doorway and from the steep decline of the ceiling beyond, he realized that it must lead to another flight of stairs going farther down into the heart of the mountain. It was too dark to venture deeper without a lamp.

Giovanni considered calling down the stairway to bring attention to himself but decided against it, since to do so might disturb the prayers undoubtedly being made somewhere below. Not wishing to start with a bad impression, he decided to wait quietly outside for the worshippers to finish: he would join them as they made their way back down the mountain. He returned to the entrance and climbed the stairway, squinting against the bright light outside.

When he had climbed high enough for his shoulders to clear ground level, something on the right caught his eye. He turned to look and in a blur saw a man moving swiftly up to him, even as a stout walking stick crashed down across the top of his head. It happened so quickly he had no time to do anything more than gasp. There was an explosion of light and he winced, legs buckling. The world vanished.

Giovanni opened his eyes to find a thatched roof above his head and light flowing in through a stone doorway to one side. His head ached. There was no door, and he could see trees beyond the entrance, framing a pale blue sky, and hear wind rustling the leaves. The walls were unworked gray stone, and the room was not large, eight paces by five at most, with little to attract his attention: it was a typical rustic building. He'd seen its type many times before. But what was he doing there?

He felt very uncomfortable and stiff. There was a lump beneath his lower back and he tried to rearrange himself, guessing dully that he must be lying on a straw mattress. But the attempt failed, the lump being too big, so he gave up trying.

Slowly swinging his feet over the edge, pushing himself upright, he winced at his throbbing head. He noticed for the first time a heavy chain running from his left ankle up to a sturdy beam that bisected the hut. The beam was high enough that a man might just be able to reach its upper edge with his fingers if he stood directly below. Confused, stretching his hand down to where the chain was fastened to his ankle, he fumbled with the heavy chinks for a moment, his fingers picking up a thin layer of dirty grease obviously intended to stop the chain from rusting. After a moment he realized the chain had been attached by a blacksmith: it had been wrapped tightly around his leg and fastened back to itself by a new link still shiny from the forge. His eyes followed the chain upwards to its source. The beam was heavy, and he could see from faint discolorations on the crudely fitted stones of the walls that it had once provided support to a wall that had divided up the interior space.

In the distance he thought he heard the sounds of children at play. Their shouts were almost lost behind the sighing of a breeze as it pushed past the leaves of the trees somewhere just outside. The voices seemed out of place. He struggled for a moment but could find no memory that made sense of his circumstances. The effort tired him so he laid back and sprawled across the mattress, without lifting his feet from the floor.

He was just going to shut his eyes when he heard footsteps in the dirt outside, so he lifted his head and shoulders instead, supporting his weight on his elbows. A boy of six or seven years appeared at the door. Apparently in surprise, the child raised his eyebrows before disappearing wordlessly, running. With a sigh Giovanni settled back and closed his eyes.

He must have slept, for when he opened his lids again it was to find the face of a man in his middle years peering at him closely. It was a peasant's face, rough with the labor of a lifetime in the fields: friendly enough, though not smiling at the moment.

"Are you all right?" the man asked politely, but not with the sort of deference Giovanni was used to receiving from peasants. Giovanni didn't answer. He was too busy recalling the events that had brought him here, events that were at last flooding his mind with images: the attempted killing, the nightmare flight, the decent into the valley, and vaguely, something to do with a cave and a religious festival. He was aware of the chain uncomfortably gripping his ankle and how it rose behind his questioner, stretching from the floor up to the beam. He felt a prickling of danger and sat up, though he tried to maintain the appearance of composure. He could think of nothing to say.

The man waited patiently for Giovanni's reply until it was clear there would be none. His manner grew a little more tense, a little more aggressive. "What were you doing in the cave?"

Giovanni wondered that himself, but he made no sign he had heard the question.

"Were you alone?" Again no reply, and now the man became noticeably angry. "How did you manage to get by the woodsman at the southern pass without being seen? Look, you had better tell me. We know all about you anyway."

Giovanni's wits cleared enough for him to settle on a story. When he spoke, he made himself sound indignant. "I don't know what you're talking about. I was hunting on the mountain and was hoping to find lodging for the night. Take this chain off me," and here he kicked his leg angrily for effect, "or you will have more trouble than you could have dreamed possible."

The man was unimpressed by Giovanni's act. "If you want to play games, that is all right with us, but you should know that it won't help you. You have threatened us all by what you've done, and no matter what lies you invent they will not set you free." At this he turned and left.

Giovanni let himself fall back wearily and lay there looking up at the ceiling, putting things together in his mind. They must be fairly certain of who he was—perhaps his pursuers had already passed through the village looking for him. They couldn't still be here or he'd be dead or on the road back to Milan by now. The villagers must be intending to hold him until they could send for someone to take him off their hands. It looked like he would be dead soon, by torture most likely, and for nothing: he had failed. He wasn't afraid, just very tired and sore. Lying back on the bed, he closed his eyes again and slept.

When he woke a young woman of about his age was just entering the hut carrying bread and a clay jug. She looked at him curiously as she approached, and when she stopped at the foot of the bed she seemed to forget her purpose for a moment. Her eyes peered at him from under a tangled mat of greasy hair, her face mottled by soot and dirt, yet the grime could not conceal the freshness of her youth. She wore a sleeveless top and skirt of un-dyed wool, long since permeated and encrusted with the substances she encountered most in daily life: animal dung, dirt and food. The garments were too coarse to give more than a hint of the body beneath and Giovanni wondered vaguely whether she was fat or thin. It seemed impossible to tell. Though her hands were dirty and her fingernails torn back to where they met the skin and sometimes beyond, the fingers themselves were long and finely shaped, sensitive. Her undisguised curiosity continued, and he became annoyed.

Seeing his reaction, she became embarrassed, and looking down she noticed the jug and loaf in her hands. She held them out towards him. "I brought you something to eat. It's not much, but for something hot you will have to wait until dinner time." Her voice was gentle.

Giovanni made no attempt to take the offered food, so she placed the bread on the bed and walking around the side she put the jug on the floor where he could easily reach it. Her movements were graceful, and he suddenly felt like touching her shoulder with his hand as she bent over beside him. It was a strange impulse, and he wondered about it. For some reason he felt as if she were a friend. Perhaps it was because of the kindliness of her tone. He realized that his vulnerability and the loneliness of his position must be affecting his judgment: he had better be careful.

Moving as if to go, the girl turned suddenly and said "The counsel is meeting this afternoon to discuss you. Don't be afraid: we are good people here, no matter what you might think, and they will be merciful. We don't want to hurt you. That's our problem, because we must protect our religion from danger, and what you've done has threatened it. I and the others will pray for you." She looked at him, her eyes pleading for his understanding, but he was determined not to let her off so easily.

"Do you really think I care what your squalid little village's counsel decides? You are nothing: peasants. The church will govern my fate, not you. I am not afraid of you! Now go and leave me in peace." He laid back and closed his eyes. After a moment he heard her leave, but he was already falling back into sleep.

When Giovanni awoke again it was after dark. There was almost no light coming in the doorway and he could see little. He lay there thinking about his predicament and trying to prepare himself to die in an honorable way. One way or another it would likely happen soon. The idea was one thing, but reality kept intruding on the idea, and the truth was that he was afraid. Every time he forced the fear from his mind by overwhelming it with brave thoughts, it would suddenly come back again fresh and raw and powerful. It seemed there was no lasting escape. But he kept wrestling with the problem, because although his attitude would make no difference to his fate, it would at least allow him to defy his enemies until the end. He didn't want to give them any more satisfaction from his death than he had to. The honor of his family was at stake, and he did not take that responsibility lightly.

Outside he heard footsteps approaching, a lot of them, and hushed voices. Dim, flickering light came through the doorway and grew brighter. A figure entered, holding a lamp. Then another and another, until it seemed the hut was full of twinkling flames, the faces above them yellowed by their light. They were men and women of advancing years, perhaps the town's counsel. They stood in silence for a moment, regarding him somberly, and Giovanni was relieved to see that they carried no weapons: at least he was not to die at this minute. He sat up and watched them without speaking. At last one of them spoke. It was the same man who had visited him earlier, presumably the counsel's leader, and now his voice was sad, regretful.

"We have considered the matter very carefully and decided that we have no choice. Something like this happened once before, and the decision of our ancestors was wise: we have decided that we should do as they did. Please try to understand that we hate the present circumstances and wish you had never come here. But you did come, and our wishes are not important. Necessity guides us." The man's voice grew more authoritative, impersonal.

"It is the decision of this counsel that you shall be blinded, then hamstrung in one leg to prevent your escape. This is done without satisfaction and is not meant as punishment: we do it with regret."

Giovanni was stunned. Death he expected, and torture was also probable. But it had never occurred to him the peasants would maim him first, so that for what remained of his life he would be a helpless cripple. He had been trying to imagine himself staring down his killers fearlessly, willing the memory of his death to haunt them until their own. The image that came to him was sickening. Now his sightless eyes would stare blankly, and they would cut him down like a dog, feeling nothing for the empty shell of a man who cringed before them. It made him furious to see these ignorant villagers standing around him, so fearful of the Church's power that to protect themselves from an unlikely eventuality they had rendered judgment of their own. It was with steely defiance he heard his voice speak.

"Blinded and hamstrung... Why not hamstring both legs? Why not take my hands too, so that I cannot hold a weapon or pull myself along the ground to escape? Do I frighten you so much? You speak of regret, almost begging my forgiveness. Do you not regret that cowardice you display at the possibility of my escape?" The elders looked at one another in confusion and dismay at his words. Again their leader spoke.

"We understand your anger at our decision, but surely you can see it could be worse. Our fear is sensible and our actions just. We have no choice besides this or killing you, which we do not want to do. If our plan seems too onerous, we will not prevent you from taking your own life, but you should think hard before you decide something like that: life is precious, and with some adjustment it can be enjoyed no matter what your situation is."

To Giovanni their attitude seemed absurd. Their eccentric wish that he accept their harsh decision, sympathizing with their petty fears was laughable. He realized there was no point in discussing the matter, and his thoughts turned to the question of whether he had seen his last of this world, of whether they would blind him that very night. "When do you good people intend to cripple me?" he asked, acidic sarcasm only thinly covering his anxiety. He dearly wished to see even one more sunrise before the sun would set for ever. And he feared the pain of what they would do.

"The decision will be carried out in twenty-two days, at the new moon," said the leader.

Again Giovanni was shocked, this time more pleasantly. He had assumed that at most he would have a day or two before his pursuers were summoned to kill him or take him away. More than three weeks before they maimed him: that meant they didn't expect the church's representatives for even longer! Just how isolated was this place? Suddenly escape did become a possibility after all. What were they thinking—these inbred, country fools!

Seeing the confusion on Giovanni's face and guessing at its cause, the leader spoke again. "This delay is necessary for reasons you don't yet understand. Make good use of it, with our blessing. Your chain is long enough for you to sit outside and enjoy the days of vision that remain to you. We will go now, and let you sleep. I'll leave this lamp for you, and if you wish you can burn it all night so that you can avoid darkness for the present." He paused, and went on. "I know it seems hard for you, but it is our sincere wish that you feel at home here. In the days ahead, try to see yourself as one of us, for although we cannot help harming you, that is how we see you."

Giovanni watched them file out, the leader stooping to set his lamp beside the doorway as he left. The depth of their stupidity, their naiveté was incredible. They were apparently so isolated that they didn't see him as a human being like themselves, or they had so little imagination that they couldn't put themselves in his shoes. They seemed to want him to see them as hosts, and himself as a guest in spite of everything. Of all the ignorant people in the world, these must be among the most ignorant. But he shouldn't let it bother him: after all, for reasons only a bumpkin could comprehend they had given him twenty-two days to free himself. If he kept a cool head and moved cautiously, that was more than enough time to find some way to get out of here.

When he was sure they were well away, he got up and took hold of the chain where it dangled from the roof beam, shaking it. It traveled loosely along the beam. The beam was old and blackened by smoke. It was one and a half hands deep and three-quarters of a hand wide: if he cut through the beam he could slip the chain through the gap. The length of chain was heavy, but not too heavy for him to gather it up and take it with him. Once he was free of the town he could find a way to break it open. As for the beam, it could probably be easily severed in two weeks if he could find a suitable tool. He just hoped the villagers were right that he had several weeks in which to act. They seemed befuddled enough to be wrong about that as well, but there was no use worrying about it.

Giovanni wanted to begin immediately, but he forced himself to be patient. He didn't know how close the other villagers lived to his hut, so he couldn't judge what they might hear of his work. It would be better to wait until he checked his situation properly in daylight. Besides, finding a tool by lamplight would not be practical, and he had to consider how to conceal the cut in the beam. It would be better to sleep tonight, and worry about things tomorrow. His head still hurt and he was exhausted, so the thought appealed to him. He returned to the bed, lay down and closed his eyes. For a time his thoughts turned to escape, but after a while he slept.

It was just after dawn when the girl returned with bread and a bowl of stew. "This is from last night. You were asleep so we saved it." He took it and began to eat immediately for he was ravenous. He had only had water since he'd arrived. "Would you like to sit outside?" she asked. "It is going to be a beautiful day." He nodded and taking up his breakfast and the jug of water he followed her outside, the chain clinking as it snaked along behind him. There was enough free play in the chain that he could move five paces beyond the door. They sat leaning against the wall of his hut an arm's length apart and he continued to eat. The stew was delicious.

For a time there was silence between them while the birds sang greetings to each other after the long night, and a few light clouds high above them were touched by the pale light of the rising sun. His hut was on the outskirts of a village, forty paces from its nearest neighbor and half hidden behind a screen of trees, so if Giovanni was careful he would be free to make a little noise while he worked on the beam, without raising attention. The girl watched him while he wiped his bowl with a piece of bread, and when he had cleaned it thoroughly and set it down, she smiled. "My name is Giulia" she said.

"I'm Giovanni." In the circumstances it made no sense to be hostile. He wondered if she was sitting there because she wanted to for her own sake, or whether she had been ordered to keep an eye on him.

"I'm sorry about...what the counsel decided," she said, looking away. "The elders have a great responsibility, and I know they are also troubled by it. If you hate us for it, I wouldn't blame you."

"I don't hate you for it." That was true. He despised them for their stupidity, but hatred was another matter. In fact, the events of the past few days seemed to have cured him of all hatred. He just wanted to get out of this town, out of Italy in one piece. The hatred that had consumed him for months no longer seemed worth the effort.

Giulia spoke, interrupting his thoughts. "The elders asked me to answer any questions you might have. Nothing will be concealed from you once you have become one of us."

Giovanni was astonished. "Become one of you? What do you mean?"

"Well, you may be blinded, but you will be one of our town and that means there will be no secrets from you. You will be an equal member of the community until you die."

"I'm sorry...Giulia...but I don't understand. When will I be handed over to the church?"

"Never. Of course never. You will never leave this valley again, you can't be allowed to. Our survival depends on it. I'm sorry."

Giovanni was stunned, and he gazed at her blankly for a moment. "What do you mean I will never leave? What does my leaving have to do with your survival?"

She looked at him long and hard, her eyes questioning him, looking into his own, studying him. She too appeared puzzled. "You don't know?" she asked. He shook his head and shrugged, bewildered at what she was getting at. She frowned. "How much did you see up on the mountain?"

"You mean when I came? I saw the cave, and the statues of the saints just inside. That's all. Oh, and the religious procession into the cave. Why?"

"You saw too much. Even if that is really all you know, it is far too much. That is why the elders have acted. If you happened to tell others of what you have seen, everything could be lost."

So like him, this village also had something to hide from the outside world. But what was it? At last Giovanni was beginning to make sense out of the peculiar attitude of the elders yesterday, and of Giulia today. What he had naturally mistaken for stupidity was really evidence of a deeper current behind what had happened. He made a guess. "You're Cathars aren't you? Albighensians." That had to be it. "It's the reason you chained me. You are afraid I will go to the church and tell them about you and they will slaughter you as they slaughtered the others in the South of France a Century ago. My God, this is irony! Believe me, you can trust me with your secret: I have nothing against your people." He was making some rapid calculations. "So you haven't heard about me, have you? You don't know who I am...?"

"Giovanni," said Giulia unsteadily. "We are not Cathars, and we have not been hiding from the Church for a century. It has been nine hundred years..."

"But that was...before the Roman empire fell apart. Nine hundred years? In this little valley? That's absurd. Who are you?"

"The Church has told lies about us, that we are evil and serve Satan. We are not as they say: we are good people trying to do something good for humanity. You shouldn't be afraid of us."

"I'm not afraid... But your religion is nine hundred years old? That's difficult to believe."

"Our religion is more than nine hundred years old: it is as old as the earth. We've only been hiding for the last nine hundred years."

"Only nine hundred!" He chuckled, then it came to him and he looked at her. "So you are Pagans. Is that it?" She nodded. "But why did you have saints in your cave?"

"They're not saints: they're Gods."

"I see. Of course. I've heard about Pagans in little towns across Europe: witches and sorcerers. I met a Benedictine once who told me that many Christians in more isolated areas still engaged in customs the church views as Pagan. I guess it makes sense that some never converted…I mean, if you are really isolated from the outside world, it makes sense. But believe me, Cathars or Pagans, I have no wish to harm you. I've been to the land of the Muslims and I know them to be a mixture of good and bad: like Christians or anyone else. I don't believe everything the church tells me. Selling indulgences for a quick and painless trip to heaven, as the Catholic church does, is both absurd and disgustingly greedy. That's obvious, even to honest Christians. And I've read some of the Pagan works: they didn't seem evil to me. Just different."

"You can read?" Giulia was surprised, and Giovanni felt a twinge of pride at what sounded like awe in her voice. Reading was a rare skill, and probably unheard of outside the cities or monasteries in this part of the world.

"Yes. My father was a merchant of considerable means. We used writing for our business concerns, and when I was young he saw to it that I was tutored in Latin, Greek, and Arabic. We lived at Constantinople then, and literacy is more common there than in Italy and Europe." His voice took on a hint of pride. "I've read more than thirty books in my life."

Giulia did not seem particularly impressed. "If you'd like to read some more, I may be able to get you some. I'll have to ask the elders. We don't usually allow books off the mountain, but they may make an exception because of your…situation."

"You have books here? How can you afford them? What have you got?" He found this even more amazing than the fact they were Pagans, since books were extremely expensive, the preserve of the richest families or the church which maintained ancient libraries for scholastic studies.

"We inherited them from the time we went underground. We've got many to choose from, so what interests you?"

"Many? How many?"

"A few thousand, I guess."

Now she was going too far, and Giovanni became suspicious. "You inherited them? A little town in the middle of nowhere? Forgive me, but that seems unlikely." Was the girl lying for some reason, or had someone lied to her? "Have you seen these books?"

She nodded. "We're not like other little towns. We were settled here from many places, particularly from Greece. We had a wealthy patron back when the village was set up who provided us with a lot of money and many books. Other books came from other places. Have you heard of Delphi and Eleusis? Our predecessors came from there and other sacred areas to guard the old ways when the Dionysian cult took over the world. We have been hiding ever since."

"Dionysian cult? I never heard of them. I know Dionysos—or Bacchus as the Romans called him, I think—was an old God of the ancient world; but if a Dionysian cult had taken over the world I think I would have read about it. I was tutored in history as well as reading and writing."

"They know themselves as Christians, but actually they follow Dionysos."

Giovanni was taken aback by this eccentric belief, but he let it stand. It was becoming clear that there were a number of oddities about the town, and not all his questions were going to be answered at once. Given that books could easily be worth their weight in gold, that was where his curiosity was greatest. It was really too incredible. "You're saying that the ancient Pagans decided to hide some of their books in this little town? Why here? Where do you keep them?"

"They are in the mountain, in the cave you entered. Not just books, either. There are things hidden there which have been in the possession of the priests of the old religion from ancient times. Some are said to have been given to men by the Gods. And we have kept alive the secrets of the old religion. I have read the histories: when the darkness came, we gathered knowledge, things and people from all over the Roman empire. That is why we call ourselves Guardians."

It seemed to Giovanni their conversation was becoming unreal. Sitting here in the dirt in a sleepy village lost in the mountains, impoverished as any he had seen, from what he could make out, and now this peasant girl was calmly claiming to be able to read! He'd heard of Italian women learning to read Latin and Greek, but that was only among the wealthiest class, where the expense of educating women made it desirable to do so: it was a means of showing that one's wealth was so great it could be casually thrown away. He had never heard of a peasant who could read: it just didn't make sense. He looked at her curiously. Was she nothing more than an imaginative liar? It was even unbelievable that a peasant could invent such an exotic story. And why would she want to? As Giovanni gazed at the girl he saw her bright, guileless eyes looking back.

Giovanni spoke in Greek to her. "Who is your favorite poet?"

She shifted uneasily and replied in Italian "Sapho, the Poetess of Lesbos."

He tried Latin. "Do you know the works of Plato and Aristotle?"

"Yes, although I don't enjoy philosophy as much as poetry." Once again she had replied in Italian. Why? Perhaps she had guessed his meaning somehow without really understanding?

He spoke to her in Arabic, asking her if she knew of Plotinus, but she looked at him blankly. "I'm sorry," she said in Italian, "I don't know that language. Is it Arabic or some Eastern tongue?"

"Arabic...but if you understand Latin and Greek, why don't you reply using them?"

"I'm sorry, but it is forbidden. We only speak the ancient languages on the mountain. It's a precaution so that travelers and others from outside will not discover what we are. If peasants spoke Latin and Greek it would attract too much attention. But it is good that you speak them. We had no idea that you were so educated. We had thought you would be like most of the other Dionysians in the outside world." She hesitated, frowning, and then smiled. "Perhaps you were brought here for a reason, since the coincidence is great. Perhaps the Gods have some purpose in bringing you to us." Her face lit up when she smiled: she was really quite beautiful.

"I don't know about such purposes, but the coincidence is greater than you think." He paused for a moment, thinking. Whatever was going on in this town, it was clear they were as opposed to the Christian church as he now found himself. As the Arabs say, the enemy of my enemy is my friend. Perhaps once they knew of his situation they would see him in that light. He needed to be cautious of course, but if their intention had been to trap him into a confession, they would not have invented such a preposterous story, and anyway proving his guilt would not be their responsibility. No, while her story might be exaggerated, it was probably essentially true: he was convinced they too were hiding from the church so there was little risk in being honest. He decided to take a chance and tell her.

"You really don't have to fear me. I am not Pagan, but my allegiance to Christianity is very weak. As I said, I've learned that Christians are no better than the Muslims. I even met a fire worshipper in the East, a Pagan like you, and he was a good and honest man. I don't care about what people believe, but what they are." He paused and looked at her to gauge the effect of his words. She gave no sign of her thinking. "And more importantly, I am in trouble with the Church. That's why I'm here. I was being hunted by the body guards of the bishop of Milan, and I came to the mountains to escape."

It was her turn to be suspicious. "Why did they hunt you? Did you do something to offend the church?"

"You could say that." Unexpectedly, he felt a little sheepish, like a child caught in a silly lie. "I tried to kill the bishop."

"Why would you do that?" Her voice told him she was certain he was lying, making up a tale to save his skin.

"It's a long story. He did great harm to my family. He used his power to jail my father and take his business, giving it to an ally in the Visconti family to cement their relationship. My father died there last year. I am the last of our family, and I have worked to avenge him ever since. My father was an honest man. When I thought of the way he suffered for the sake of another man's ambition, I could do no less. There was no redress under the law, of course, so I had to do it myself. I hid my family name and succeeded in being retained as a bodyguard last month. I didn't want to die, so I waited until the situation allowed me to strike and escape. Do you know what has been happening between the church and France recently?"

She nodded. "Pope Boniface VIII has been trying to make himself supreme in Europe by demanding the right to appoint kings to their thrones: he wanted them to be dependent on him. If he had succeeded, it would have been the highest pinnacle of power the church had ever achieved in Europe, but Philip of France had him seized. He has escaped and is near Rome somewhere. It is not yet clear how the matter will end."

"Exactly. The bishop of Milan is on his way right now to visit the Pope. For me it was the perfect opportunity: I knew his route; he would be out of the city; his retinue was reduced in number to attract less attention; and they stayed off the main roads for the same reason. I traveled with them part of the way, but once we were near the mountains I deserted my post so I could set an ambush." He paused, and looked at the ground. "I missed, but escaped with them only minutes behind me. That's how I ended up here."

She had watched him closely while he talked. She spoke now, her voice taut. "Did you lead them to this valley?"

"I don't know. I hadn't seen any trace of them for many hours before I came to your mountain, but they could have been close."

"How many were there?" she asked in alarm.

Giovanni looked at her curiously. "Five, I think. But they may have given up and gone back to rejoin the column."

"I have to talk to the elders about this. If the Church's men are in the area, they could arrive at any time." She got up as she finished speaking and was already leaving him, at first walking briskly back towards the main village area, but running by the time she disappeared behind the trees.

When she returned a few minutes later, she was accompanied by several of the elders he'd seen the night before. They quizzed him carefully about his story and left hurriedly, heading up the mountain. Before they left, they sent Giulia back to the village with instructions to warn everyone that outsiders could be about, and she ran off leaving Giovanni alone. He wasn't unduly worried: he was sure they were overestimating the risk they faced. And it suited his purpose that they might end up being grateful to him for the warning.

Once he had been left alone, Giovanni went carefully over the ground within the perimeter his chain allowed him, picking up stones that had sharp or serrated edges. He managed to find a few because the local rock was a hard and angular slate, and there were stones of that material scattered everywhere. Taking them inside, he hid the rocks under his mattress. Luck seemed to be on his side, for once. He would soon be free, whether because they released him or because he would free himself.

Feeling confident, he went back outside and again sat down against the wall. It was a beautiful day. Tonight he would begin. And although he thought his hunters had long since given up, it was a relief to know the locals would do everything they could to conceal his presence. The threat of blinding seemed especially remote now that he had a plan ready to execute, and he reflected with satisfaction that, all things considered, he had stumbled on the best place to hide in all of Northern Italy. If the opportunity to escape had arisen that day, he might have turned it down and waited. In a few weeks his chances in the outside world would be much better. He decided he would grow a beard, as well, in case he came across someone who had known him: the better disguised he was, the more certain that he would make his escape permanent. The idea of trying once more to exact revenge made him cringe inwardly. He had done what he reasonably could, and his death would just increase the harm that had been done to his family. Perhaps the reality of death was very near to him after the events of the last few days and that had made him more circumspect, but whatever the cause of it, he no longer cared to exact revenge. Life was too precious to risk, or indeed to take. Hatred was a kind of suffering, and he could see now how miserable he had been in the preceding months: he hoped he would never go back to it.

In mid-afternoon several of the elders came by. They asked him to stand and made him swear an oath of secrecy. It seemed rather quaint to him, but he went along since it was a simple enough matter. "I swear by all the Gods and by my life to protect and preserve the mysteries of the Gods, and to keep their secrets from all who have not been initiated." That was it. The elders explained that they were obliged to have him swear by tradition and by oaths they themselves took when they were old enough to begin their own schooling. By doing so he had made it possible for others like Giulia to speak frankly to him. Everything he learned in the valley was to be considered secret by him. They asked him again about his pursuers and the attempted killing, seeking a few additional details to add to those he had already offered. Then they left. He watched them go, smiling to himself in the memory of their solemn manner. He would honor their oath, but not in such close proximity as they imagined.

That evening when Giulia came with his evening meal they sat outside under the stars. It was cool and she suggested they have a fire. She left and returned a few minutes later with a bundle of kindling and firewood in one hand, and a half burned stick smoldering in the other. Together they built up the fire until it burned cheerfully, snapping and crackling as it consumed the wood. They sat beside each other and watched it without speaking for a time. Overhead the stars sprawled across the sky, bright as the sparks from the fire but infinitely more serene. Although he did not look at her, Giovanni was very conscious of Giulia sitting next to him. He no longer was put off by her peasant appearance. He saw beneath it a young intelligent woman of considerable beauty and he was glad to have her beside him. He had been hoping she would return that afternoon and was rather disappointed that he'd had to do without her company. Besides, he had many questions he wanted answered. He picked up some twigs and began to casually throw them onto the flames, watching them smolder for a moment and flare up brightly against the hot coals. Without thinking, he spat into the fire and sensed Giulia stiffen. He looked over at her to see what had caused her to react, and saw that she was watching him, as if debating with herself over whether to say something. "What is it?" he asked.

"We don't do that to the fire here," she said slowly, searching for the right words. "Not all fires are the same. Fire in this valley is unique, and although there are no rules about it, treating the flame with disrespect is not normal." Her voice was tense.

"I'm sorry. I don't mean to offend your customs. What is so unique about fires here? Do you believe some God watches over them?"

"Yes, but that's not it. It's a symbol of something very ancient...in fact it is very ancient."

Giovanni was confused. "What do you mean?"

She hesitated briefly before replying. "Life is passed from generation to generation. All living creatures gain their life from other living creatures who came into this world before them. The life in you and me is very ancient, going back thousands and thousands of years. Each person is different, but the life in them is the same, coming from the same source, and it is a gift from the Gods that should be treated with great respect whether it burns brightly in them or merely glows dully like a fire reduced to smoldering coals. Life warms our bodies and keeps them supple. When the fire of life goes out, the body becomes cold and stiff. When the fire of life goes out in some person, it is gone forever, and every man's death is a loss to every other.

"Wisdom is similar, but where some lives burn brightly, some are dim. The brightness of wisdom is not always present in everyone. Most in the world smolder hot and red, but never burst into that brilliant flame which is wisdom, illuminating everything around them. Wisdom is the greatest expression of the flame of life, and it was discovered long ago that while the lesser sort of fire is lost forever when a mortal dies, the flame of wisdom continues forever if it burns brightly enough."

"But if it is truly like a fire, then how could wisdom survive when the body grows cold? Flame does not survive when the embers grow cold."

"You are right, Giovanni. And in ancient days our ancestors despaired at the inevitability of death. But wisdom cannot really die. Even in death the light of life can shine if wisdom is present. Just as the sun turns red and sinks below the horizon to the West, but the moon continues to glow brightly in the night, so too can wisdom survive, its light now cool but brilliant. And there is great beauty in the moonlight, beauty that is hidden when the moon's light is unseen." She rearranged the wood on the fire so it burst more brightly into flame. "And there is also the fire of the sun which is transformed into wood by the living trees, and which is then released again when it burns. The seeds are also fire, and new life comes when that fire is buried in the earth and joined to the soil by water."

"Perhaps I'm pressing the first metaphor too strongly, but if wisdom is like moonlight, it is not so reliable: it comes and goes throughout the year. Do you believe that wisdom also comes and goes to those wise people who have died?" There was a hint of amusement in his voice, but if she heard it she gave no sign.

"This may seem strange to you, but in time you will come to understand. Wisdom does not come and go: wisdom is the coming and going. Mortals are at war with change, always seeking security by stopping the natural cycles of things. Mortals wish that summer was eternal, that the moon was always full, and the sun was always bright and warm. But that is not the nature of things. Change is the nature of things: the seasons come and go. You can war against nature, but you will never defeat it, because you are its child and fated by it to death. Wisdom does not resist nature: it comes from accepting the necessity of change and transformation. Instead of fighting the flow of time, the wise move with it, becoming one with change. They hold onto nothing, changing moment by moment, dying to the past, careless of the future, always fresh and new and free of struggle. In this way they embrace the Truth and are therefore True. They do not actually become wise: they are wisdom. Wisdom is a light that can never truly die, as the moon can never die. Sometimes it is seen, sometimes it is hidden. Even in the darkness of death when its light is hidden from mortal eyes, it lives. And while a mortal dies and loses everything, the wise die and by the light of their wisdom they transform death into creation. Death becomes life becomes death becomes life. Forever."

Giovanni was impressed by Giulia's confident words even though he doubted what she said. There was a certain music in her voice as she sat beside him, one side lit by firelight the other in darkness, and she seemed more beautiful than any woman he had ever seen. She was glowing, in the soft light that danced before her. How delicate she was, and feminine!

He found himself wondering idly if he could take her with him, but dismissed the thought immediately. He was letting his fancy endanger his plans. If he confided in her, she might betray him. He barely knew her. Even if she felt this attraction for him that he seemed to be feeling for her, her loyalty to the village was probably too strong to be shaken. And anyway, what made him think she shared his romantic feelings? She was beautiful, but he was nothing special. What was more, he was letting himself get carried away. She was exotic, yes, but would that last? He would be a fool to risk his life in the expectation that it would: loneliness was making him foolhardy. He put the thoughts from his mind, and returned to their conversation, following something she had said earlier which he did not understand.

"I think I see what you're saying about the light of wisdom, but what about this fire? You haven't really answered my question about why you treat it with respect. Is it that the fire is a metaphor for wisdom and life?"

"It is that, of course, but this fire is older than you imagine. I brought this fire from the embers in my family's home, and my parents got it from the common hearth of the village. The village fire was taken from that in the sanctuary on the mountain where it has been kept burning for nine long centuries. But it is older still. The sanctuary's flame was brought here from Delphi, and the flame at Delphi came, more than two thousand years ago, from the island of Delos in the Aegean sea. But it came to Delos from an age long before, and it comes originally from the hearth of the Olympian Gods. It was brought to earth at the same time as human life by the God Prometheus, or so they say, back in the days when the world was new. It has been fed and protected, shared across the generations of humanity ever since.

"We venerate its age, and the things it has seen. In Greece, when the old religion was still respected, all of the cities brought their flame from Delphi. Alexander the Great has seen this same fire, and Socrates, and Homer. King Priam saw its light in the fields before Troy, and Achilles and Agamemnon sat beside it in the Greek camp and talked, just as you and I are doing now. We are the guardians of the ancient ways, and of the ancient flame."

Giovanni didn't consider himself a dreamer. He was a believer in action and common sense. But as he sat feeling the warmth of the fire and seeing its reflection twinkling in the eyes of the girl as she gazed into it, he felt the hairs on the back of his neck prickle and stand on end. A shudder passed through him. Giulia's words had touched something deep inside that he could neither see nor fully understand. The idea of this same flame in the plains of Troy, in the hearths of a million homes, whispered to him: he felt the presence of the multitudes of men and women who had come before, heard their voices and seemed to see their faces: and the joy of their coming, the sorrow of their passing, was as bright and new as if it had happened that very night. He felt breathless and confused, excited and full of grief, happy and somber, all at the same time. Unexpectedly, tears flooded his eyes, and he looked away, shaken. How strange he felt!

For a long time they didn't speak, and gradually Giovanni grew calmer. Little by little the feverish impressions passed until again he was himself, a young man sitting by a fire in the night with a young woman sitting beside him. Their silence was somehow comfortable, as if they were old friends, and he felt no need to talk. It was Giulia who spoke first, responding to some troubling train of thought.

"I don't want you to think I am claiming wisdom for myself," she said with obvious embarrassment at the thought. "I know very little...and I may never become immortal because I too am at war with the world." She picked up a twig and held the end of it in the flames. Looking at him then, it was as if a cloud fell across her brow, while her eyes pleaded forgiveness in the flickering light. "For example, I can't... I don't want... What we will do to you...hurts me. I'm so sorry, Giovanni. I'm glad I had the chance to meet you, but I hate it too, because we are being so cruel. I don't think you deserve this." She dropped the burning twig into the fire and reached over, her hand warm against his knee. He looked at her and saw tears shining on her cheeks. It made him feel deeply too, and he put his hand on hers.

"Thank you," he said quietly. He squeezed the hand and let it go. She withdrew it, and he wanted to put his arms around her but he resisted. He didn't feel he had the right, his mind too committed, as it was, to making plans for his escape. Besides, she might not like it. He sighed and decided to change the subject. "I've seen Delos," he said.

She looked at him, wiping away the tears. "What?"

"I once sailed past that island you mentioned, Delos, in the Aegean. We were quite close but it was very small so there wasn't much to see."

"Have you been to Delphi?"

"No. It doesn't exist anymore. I have been to Athens on business, though, and seen the Parthenon."

She was curious. "What was it like?

"Very beautiful. The rock it's built on is strange: it is pale yellow, and seems soft and smooth like butter where people's feet have polished it. The old temples are still standing, and from the walls you can see all of Athens, right down to the harbor."

"You're so lucky! I've never been out of this valley, and probably the only time I will leave it is when I go to adopt a child. I have read about so many things I will never see! Did you go to Eleusis?"

"No. I read about it in Pausinias, but I'm not even sure if it's still there. I was only in Athens for a few days. What do you mean about adopting a child? What makes you think you can't have one of your own? I mean, you're not married, are you?" This last was said with a hint of anxiety that Giovanni tried to conceal. It was silly of him to feel like that about something that was none of his business.

She laughed, her tears now almost dry. "Of course not! However, we guardians have to be careful because we are so small in number. It depends on the situation, but when a couple is married they are usually only allowed to have two children, one of them adopted. The fresh blood helps us avoid inbreeding and keeps our village healthy. We can't marry outside our community because it would be too risky. Besides there's no chance since we always stay apart from the Dionysians. Furthermore, every generation has to be the same size: too big and we cannot feed ourselves, too small and we don't have enough people to keep alive the knowledge we protect. I'm certain it's a lot more complicated than it is where you come from. After I'm married the elders will tell me how many children I can have and how many must be adopted. The sex of the adopted children is decided by the town's needs, of course. But they always try to make sure a couple can have at least one child of their own. Adoption is good for the children, too. Orphans are looked after by the Church in the outside world, but their lives are very hard and their prospects very dim. No institution can take the place of a family. We give them love and raise them as one of us. It is forbidden to speak to anyone about whether a child is adopted or not, so who was and who wasn't is quickly forgotten. Everyone here is born equal in responsibilities and potential."

"But surely it must be difficult having others decide about your family."

"It is, but there's no choice. It is because of our situation. If we did not do it, we would be destroyed within a few generations. The elders don't decide based on their own preferences: the decision is based on necessity. And when there is uncertainty, for example when only one of five couples can have three children, the lucky couple is selected by lottery. The matter is left up to the Gods to decide."

"Where do you get the children you adopt?"

"We go to nearby towns and cities. The husband and wife go together, telling the outsiders they are a childless couple. It's quite simple. The biggest problem is selecting the right child. We need to pick the brightest and most healthy we can find so that they can give intelligence and strength to future generations. Often couples bring one or more of their parents or the elders to help them make the choice."

She looked at him and smiled. "Do you want to hear a story?"

"All right."

"It's a story my parents told me when I was a little girl. A long, long time ago, a man named Marco lived in this valley. After he married, he and his wife asked one of the elders, a wise man called Vincenzo, to come with them to find a boy to adopt. The three of them went all the way to Milan and asked a priest who was in charge of orphans if they could have one because they were childless. The priest was very kind. 'Of course,' he said. 'Let me find the best one for you to take back to your village.' They agreed. He went away and came back a few minutes later with a beautiful boy two years old. The young couple loved the child on sight and would have taken him without hesitation, but the elder said they had better not. When they asked him why, all he would say was 'He has the eyes of a Dionysian.' The couple thought that was foolish: the boy's eyes looked beautiful to them, so they decided to take him anyway. 'As you wish," said the elder, and they returned to Sanctuary.

"The boy grew up and he was very handsome, so every girl wanted him for her husband. Now the elder Vincenzo was still alive though he was very old, and his granddaughter fell in love with the boy. She told her grandfather of her wish, but he said she had better not marry him. When she asked him why not, all he would say was 'He has the eyes of a Dionysian.'

The girl thought he had grown senile, for the boy's eyes seemed very handsome to her, not at all like those of an ignorant outsider. When he asked her to marry him, she agreed immediately and told her grandfather of her plan. 'As you wish,' said Vincenzo.

"They lived in Vincenzo's house and he was very kind to both of them. When the time came for the couple to get a child of their own, the young man told his wife they would go alone. 'We don't need help in choosing her,' he said. She was uncertain, but she agreed because she was very much in love. They were gone for several weeks, and came back with a beautiful little girl. How happy the family was!

"But later when the wife was pregnant by her husband she became very sick, and a little later the husband grew sick also. The physician came to their house and realizing what was wrong he asked the husband many questions. It turned out that while they were among the outsiders, the husband had slept with one: she had made him sick. He had given the sickness to his wife. The unborn baby died, and the girl never had another. She and her husband grew sicker and sicker, and eventually they came near to death. The family gathered, including Vincenzo. The girl's parents were very unhappy, and kept asking 'Why?' The daughter heard them, and she too began asking 'Why?' Vincenzo looked at the three of them together, and shook his head sadly. 'As you wished,' was all he said."

Giovanni laughed abruptly. "That's a terrible story! Vincenzo sounds like a heartless man who cares nothing about the well being of his family. If he really could tell what was going to happen, why didn't he order them to do as he said, or at least warn them?"

"You are missing the point," said Giulia. "He did warn them, because he did care. But one who is wise speaks softly and is too gentle to quarrel. Though they knew he was wise, they refused to listen, and it was not in his nature to disagree. The parents decided to let a Dionysian priest choose their son, and the girl later followed her own love-blinded heart. Then she let her husband wander freely among the outsiders, without guidance from someone more stable. It was all their own choosing. The wise speak softly and resist nothing. We must listen for their meaning very carefully. If it is not in our natures to listen, then fate will take its course."

Giovanni shook his head with wonder at her reasoning. "What is the point of wisdom if it cannot save a wise man's family from disaster? I still think it is a terrible story."

"I understand," said Giulia. "When I was young it sounded terrible to me too. There are many stories told to children about Vincenzo, and many are like that one. The more you understand, the kinder and more loving Vincenzo becomes. I don't know if he was a real man who actually lived here or just an old invention, but he has taught me much about the world in either case." She got up suddenly and he rose with her. "I have to go to bed now," she said.

They said goodnight, and Giovanni took her hand briefly before she went. He noticed that he was feeling a subtle euphoria as he watched her leave, like a fire burning deep in his soul. At first he thought it might be infatuation for the girl, but it seemed unfocused and lasted long after she had vanished through the trees back towards the village, so he decided the strange conversation and a peculiar reaction to the stress of his circumstances was probably the cause.

That night Giovanni began his escape. He jumped up, catching hold of the smoke-blackened cross-beam with his hands and heaved himself up onto it. He pulled himself along the beam until he was at the end, by the wall near the doorway. This was the safest place to work because only someone standing in the doorway could see where he was. That afternoon he had also noticed that it was the darkest region of the beam: farther in, away from the doorway, the daylight reached up and touched it, but here where the beam ended barely an arm's span from the door its light passed by and left it in shadow. Making himself as comfortable as he could, Giovanni began to work on the upper edge of the beam, tearing through the fibers of the wood with the sharp stones he had collected earlier. It was slow going, but Giovanni had expected as much. By the time the first birdsong rose into the still dark sky, Giovanni decided with satisfaction that his work had progressed well. He estimated he would have four or five days to spare by the time he was through. He hopped down and went out to the ashes of last night's fire, gathering a handful. Returning to the interior of the hut he mixed it with water to form a thick black paste. Piling it carefully on top of the beam, he jumped back up and smeared it in the crack he had gouged along the upper edge, smoothing it carefully. The result was not bad: even from close up, the beam appeared untouched.

Giovanni laid down in the bed well pleased with his work but could not fall asleep, for too many thoughts crowded his mind. Going outside, he sat leaning against the wall and watched the stars slowly turning and fading as dawn poured its light across the sky.

An hour or two later, Giulia brought him his breakfast. She explained that she had work to do, but if he didn't mind she would like to come back and visit with him again later in the day. He was glad of the free time for he was very tired, and a few minutes after she left he went to sleep, remaining in bed until midday. All afternoon he sat outdoors, lazily looking around at the trees while he daydreamed in idle comfort, and watched as the villagers occasionally went by on some chore or other. As they passed he called out cheerful greetings, and for the most part they responded in much the same way. That strange sense of euphoria he had felt the night before was with him still although it had faded a little: he could not remember when he had felt so happy and at peace. From time to time he tried to make sense of his feelings but he could not, so he let it go, resolving to enjoy the unfamiliar sensation so long as it did not lead him to let his guard down and risk discovery of his escape.

As the sun was setting Giulia returned with his dinner. While he ate it she went to get firewood and a smoldering stick as she had the night before, and built up a new fire. They sat together in silence and watched the light fade, leaving the world in shadows. The flickering flames lit up the clearing and the surrounding trees with its dancing light.

"Giulia, I've been wondering something."

"Yes?"

"Have you been chosen to spend time with me, or is it your idea?"

"Both. I am of marriageable age, but I am not yet engaged to anyone. It was decided that I might be the best person to introduce you to our community, and I was happy to agree."

Giovanni was surprised at her candor, and affected annoyance, although he noticed that her words gave him a burst of pleasure he found difficult to conceal. "You didn't even know me but you were already considering me for marriage? Is that it? I would have thought you would prefer not to marry an outsider."

"But you are not an outsider any more. And every person in our village must marry if possible to continue the generations. I was not assured of finding anyone since there was a young man who died a few years ago in my generation, leaving one girl without a potential partner. As it happened, that turned out to be me. Unless an older man was widowed I could not hope to marry until you came. Normally if young people don't choose a willing partner on their own, it is decided by the elders who should marry whom, but since you are only new to us here, I will not be forced to marry you and you won't have to marry me." She laughed teasingly. "Anyway, I really only want to learn from you about the outside world: we don't have to get married just for that, do we?"

Giovanni wasn't feeling playful. "There isn't much chance of you wanting to marry a blind cripple, is there?"

Her smile died. "Let's not talk about that, all right? Please, Giovanni: I can't bear to think of it. And anyway, such things are not important where love is concerned. If I love a man nothing else matters. And I am not so beautiful that I can afford to make appearances important."

"You are very beautiful," said Giovanni with unexpected force, but then he blushed and looked into the fire while he wondered what to say next. Nothing occurred to him, but she didn't speak either so he glanced at her to see what she was thinking. She was staring straight into the flames with her head lowered, and he couldn't make out what her thoughts might be. They were both silent for a time.

It was Giovanni who broke the silence. "Last night you said it was Prometheus who brought this flame from the Gods and gave it to men. I remember him vaguely from myth, but if you don't mind telling me about him, I'd like to hear his story again. He's the God who was chained to a rock, wasn't he? What was that about?"

Giulia stared into the fire while she spoke. "Prometheus means forethought. He has the power to see things before they happen. His brother is Epimetheus which means afterthought. He only knows what has already happened. The tale of the two brothers is the tale of the creation of mankind, not just in the distant past but now, with every newborn child as he takes his first breath of air.

"Prometheus and Epimetheus are both Gods of air. Air is the element the soul is made of. The soul is the seat of all thought. Prometheus is air when it travels free and full of light like in the daytime sky. Epimetheus is air in darkness, as it is inside the human heart, hidden away behind flesh and blood. Prometheus and Epimetheus are twins, two aspects of a single thing—one mortal, one immortal.

Perhaps you have heard of Pandora? Her name means All-gifts. She is the mortal body. In myth Pandora is given to Epimetheus as his bride. The soul joins the body at birth. As her dowry Pandora brings all the diseases that afflict mortals, for that is the price soul pays when it becomes joined to flesh: it must be tormented by the qualities of the body. And the body is the thing which submits the soul to the sorrows attached to time. She also brings hope in her dowry: hope is only meaningful for those who are blind to the future and cannot see for certain whether it will be good or bad. It is a chain that binds all mortals to their bodies, making them endure.

"Some myths say Prometheus was responsible for his brother's wedding, some even make him the creator of Pandora. But he loves his blinded brother and wishes to help him, so he is the God who first showed mortals how to reach out to the timeless world of the divine with their longing, through the use of sacrifice and prayer. He could not grant immortality to mortals, but he began the process of dialogue between Gods who are beyond the reach of time, and men who are its slaves. Thus he brought life to this world and then found a way for it to communicate with the other world from which it originally came.

"It is said that Zeus, the greatest sky God, was angered by Prometheus' efforts to raise up individuated souls, and had Prometheus bound to a rock where an eagle—Zeus' symbol—ate his liver as the moon grows smaller. As the moon grows larger again, the liver grows back. So Prometheus was greatly tortured for many centuries.

"You should know that Zeus could never despise another God or do him harm. On the surface, myth has Gods engaged in terrible things, but this is only to conceal the real meaning. The story of Prometheus' bondage is not of vengeance by Zeus but of the inevitable consequence when a portion of Prometheus becomes Epimethian by being bound in flesh. Prometheus' punishment is self-inflicted. Prometheus sacrificed himself to bring life to this world, that wonderful spark of divinity which is in all mortals. Before his sacrifice, this world was truly dark. Afterwards it has been filled with sentient life."

"What is the significance of Prometheus' liver?" asked Giovanni, wondering if every detail of myth was meaningful, or if some parts were just included because they made the story better.

"The liver is the organ used in ancient days to tell the future, and its link to the cycle of the moon is because the moon reflects the seasons, the inevitable movement of mortal time from beginning to middle to end. Prometheus, chained in Epimethian form to earth, to flesh, suffers from its blindness of the future.

"Prometheus suffered a very long time, but in the end the Gods found a way to free him. Herakles, beloved devotee of Zeus' wife Hera, mastered the cycle of time from within it, and thus freed Prometheus from his suffering. Perhaps you know Herakles and Hera by their Roman names, Hercules and Juno."

Giovanni interrupted her. "But Hera was the sworn enemy of Herakles in the myths I have read."

"That is the surface description. To understand, you must go beneath appearances. His name reflects Hera, and without her encouragement to master the various aspects of time's cycle, he would never have found the way for mortal men to look beyond the past and present. After his labors here on earth were completed, he ascended to Olympus, symbol of the world of the Gods, and took Hera's daughter Hebe, which means Youth, as his bride. With

Hera's assistance he had achieved immortality and eternal youth through wisdom.

"Where Prometheus had found a way for men and Gods to communicate between their worlds, Hera and Herakles found a way for mortals to reflect the natures of the Gods here on earth, and that is how the age of heroes began. Later still Dionysos would find a way for wisdom to free mortals from death altogether. So, bit by bit, by gradually increasing understanding, mankind has grown closer to the Gods, closer to Truth."

Giovanni was amazed at the growing realization there might be a vast world of hidden information concealed in the myths he had read years before. At the time they had seemed like foolish tales invented by simple people, a chaos of conflicting stories that were amusing but in no sense profound. Giulia had caused one of those stories to be rearranged and ordered in his mind, and it amazed him to think that he and others had missed the deeper meanings that were there for all to see. The myth of Pandora certainly seemed to fit the explanation Giulia had given him, and it made Giovanni reflect that this village really might have a direct link to something far older than itself. His doubts about its lineage were fading.

"What is the world of the Gods?" he asked.

"The Gods live beyond time, in a world from which ours arises. Although the Gods are in a world beyond time, they shape the characteristics of this temporal world. Just as the sun affects this world yet is unaffected by it, so the Gods affect this world but are unaffected by it. Indeed, this world is shaped and sustained by them. You could say their world is parallel to our own, and dictates it. It is the qualities of the Gods that give rise to time and every other natural phenomena we know, although they themselves are entirely free of them. Our world is formed by the shadows cast down from their world: their world is Truth, but our world is shaped by the shadows of Truth. Their world is Order, but our world lies half-way between Order and Chaos. Their world transcends the cycles of time, but ours is permeated by those cycles.

The two worlds are very different, and transferring the Truth between them is not so easy. Although the Gods have worked to bring the Truth to us, it takes only a dim form here, like a dream. It is difficult for creatures in a world possessed by time to understand Truth, which is timeless: very difficult.

"It is the Gods Prometheus, Herakles, Hermes, and Dionysos who have most notably expressed the will of the Gods to span the divide between their world and this one. There is a bridge that has been opened up between the worlds, and that bridge is known as wisdom. In ancient times this bridge was only open to the Gods, but as humanity learned from the Gods, eventually some of us learned how to find and cross the bridge. When, through wisdom, a mortal finds the timeless present in this world, it is as if a bridge is opened up and he or she is then in direct contact with the world of the immortal Gods, living in both worlds at once.

"I mentioned those four Gods as benefactors to mankind, but actually all the Gods are kind to us. Hera, for example, is not the enemy of mortals that a surface reading of myth suggests. On the one hand, she is the clouds which join earth and sky together through the falling rain, and in this way she works to create new life. Then again, she is the water that brings the benefits of the Gods down to earth. Water is the element which allows things to be joined together: man and woman, heaven and earth. That is her material expression, but she has another, deeper meaning. She transfers the fruits of heaven to this world. When they arrive here, they are mere shadows of what they are in Olympus. But hidden in them, for those who understand, are intimations of that world of Truth.

"That's why she is so important in guiding Herakles through his labors. Those twelve labors represent his struggle to overcome the distorted form divinity appears to take in this world of shadows. And thereby to discover the True forms that gave birth to them. By destroying the false distortions that appear in myth as monsters, Herakles sees the true forms and achieves wisdom.

"So Hera brings the shadows to earth, but she does not do it to harm us: she brings them to us so that we can look past the distortions and see the Truth that lies behind the shadows. She brings shadows because that is all she is able to bring from the other world. She is like the teacher who reveals the Truth in her words, but who must constantly struggle with her pupils— Herakles and the rest of us—to make us see past our own delusions to the heart of what she has revealed.

"You should know, Giovanni, to understand myth you must realize the things described are not as they appear. Myth uses symbols. Two apparently conflicting myths may not conflict at all once you understand their true meanings. Even ascribing the same achievement to two different Gods acting in different ways is not a contradiction, because the Gods we know in our thoughts are not the real Gods: they are metaphors, shadows of Gods. No metaphor is perfect and the Gods are not clearly known through metaphor.

"Only the wise who can see the Gods directly know their true nature. And such people have very strange ways of trying to describe what they see. If they are pressed on the point, they may even say there are no Gods at all, or that there is but one God from which all of the others appear to come. They have told us that in this world it is proper to speak of Gods and see them as separate, but when wisdom looks from the other world there is no separation, no distinction, and in that place the Gods are one. It is a mystery that cannot be taught but only seen directly."

It was surprising to hear of such a strange philosophy underlying Pagan beliefs. Giovanni had never thought the religious Pagans believed in such things, though of course Pagan philosophers like Plato certainly did. The old religion was vastly more complex and beautiful than he had been led to believe. Giovanni scratched his chin thoughtfully before he spoke.

"You said our world lies halfway between Chaos and Order. By Chaos do you mean evil?"

"Oh no, certainly not! But so-called 'evil' actions often come from Chaos, as does the belief in evil itself. Evil is a word which really means 'that which I don't fully understand and which deeply frightens me'. Evil comes from ignorance: it does not exist in any absolute form."

"So if I murder you, my action is not evil?"

"That's right: not evil, just ignorant, insane. By harming others you harm the life within your self which is a fragment of the same whole. Only an ignorant and tortured man would harm himself willingly. When you tried to kill a man, did you not feel the ugliness of your act? You were very fortunate to have failed. All over this world people are harming each other constantly. They do this because they imagine the profit exceeds the price, but they are wrong: they are ignorant. Many are so confused that in their lust and greed they tell themselves there is no price to be paid for harming others, only profit to be gained. Believing this lie, they destroy themselves by extinguishing that tiny flame of wisdom that is every mortal's birthright. Instead of rising into the radiance of full wisdom, they sink into the darkness of Chaos. Such madness is to be pitied, not emulated."

"One thing I don't understand," said Giovanni, "is why no one knows about these things. We are taught that Pagans were like children deluded by devils, with only a few exceptional thinkers who foresaw the coming of Christ. If these ideas are as old as you say, why are they not well known?"

"The Christians view us as their enemies, and they have tried to make us look foolish, so that is one thing. But much more important is the way our ancestors thought of wisdom and the knowledge that leads to wisdom. They believed most people should have some knowledge, but only some are suited to have more. Just as wisdom sent from the world of the Gods is a mere shadow when it arrives here in our world, a metaphor for Truth, so were these metaphors rendered as shadows yet again for the majority of mankind. So most people in ancient times were fed metaphors of metaphors, shadows of shadows, reflections of reflections. These shadows are called myths. Hearing a myth, most people thought they knew its meaning, though all they really knew was the shape of its meaning. Those who truly understood were few and sworn to secrecy. They kept their secrets hidden.

"Our world is parallel to the world of Truth, so myth is parallel to Truth. The world of the Gods is hidden from this world, so knowledge of it is also hidden. Myth gives up its secrets only to the few. In this Dionysian age, we of the sanctuary are the only ones left who still truly understand. Everyone here is initiated into the ancient mysteries to whatever limit they are capable of."

"Why do you keep referring to the Christians as Dionysians?" asked Giovanni, for he no longer felt comfortable in his assumption that this was a simple eccentricity.

"We are not the enemies of Christians, though in their delusion they imagine that we are. We know who Christ is, and why they follow him. We follow him too. He is the God we call Dionysos, and he leads mankind through a time of forgetfulness and ignorance so that wisdom can grow stronger in the world."

"But Giulia, that's crazy: how is it possible for ignorance and forgetfulness to lead to wisdom?"

"In this world of ours, the way forward is never straight, for time contains within its nature cycles. Creation is always eventually followed by destruction. It is the Law. When the cycle is resisted, when death is resisted, destruction is total. When it is embraced, accepted, it becomes the seed for rebirth in a higher form. By following Dionysos, mankind has accepted the will of the Gods and prepared the way for future greatness.

"The ancient religion grew old and its death approached. But the Gods were kind and guided mankind into this death, so it was not total. Everything is not lost, though the light of knowledge has grown very dim. In time, a rebirth into a higher life will come because the spark was kept alive. Dionysos is the God whose secrets guide such things. He brings his initiates into death, but keeps the living spark alive during that difficult and dangerous time, so that when the cycle has turned again, they are reborn."

So it went, Giovanni asking questions, Giulia answering while the evening fled past and it grew late. It was after midnight when Giulia went back to her house to sleep, leaving Giovanni with a mind full of strange new questions and answers, and the task of freeing himself to occupy his hands while he considered them.

wo weeks passed, their hours following the same pattern: relax and sleep during the day, talk with Giulia during the evening, work through the night. In this way Giovanni slowly grew more knowledgeable of the Sanctuary's ways, even as he cut his way slowly through the beam. His affection for Giulia grew, and with it the sense of exhilaration that followed him day and night. He had to acknowledge eventually that the feeling came from her, though whether it was infatuation or love he could not tell. He preferred to think of it as infatuation. He kept his life in separate compartments, for when the parts collided it brought him pain. Escaping was good until he thought of losing Giulia; infatuation with Giulia was good until he thought of escaping. Life in the village was good until he thought of blinding; blinding, of course, was never good. So actually he had no choice. It was best just to follow each goal separately and not to mix them.

For the most part, Giulia was his only companion. Several times he was visited by an elder or two who did little more than politely ask if he was comfortable before leaving. Though Giovanni said nothing of it to Giulia, it seemed clear to him that this was a matter of policy developed by the elders, though what their exact thinking was he could not say. It seemed they were content to let Giulia be the spokesperson for the village, and everyone else went about their business as if he barely existed.

Once, two weeks after he had arrived, an elder came and told him they had investigated his story about the attempt on the bishop's life. There was no evidence to support what he'd described. If it had happened as he said, the Church was keeping it secret. Of course, given the problems the Church was facing at that time, it was very possible it had concealed the event, but there was no way of knowing. Therefore, with regret, the counsel had decided it could not accept Giovanni's story, and it could have no effect on their decision. For Giovanni's part, the Church's secrecy was good news, since it would mean once he had escaped he would be fairly safe as long as he stayed away from Milan and kept a low profile. His beard was coming along nicely, and he was becoming increasingly confident that he would see this difficult period through without harm.

When his blinding was still six days away, scheduled to coincide with the new moon, the beam began to crack under his weight: he asked for and received a stool, claiming he wanted it for sitting but actually using it to stand on while he cut the beam down to its final few fibers. At last he was ready. From now on he could sleep through the nights. He began to set aside bread, letting it dry out so that it would not go bad and he could take it with him when he left. Originally it had been his plan to leave as soon as the beam would allow it, but he felt hesitant. He told himself that he was tired and needed several days rest, and that it wouldn't hurt to stay around for a little longer to talk to Giulia. No one had ever inspected his chain or the beam, and even if they did, he was confident that they would find nothing unless they actually tried to climb up and have a look. Besides, the more time that passed in the outside world, the less likely that he would be discovered by his enemies, so waiting made sense.

It is perhaps ironic that on the morning of the fourth day before his blinding, after a long night spent only in slumber, Giovanni slept in. For the first time since he had begun working on the beam, he was not outside ready to greet Giulia when she brought him his breakfast. Naturally she came in to wake him. When he opened his eyes, she was at the foot of his bed, beside the chain where it dangled from the beam. He smiled at her and she laughed at him, taking hold of the chain and suddenly trying to shinny up it for fun. Giovanni had no time to react: as soon as her weight was upon it, the beam cracked loudly and gave a little, though it did not fall. The cut had been severed, and the longer portion of the beam had rotated downwards slightly, slipping along the cut edge several finger's width before wedging itself in again. Giulia looked up in surprise as the beam came to rest at an angle, and a shower of ashes dropped from the crack. Giovanni was transfixed, looking at Giulia, forgetting to breathe.

For a moment they seemed frozen, the two of them, and then Giulia looked at Giovanni, her face pale, her eyes wide with comprehension and concern. "Giulia," he started to say weakly, but before he could go on she had turned and left.

Giovanni cursed and started up to go after her, but instead kicked the wall and began to pace back and forth, looking wildly about, now at the beam, now at the door, his mind racing. Should he risk fleeing now, or wait until nightfall? He did not know what to do. Again he cursed, and kicked the wall angrily at the thought of his stupidity. He felt powerless.

After a time he calmed down a little, though he was by no means at peace, and he realized that there was a chance Giulia would say nothing. He knew she had grown fond of him in these past weeks and that she would probably trust him to keep the village's secrets. Even so, he kept listening for the sound of footsteps outside, but to his gradually growing relief they never came. He went out and looked around, sat for a minute by the ashes of the previous night's fire, and then went back in to look at the beam again. He might as well assume she would keep his secret. If she didn't, he would have to deal with that when it happened. Leaving in day light was almost certain to lead to his recapture, given that he would be encumbered by the chain and unfamiliar with these parts, so it wasn't worth the risk. And if she was going to keep his secret safe, there was no time to waste: he had better make sure no one else would stumble on his work.

Pulling the stool closer, he climbed up and inspected the cut. The beam was held in place by gravity: the two pieces were no longer connected. He went outside, looking around until he found a flat stone the width of the original cut. Bringing it in with him, he climbed up on the stool and put his head under the larger section of the beam, pushing against it to lift it up, and slipped the rock into the gap. Letting the beam go again, he saw that it was once again running horizontal. He went outside and gathered some more ashes, being careful to ensure he was not being watched. Back inside, he mixed them with water and smeared them into place. Once again everything looked normal, and it made him feel better. Then his eye fell to the ground and he saw the pile of black ash that had fallen in clumps when Giulia broke the beam. God, what a fool! Cursing again, he got on his knees, gathered them in his hands, and threw them outside into the remnants of the old fire.

There was no sign of Giulia all day. It was the most anxious day he had ever spent. To be waiting, helpless, wondering what would happen, was agony. Obviously she had said nothing to anyone or they would have come already. But as far as he knew she was deciding whether to tell or not. Surely if she had decided to keep his secret she would have come and told him so. She held his destiny in her hands, and he was unable to speak to her, to help her see his point of view. Though he hated it, there was no choice but to wait.

At dusk Giulia returned, carrying his meal as always. She walked up to him, and he noticed her face was contorted a little: it was obvious she was making an effort not to cry. Silently she handed him a bowl and some bread. Then she sat down beside him and watched while he forced himself to eat. Something in her manner told him he had nothing to fear: his secret was safe with her. But somehow that did not make him happy. In fact, he felt miserable.

"What else can I do?" he asked, finally. "I'm sorry Giulia, but what else can I do? I don't want to leave you. I have even come to like your village and respect it—the things you are doing, your beliefs—but the life I would have here is too terrible to contemplate." He looked at her a moment, and when he spoke again, he was pleading. "Come with me. We will make a life together somewhere else. I don't want to lose you. I will look after you: we can be happy together. All day I have been afraid, terrified that you might tell someone, but even so, despite everything, I have felt the same...joy, the same joy I've felt ever since the day I met you. It has been everywhere for me, in the air I breath and the water I drink. Whether I'm sleeping or awake I feel your presence. When I see you I am shocked again to discover that you exist, that you are not some dream. Please don't make me be alone again: I love you. Please come with me. I will do everything I can to make you happy. Please don't refuse..."

When she spoke, her voice was thick with resignation: she sounded very tired, dull. "I know you love me, and I love you too. I am sorry, Giovanni, because I let you down. I have been very selfish, thinking only of what I wanted. I told myself that our love could make everything all right, that everything was for the best. I...it's terrible, but I even imagined us living together with...pleasure, me looking after you, reading to you, being your eyes. I'm so sorry...I have been like a selfish child.

"I'm glad you are going to leave. It is much better this way. I don't know how I could have believed otherwise. You belong out there, in the world, as I belong here. I know your heart is true, and you will never betray us. And that is all I ask from you, that you take our secret to your grave.

"The best way to go is down the path, out of the mountains. Within a few hours you will be beyond the range of our village. The stream that runs through this village empties into the Taro river, and that marks the edges of our land. They will attempt to follow, of course, but you will be in your territory, not ours, and they will be far more cautious. Get off the main path then and hide for a time: you will have the advantage. If they don't find you within a few days, they will return to assist in covering the cave and concealing all evidence of the sanctuary. You will be safe. Follow the Taro downstream and you will come to the Lombardy plain in about a day." She paused and remembered something. "Look, I brought you this." She took a short bladed knife from her under dress, releasing the bindings where she had tied it above her knee, and handed it to him. "I should have brought it a few weeks ago. I'm sorry. And if there is anything else you need, I'll try to get it."

"Come with me," said Giovanni. "I need you."

"I can't. I belong here. I know we would be happy at first, but it would eat at me. I can't run away from my responsibility, no matter how much I want to, and please, don't ask me. It only makes it harder." She reached over and took his hand. "You go. You will always know where I am when you think of me. And I will never forget you. I will think of you out there in the world, seeing all the places I have read about: it will make me happy just to think of it. You don't belong here, Giovanni, but I do. Please, let's not talk about it any more."

They sat together holding hands while the stars came out. The moon was a sliver to the West that followed the sun down below the horizon almost before daylight had fully passed. This night they had no fire, and the stars blazed so brightly that they cast faint shadows beneath the trees. Giulia moved closer, and put her arm around Giovanni's shoulder. He could feel the warmth of her body beside him, and he turned his head and kissed her, softly, on the mouth. Her lips parted and he shuddered as his longing for her seemed to tingle across his skin and pull her closer. He felt her breath, her tongue, her delicate body, straining as he was—to be closer, to be one. Oh God: why was this happening to him now?

Suddenly he felt her pull back from him, and he let her go, confused. She stood up, but then reached for him, and taking his hand without a sound led him gently into the hut and onto the bed.

Giovanni had lain with women before, but not often. With his circle of friends he had experienced sex in the houses of love in Constantinople and Venice, but he had not found much pleasure there. What followed was nothing like it. It was as if everything he had known before was thrown aside and for the first time he was home. Dully he wondered several times, his mind thick with passion, where she began and he ended. He really did not know. And from her tender sighs and gasps, as from the expression in her eyes and face, he saw she was equally confused. What would he not do for her? What would he not risk?

Once, in a lull as they breathed close in each other's arms, smiling the secret of their closeness, he spoke the new thoughts that he could no longer deny. "Perhaps I should stay," he said, in a voice he had made reasonable, steady.

"Oh no," she said quickly, but it finished like a drawn out sob. Tears choked her and she turned away from him struggling to breathe. "Don't say that. Don't ever say that..." And she cried so bitterly that it made him feel frantic and afraid.

He held her for a time, soothing words of reassurance spilling from him in an even flow. As the minutes passed, to his relief her unhappiness seemed to fall away behind them, smothered in forgetfulness, and they returned at last to the joyful pleasure of their sharing. So the hours passed in dreamlike love, until Giovanni fell asleep, telling himself she would come away with him after all. Telling her in his heart that he loved her...

When he woke, it was dawn. Her scent lingered, but there was no sign of her. He rose and went outside to wait. Overhead, a few clouds spilled across the mountains and covered half the valley beneath their soft white billows. The sun rose, but Giulia did not come. It was midmorning before a giggling girl arrived with his breakfast, saying that Giulia was sick that morning, and had sent a note for him instead. The girl was about six and seemed to want to talk, but Giovanni couldn't conceal his disappointment so she left before long. As soon as she had gone, he unfolded the cloth he had been given and read the note scrawled on it.

'Giovanni, thank you for last night. I have always been curious about love, and now I know. I also know that you don't belong here, and that we are not right for each other. You were raised among the outsiders and that is where you belong. Anyway, even if you were one of us it wouldn't have worked. I'm sorry for misleading you, but I was mistaken: I don't love you. I realized that last night. What I thought was love must have been desire, because after I left you I didn't feel anything. I still don't. When I think about it, I realize I don't want to see you again, perhaps because I feel a little foolish when I remember the exaggerated things I said. Please try to understand that you were exotic to me, a kind of adventure. I regret now I realize it was nothing more. I am sorry if my insincerity has hurt you, but you should realize I am still young and inexperienced. I tell you all this because I think you should know that if you fail to escape there will be no one here to care for you properly. I feel bad about that, so I hope it doesn't happen. Therefore I wish you good luck.'

Giulia.

Giovanni read the note twice again, his hands shaking. Was it true? Was last night a matter of such little importance to her? Or was she simply trying to encourage him to escape because she didn't want him to suffer? A darker thought occurred to him. Perhaps she had decided a blind and crippled husband was something she didn't want—if so, who could blame her? He thought back over the previous weeks, looking for hints in her behavior. There was nothing that could be taken as clear evidence either way. She was young. She was devoted to her community. He had to admit there was no clear reason to suppose she was lying about her feelings. And if she really loved him, why wouldn't she come with him? He would have died for her: if she felt as he did, she would not hesitate to follow him anywhere.

He returned to the hut and lit the cloth with the lamp, holding it until the writing had all been consumed. Then he laid down on the bed and his heart grew unbearable within him, flooding his mind with a torrent of anguish. Tears came, and for hours the grief was unrelenting. As the previous night had been heavenly, so the morning had become like living in hell. Sometimes he was furious at her, sometimes pitying. It made no difference: everything was a whisper compared to the fierce grief that had seized him.

In the early afternoon there were times when he grew calm and reasonable in his thinking, and he thought the worst of it might be over, but then the sorrow swelled afresh and he again felt the agony and hated everything in his life. He fought hard for lasting composure, but it eluded him. Every time he thought he had discovered the right way to interpret what had happened, a way that granted peace, a fresh thought would come to him with such immediacy and strength that he could not find the means to fend it and it would smash his previous conclusions to fragments.

Yet slowly, very slowly, as the afternoon moved on, a feeling of deep disgust grew in him and remained. He was weary of this village, of their vain hopes for the future, of their obsession with preserving the past. They were harmless enough, but whatever their origins, it seemed to Giovanni that they had grown very small in their thinking. He could barely wait to be free of this place. And by early evening he noticed, with relief, that this attitude prevailed. His love for Giulia, if that's what it was, had been misplaced. Since he seemed to have recovered from his disappointment in a single day, it could not have been too powerful an affection. Perhaps he would soon be free of any lingering regrets, fortified by the knowledge of her shallowness. It was good to know this now, before he left, so he would not have to suffer doubt in the future. And he should learn this lesson: that he was a fool, easily weakened when he let down his guard.

A young man brought him dinner, announcing he was Giulia's brother. He was a handsome boy of eighteen or so, and his manner was formal. After politely handing Giovanni his food, he stood awkwardly in front of him for a minute, one hand fidgeting with his belt buckle. When he finally spoke, it seemed to Giovanni as if he was delivering a speech.

"I just thought you should know, my sister has told the elders she will not marry you." Giovanni smiled acidly, but kept silent. "I have been telling her she should avoid becoming too involved with you, and I'm glad she has come to her senses. A crippled husband is not suitable for her. What sort of a husband do you think you would make? She has a good heart, and you have upset her. Have the decency to accept your fate without dragging her into your problems. I could not speak before because the elders had given her their permission, but her decision frees me to speak, at least for now. What I'm trying to say is that she is kind hearted, and she may later pity you and feel she should marry you. I know you are an outsider, so you probably have little respect for anything but yourself. We of this valley are raised to devote ourselves to something greater than ourselves. Self sacrifice is in her nature: I beg you in the name of honor, if she changes her mind, please don't take advantage of her. Let her live a happy life.

"She asked me to give you this." With obvious reluctance he took a necklace from around his neck with a small pendant attached. "It is very old, a family heirloom. It is proof of the guilt she feels, and I don't think you should accept it."

Giovanni reached out and took the necklace. He glanced at it briefly, noticing the pendant's tiny yellow thunderbolt falling from a blue cloud against an black, oval background. The gemstones had been well cut, and it was a beautiful piece of jewelry, though not particularly valuable. "Why not?" he said, placing it around his neck. "Guilt is good for people who are guilty. I'll keep this to remind me of what she and all the rest of you have done."

The brother curled his lip in disgust and turned and left without a backward glance. Though Giovanni's face was impassive, he felt a deepened revulsion as well. These were petty little villagers indeed, for all their education. It would be a pleasure to be free of them at last.

That night Giovanni waited until the hour was late. Rising from the bed, he climbed up on the stool and lifted the beam, pushing it to the side. Unhampered, it swung freely, and he lowered the free end carefully, fearful of noise, until it came to rest at a steep angle just above the ground. While he was doing so, the chain slid off of its own accord. He began with the end that was attached to his ankle: leaving enough slack to allow him free movement, he wrapped the excess chain fairly tightly around his waist. By the time he had reached the free end and tucked it securely in, the bulk and weight was considerable, but not too much for him to handle. He jumped a few times to test how noisy it was, and was pleased to note it made little sound, thanks to the layer of grease that still coated the links.

Donning his cloak, gathering up the bread and placing it in his tunic against his skin, he tied the knife to his leg as Giulia had done. After a final glance around the hut to be sure he'd done everything he needed to do, he turned and left.

It was dark outside, very dark, with no moon and a slight haze dimming the stars. A perfect night for what he had to do, although it took a few minutes for his eyes to become adjusted to the blackness after leaving behind the lamp that was still burning in his hut. Very slowly he passed through the village, with every step taking care to move silently. It took him ten agonizing minutes to pass, but to his relief there was no sign of anyone stirring. At the far end, where the houses came to an end, there was a hole in the tree line with a path disappearing into it. He entered, and cursed. He could see absolutely nothing in the darkness. Crouching, wondering if he should risk waiting there until the first light or push on downwards blindly. He had just decided to keep moving when he made out the faint outline of the path stretching before him. Looking up he saw that the mist had parted and the stars were now brilliant above the treetops. Standing up, he began following the trail as fast as he could. It was no easy task, for the light was barely enough to assist him, and several times he took wrong turnings where he mistook a patch of moss or a line of stones for the path. More than once he had to retrace his steps until he was once again certain he was on the trail. But at least it was well-trod, and after a little he discovered he could check whether he was on it by reaching down and feeling with his hand to determine if there were any plants beneath him. The trail was dirt and stones, and plants had been trodden to death, so this turned out to be a reliable method to stay on track. Having made that discovery, his progress became more rapid, though not as much as he would have liked. He still went no faster than a slow walk.

By the time dawn had come, he found he was following the banks of a small river which he assumed must be the Taro. Before the sun rose, he left the path and crossed over the stream without difficulty, for it never reached higher than his thigh. Feeling Giulia's necklace suddenly pulling on his neck, he tore it free and threw it into the current with a shudder of disgust. It splashed and vanished, swept away downstream. He felt a fierce pang of sorrow, as if it were not merely a necklace but the whole of his happiness and freedom that had been lost. He stared in a daze at the tumbling waters for a moment, fighting to turn away. When, with a shudder, control at last returned, he walked quickly over the jumbled stones of the river basin on the far side and climbed the gentle incline there. He guessed that about this time they would discover his absence, but they might have done so earlier. Rather than continue on his way and risk discovery, it would be best to go to ground. Looking around, he spotted a big tree nearby, which seemed likely to offer a commanding view of all approaches. There were low shrubs around its base to provide shelter, and he made for it.

He had just settled himself in, sitting on a large stone under the shelter of the overhanging branches, when he saw movement on the far bank of the river. He made out five figures running quickly in single file along the line he presumed the path followed, heading downstream. It made him feel dizzy to realize how close he'd come to being overtaken. He shrank back into the shadows and watched them pass. Every now and then one of the figures would head off at right angles, running down to the river or up the steep valley side to reconnoiter and then sprinting quickly to rejoin the others. They were deadly serious in their work and it was only a matter of moments before they disappeared from sight downstream. He was shaking as he watched them go. They must have discovered his escape before dawn.

After a time he became calmer, realizing the immediate danger had passed. He rubbed his ankle where the metal had chafed it as he walked. In several spots his leg had been rubbed raw and was oozing blood: he looked forward to the time when he had the means to remove the chain. For a while he pondered his next steps, but he concluded there was little to do but wait for nightfall, and he soon began thinking of other things. He picked up a section of dead branch and taking out the knife, began carving it absentmindedly while the morning passed.

The events of the past few weeks were amazing. He thought of the village, of its extraordinary secrets, and eventually, reluctantly, of Giulia. It was strange indeed, but that peculiar euphoria was with him even now, quietly burning in the background of his mind, like a warm yellow candle lighting a cold and empty room. It had never wavered, not even when he was absorbed by the peril of his escape. Perhaps it wasn't love at all. But then what was it? It shone brightest when she was near, but it shone always, whether he was angry at her, frightened, or thinking of his escape. It shone now, when he had sensibly left her far behind. It was as if his heart and mind were two separate creatures that hardly knew each other. His mind was practical and clever, always digging into the problems he faced, but his heart was stupid as a cow, a slave that never wavered in its devotion to her. How had something so foolish come to pass? When he was with her his heart had sat silent and happy, pleased—no: ecstatic—just to see her. When he had read her letter, his despair and anger had not touched it: looking back he realized his heart had gazed upon the cloth where she had written the note, smiling happily in its simplicity.

Now that he was away from her the euphoria continued, but that devoted fool of a heart had also begun to ache. "Idiot!" muttered Giovanni angrily to himself. "She doesn't love you, but you don't care, do you? She is danger, but you think she is an angel. Grow up: let her go!" The dumb beast did not heed him, however. Or if it did, it sought out greater perversity, for its aching only increased, and its ridiculous joy was simultaneously undiminished.

The more Giovanni reflected on it, the more he came to feel he had been saddled with an extra burden, a child that knew no sense, or rather a retarded man with the brain of a child: big, stupid, dull. And though his mind was free to think wherever reason took it, traveling now here, now there, his heart never moved. Where his mind was loud and forceful, his heart was always silent, so he could easily overlook it for a time. But in the end his heart was the stronger of the two, for it never hesitated, never changed. Bit by bit it steered his mind back to Giulia, to her and her alone. And where his heart looked upon her blissfully, his mind perceived only fear.

When the morning sun had risen high in the sky, and its bright color had turned his shade to deepest blue, Giovanni became aware of the thing he was carving for the first time. It was a man's face, his own perhaps, contorted as if in grief: the eyes were large and staring at nothing, the mouth turned down in misery. He chuckled out loud, tossing it into the air and catching it again, as if he were weighing it. "Fool," he said, and tossed it away. A moment later he fetched it back, and set it on a stone facing across the river, its sightless eyes staring back the way he'd come. "There you go, fool. There is where your sorrow lies: look long and enjoy your misery." Then he sat down again, this time facing away to the West, where the carving was out of his sight. He put the knife away.

The day passed as he sat there, only rising to relieve himself. He didn't see his pursuers, but then he wasn't looking, confident that if he remained where he was they would never find him. Though he sat quietly, beneath the surface the war between his head and heart raged unabated, and progress in resolving it seemed impossible. His mind was on the side of the facts and was open to any sensible argument, of which there were many. His heart cared nothing for facts, greeting every attempt at reason with total indifference. In mid-afternoon he moved the carving, turning it to face down the valley in the direction of freedom. "This is what lies ahead of you," he said. "You need two heads little man, both full of sorrow: one for where you've been, one for where you are going. But since you are headed down the river, perhaps you should face the loneliness that lies that way."

In the dusk Giovanni made his way stealthily down to the river for a drink. He had intended to follow its banks downwards, but as he started out he could not bear the thought that every step carried him farther from Giulia, and that he would never see her again. Perhaps a night's sleep would settle the matter. He returned to the tree and lay down, shifting his weight several times in a vain attempt to make himself comfortable. The chain was still wrapped around his waist: he had been afraid to take it off during the day in case he had to escape suddenly, and now it was biting into his side and back painfully. In the end he unwrapped it from his waist and lay down beside it. Before long, he was asleep.

Giovanni awoke before dawn when a bird began to sing in the branches of the tree overhead. He had been dreaming, something very beautiful, though he could not recall what. He tried to remember, because it had left him feeling happy and full of hope. Something about Giulia... Suddenly he sat upright, excited, wide awake. Perhaps there was a way after all! Restraining himself by an act of will, he considered it carefully, fearful lest the dream was confusing his reason. He sat for a moment thinking. But no! It was obvious!

The villagers sought to blind him because they feared he would tell the outside world about their presence. They couldn't trust him: they would be fools if they did. He couldn't prove that their secrets were safe with him because he'd had no chance to prove it. But now that he had successfully escaped, if he returned to them of his own free will they would know he could be trusted. The blinding and hamstringing would be unnecessary. They were not bloodthirsty people: once their fear had been set to rest they would offer him no harm.

But what if Giulia didn't want him? Even if she had been sincere in the things she said in her note, that didn't mean there was no hope: if she had changed her mind because a handicapped husband had seemed too onerous, that was no longer a problem. And if she was truly not in love with him, even that might change with time. She was young, after all, and hadn't she said there was no alternative choice for a husband besides him? Faced with a life alone or one with him, she might be persuaded to change her mind.

There was no immediate rush, and in fact returning too quickly to the village would be dangerous, so he would remain for another day and night in this place. The extra time would assure the villagers that he had been safely away before he went back to them. He noted with relief that the knowledge of his decision to return seemed to have soothed his heart, for the ache had faded even as the decision had been made. He settled himself to wait.

And suddenly Giovanni knew that this had always been the course he had to take. It didn't matter whether she loved him or not: he had to remain as close to her as he possibly could. As foolish as its urges might be, his heart would give him no rest until he gave into it. But there were other reasons. However misguided their goals might be, he had no argument with the village's religious views, and it was obvious that they were by and large honorable people, which was more than he could say of most of the people he had met in the world outside. And until he was free of the regions dominated by Rome, he would always be at risk of discovery. Perhaps his actions had been kept secret from many, but some at least knew of the attempted murder, and if he came across one of them his life would be worth nothing. Here his life was not in danger. The valley would be a sanctuary to him as it was to the ancient Gods.

iovanni got up the following morning and started to walk back towards the river, forgetting in his haste that the chain was no longer secured. After a few steps it began to drag, and it dug into the wounds on his ankle that had been formed two days before. It had not had enough time to heal. Cursing, he went back and again wrapped its length tightly around his waist. As soon as he'd tucked in the end he set out again, walking at a brisk pace, limping a little from the pain. Something occurred to him and he stopped to remove the knife and its scabbard from his leg. Then he tossed them as far as he could into the bushes: he didn't want anyone to realize Giulia had known of his plans for escape.

He crossed the river again and rejoined the trail. As he walked along it, his thoughts were full of Giulia, wondering what she would say and do when she saw him once again. The trail seemed different in daylight, and at one point he stopped in confusion, wondering if he had taken the wrong turn. But no, up ahead in the distance he could see where the valley narrowed, and the mountain he'd climbed over the day he'd first come. Relieved, he set out again.

His ankle was hurting badly and his limp was getting worse. It was difficult to tell, but he thought he must be still an hour's walk from the village. He heard a branch snap somewhere behind him and he turned and listened. Was someone coming? He braced himself, for the moment of truth was coming. Not wanting his back turned when they overtook him, be began to walk back down the path the way he'd come. Just as he rounded a sharp turn, he almost stumbled into three men coming fast up the path. The one at the fore saw him first and grunted in surprise, but he barely slowed before hurling himself on Giovanni, knocking him over into the bushes.

There was nothing Giovanni could do but curl himself up as the blows rained down on all sides. "I surrender!" he shouted several times before his attackers got control of themselves. Then they bound his hands behind his back and dragged him bleeding to his feet.

"I came back to surrender," he said, but no one paid any attention. Their profound relief at having him again made them break out laughing and slapping each other on the shoulders, excitedly recounting the capture and describing in detail what parts they, personally, had played. Giovanni listened in silence, understanding fully, for the first time, the degree of danger the village must have thought it faced. It occurred to him that in nine hundred years he probably seemed to them the greatest danger the village had ever encountered, but he knew this was not the time and place to try to convince them otherwise. He would wait until he met the elders. It was several minutes before one of his captors calmed down enough to suggest to the others that they go back to the village and share the good news.

Over the next hour or so, Giovanni was marched rapidly up the valley. He tasted blood in his mouth, and one eye was swelling from the blows he had received. His ankle was freely bleeding by now, and he winced with every step, the pain radiating up his leg and almost robbing him of the power to walk, but his captors seemed not to hear his frequent requests that they slow down. They pushed and pulled him when he lagged or stumbled at the rougher spots along the trail, and continued to speak excitedly among themselves. It was as if they couldn't hear Giovanni at all.

When they finally broke from the trees and walked into the village, Giovanni almost sobbed with relief. He was shoved to the dirt, and within a few seconds a crowd materialized. Like his captors back when they had taken him, the crowd became very excited and the lucky three were congratulated, embraced, patted, kissed: at one point everyone cheered them as heroes. Despite being at the center of all this enthusiasm, Giovanni felt almost invisible. No one spoke to him, and it was as if he was a trophy, not a man.

Finally the crowd parted and made way for the elders. They too were smiling and offering their thanks to his captors, but after a few minutes they turned their attention to Giovanni. They gathered around and regarded him for a moment, and the crowd fell silent as if by magic, everyone waiting to see what would happen. It was the counsel's leader who spoke.

"You will be blinded and hamstrung at sunset today. I think you can appreciate that we no longer feel much regret at this fact. You have endangered everyone's life, and more importantly, the purpose to which our lives are dedicated." Noticing the state of Giovanni's leg and face, he turned and called to someone to fetch the physician. He was told the man was away at the Southern pass looking for Giovanni, and would not return until later that afternoon. Turning back, he was silent for a moment, and then he frowned. "Have you anything to say?"

At last someone was paying attention to him: Giovanni felt grateful to the elder for that. "I was returning here on purpose. I have decided to live here."

Some among the crowd burst into loud expressions of disbelief, but the elder maintained a dignified calm. "Why would you return, knowing what you would be forced to endure?" Giovanni could hear the skepticism in his voice.

"I was free...clear of your valley. No one could ever have found me. I watched some of you from across the Taro river as you hunted me. I sat under a big tree and watched, perfectly safe. You said you wished to blind me because you thought me dangerous, but by returning I think I have shown I pose no risk. The truth is that I don't fear your religion, and although its continuation doesn't seem too important to me, I do not wish to see your village destroyed by the Church. The Church is now my enemy too, and while you threaten to cripple me, they would kill me if they could. I have no wealth, no family, no close friends left in the world outside. I have no real wish to return there. I know it seems strange, but since I have come here I have felt a deep sense of peace: I want to remain." He thought about mentioning his greatest reason for returning, but since she had rejected him, he thought it might do more harm than good. Besides, unless he could get her to change her mind, returning for her sake would make him sound a fool, though not for an instant did he feel like one. In fact, he kept scanning the crowd to see if she had come. She had not.

The counsel head asked the men who captured Giovanni the circumstances in which they had encountered him. They explained that he was heading away from the village and stumbled into them by chance. Presumably he had gone to ground somewhere nearby and only today felt safe enough to head down the valley towards freedom. Giovanni heard their description and realized their assumption was very reasonable. In their place he would see it the same way. His confidence began to drain away, and suddenly he felt sick. When he spoke, his voice was thin and ragged, and even to his own ears it seemed like the voice of a liar.

"I was heading for the village, but I heard a noise behind me. If I was really trying to escape I would have hidden, but instead I turned back to surrender myself. I give you my word."

"What noise did you hear. Were these men talking? What did they say?"

"I heard a branch break."

One of the men who had captured him vehemently denied having made any sound, and the others backed him up. They seemed to Giovanni to be sincere. Who remembers a thing of such little importance as a snapping branch underfoot? There was no reason they should remember it.

"Giovanni," said the elder, "we have no proof the Church is your enemy. For the truth of that we have only your words to rely on. And you were not taken heading towards our village, but away from it. We have only your word that you heard something and had turned back to greet our men. We know that you escaped, and that even if one of us were facing the same situation, we might be tempted to flee to the far corners of the earth to escape. To be blind and crippled is a terrible thing. Furthermore we know of your affection for Giulia, and we know that her rejection of you stripped away the only human bond that you had with our village. Unless you have something to add, the counsel will meet now to consider the circumstances yet again, but you should know there is little chance of a change in our decision."

"I love Giulia, I wanted to be near her..." Giovanni's words were so weak that he himself could scarcely believe them. He was very tired, and suddenly he just slumped and let it all go. Let them blind him. He was past caring. His leg hurt, his face and body ached, he was surrounded by enemies. It was madness that brought him back for this. The only thing left that seemed to matter was this absurd urge to see Giulia, his dumb heart's wish, nothing else important to its stubborn will but that.

The elder made no reply to his profession of love, and no one else appeared to think it worthy of a response. The elders walked away, taking most of the crowd with them, leaving only those too young to have a vote in the counsel. After looking at him curiously and chattering to each other, they too moved off, sitting together twenty paces away in a rough circle, talking and laughing excitedly. But they did not forget to look at him often to make sure he was not attempting yet again to escape. Giovanni was left sitting on the ground, arms bound, bleeding still from the wound at his ankle, his face dirty and crusted with dry blood from the blows he received earlier.

He sank down, grunting with the pain, collapsing slowly to lie uncomfortably on his side in the dirt. After a moment he closed his eyes. He did not sleep, but nor was he fully conscious of what was going on around him. He seemed to ache everywhere, he was thirsty, and nausea came and went in waves. With his inward eye, he watched himself suffering like a wounded beast, and for a long time that was all he knew.

How long it was that he laid there he could not guess, but suddenly he was aware of something touching his face. It hurt. He flinched away, fearful of more blows, opening his eyes wide in shock and fear. And then the fear seemed to melt away.

Giulia was there, her face a mix of concern and sadness, pushing his hair back from his face. "Oh Giovanni," she cried in anguish, "why could you not get away?"

He tried to answer, but he could not make his tongue and voice produce more than a croak.

"Don't speak," she said softly, "I'll be back." She disappeared from his sight and he laid there unmoving, his eyes gazing blankly at the ground before his face. A moment later she was beside him again, with water in a bowl and a damp cloth. She held his head up so he could sip the cool liquid, and when he'd had a little she used the cloth to wipe his face. "Where does it hurt?" she asked anxiously.

"Everywhere." He tried to smile, but his lips hurt, and he must have broken open a fresh scab, for he tasted blood again. Giulia dabbed at the corner of his mouth with the cloth. "I came back," he said.

"Why? Why would you do something so stupid?" She seemed angry and pitying at the same time, and afraid of what he would say.

"For you. I couldn't leave..."

"Oh Giovanni, you are a fool."

"I know, I know. It's my heart...it's a cow." He tried to laugh, and she stared at him uncomprehendingly. "Giulia, I had to come back. But I thought since I was returning of my own free will they would realize I was not dangerous and they wouldn't... Giulia, you don't have to love me, I don't blame you: I couldn't leave. Being near you is enough. I'm happy now. Just seeing you..." He smiled, and the pain seemed to have dimmed. "I know it's stupid, but I'm happy. I should be worried and regretful—and I am—but I'm also happy. I love you."

He could see she was confused as she looked at him, but when she spoke her voice was clear, sad. "I love you too, you foolish boy. And I'm sorry about the letter, the things I wrote. I didn't want to see you harmed. I was afraid."

"I wondered if you meant it."

"I meant nothing I wrote: nothing. I wanted you to escape, but then when you were actually gone I kept hoping you would be caught: I'm sorry, but I couldn't help myself. Even now, I'm sorry, but even now when you are so hurt, I'm just glad to see you. I can't help how I feel."

"It's the same with me. Don't feel sorry."

"I should have come with you. I haven't slept since that night... Sometimes it has felt like I'm going insane. I was planning to leave tonight. And now it's too late. I was going to find you. It seemed hopeless, but I had to try. Only now there is nothing I can do. I'm sorry, Giovanni: I failed you."

"You have nothing to regret, nothing to feel guilty for. If I was someone else, that might be true, I don't know. But I am not. It sounds strange, and even if you don't feel it too, I still feel this way in every corner of my being: I am not separate from you. What you want I want, what you do I do. If you wanted to take my life, I would help you to take it. I will lose my sight, but if I can just hear you, or feel your touch, I will be happy."

"I will never leave you, my love, never again let you go. It's the same with me: Aphrodite has joined us so closely you are like one side of a single person and I am like the other. That is how it feels. When you left and I stayed, that person was torn apart and lay dying. I will never do such a terrible thing again as long as I live. I will never! By all the Gods, I swear it."

She cleaned the wound on his ankle while he lay there, and fetching herbs and rendered fat, made an ointment that she smeared over it. Then she worked a thin strip of clean linen under the chain and bound it, providing some protection from the hard metal. She cut the cord that bound his hands behind his back, unwrapped the chain from his waist and he stretched out, his cloak beneath his head. Slowly she bathed him, despite his protests, dipping the cloth in water, wiping away the dirt and blood from his face, his arms, his feet. It took a long time, so careful was her work, and she was not yet completely finished as the elders returned with the rest of the counsel. As they walked up, they looked at her curiously but no one said anything.

The leader spoke once everyone had gathered around and Giovanni had pulled himself up to a sitting position with Giulia's help. His voice was guarded, neutral.

"Sunset approaches, but there is one thing I must ask before the decision is carried out. Is there anything, anything at all that could prove to us you left this valley and returned before your capture? Did you leave any evidence that you were there? Think, Giovanni, before you answer. Justice demands it."

Giovanni wondered what he was getting at, and started to say that he had already told them all there was to tell, when he remembered the little bust he'd whittled. Had there been time for someone to find it? "I made a carving. A self portrait, sort of. I left it under the tree where I sat, facing north." Would they delay matters while they checked his story? He should have thought of it earlier.

The elder looked at his colleagues, and they nodded. Then he turned to Giovanni again. "The Fates have been kind to you." He held out his hand and opened it, and Giovanni saw the little carved head lying in his palm. "We sent some hunters immediately to go down and check out your story. We felt it sensible to make our final decision while in possession of all of the facts. They ran all the way, both there and back. They were sent to see if there was evidence of someone sitting by a tree beyond the Taro, and they found it, but they also found this. It was more than we expected, for it is proof. But it was not enough.

"While they were gone, the counsel debated the matter. Even if we knew you had come back, did that mean you were safe? We have been afraid of you, Giovanni. Deeply afraid. When we caught you, many of us felt like blinding you on the spot. Some of us even wanted to kill you. And while we were waiting to see if your story was verified, many of us felt it would make no difference if it was. Please forgive us, and understand the reason.

"I think our fear was greater than our reason and compassion, and we would have voted against trust, but you have a friend you've never met. One of the wise came down from his home farther up the valley when he heard of your escape. He attended the counsel. He is called Giorgio, and he listened quietly while every voice was raised against you. Then, just before we voted, he spoke.

"He didn't say much, only that you sounded to him like a decent man, and perhaps the Gods had need of your legs and eyes in times to come. Otherwise, why would they have taken the trouble of having you leave and then return? Better just to have kept you here in the first place, if blinding was their will. He also spoke of the founding of Delphi, and of Aias of the Deukalidae who was an outsider like you when he discovered that place at the end of the previous dark age. Aias played an important role in the re-establishment of civilization, though his name is known only to a few. His blood still flows in this village, for many here are his descendants. Giorgio said that the time is coming when our secrets will again go out into the world, and the wise had been expecting someone like you for many years. Though he didn't say what your role would be, he believes you are to be like Aias was, those many centuries ago.

"The wise rarely come to the village, and more rarely still do they speak in the counsel. We did not debate the matter further, but unanimously voted to set you free, provided you could be proven to have told the truth. Your words are proven, so you are free. We regret your rough handling, and the way you were imprisoned after you arrived in this valley." He paused and shook his head as he regarded Giovanni's wounds. "Please take our hands in friendship, for you are welcomed here as one of us." He held out his hand, and Giovanni took it. The elder pulled him forward and up, and with Giulia's help, Giovanni found himself standing unsteadily on his feet. At the suggestion of one of the elders, the villagers solemnly formed a line that slowly passed him, shaking his hand while each offered brief words of welcome. He felt a vague sense of unreality at the change in his circumstances, but he pushed it aside and paid attention to the people who passed before him. Some were cool and formal, but others seemed genuinely happy at the turn of events. Only a handful were transparently suspicious, and he did not begrudge them their doubts. He would prove them wrong in time.

The elders were beside and around him, Giulia with her hand supporting his arm. Giovanni turned his head to look at her, and they both smiled. And at that moment, while he stood in the dust aching and bloodied, a boundless joy burst like a shout from somewhere in his heart, and all the world seemed gladdened by its song.

iovanni saw only his own life at that moment, and gave no thought to history's ebb and flow—the enormous tidal currents of the centuries that sweep humanity helpless before them. That is how it often is with mortals, but it is never the full story.

Far away in the land of the Greeks where the remnants of the Eastern Roman Empire still survived, twilight was deepening around a rugged mountainside even as Giovanni stood greeting his new neighbors. It was a beautiful spot, but no one paid much attention to the place: it was just another mountain in a land of many mountains. But it had not always been so.

Long, long before, there had once been an age like Giovanni's, when a time of darkness was slowly giving way to one of light, and civilization was quickening in the hearts of men and women. In that distant time, followers of the God Apollo sought out a place to found a sanctuary, a place that would give voice to their vision of Truth and lay the foundations for a glorious new age. It was here they would come, to this silent Greek mountainside, more than two thousand years before Giovanni's day--a place they would come to call Delphi.

Under Parnassos: The Tale of Aias and the Womb of the World

(Delphi, Naxos and Delos, 933 - 932 BC)

The shadowy interior of the hut was cramped, barely enough room to hold the narrow cot where the dim shape of a man lay unmoving, breathing irregularly. On a low shelf beside him an oil lamp burnt with an almost insignificantly tiny flame, releasing a thin steady stream of smoke towards the low ceiling where it hovered, forming a dark haze that nearly obscured the roof beams and thatch from view. The floor was dirt; the walls had been fashioned of sticks caulked with mud. The doorway was even cruder, though it did keep the light out: it had been draped with a motley collection of worn leather and cloth pieces roughly stitched together. There were no windows, and the overall effect was unrelentingly squalid and claustrophobic.

At the foot of the bed, almost indistinguishable from a shadow at first glance, a boy squatted in the dirt with knees drawn up, arms holding them tightly against his chest while he rocked nervously back and forth. Every now and then he paused to crane upwards over the edge of the cot and inspect the sleeper.

At such moments the light caught his face. It was dirty, his skin an unhealthy pale color, and the flesh of his cheeks sagged slightly with exhaustion. Tension around his mouth had narrowed the lips, while his eyes had a frightened, anxious look about them as he frowned through the shadows towards the sleeper. And yet it was clear that the boy was basically attractive, that with rest and pleasant surroundings he would actually have been quite handsome. The bones of his face were generous, strong, as his lips were disposed to be at other times, and yet around the eyes an appealing sensitivity prevailed. He wore a cloak of rough-spun wool over a long, loose-fitting tunic. Around his neck a thong had been tied with a pendant attached. The pendant was small, a black oval that had a beautiful little cloud of blue and an amber lightening bolt set in it. His ample black hair was bound back with a strip of cloth to keep it from his eyes. Beneath the leather bands of his sandals his toes were just visible in the shadows, and he clenched and unclenched them steadily, his skin sliding smoothly over the damp soles.

His name was Aias, and he was barely twelve.

They had arrived in the village near sunset some time ago and Aias had helped the sailors beach the ship, plunging stiffly into the calm water, his sandaled feet stumbling over the smooth stones while he tried to help maneuver the heavy boat across a shallow sandbar.

Once the ship had been pulled a little way up the beach Aias had sought out the village elder, and after some negotiation offered him a small piece of silver he had taken from his teacher and stored safely in his mouth even before the village had come fully into view. The elder had promised they could stay as long as they needed in an old widow's hut, situated out beyond the town's refuse pile. Then he had disappeared behind the trees and returned a little later to tell Aias that he and the unconscious man could move in now, for the widow had already moved her few belongings into a goat shed nearby.

The sailors took Alcidas from the boat, carefully lowering him over the side in a large cloth meant for patching sails. Several villagers watched silently from in front of their huts, some still holding the weapons they had taken up on hearing a ship was approaching. Fear of pirates would make any sane man suspicious of strangers.

Two of the bigger sailors carried the unconscious man along the grassy path that led to the widow's home while Aias moved anxiously around them, carrying the bundles belonging to Alcidas. The boy thanked them repeatedly for their assistance as they went along, apologizing for the inconvenience. The sailors ignored him.

After laying Alcidas down in the dust just outside the hut, one of them, a tall, balding man burnt brown by the sun, reached under the inert man's cloak and broke the string holding the small sack he had strung to his shoulder. It was the little sack containing their remaining pieces of silver.

"Wait!" Aias had said, reaching out as if to stop him, but the sailor straightened slowly and turned to face him, putting his hand on the pommel of his knife. The man's lips were stretched into a hard smile, his eyes cold.

They stood there a moment, watching each other, and Aias felt himself beginning to shake uncontrollably, though with fear or frustration he did not know. The sailor's mouth slowly twisted open and he chuckled while Aias looked down, his ears growing warm with humiliation. His mind seemed choked with noise and he felt paralyzed, confused.

He hardly noticed when the sailors turned their backs dismissively on him and walked away laughing, disappearing towards the beach. Instead he became aware of Alcidas' figure lying motionless in the dust. He felt the urge to explain to the unconscious man that there was nothing he could have done, that he had no weapon, that there were two of them... but Alcidas scorned anyone who did not defend his possessions from others, regardless of the circumstances. He would almost certainly side with the sailors when he recovered and found out what had happened.

Belatedly, Aias had thought to appeal to the captain for justice. After all, he had been Alcidas' drinking companion since before the ship had sailed. Aias had run down to the water as fast as he was able, full of hope by the time he got there that everything might soon be put right.

He arrived in time to see the captain tying the sack to his waist-belt while the sailors wrestled the ship back into the water. When they saw him they paused in their work and jeered. Seeing Aias standing helplessly by the water's edge, the captain tapped the sack with his hand and called out smiling: "I'll keep this for Alcidas, since you're too young to protect it properly. He can collect it when he's better."

That made the sailors' laughter strong, and Aias watched numbly while they heaved the boat into deeper water, scrambled aboard, set out their oars, and began pulling away to sea. He watched after them for a moment and then turned and went back through the silent village, ignoring the impassive faces of the town's folk and dreading the unconscious form he had left lying in the dust.

When he got back to the hut, Aias half carried, half dragged Alcidas inside and onto the cot. He kept hoping the man would stir, but it did not happen. Filled with fear, lost, he took his place at the foot of the teacher and began his vigil, getting up only when the lamp needed refilling from the little clay jug he found stored beneath the bed.

*T*here had been no sight or sound of the villagers for hours. It seemed as if the world beyond the ragged doorway had disappeared and only the dim four walls of the smoky hut remained of the world Aias had known. He rocked back and forth, his mind numb, listening to the breathing of the man who lay on the cot while the hours moved steadily on.

It was a great shock to him when suddenly the door cover was thrown back from outside and daylight rushed in, forcing him to squint. The night had come and gone. A deeply lined face appeared, no doubt the widow's whose hut this was, partly silhouetted against the bright sky and sunlit trees outside. At first she did not see Aias, blinded as she was in the dark interior of the hut. After a few seconds, however, she became aware of his pale, careworn face peering at her from the dust at the foot of the bed. "I am Tisiphone. And you?" She seemed shy, the sympathy in her words apparent despite her peculiar Dorian accent.

"Aias of the Deukalidae at Naxos" he said, and cringed inwardly: awkward, uncertain, his was a voice halfway between youth and maturity; it made him want to retreat farther into the shadows until the woman had left. He battled the impulse while she regarded him curiously for a moment.

"I brought some gruel for you." she said at last. The flap fell shut leaving the hut briefly in darkness, and when it reopened she passed him a small wooden bowl filled with cold thick fluid. He took it silently, politely taking a small sip before setting it on the floor in front of him, wiping his mouth on the back of his hand. He was not hungry. Smiling, wiping her hands on the front of her ragged dress, the old woman left, and Aias was alone again with the burden of his thoughts in the smoky hut.

More time passed, some hours certainly, before the door-flap was once more opened. This time, a painfully bright barb of sunshine reached into the womblike darkness to fall on Aias, blinding him with its intensity. This time it wasn't the old woman. Instead, three women he had not seen before came in, one after another, to stand beside the cot where Alcidas lay. Feeling overwhelmed by so many people in the tiny space, the boy got up sheepishly, looking at the floor. The women ignored him, standing and looking at Alcidas for a minute, glancing at each other when his breath rasped a little in his throat. Aias, realizing they were not interested in him, took the opportunity to secretly look them over. It seemed that they might be mother, daughter, and grand-daughter, given their ages and certain physical characteristics they shared in common, but he couldn't be sure. The middle-aged one spoke first.

"Pull back his cloak so we can see him better", she said to the eldest. The old woman glanced at Aias, as if to see whether he would raise any objection, and then reached out and gingerly lifted the edge of the cloth with her thumb and index fingers, and with a sudden flick lifted and threw the cloak towards the wall.

Although he was bloodied with several minor cuts, it was difficult to see what Alcidas' problem was as he lay there. The girl edged to one side to let in more light from the door-flap she was holding open. It didn't help much, though they peered closely, studying: the lump was hidden on the back of Alcidas' head, beneath him. "How did this happen?" the old woman said, not turning to look at Aias, though both of her companions did.

Aias felt hollow, his memories seeming to echo through his head. "He fell on the ship, fell from the mast." Aias looked up after he spoke, wondering if his words would satisfy them. Apparently they did, for they went back to observing Alcidas. He was surprised that such a simple explanation seemed sufficient for these strangers. Were it not for the presence of Alcidas' inert body, he would have thought the whole thing a terrible dream. But the unconscious figure lying before him made that impossible.

Alcidas had always been prone to displays of prowess. He had been drinking with the captain, a stout man of middle years with a withered leg, speaking fondly of the wars of his youth, when a rope had jammed in its track at the top of the mast, preventing the sailors from taking advantage of a freshening breeze. They were about to send their lightest crew member aloft, when Alcidas shoved the young sailor aside, proclaiming that such jobs were better left to men. After offering a torrent of friendly abuse to the captain and his men, he had begun to shinny up the mast.

Although forty-five years had left their mark on him, Alcidas made swift progress. The sailors gathered below to watch, and took to cheering him on with laughter and insults. He reached the top without incident and freed the rope, but relishing his position he began to clown for his audience, pretending to scan the surrounding waters as sailors did in dangerous seas, shouting out warnings and pointing to imaginary rocks. At the time it seemed funny and everyone laughed, even Aias. Alcidas might have carried off his prank without harm but he was holding on with only one hand, pointing with the other, when a particularly heavy wave struck the side of the boat.

His hand losing its grip, Alcidas swung upside down, his legs tightening as he fought to regain his position. For a moment it looked as if he might recover, but then he began to slide down the mast with increasing speed, suddenly breaking free and plummeting to the deck below. He was unconscious when Aias pushed to his side through the press of sailors. The captain ordered water thrown on Alcidas' face, but it had no affect. Aias began to pray.

After slapping Alcidas a few times across his face, shouting his name loudly into his ear, the sailors started moving him to a better position in the belly of the ship. It was then that they discovered a large bump was forming where his head had snapped back against the deck when he fell.

A little later when the captain told his helmsman to make for shore, it dawned on Aias that he meant to abandon them. "Can't you wait?" Aias had asked. "Alcidas will be all right soon: it's just a bump on his head. He thought of you as a friend, and we have no other way of going to the west or getting back to Megara."

But the captain had already made up his mind. "I'm not having a man die on my ship if I can stop it. Nobody made him go up there, and I haven't got time to waste waiting to see if he lives. We have much to do before the annual North winds force us to winter on shore."

He looked down at Alcidas and added reflectively: "Anyway, his chance of surviving will be better on land." Abandoning them (and indeed, later stealing Alcidas' property) was nothing personal: a traveler could only make claim to the things he could take and hold. Aias knew that the captain was honorable, but that honor rarely benefited the weak. Ultimately the fault for his difficult situation was his alone. Were he more forceful, they might still be on board the ship. If he had shown more bravery when challenged over the purse, it was true he could be injured or dead, but then again he might have managed to save the silver; in either case his honor would be intact. When Alcidas recovered, he would certainly thrash Aias for his cowardice.

Aias became aware that the three women were discussing Alcidas' prospects. As they did so, they ignored him. "Look at his stomach" said the older woman, "It's swollen." The other two bent forward a little to see in the lamplight.

"Do you remember, mother, the time that sheep fell from the cliff?" the middle-aged woman said thoughtfully. "He survived the fall, but his belly swelled and he died the next day." Apparently she did, for she nodded.

"This man's skin has lost its color, and he's shivering too." said the youngest to her grandmother, her voice inquisitive, uncertain. "Surely his fires are burning low?"

"You are right, child, and look: water is pouring from his face, driven by the battle within. It will certainly extinguish his life before long."

Aias could see their observations were true: Alcidas' belly was indeed bloated and had been since last night; his face was bathed in sweat and very pale. Only the difficult rise and fall of his chest showed he was alive. Yet although he had no reason to doubt the wisdom of the old woman, he found himself unable to accept the possibility that Alcidas might die. If it were true, he might as well be dead himself: how could he get home? Anything could happen: murdered by bandits, enslaved by householders, starved to death, lost in foreign parts. The land of his birth seemed as far beyond his reach as the moon.

Apparently satisfied that there was little more to discover, the middle-aged woman looked inquisitively at her elder, then nodded. The old woman reached over to the cloak and tried to drag it back on top of Alcidas. Her effort was half-hearted at best, leaving him mostly exposed, but Aias could see that she was not doing this intentionally: she did not want to be tainted by a body which would, in her opinion, soon be earth-bound. Rubbing the fingers of her hand on her tunic, the old woman turned towards the door and waited impatiently while the other two filed out. In a moment they were gone, off to tell the other villagers, Aias supposed.

Aias walked around the cot and after adjusting the cloak across him, leaned over to look closely at Alcidas' face. He hovered there for a minute, studying the eyelids, the mouth, the perspiring forehead for signs of returning consciousness. There were none. He reached under the cloak and felt the distended belly with his fingers. The skin was cold and wet. It frightened him.

He turned and walked back to his spot in the corner and was just settling wearily to his seat when the door-flap opened again, this time revealing the face of the widow. She regarded him somberly for a moment, glancing at the still untouched bowl of gruel on the floor, and then her face softened into a shy smile.

"Come away and have some dinner with me." she said quietly, firmly. "You need food if you are to look after your father."

"He's not my father" replied Aias.

"What then?"

"My uncle, I suppose, but also he is my teacher, a member of one of the brotherhood of poets at Delos."

"Then for your teacher's sake, come away and eat."

"I can eat here."

"Will you make me run back and forth with food you won't touch?" She pointed at the bowl, and then waved toward Alcidas: "You can do nothing for him. Let the Gods settle the matter as they see fit."

Realizing she was not going to give up, feeling foolish, he rose, picked up the bowl of gruel and followed her out through the doorway, stumbling a little in his stiffness. It was not as grim outside as he remembered. The late afternoon sun streaked down through the trees from the west, and a pleasant breeze was blowing from the sea. Tisiphone led him around the hut to a path leading farther from the sea, along beside a tangle of low trees, their trunks obscured by dry, knee-high grass. He could see the smoke of a fire rising from behind some higher trees ahead, and they made for the spot.

The fire burned before a low thatched roof without walls, a shelter for goats when they were brought down from the pastures on the mountains. Surrounding the shelter and the ground out front of it was a badly made and maintained stone wall built of angular grayish rock. Beside the entrance, really nothing more than a hole in the wall, leaned a sturdy wood section that could be lifted into place to cover the gap. They walked past this, into the enclosure, and Tisiphone stopped at the fire to peer into a small blackened clay pot that sat beside it keeping warm. She looked at Aias and smiled, the deep furrows of her face rearranging themselves to reveal a mischievousness he had not noticed before. "Onions in broth" she said.

Life had been hard for Tisiphone, as it was for most people living on the mainland. On the whole, her appearance was typical for a woman who had made it to her sixties. Most of her teeth were missing, her face lined like an ancient river valley, scored deeply by the passing years. She was hunched over from too much labor and too little good food, and her hands were coarse and stubby, fingernails torn, fingers callused. Her hair was mostly gray and the dyed black cloth of her clothes was so frayed and torn that it seemed entirely possible they would not survive another month of use. Clearly she was one of the poorest people in a very poor town. Yet there was an essential good humor emanating from her eyes, and they moved with unexpected swiftness and decision, giving the impression of a person whose mind had grown more sharp and balanced with the years, not less. While Aias ate, she observed him quietly from the far side of the fire, so that he grew quite uncomfortable and was very relieved when she broke the silence and spoke.

"What will you do?" she asked.

He spent a long moment looking into the fire where a tongue of flame was licking against a stick, caressing its bark so that it peeled away in irregular patches and dropped burning onto the hot coals below. He could find no answer.

Suddenly, absurdly, he felt the urge to throw his arms around this woman and cry. The temptation outraged him, and when his bottom lip threatened to tremble, he pressed both lips together while looking at the fire, an action he hoped would convey thoughtful reflection. Trying to sound confident, he spoke without knowing what he was saying, his words thrown out like a billow of smoke that he prayed would be thick enough to cloud her penetrating eyes.

"I don't really know," he said slowly at first, his voice taut. "I've got to get to Megara, and I don't have any goods to barter, but something's bound to turn up. Anyway, Alcidas, that's my uncle's name, will probably get better." The boy glanced shyly at the old woman, but her face showed no reaction. "So it's too soon to say. I suppose I could perform with Alcidas' lyre for food along the way: I have trained under him for seven years now and my other uncle says the Muses have helped me in my training." He was aware that he was rambling, but he couldn't stop the increasingly forceful rush of words. "I'll be thirteen soon, and in seven years I'll be a full member the assembly of our brotherhood. One day I'll sing there, when I am a poet. Alcidas says I will never be a good poet, because I am a bastard, but my other uncle, Eumaeus, says that the muses can even use a bastard's voice, when they want to...my mother was a Pan-girl: Alcidas said she was inflamed by

Aphrodite at the sacred rites and in a single evening was joined with many men…but I never knew her…she died when I was born."

He suddenly realized what he had been saying and the shock of it silenced him. What was he doing? He felt a flush of shame: he must be feverish to reveal so painful a past to a total stranger who had merely shown him a little kindness. He looked at her, bracing for the scorn she would surely feel.

The widow only nodded, her smile sad as if she were touched by thoughts of her own. She seemed to weigh her words carefully when finally she spoke. "You are lucky" she said at last, "to have had a Goddess and God presiding over your conception. I think your other uncle is right: the muses would gladly use the voice of so favored a bastard. "Men forget the womb, caring only about the source of the seed. But though a single seed may in time create a thousand more, though a flame may be passed to a thousand other fires, the Mysteries of the Gods can only be found when a flame enters the earth, a seed into the womb of the mother. Every life begins in that sacred mystery and is brightened by it. It seems strange to me that Alcidas did not know this, since he is a poet."

Aias was distracted from his worry, surprised at such well-considered words being spoken in an old goat-pen, by a strange old woman. He glanced at her, and his look lingered. "But where did you learn this?" he asked.

She shrugged, her deep-etched palms held open to the sky. "I have served in the train of the God Dionysos since my youth."

Despite his distance from home, despite his desperate situation, Aias was suddenly aware that he was in the company of a bacchant, of someone who might understand him. Like the members of his brotherhood she was an initiate to the Mysteries.

She asked him the purpose of their journey, and he welcomed her words, replying with as much candor as his obligations allowed.

"Do you know of Delos?" he asked her.

"I have heard of Apollo's sanctuary there."

"And do you know about the crane-dance of the God?"

"Of course. Dionysos' consort, Ariadne, was practiced in those rites, though she preferred to use the labyrinth when she entered the house of the dead to find and bring back the mysteries hidden there."

Aias picked up a small stick and placed it on the fire. "Last mid-summer, as was customary, a prophet of the God performed the dance at Delos. As he moved in rapture beyond the moment of his death, he fell to the ground shaking and the God began to speak through him, addressing those who watched. He told them that the assembly of the Gods had determined they should send out their poets to find a new sanctuary for Apollo's flame. It was to be established in a forgotten place

> *Where the mead-makers hide,*
> *In the burrows of the serpent*
> *Who dwells in the stone.*

"Of course the mead-makers are the honeybees, but no one has ever seen the burrows of a serpent who lives in stone. Perhaps it refers to a cave somewhere.

"The God also said the poets must be able to answer a second riddle, as proof they had found the right spot.

> *Is the center of earth*
> *At the earth-umbilicus,*
> *Or the womb of earth-mother Gaia?*

"No one is sure what the answer must be. Some say one thing, some another. Alcidas believes it must be the earth-umbilicus, since umbilical cords are at the center of the body, where the soul is housed. Based on the words of the traders who came to Naxos, he had decided it would be best to seek the center in the barbarian lands to the west. We were on our way there when the Sea-Mover, Poseidon, brought us unexpectedly to your village." Seeing the old widow looking at him with a peculiar excitement, Aias felt compelled to continue. "I don't know what I will do: although I have had some training, I am not yet a poet: therefore I can play no part in the finding of the sanctuary...until Alcidas recovers. Anyway, without money we will never find our way to the West across the sea. Others will have to go there and win this contest."

"Alcidas will not recover." said the widow quietly.

Aias paused, remembering his pain. "No-one but the Gods can know for certain how long anyone will live."

"Perhaps, but Alcidas will die here."

Feeling a wave of dread, Aias looked at her. "How can you be so certain?"

"I have had dreams over the past four years, growing more frequent in recent months. They are always the same: Poseidon's bull drives two shepherds onto our shores, one to die, one to sing, and all the Hellenes gather to hear the singer's voice. Given your uncle's condition, I must assume you are to be the survivor."

He replied, quoting from the words of his uncle: "Prophesy is always tainted by its mortal vessel: all prophesy is uncertain, especially the prophesies born of dreams." He paused and added with a hint of relief: "And anyway: I am not a poet so I cannot sing."

She smiled. "But what else can I think? I guessed the answer to the Delian riddle the moment you told me of it, and the place the God spoke of as well. Your uncle cannot go there so you must."

He looked at her with a mixture of doubt and fear, each badly concealed. He could think of nothing else to say except to ask about the thing he did not want to hear. "What is the riddle's answer?"

At this she laughed, and it sounded to Aias like a raven's croak repeated over and over with less and less force until it died away altogether, leaving her slightly breathless. "Should I do all your work for you? What are poets for, if not to answer old riddles and discover new ones to amaze the uninitiated? Did the God say 'Find an old woman and she will make things easy'? It is given to you to do the God's work: I may be here to show you the way to go, but it is you who must go there."

Aias suddenly felt uncomfortably hot, and pushed himself back from the fire a little. "What way would you show me?"

She held out her knobby hands to the coals, warming them despite the heat of the day. "A place, a towering mountain, split by a deep cleft. At its base: a spring. And your road home will take you near it."

"But why would you show me that particular one, among all mountains in the world?" As he spoke, Aias was aware a pleading tone had entered his voice.

"For many reasons, Aias, but deepest is this: since my husband brought me here from across the Corinthian Gulf in my youth, in my dreams I have often heard music, the sounds of pipes and drums flowing down the valley like water. They always come from the mountain." She turned and pointed to a wall of great cliffs in the north east, some hours walk in the distance. Looking back at him, she saw something in his eyes that made her add "it doesn't matter whether you believe my dreams, Aias, or whether you believe yourself a poet: what matters is that you go there so the God can show you the things you need to know. If I am wrong, you will find nothing. If I am right, you may begin to discover the substance of your fate. In either case, you really have no choice."

He didn't believe her. He couldn't. He needed time to think: not hours or days, but months and years. He was too young to bear this responsibility, too young to be here, to be left alone by his uncle's death. He was too weak even to look after himself. It seemed to him that events were stripping what little shelter he had against the confusions and responsibilities of adult life. Nowhere could Aias see an escape from them.

Why wasn't he the one who must die? Why should he be spared? Though Alcidas had been hard on Aias over the years, he enjoyed life. The empty night of Hades would better suit the shade of one such as Aias, of one who hated life. Justice demanded that if the Gods wanted a death, it should be Aias. Alcidas must live.

The thought grew strong in his mind, like a voice raising in song. It grew like a revelation. A prayer materialized, and without even noticing what he was doing, the boy began to breath it: "Alcidas must live, and I must die. Alcidas must live, and I must die..."

Suddenly he longed to escape from Tisiphone, to return alone to the welcome darkness of the hut. He rose and began to back away, trying to force a smile onto his face. "I must go now; I must be with Alcidas in case he wakens and needs anything; thank you for the food and conversation." For a moment it looked as if she might get up too, so he turned and walked quicker, speaking to her over his shoulder until he was free of the goat-pen: "You may be right, we'll see; your words were well spoken Tisiphone."

He waved a final time and walked away, avoiding the distant ribbon of towering stone with his eyes. Tisiphone said nothing, just sat quietly, gently sucking her cheeks in and out, watching him go.

The following hours passed in shapeless succession, a blending of one moment into another while the flame of the lamp burned smoky and dim, creating shadows from its niche on the wall. In Aias' thoughts, the sun outside slowly sank towards the West and disappeared forever below the horizon. It would not be given to him that he should see it again. The Gods would grant his prayers and take his life. He felt relieved to be free of the burdens of the last two days, indeed of a life that had been more pain than pleasure. The calm entered him like a soft breeze, smoothing out the roughness of an uncaring world. Delighting in his unexpected freedom, Aias closed his eyes and imagined himself in Alcidas' place, lying on his back, sinking closer and closer to death. The image was sweet. It soothed him. At one point, his head rolled back against the corner where he leaned, and he slept.

Some time later, the lamp sputtered a little and then went out. Disturbed in his dreams by unnaturally loud, strangled sounds issuing from the darkness, suddenly shocked awake when he remembered where he was, Aias fumbled through the blackness to the side of the dying man. As he strained to listen, fighting panic, Alcidas' breathing grew increasingly labored. Then, at the end of a drawn-out sigh, the room fell silent. Aias was alone.

For better or worse he had no choice now: he would have to find his own way home.

Lifted by the surge of a cresting wave, pressed forward by a stiff breeze, the ship ran up onto the beach, crunching and scattering drifts of shells and pebbles as it went. Before its forward momentum was lost the sailors leapt down, shouting and hauled hard on their ropes, struggling to bring it still higher up the beach as it settled. A small group of children ran up to watch their exertions. One of the older and braver of them touched the soaking, weathered planks on the side of the ship's hull until the sailors bellowed at him to stand clear.

Behind the beach stood the town, its jumbled buildings bright in the afternoon sun, its alleyways narrow, haphazard and steep. With evening not far off, cooking fires were being lit in some of the wealthiest houses, their smoke blowing inland towards the rocky hills behind the town.

The children were not alone in welcoming the ship. Farther up the beach, arms folded, a heavy middle-aged man surveyed the scene, frowning. Catching sight of him, the captain hopped lightly over the side and ran across the sand to the watcher. Greeting one another formally, they spoke for a minute. Then the captain began to walk back down to his ship. After taking several steps, however, he paused and half turned as he yelled something else over the noise of the sea while pointing at the vessel. Then he continued on his way.

The other, who until then had seemed about to make his way back to the town, instead paused and again regarded the ship.

A figure, previously invisible in the jumble of cargo, got up from the rear of the craft and stiffly picked his way across the clutter to the side. He leaned over the gunnel to place a sack carefully in the sand, and jumped down after it, keeping a hand on the ship to steady himself as he landed. It was Aias. Retrieving the sack, he made his way up the beach and would have passed a good thirty paces from the watcher had the latter not walked across to intercept him.

Aias was taller now, and stronger-looking than when he had left. In the year since Alcidas had died a great deal had happened, as evidenced by subtle differences in his face and manner. Though he had not lost his sensitivity, the painful timidity that had given him such anguish was no longer visible. Well-rested and well-fed, he stopped and stood politely, waiting for the other to speak first.

"You made it back," said the merchant, his face impassive, his posture confident and commanding.

"Greetings, Thoas," said Aias. He tried to smile, but finding it impossible, settled instead for what he hoped was an appearance of good humor.

"We heard about you and Alcidas from a trader two months ago. You've been at Megara..." Thoas let the statement trail.

Aias made no effort to accommodate the older man's unspoken curiosity, managing instead a partial smile, but saying nothing. Both were silent for a moment. Aias shifted his bundle from one hand to another. Thoas frowned.

Suddenly the merchant flushed, and began speaking in a mock-friendly, conversational tone, made sharp by too much intensity. "How clever you must have been to make a few stupid Megarans pay to hear your music. But I wonder why you returned. Without Alcidas there is nothing for you here: no wife, no friends, no family worthy of the name. And though of course it doesn't bother you, by your presence you shame our town."

Thoas looked at him, but Aias did not reply. A moment passed before the merchant wrinkled his nose. "There is a bad smell on this beach, so I'm leaving. I hope that whatever wind brought it here has the kindness to carry it off."

Giving Aias no chance to answer his insult, he turned and walked slowly away, his sandals flicking little wisps of sand behind him with every weighty step. Thoas hadn't changed a bit.

Aias waited a moment giving the other a chance to get clear, and then began once again to walk towards the town. The laughter and shouts of the children were carried to him by the wind as they played by the foaming sea. He did not look back.

Aias entered the town and made his way upwards through the twisting alleyways, overcome at the sight of so many things familiar yet somehow strange. He was heading towards the top of the hill to the house of his surviving uncle, but the route there was by no means direct. Over the centuries the buildings of the town had been constructed without the benefit of an overall plan, thrust up in whatever space was available. The result was chaos. In times of war this had benefited the town, as invaders had run around in circles on the footpaths below, lost, and the Naxians had loosed arrows down on them from the rooftops.

It took five minutes of skillful navigation for Aias to arrive at the right doorway, slightly breathless with the climb. He paused, absorbing the view from the street, and then went in calling his uncle's name. The house was silent, gray in the light filtering through the narrow windows. He removed his sandals by the entrance.

It was a pleasant house though somewhat worn. Comfortable and large, the ancestral home of the Deukalidae on Naxos was a product of Aias' grandfather's success in trading when he had moved here from Crete many years before. Along the wall of the living room where meals were customarily taken, brightly colored geometric designs decorated the space near the ceilings and floor. Underfoot, tiles provided a hard, cool surface. Very little furniture was in evidence: just four roughly finished wood-frame sofas for lounging on, each with a thin straw mattress, well stained and lumpy. Aias walked over to one and set down his bundle. Hearing a footstep at the door behind him, he turned.

Eumaeus and Aias exchanged greetings with great warmth. The last two members of the Deukalidae family on Naxos were very fond of each other. Had Eumaeus not delivered a sacred oath many years before that he would have no children to continue his seed, he would certainly have legitimized his nephew by adopting him as a son. But although a formal declaration was impossible, they were very close and Eumaeus had raised his nephew as both son and friend.

When, over the years, wine became more and more the foundation of his uncle's life, Aias felt the tragedy strongly. He lived the pain of each fresh humiliation which Eumaeus delivered to himself; the foolishness, the growing indolence, the frequent bouts of nausea. It was with some relief that he now observed his uncle's sober if disheveled state, a consequence of the older man having just risen.

After embracing his nephew and waving him down to one of the couches Eumaeus sat on the one beside it, smoothing his tousled hair and beard as he did so, and wiping his hands on the front of his tunic. Eumaeus' habit of cleaning his hands on his clothes-front was plain from past stains made by fingers and hands dragged across his chest as he was doing now.

Other than these tell-tale marks, his clothes were clean. He was a portly man, easy to smile, but not especially happy. The death of his wife at the dawn of his adulthood had left its mark on his face, particularly around the eyes, which even when he laughed were never fully free of sorrow. His hair was well advanced toward turning gray, his beard, in particular, heavily salted with white. The alcohol was having its effect, especially in his complexion which was too ruddy by far.

"We heard news of you in Megara this past year." Eumaeus said. "Everyone is proud of your success there." It was typical of Eumaeus to ascribe kindness that did not exist to his fellow human-beings, his optimism always at war with the truth. In the past when these related to Aias, the boy had often become irritated. Whether through the passage of time or the addition of the experiences of the past year, Aias felt only regret.

"Thank you, uncle" said Aias, and paused, looking for the right words to continue. "What have you heard of the death of your brother?"

"Not much, but enough. Alcidas was a fool—oh, I know that I am considered the fool in this family, but you of all people must know I'm not alone—and I suspect that he brought his death on himself through some nonsense or other. Am I right?"

He looked at Aias who stared blankly back, trying to think of a suitable reply.

Eumaeus chuckled. "You see? He did bring a fool's death on himself. The details don't much matter: the important thing is that the Fates had their way in the end. There is nothing for me to add.

"In a way, we weren't really brothers, far less friends: he lived only for himself, for his own glory, his own pleasures. He treated both you and me harshly, letting shame dictate his behavior to us. If he had stood by us none would have faulted him, and our lives would have been far easier. The Deukalidae family name would have retained much of its honor.

"I didn't grieve for him, and I hope you weren't silly enough to. It would be like lamenting the rust on the knife that cuts you.

"Of course, I will continue to mourn him as custom dictates: I won't desert my obligations on his behalf."

Aias studied a small nick in the fabric of his couch, pushing his fingertip into the little hole, then pulling out a small piece of straw that protruded. He played with it, rolling it between his fingers while he spoke. "It seems so strange to be back. What news have you uncle?"

Eumaeus thought for a moment, then smiled slightly and nodded. "Just one change since you left: I have been ordered to avoid the assembly of Naxos when drunk. I have no memory of the event, but apparently I went there when I could hardly stand up, interrupted the speakers and then threw up on two of our more important citizens."

He had adopted a casual, joking manner when he spoke, but Aias was shocked. To have disrupted the assembly in so scandalous a manner was a thing that would be spoken of for many years to come. Eumaeus had committed an act bordering on sacrilege.

Seeing his nephew's reaction, Eumaeus responded, his manner more serious. "I know it was wrong, Aias, but when you become a servant of wine you cannot always be expected to act wisely. Since that time I have attempted to keep within these walls when I am drunk, no matter how great the temptation to go out. I even tried to drink less for a while, but I wasn't able. Don't feel badly about it: it doesn't reflect on you." Aware of his uncle's pain, Aias forced himself to smile, but they both knew it was no good. They fell silent for a moment, each pursuing his own thoughts.

Outside in the street a dog started barking, his voice badly distorted by the narrow alley and muffled by the house's walls. Someone shouted at it and it fell silent.

Aias looked at his uncle as if about to speak, but instead reached over to his sack and fumbled with the cord tied around its top. Freeing it, he reached into the bag and carefully lifted out Alcidas' lyre with his right hand, using his left to insure the instrument didn't catch in the loose material at the top.

The lyre was very old, the priceless possession of many owners for as far back as the Deukalidae could remember. Its base was an empty tortoise shell with breastplate and backplate still joined. Sections of reed had been stuck to the outer surface of the breastplate to act as a bridge from which seven sheep's gut strings were stretched. These strings terminated at an oaken crosspiece called the yoke, which was in turn connected to two goat's horns firmly rooted in the shell.

After watching Aias produce the lyre Eumaeus stood up saying he had to relieve himself, and went out. Aias looked down at the instrument, holding the cool curves of the blackened horns in his hands. He did not want to part with it.

With Eumaeus gone, Aias tapped lightly on the lumpy back-plate of the lyre with the fingers of one hand, hearing the faint echoes that issued from the empty shell beneath.

The shell was the silence of feminine earth, its hollow an empty, womblike cave. Aias closed his eyes, his hands moving gently, fingers investigating the ancient instrument.

The reed bridge was mortality: reeds grew in water, and water stilled the fire of mortal life. The lyre's oaken crosspiece was the great vault of the sky. Strings of sheep's gut evoked the Fates, sisters who wove destinies from the wool of divine sheep. The strings numbered seven, one for each of the great lights, the planets, moon and sun that wandered the sky, divine patterns to guide all that happens below. The horns were moons, both old and new, bracketing the full moon implied by the strings.

Alone these parts were magical, but together they described for all the brotherhoods a sacred Mystery: the seven great lights were of seven Gods, representatives of Olympus. When stirred by the power of the Fates, they reached down into mortal life and by mortal death still farther, into earth. At last they touched the Earth-Mother's womb, releasing their sounds in the darkness. As the Mother then willed it, new lives might begin or new wisdom be born. All of Creation might find its rightful place.

Music carried wisdom, and for that Aias loved it. Music grew from silence when divine will touched the earth and set it trembling, stirring in the mortal heart a memory of Order, of Harmony. For every note a God, for every song an Olympian assembly; the memory of great things said and done in time beyond human memory.

Aias knew well the divine Order in the lyre he held and well-recalled the delicate beauty of its music. In skilled hands, it could send out power and wisdom like a light. He gently plucked a string and felt the shell vibrate. It faded softly into silence.

Too soon, Eumaeus returned and padded across the tiles, lying down on his couch. It was time to do as honor dictated. Battling his reluctance, Aias held the lyre out to Eumaeus. His face was a little too eager, his voice a little too strong: "It is yours, uncle. Your brother would have wanted you to have it."

At these words Eumaeus laughed, waving the lyre away with one hand. "Alcidas would not have wanted either of us to have it, of that I'm sure. But you ought to keep it. You were his apprentice. I already have a lyre, one less illustrious it's true, but I no longer play it. Mice have already gnawed away the strings while it sits in storage. This instrument is too valuable for that kind of treatment.

"Look after your lyre, Aias, and one day you may help rebuild our family's pride. No, don't thank me: you have talent, boy, and the Muses will certainly guide you to victories in the years to come. I deserve no gratitude: it is proper for me to assist you."

But Aias did thank him. Over the past year he had often gazed at the lyre, holding it to the light, studying the countless little scratches picked up over centuries of use, the idiosyncrasies of the materials, the minor details of its construction, its musty smell. He had practiced in every free moment. It had become an obsession to him.

At first he had wanted the instrument to serve his career, to bring him fame among the brotherhood. With it to inspire him, he felt he could do great things. But in time it was the opposite: he longed instead to serve the lyre, to draw out its beauty for all to see. With this new maturity he found himself playing better, sensing more of the potential nuances in every tune, at times moving beyond mere technical skill into possession by the music, into inspired discovery.

With the death of Alcidas, the lyre had become his teacher. He had often prayed Eumaeus would somehow let him continue in its service, and now his prayers had been answered. He felt complete, certain of his destiny.

Eumaeus seemed embarrassed by the intensity of Aias' gratitude. He looked at his feet for a moment, then glanced at his nephew and changed the subject. "That's enough of that. Tell me what happened to you since you've been away. When my brother died, he must have left you in a difficult position. How did you find your way to Megara?"

*T*he question of what he should say at this moment had been troubling Aias for months. It was one thing to prepare a poem, compose music, and quite another to end his silence of a year and describe what he had seen to another person. The right words eluded him.

Feeling very awkward he began by mumbling, caught himself immediately, and started at the beginning, or near to it.

"When uncle Alcidas died, I had nothing of any value to use in barter." He paused, glancing under lowered lids at the older man. "It was my own fault, not Alcidas'. Anyway, I was afraid that I wouldn't be able to get back here. The home where Alcidas came to the end of his thread belonged to an old widow, a bacchant. She was strange, and made me a little nervous. As you know, we were headed to the barbarian lands to the West when Alcidas fell. He believed the place of which the God had spoken was there. This widow seemed to know what we were doing from the first, and she told me that she had dreamt we would come.

"She said the place we were seeking was nearby, a mountain to the north of her village called Parnassos. The people there thought the place was sacred to the Earth-Mother, but no-one could say why. They mostly avoided the place, fearful of its power.

"I performed the funeral rites for Alcidas, and the whole village was helpful out of respect for his occupation, it being a civilized area where traders sometimes stop. After making offerings to the dead and the rightful Gods, everyone feasted well.

"The next morning I rose early to walk back towards Megara by the land route. It was about a week's walk, or so I was told, and I had a vague hope I might be employed at Megara when I got there so I could pay for a passage home. The widow saw me off. When she realized that I was not intending to investigate the mountain, she refused to let me go until I swore to her that I would. It did no good pointing out that I was not a full member of the brotherhood, nor that I was too young. She refused to be persuaded. In any case, I felt beholden to her as her guest, so in the end I swore."

Aias paused and looked across at his uncle, who had started smiling broadly. "Every village thinks the Gods live on a molehill in its back yard, and not on Olympus" the older man said stroking his beard. "You let the widow trap you, didn't you? Nothing like walking all over the place in answer to the longings of some frustrated old woman."

Aias didn't disagree, but shrugged his shoulders and raised his eyebrows, smiling apologetically as if to say such things do happen, whether or not they did in this case. "I felt a little annoyed, at first" he conceded. "But the mountain was extraordinary. Even when I began walking from the village I was impressed with the way its cliffs looked: a huge mass of rough-shaped rock rising steep and blue through the morning haze and into the sky.

"All morning I followed a river running towards the mountain, turning eastward past its base. Where it turned I found a small creek and followed it up the slope towards the cliffs above. Until then I had been following the trail that runs by land towards Athens and Megara, a path well-frequented, but from that point on I followed no trail.

"Perhaps it was the reputation of the mountain's sacredness, but I saw no sign of anybody at all until I returned to the river in two days time. As for my route to the mountain, it was fairly gradual, but not a particularly easy walk: the scrub and low trees living there made progress more difficult than it had looked from the valley floor. A little after midday I stopped to wait out the heat and lunch on a little of the goat's cheese the widow had given me. The day was hot and I was not yet well rested from my vigil at Alcidas' death-bed, so I slept where I was, under an old oak.

"When I woke it was late afternoon, really almost evening, with the sun just over the tops of the mountains to the west. I was very angry with myself, since I had planned to investigate the mountain and return to the valley below before dark. The truth was, the widow's words had made me nervous, and I thought it would be better to sleep elsewhere."

Seeing that his uncle was once again finding amusement at his words, Aias went on hurriedly: "Of course, I knew that I had nothing to fear from the Gods and spirits of the place, but there could have been robbers around. You know there are many on the mainland in these days."

Eumaeus took this comment with good humor. "There are many indeed. But perhaps most of them prefer to do their work near pathways? I don't suppose they can often run across boys in the hills, especially not boys like yourself, loaded down with a treasure in goat's cheese. Not often enough to make the nuisance of coping with wilderness worth the booty, surely."

He paused, enjoying his joke, but realizing Aias wasn't laughing he hastily continued: "You shouldn't feel bad about getting nervous. Alcidas didn't ever feel uncertain, but we agreed he was a fool. To fear the Gods is wisdom, not shameful. It doesn't hurt to respect the spirits of a place, and there are many places I would prefer to avoid after nightfall, spirits or not. I was just having a little fun with you. I don't often get a chance to speak with someone like this: most of our neighbors get very busy when I'm around. Please go on. I won't interrupt you again."

Aias was glad to get back to his story. He was not finding it easy to find the right words, but it seemed very important to him to succeed, to convince his uncle of the truth of his discovery.

"I decided to sleep where I was, well away from the cliffs. I had some more to eat and looked at the view as the sun went down, light fled the sky, and night came. There was no moon, but it was very clear so I was able to see easily by star light.

"From the other side of the valley another mountain loomed dark and broad, but not menacingly: it seemed kindly, watchful, like an old friend. Mostly my thoughts were not on the things around me. I wondered only how I would get home, how I would find the means to command passage from the mainland. Everything about my situation seemed too overwhelming, too heavy for me to bear. For hours I worried while the stars slowly swung around in their heavenly course, and Orion tipped down towards the horizon. Eventually I fell asleep.

"I woke with the coming of Eos, the dawn. She spread herself across the sky, quickly giving way to the day, and I rose and began the final approach to the cliffs. It was a pleasant walk. There was birdsong and cool air before the sun found its way around the peaks to the east. The quiet babble of the brook soothed me—after the preoccupations of the night before, a kind of peace had settled over me. I was prepared to wait and see what pattern the Fates had woven, rather than chase after their wills with a fevered mind. The cliffs grew increasingly impressive the closer I got to them, and I began to pick out more and more details of the rough rock walls.

"I followed the creek steadily upwards. At last it disappeared beneath a dense tangle of trees and scrub at the base of the cliffs where the rock wall was severed by a deep cleft, but I could see no evidence that the stream had passed down it. The cleft was dry, near-vertical rock.

"I made my way with difficulty through the snarl of low branches and tumbled stones, twice having to stumble along the slippery rocks of the stream before I stood beside its source: it issued straight out of a hole in the stone, gushing from the heart of the mountain itself.

"I have seen sacred springs before, carrying their secrets up from the underworld where the shades of the dead whisper in the eternal darkness of the hollows, but never had I seen one bubbling up so strongly from a hole in solid rock, though I had heard of such things.

"I said a prayer for the nymph, the lovely spirit of the spring, and the beauty of the place overwhelmed me. I remained by the cascading waters for some time.

"When I felt I had properly respected the spirits of the place, I crouched by the stream and bathed, cleaning away the impurity of my travels. Then I drank from it, the sweet cold water, and felt greatly refreshed. It was with eagerness that I went to explore the rest of the area, for I knew that whatever place I had come to, it was surely sacred.

"I wandered to the west along the same elevation, planning to go up to the cliffs and walk along them on my way back to the spring. Seeing a rough-shaped pinnacle of stone through the trees, rising from the rocky soil and dry grass of the slope many paces above me, I made my way to it. It was about my height on the uphill side, but somewhat more if approached from below, which I did. Rather than walk up onto it, an easy thing to do, I walked around the rock, reaching out and touching its rough surface with my hand from time to time.

"On the base of the pinnacle on the downhill side I saw a hole in the stone, about one and a half fingers wide, and smooth: like the worm holes in the drift wood that sometimes appears on the beach, down below our town. I had seen similar holes in the rocks throughout the area, but hadn't given them much thought.

"It was only when I heard a buzzing sound and saw a large black and yellow insect swoop past my head and alight at the entrance of the hole that it occurred to me I might be standing in the presence of the riddle's answer. As I watched the bee shook its wings and entered the dark opening. The answer to the first part of the God's prophesy lay before me.

Where the mead-makers hide,
In the burrows of the serpent
That dwells in the stone.

"It made me feel dizzy with wonder, and I stood for a moment with one hand on the rock to steady myself.

"What happened next was stranger than anything that has ever happened to me before or since. It seemed that dreamlike, drawn like a wisp of steam, I felt myself fading, thoughts curling downwards, into the entrance of the hole. I was powerless to resist the magic that possessed me.

"Down past the light that filled the opening, down the twisting passages, beyond the bee as he hurried to his subterranean nest; I was pulled ever deeper through the tunnel of rock, down into the chilled stone heart of the mountain. At last I came to a huge cavern in the heart of Parnassos, and there I stopped.

"Invisible in the darkness, I heard the sacred stream passing near me, gurgling soft and cold. I had come to a halt on the damp stones by the side of that stream. In the close unending night I waited, seeing nothing, hearing nothing, waiting for what I could not say. I felt a strange inability to move, even to think. It seemed like hours passed: I vaguely wondered if I would ever come away from the banks of that stream and see the light of day again.

"I was startled suddenly, like a sleeper by the flash of lightning in the night. Abruptly I sensed the flickering shadows that filled the cavern and I knew instantly, though I cannot say how, that they were the shades of the dead and this their abode. They were crouched in silence all around me, listening as I was, hidden for ever in eternal night. I felt them edging closer, drawn towards me by the fire in my blood, longing for the life that was no longer theirs. I felt the fingers of the nearest on the skin of my arms and the back of my neck, caressing the warmth that lay beneath, willing my fire into its soul...

"With a shock of fear I pulled back gasping.

"When my reason returned, I found myself in the late morning sunshine beside the rock pinnacle, panting, sweat rising through my cold skin. I backed away across the uneven ground, until a low shrub half obscured its base from view. There I knelt and prayed to Apollo to protect me, for I felt my end very close. Never have I had so terrible an experience: if it had not been daylight I think I might have died of fear. Look: even now the memory makes me shake.

"I prayed until I grew calmer while the sun moved a little across the sky. In time I felt that I should continue my investigation and I went uphill towards the cliffs, walking around the pinnacle at a safe distance. It seemed to me that I had already seen all the place had to offer, so I was unprepared for what I saw next.

"About sixty or seventy paces above the pinnacle the ground beneath my feet seemed surprisingly flat and solid, and I looked down to find that I was standing on the edge of a circular stone terrace, worn by countless years. Stones and boulders of all sizes littered its surface, and several trees and many bushes had reached down through the cracks, the relentless pressure of their roots buckling the carved stone floor. So great was the clutter that at first I didn't notice the central stone where it sat, still on its carved six-sided pedestal, resting where men or Gods had set it in some distant age.

"The central stone was white, beehive shaped, but otherwise not particularly noteworthy, yet I felt a sense of awe: clearly whoever had set it there knew it had great significance. Was it the umbilicus, the navel of earth? I must admit that I never had any doubt that it was.

"I recall a sense of awe mingled with raw excitement, a near-ecstasy that followed me all day as I walked about exploring. I found little more of note as I explored the area, returning several times in the course of the afternoon to the white stone, even clearing away some of the rocks and grass that littered the terrace around it, and offering prayers in its vicinity.

"When dusk came, I began to feel nervous about spending the night there, so I walked over to the stream and crossing it, walked down the slope at an angle towards the southeast. About a thousand or more paces from the spring I felt far enough away to be safe, and I cleared a place to sleep in the loose pebbles and dirt. I had not eaten all day, but I still was not hungry, so rather than eat, I lay watching the view across the valley as the day gave way to night.

"I don't know when I fell asleep, nor how many times I awoke during the night. I do know that despite being exhausted, I did not sleep well.

"Sometime towards the dawn I had a dream that troubled me deeply. It came to me softly, like any other dream, but even from the first it was very intense, as real to me then as you are now.

"I was in a strange landscape that was neither light nor dark: the sky was uniformly gray, without clouds; the earth beneath my feet was gray rock, without trace of plants or any other living thing. All around the atmosphere was crackling with scarcely controllable power so that at any moment it seemed it might explode, shattering the very fabric of the world.

"I felt no fear, though I knew myself to be a tiny fragment, a spec of dust that could be swallowed up in an instant by earth or sky. It occurred to me then that I was standing by the edge of the cliffs I'd been exploring the previous day, and they were towering above me with a deep and foreboding silence. Oddly, the cleft where the spring arose was nowhere to be seen.

"I knew, I don't know how, that the rules of time did not apply: that the moment was ancient and new at the same time, that it was a part of every moment in every age and yet defined them all. It was the heart of the sacred: the instant of creation.

"A woman stood near me, her back turned, looking at the cliff. From where I was I could see a goat skin thrown across her shoulder, its fur forming tufts and in between these, the hide itself a strange translucent blue. She ignored me, but I felt that it was she who had brought me here. Despite her presence, it seemed as if I were the only person in an empty world.

"The hidden power in the sky above seemed to grow imperceptibly at first, then to surge suddenly to an unspeakable intensity, and to drive down like a massive column of flame into the base of the cliffs near where I stood.

"It was then that the rock split and the gorge appeared, water welling up from below.

"I was near the spring and saw the roaring pillar of fire thrusting down from the sky and into earth where the water flowed. It seemed to be fusing the two together. Rushing from the point where it entered the earth countless things flickered past, spreading out. It was as if all the seas and mountains, the rivers and plains, all the things that lend shape to the universe were issuing from that place at that moment. The noise and motion were thunderous and seemed unending.

"Then I saw amidst the whirling light and noise a man's figure emerging from the flame. Flame himself, he turned and raised his arm. I saw a sickle in his hand; I saw the arm fall, and in the blinking of an eye the light was gone back up into the sky and the rush of creation was over.

"Only the shadowy figure, his sickle dripping blood, remained crouched in the crevasse. He was dimmer now, glowing red. There was a moment of unnatural silence, and then the earth moaned, as if straining to be free of some burden. I felt a terrible sadness I could not explain. It was the earth's turn then to reach out and fuse, sending forth, as if reluctantly, the shape of a woman with dark hair and flashing eyes. They mated, the figure from the flame and this woman, six times.

"Nine months passed while the earth beneath me writhed, then the woman gave birth. Six infants she bore, but the figure from the flame devoured each in its turn. All, that is, except the last: for the woman gave him a stone to eat instead. It was the same bee-hive shaped stone I'd seen on the platform.

"The figure ate the stone, darkening with rage as he realized her trick. But it was too late, for the babe had been born and stood before him as a youth, a wheel in one hand and a lightning bolt in the other, and the power flowed across from father to the son. The youth became a man and rose like a brilliantly shining sun from the crevasse, leaving his father behind.

"Again I was standing behind the woman with the goat-skin, looking at the cliffs beyond, but now there were trees and birds, and the world was alive with sounds. The sun rose and fell, the rains came and went, night became day; day became night.

"The woman turned, but though I wanted to see her face, I could not bring myself to look directly at her. She beckoned me to look farther up the valley, towards the East. I turned to look, and instantly I was standing on the far side of a distant mountain beside a muddy bank. The woman was still in front of me and she pointed at the red clay, saying softly in a voice that was rich with music: 'There lies the body of man: his beloved wife, Pandora'. I didn't know why, but I was crying and felt such sorrow I could scarcely breathe.

"And then, as if drawn from the air around us, the figure of a man appeared, radiant like the midday summer sky, his face intent and kind. He took a little of the thick red clay and skillfully molded it into human shape. He warmed it, breathed on it, and the figurine, glowing softly, started to move about in his hands, and to cry out from time to time, now in sorrow, now in joy. Unbearably tiny, it was fragile in its maker's hands. Yet sometimes it shouted in rage or pride, unaware, it seemed, of its helplessness. Again I felt sadness, but happiness too, for it was the most beautiful thing I have ever seen.

"I reached out to touch the little thing, but as my fingers came close I awoke to find the sun was shining on the clouds above me and the day just beginning."

Aias was leaning forward in excitement. "Do you see this uncle? Does it not seem that the riddle has been answered?

> *Is the center of earth*
> *At the Earth-Umbilicus*
> *Or the womb of the Earth-Mother Gaia?*

"Both are found at the center. The stream at the cliff issues from the womb of the earth mother; the stone on the terrace is the Earth-Umbilicus. Both are in the same place because womb and navel are found together at the place of birth. The navel is the echo of the father's phallus in a mother's womb, and the sprouting stalk from which a man is harvested at the dawn of his life. And the navel of that place is our fate-stone, for it ties us all to the Mother. As a birth place of all the things in the world, it is natural that the God Prometheus made our flesh for his foolish brother's wife from clay nearby."

When he finished this last summary of his discoveries, the boy's eyes were bright. Throughout his narrative, Aias had been aware of his uncle listening intently, frowning with thought.

When Aias was done, Eumaeus, as if startled on realizing no more would be forthcoming, leaned back a little, clearing his throat. He paused for a moment, started to speak, paused again. "Have you told this to anyone?", he asked. When Aias shook his head, the older man seemed relieved, and nodded. "You must keep this to yourself. It would not be believed, and if you wish to continue your training you must remain silent. Your position is already difficult in the brotherhood now that Alcidas is dead: in fact, you would probably be sent into exile by the council and never allowed to return if you told them what you just told me.

"I believe you, or at least believe that you believe because I know your heart, but there is no-one else who would take your side. You would be seen as a promoter of self-serving sacrilege, and only your youth would preserve you from more serious punishment. Who will believe such epiphanies were granted to a mere child?"

Aias was not surprised by his uncle's reaction: he knew well what he must expect from others. He looked at his hands, searching for the right words without finding them. His thoughts were jumbled: there was fear and pride, longing and uncertainty, and he could not seem to separate out the streams of ideas, to order them.

Suddenly he became aware of himself speaking calmly and with precision. "You are right, uncle. I know you are right. But I cannot hold silent: if these things I have seen are only dreams and the fragments of dreams, then I am doomed by what I must do. If they are things shown to me by the Gods, however, to hold silent would be even worse: that would be the greatest sacrilege. I must say what I have seen and hope I am right, and that others will think me so. If I did any less, I would be breaking the oath I took when I entered Alcidas' service, to place my self last."

Eumaeus looked at him silently for a moment and seemed as if he were about to speak but instead he jumped up and walked into the next room. He returned a moment later with a skin bladder full of wine. When he spoke, Eumaeus seemed outwardly cheerful, though Aias knew him too well to be fooled. "Perhaps it will go well. Certainly: why not? The Gods may favor it. But in case things don't go as they should, I ought to visit with Dionysos, to die a little with his wine, and see about preparing a place for you to go when our brotherhood has finished with you."

Chuckling dryly at his attempt at humor, he carefully splashed a little wine onto the tiles beside the couch. Then he inserted the bladder's nipple into his mouth and threw his head back, squeezing the wine out hard with his hands. Like Alcidas he was a thirsty drinker, so Aias waited patiently listening to the sounds of the wine gurgling down his uncle's throat. Eumaeus offered Aias no wine, and none was expected. The older man knew his nephew only took wine at meals and when ritual demanded.

When Eumaeus slowed his fierce drinking at last, pausing to regain his breath, Aias spoke. "Exile is not so bad, uncle. In Megara I was better treated than I ever was here on Naxos."

Eumaeus grew angry at these words. "Don't be a fool. This is your home. In any other place you would be a stranger without friends. You have nowhere to go."

Aias nodded, but not in agreement: he too became angry. "I may have nowhere to go, uncle, but I am a stranger here as well. I have never been accepted and I never will. Who would give me his daughter to be my wife? How can I be a part of this place? I cannot even join the assembly, because my father was not a Naxian. I have been in exile here from the day of my birth. Perhaps if I wander, I will find a place to make my home."

In response to Aias' passion, Eumaeus waved his hand vaguely, even beginning to laugh. "Let's not start you fighting before you must. I know that you will do what you believe you have to, and if I were in your position I might take the same actions. Just be careful, Aias. This matter is sensitive, and you have many enemies."

"I have thought very hard about how to do it, and I've decided to try to perform at the festival on Delos." Eumaeus winced. "I know it will be difficult to gain permission, and that everything will depend on that one performance, but I believe the Gods will help me, that it is their will that I do this. And if I am wrong, I deserve to fail." He paused, and looked probingly at the older man for a moment. It seemed at that moment as if his childlike uncertainty was back, but in the end he went on and his self-possession returned. "I have already prepared my poem", he said. "I will perform for you if you like." But when he began to reach for the lyre, his uncle raised his hand, to restrain him.

"No, nephew, not now. Save it for the festival. I don't know which I am more afraid of: that your song will be bad, the product of delusions sent to destroy you, or good, and evidence of the favor of the Gods. I am only sure that I am afraid. If you are too, that is all I can ask for. I don't know what else to think. It seems to me that Apollo and the other Gods could have chosen a more respected vehicle for their revelations, but I cannot claim to know why they act as they do. Naturally, I will do what I can to help, but as you know, my reputation with the brotherhood is no longer very good, so you and your visions are in the hands of the Gods. Tomorrow I will make an offering for you."

They spoke at length that night of other things, Aias describing his stay at Megara and catching up on old news of the town. Eumaeus fell asleep near midnight, sprawled on the couch snoring.

*O*ver the following weeks, they did not discuss Aias' plans again. At his uncle's bidding, Aias worked in the Deukalidae vineyards near the town while he awaited the festival. He soon grew used to living under the hostility of many of the townspeople again. In some ways it was as if he had never left, but even so his resolve was never shaken.

Tending the grapes gave him great pleasure. Sometimes he went along the rows and pulled up weeds. At other times he tied the new tendrils to the two wood crosspieces that had been fixed to their central stakes. By supporting and spreading the vines the crosspieces made cultivation easier. They also made each vine look as if it were growing up the mast and along the twin booms of a ship, reminding him of his adventures over the previous year.

It was not the season of Erigone, the season of the new-born grapes, so he could not tend them as the satyrs came on the wind to impregnate them with their seeds and softly swing them back and forth on the stalks of the father-vine. Yet he sensed the grapes rising, growing out of the father's union with the earth. Sometimes when he was alone with the ancient vines he felt a sacred presence that lingered as he worked the soil and moved among the rows.

Several weeks after his return, Aias struck up a friendship with an Ionian trader, a remarkable man who devoted his leisure to the refinement of his mind. Though they behaved outwardly as friends, the trader became his teacher. He provided answers to questions that Aias had not known existed, answers that gradually and subtly transformed the young man's art.

Once, during one of the town's festivals when they were still little more than acquaintances, they decided to walk together along the beach while the sun sank low over the horizon.

The trader was a thin, dark little man with narrow lips and a remarkably bony nose. Though he was far from beautiful, he was so animated, his eyes so quick and warm, that everyone he met could not help liking him, and Aias was no exception. As they walked along talking about the occupations that consume men's time, the trader mentioned that his real pastime in life was discovering the smoke of things. Aias was unfamiliar with this phrase, and asked him to explain.

The trader smiled. "When we make sacrifice by burning, the portions are divided according to sacred law. Not just those separated out by the priests—fat, bone, and flesh—no, the sacrificial flame completes the division of the portions we offer the Gods. The earthen part remains as ash, meat warmed by the fire is fitting food for mortals tied to their fleshy frames, while that which is airy ascends to heaven in the billowing smoke. All things on earth combine the three parts in their being: through sacrifice the Gods have taught us how to divide them.

"While earth is the mother that nurtures what is, fiery smoke lends the substance of wisdom and life. For this reason I seek the smoke of things."

Seeing that Aias was not yet satisfied with his words, the trader stopped, reaching into his clothes to pull out a piece of twine with two sticks tied on either end. He inserted one stick into the ground. Stretching the string taut, using the other stick as a stylus, he carefully inscribed a circle in the sand with the first stick at its center.

"What is this I've drawn?" he asked.

Puzzled, Aias replied "A circle."

The merchant raised an eyebrow quizzically, smiling. "Is it really? Look at this side, where my hand and eye were unsteady, and here, where the shell pushed the line inwards. Is it really a circle, or only nearly?" Aias conceded his point, though still not yet clear what his companion's meaning was.

"And is this a circle?" The Merchant showed him a ring on the finger of his left hand set with a beautiful, circular blue gemstone.

Aias was about to nod, thought better of it, and looked more closely, taking the merchant's hand and holding it steady before him to be certain. "No" he said, catching the merchant's eye.

Nodding and putting away the sticks and string, the merchant began to walk again. He asked "Have you ever seen a real circle anywhere on this earth?"

Aias thought for a moment and shook his head so the merchant continued: "Yet your mind knows a perfect circle?"

"It seems so."

"Perhaps if a perfect circle existed in the world it might blind your mortal eyes as the sun would if you looked upon it. Thus it is said that the eyes of the wise are rendered blind in exchange for their wisdom.

"So your earthen nature has never seen a real circle, yet your mind, your soul, knows it well. The perfect circle is the smoke of all circles, and your mind is the part of you that knows it."

Aias became excited, reflecting on the knowledge Alcidas had given him that soul was a form of air. It seemed fitting that only air could know the nature of air, and only soul the smoke of things. He asked the merchant if smoke only referred to shape.

"Oh no, not at all. There are many kinds of smoke." The merchant held out his hand with several fingers hidden. "How many fingers do you see?"

"Two."

"Now burn away the fingers so that only the two is left. It is the same two whether it refers to two cows, two Gods, or two fingers. So your mind knows the pure two, doesn't it?" Aias nodded and the Merchant continued.

"Shape and number: we've considered them, but what do you think is the smoke of substance?"

For a moment Aias looked down at the damp sand beneath his feet as he walked. Then it came to him. "The trinity of earth, water, and air."

"Exactly. All things, even the Gods have the smoke of substance in them. It is the smoke of substance that determines their character."

Aias frowned and interrupted the older man. "But the characters of Gods are surely free of influence?"

"No, no;" the merchant said firmly, "just as men can burn with anger, or be still as earth in their hearts, so it is with Gods. Smoke is the pure and true way of considering what all things are and what they do. Smoke is the way the Gods themselves see all things.

"But perhaps you should consider what the smoke of music is since music is your trade. Doesn't smoke lie behind the crudeness of our human sounds, the pure smoke of harmony such as no mortal ears can hear but mortal minds can know? Isn't that the root of your art, the secret the Muses grant their followers? Don't you offer up the smoke of Harmony as you sing? Are you not the musician, that fluid creature, who joins the earthen instrument to its rising sounds?"

Aias was delighted by the merchant's words, his face breaking into a smile, but the merchant went on without noticing, himself entranced by the ideas that lay behind his words.

"There are always at least two ways to perceive the things of this world. Low or high; Earth or Smoke; the manifest or the hidden; Public religion or sacred Mysteries; myth or its hidden meaning; complexity or simplicity: physical experience or pure thought. It is given to free men to reach towards the high through initiation into mysteries revealed by the Gods, and at the same time through the discoveries they can make with their minds."

As they walked along the beach talking, the sun disappeared to the west and the stars came out, but Aias hardly noticed, lost as he was in the discovery of a new world. They would speak of such things many times in the days ahead.

The weeks passed, bringing Aias hard work and long walks with his new friend while the days grew longer and the midday sun rose higher in the sky. In time the poets' festival drew near.

Early one morning Aias and his uncle took ship with several other members of the brotherhood from Naxos. With a stiffening breeze the vessel put off from the beach, rounded the point and turned northward to make the swift journey to the sacred isle. It seemed to Aias as if his time of waiting was finally drawing to a close.

*C*ong ago the Goddess Leto, keeper of the gateway into death, wandered the earth in search of a haven where she could give birth to the twins she carried in her womb. Yet she could find no place, for she was hounded by the serpent Pytho: he knew her unborn son would one day illuminate secrets concealed in his dark lair.

The sky God Zeus, whose fiery seed she carried, guided Leto to a floating island in the Aegean Sea, the little isle of Delos: since it did not touch bottom, it would provide no passage for the mind-clouding snake. To make the birthing-place steady, Zeus fastened the island to the bottom of the sea with chains so strong even Pytho could not pass through them. There, at last, Apollo and his sister Artemis were born.

Apollo became lord of the gateway of Light into Earth, illuminating the wisdom hidden in the dark realms beneath; his beloved sister became mistress of a darker portal where the life-extinguishing waters seep earthward, calling all mortals to their doom.

In the appallingly violent age of darkness that followed the Trojan War, the little pockets of civilization that survived scattered around the Aegean Sea made tiny Delos their meeting ground, the center of their world. It was there they went to trade pottery, grain, and the mysterious new metal from the east, iron. At Delos they shared the worship of Apollo and Artemis, and of all the other Olympian Gods, a common heritage of shared myth and meaning.

There too, they lodged a sacred flame through the centuries, never allowing it to go out, a flame said to be as old as the human race. There they tended to it, feeding it fragrant wood. It had been brought from the hearth of mount Olympus by a God and given to the peoples of Greece. Once a year, in the spring, a great festival took place at Delos. From all over the Aegean representatives came from every civilized town and village to join in the festivities and then to return home with a little of the sacred flame kept alive in their ships. From these small fires the common hearths of each community were lit, and the hearth in every home in turn.

As the Gods were diverse, so were the Hellenes. As the Gods were united around their hearth in Olympus, so it was with the civilized Greeks around their hearth at Delos. Alone among the peoples of the world, the civilization of the Hellenes was based on this God-given custom. They were a proud people, and in the time of Aias their pride was centered around the sacred isle of Delos.

*W*hen the ship bearing Aias and Eumaeus pulled up on the Delian beach to the West of the enclosure sacred to Apollo, there were already many ships before them. This was the time when all of the brotherhoods, assemblies of poets, met at Delos to induct new members, mark the passing of old ones; to discipline and regulate themselves and reaffirm their sense of greater community through general assemblies and contests. Given the religious nature of their calling, it was natural that ritual, prayer, and prophesy played an important role in all their activities.

After helping to beach and stow the ship, Aias and Eumaeus walked inland with the others to the location traditionally set aside for their brotherhood. There they found the tents had already been pitched, and after a little searching Aias found one with several sleeping spots still free. As was customary, he and Eumaeus gathered dried grasses from nearby and laid them out as a foil against the uncomfortably hard and rocky soil.

By early afternoon they were finished and ready to look about. Eumaeus had a few old friends he was anxious to see, so while he headed towards the market area (which doubled as a meeting ground), Aias wandered along the bed of the little river called Inopes towards the base of Kinthos hill, the highest point of the island. He had several hours to pass before the first formal meeting of his brotherhood was to occur, and no wish to return to the meeting place early, knowing from experience that the other apprentices would not welcome him. The tale of his family's indiscretions was long since well known.

It was a beautiful summer's day, surprisingly cool despite the advanced season, and fresh under a brilliant blue sky. Leaving the Inopes, Aias made for the north flank of Kinthos and within a few minutes was at the top where a tiny, ancient shrine had been set up. There were others there already, so Aias did not stay long, pausing only to look at Naxos in the distance and straining to see the mainland, which he could not through the haze. Then he turned and walked back a little, the way he had come.

After some searching, Aias found a rock not far below the top, overlooking the harbor and marketplace, and he sat down in front so he could lean back against it. He adjusted his weight until he had made himself comfortable, and wiping the sweat from his eyes he looked out over the sparkling sea to the west. In the distance, the dusty hills of Syros seemed to luxuriate between the warmth of the sun and the cool waters of the Aegean. A breeze from the south softly fanned his cheek.

Feeling sleepy, Aias heard the general buzz of voices rising up from clusters of men below. Here and there a voice stood out, its owner laughing or shouting above the others. Once or twice Aias squinted against the light to see if he could trace the source of such exuberance, but he failed, in part because he was unwilling to expend the effort.

When a movement caught his sight a little to the left, his eyes followed it: it was a lizard skittering pell-mell across the loose rocks before disappearing from sight farther down the hill.

While the minutes passed, the sun's heat flowed across him in waves. His eyes at last fell shut. He felt great ease in the warmth that surrounded him, in the sun that dazzled even behind his closed eyelids. Slowly, unnoticed, everything started to fall away: the distant voices, the rocks beneath him, the memory of his purpose on that day. At last only peace remained as Aias drifted quietly into sleep.

*W*hen he awoke suddenly, the sun was already well advanced in its long slide towards the western horizon. He glanced down to the marketplace and started. Already the general mass of bodies had broken into groups and moved off some distance towards the spots tradition had bequeathed them. He could see his own brotherhood gathering at the spur of land overlooking the harbor where the boats lay. They had not yet convened the assembly, but they would do so at any moment. He would surely be late. Speedily he got up, slapping his clothes to relieve them of their dust and hurried downwards, ignoring the pebbles that collected in his sandals as he moved down the slope.

The assembly was in prayer when Aias arrived at the outer edge of the group. He could not see Eumaeus, so he sat where he was, at the fringe of the crowd. An elder was preparing to sacrifice a goat, and the sacred fire where its flesh was to be roasted was already burning by a low stone altar.

As the victim was being led forward on a leash by one of the older apprentices it suddenly kicked and jerked free, darting forward to stand with its back to the alter, its head bobbing a little from side to side, its eyes and nostrils flaring. Yet when the handler came forward to again take hold of its halter, it seemed to surrender easily: it was even said later that it had pressed its own neck into the blade, but Aias was too far back to see this for himself.

Great things seemed to be in the air that day and like the others Aias eagerly offered up prayers with the sacrificial smoke, longing for success in his purpose.

After the ritual offerings were made the meat was roasted and divided among all present. It was said by all to be unusually good and everyone agreed the omens were excellent for the assembly.

In late afternoon the first business of the assembly was begun, with the events of the previous year being formally discussed in detail. As individuals the brothers were already aware of most of what had taken place: most had been on Delos for at least several hours and informal exchanges of news had already taken place. However, the Greeks had a strong sense of what was right and fitting in such situations and a more ordered reporting was thought essential.

There had been two deaths; Alcidas of course, but also the apprentice of Idomeneus of Crete. Alcidas was the more fortunate of the two. Idomeneus had been traveling in Macedon where his pupil was captured and eaten by the hill people before they could be offered a ransom. Such mishaps were still quite common: those who brought civilization sometimes paid a heavy price.

Not much was said of the apprentice since he was very young and few knew him well, but Alcidas' passing was the source of general regret, and much was said on the topic in the assembly.

Diokles, an old friend of Alcidas, formally requested leave of the assembly to deliver a poem in the dead man's honor. This was freely granted, and all agreed he should present it the following morning at the beginning of the contests. Then a Samothracian stood and asked whether Alcidas' apprentice was present, so Aias was obliged to stand up and receive many statements of pity from those around him.

One speaker offered to help him should the need ever arise and others rose to agree, caught up in the prevailing mood of sympathy and regret; insisting Aias should tell them if they might help in any way. In this way they expressed their love for their dead companion.

The warmth towards him, though only incidental, came as a shock to Aias, but even as he felt himself moved deeply by their words he realized that no better opportunity would ever come. Though the usual time to request a place in the contests had not yet arrived, Aias decided to immediately test their words.

Finding a moment of relative quiet, he looked around at the faces. "There is something" he said. While several frowned at this, most were curious and some were even pleased, smiling enthusiastically, encouraging him. "I would like to sing tomorrow." He felt himself blushing and looked down. "If the assembly will allow me to, that is."

Someone not far off spoke up, asking Aias what he wanted a voice for while still so young, but those beside the questioner silenced him, made him sit down. The friendliness of the crowd had encouraged Aias a little, so he decided to answer.

"I want to describe what happened in the far-off place where Alcidas died." Then, with the words out, Aias could barely bring himself to look up, fearful of an angry response. But his words were greeted with more and broader smiles, with kindness even. It was quickly agreed that he should have his moment early in the day.

After his unexpectedly easy success, Aias heard little of what was said as the assembly continued. In his mind he rehearsed his poem, laboring even at that late moment to perfect its form. When the assembly was over Aias made for the hill and sat as darkness fell, watching the fires below and the brilliant stars above while he thought. It was very late when he went back down and came across Eumaeus just as he was leaving their tent, apparently heading towards the boats.

"Where are you going uncle?" asked Aias.

Eumaeus seemed almost as if he wanted to walk by without answering, but as he was passing, he turned and smiled dryly. "For a walk, my boy," he said hesitantly.

"Can I walk with you? I don't know if I can sleep yet."

But his uncle shook his head. "You'd better try and sleep. Things may not finish so well as they have begun."

Aias thought for a moment. "It did go well, didn't it? I had a speech prepared but there was never any point in delivering it, they gave in so quickly. Do you think the Gods had a hand in it?"

"I don't know. You're lucky Alcidas had so many friends." Eumaeus sighed. "Still, I never would have expected them to vote you a voice while years are left on your apprenticeship. Alcidas would have been furious if they'd tried such a thing while he was alive, especially for you." Guiltily, Aias wondered at how the man's death had changed so much for him. It did seem as if divine fortune was working on his behalf.

They said good night and while Aias entered the close blackness of the tent, full of snoring bodies hidden by the dark, Eumaeus made his way down to the beach in starlight, walking faster as he came nearer to it.

The boats were there, perhaps twenty of them, beached so that their sterns were just clear of the gently lapping waves, dark shapes he could barely make out against the sand. He searched among them for a moment until he located the one that had brought them from Naxos and heaved himself over its side. Fumbling briefly with his hand beneath an oarsman's bench, Eumaeus brought out a goat-skin bladder. He unfastened the thong at its throat, and sat down heavily on the bench before squirting a small offering onto the sand and taking a deep drink of the liquid inside. It did not seem as if he could swallow fast enough. Barely pausing for breath in between, he poured several long draughts down his throat, until the skin was almost empty. Then he sat in silence, a little breathless, and waited. Minutes passed while he grew warm and comfortable, sprawling across the bench with his head on the gunnel, gazing at the stars.

Suddenly Eumaeus froze, the sound of voices from a short way off coming clearly to him in the calm night air. He slipped off the bench, down on his hands and knees in the belly of the ship, the skin half crushed beneath one hand. The voices grew louder as their owners walked nearer.

When they were scarcely ten paces from the boat, one of the walkers suggested sitting in the sand while they talked. There was laughter at that from his companions, and Eumaeus smiled as well. He recognized the speaker as Prothoos the Magnesian, a man of huge proportions well known for his dislike of exertion. Eumaeus knew the other two as well, for their voices were equally distinctive: these were Alcidas' friend Diokles and Talthybios of Rhodes.

Eumaeus was not fond of these men, but since he was hidden he began to take pleasure in their conversation and in the stealthy way he had become privy to it. Then too, the wine was having its effect.

Apparently they had been discussing Athenians: once they had made themselves comfortable in the sand, Diokles described how that very spring an Athenian delegate had tripped and fallen while he was walking to the boats so that his portion of the sacred flame went out in the sand. He, Diokles, had seen the old man fall; blue-veined legs waving in the air while he rolled around on his belly and back, trying to catch his breath. The Athenians had to begin the ritual grafting of the flame from the beginning. The three friends laughed together for quite a while, here or there adding a comment when their mirth seemed about to die down, keeping the moment going until at last they were too drained to go on.

Then there was silence but for Prothoos' noisy breathing, and it seemed as if the delicate lapping of the water against the beach absorbed everyone's attention. It was Diokles who broke the silence, the edge in his voice suggesting that his thoughts had taken another course. "Speaking of veins, the drunkard Eumaeus has put a few on his face in the last year." He laughed unpleasantly, and Eumaeus sat upright, straining to hear what else might be said. A moment before he had shared in the general amusement, but his pleasure was changing fast, being replaced by a flood of anger at the words of Diokles. "That bastard nephew of his is sure to make a fool of himself: I could hardly believe it when I heard him ask for his voice before the assembly. We should have sent him home for his presumption."

"But I've heard he is very good for his age," Prothoos protested.

Diokles was in no mood for such ideas. "Who told you that?" he demanded.

"Several of the brotherhood... but you may be right even so." Prothoos shifted his weight a little, grunting quietly as he did so. "We should be considerate of the boy: he must find a new master to serve, and there can be little harm in his efforts to show the assembly what he can do. Perhaps I will help him. My apprentice is almost ready to become a full member of the brotherhood, so I could take the boy in without too much trouble. It is always good to help the young with our skill and knowledge in their time of need."

Talthybios chuckled. "Always ready to help a new boy, Prothoos? The kind of help you offer your apprentices might result in him being smothered to death between your roles of fat. Perhaps you are too kind for his good." Prothoos' pronounced taste for youths was well known.

"Good riddance, if he were to die" was Diokles' comment, his tone spoiling the effect of the other man's good-natured ribbing. There was a moment of silence, and then Diokles added quietly to Prothoos: "Better you should use him for your pleasures than that drunken uncle of his, anyway. It would keep the family from any more shame."

At these words Eumaeus was outraged. Leaping up he moved violently towards the side of the boat, roughly setting down the skin as he did so. He had just begun to shout insults at the surprised men, when he tripped and fell sprawling to the bottom of the boat. Rather than subdue him, this mishap made him even more angry, and barely slowed his progress as he scrambled up and over the side. He was a little unsteady on his feet as he rushed, yelling loudly, over to the companions, managing to reach them just as they got to their feet.

It took them a moment in the darkness to realize who was confronting them, but the knowledge seemed something of a relief: Prothoos settled back down in the sand to watch what would happen in comfort and Talthybios belatedly joined him. Diokles, on the other hand, continued to stand, his arms crossed in front of his chest. Eumaeus' boldness was beginning to ebb, his words sounding thin and shapeless in his ears. The other man's strength stood in powerful contradiction to his own weakness.

Finding a break in the confused stream of invective from Eumaeus, Diokles spoke with quiet contempt. "Drinking again? With the death of Alcidas there is none in your family of any worth. Even now, while the brotherhood meets, you cannot control yourself. You are not fit to be here." He spat on the sand near Eumaeus' foot and went on. "What were you doing just now, besides drinking? How dare you spy on us, members of your own brotherhood? I should raise a motion tomorrow to have you and your sister's bastard thrown from the assembly."

Whether it was the words of Diokles, or the return of normal habit, Eumaeus' anger fell away altogether, leaving him feeling exposed and foolish. There was some truth in Diokles' comments, and he could see it now. He had been spying, and drinking too.

Eumaeus became a little fearful that he might have done some harm to Aias' cause: the boy was already in trouble enough, without his uncle's antics. When at last he spoke in reply, it was with the smiling, bantering manner he usually adopted among the villagers of Naxos. You've seen through me, sure enough. Thought I'd have a drink on the boat until everyone was ready to go home to Naxos." He paused for a laugh, slightly strained by nervousness, then went on: "I asked my nephew to join me, but he won't have anything to do with wine, or any other nonsense, either. A very serious boy...

"You're right, what you said about me being fond of the vine, but there's no confusing Aias with me. And by the way, on behalf of my family, and Aias in particular, I want to thank you for honoring Alcidas' memory. It lessens our loss to see how much he is missed."

Diokles had been watching, intently but impassively, giving Eumaeus no hint what impact his words might be having. When Diokles began to speak, it was in a hard, cold voice. "I'm going to call for the dismissal of both of you from the assembly tomorrow. Talking nonsense won't change that. That brat of yours thinks he will one day be an honored member of the brotherhood? Not while I remain in the assembly. It was foolishness letting him praise Alcidas tomorrow, and now my work will be cheapened by competition with an untalented boy. It's an outrage."

Talthybios, who until then had been lying back in the sand the better to observe the two men standing over him, suddenly sat up and addressed Diokles. "So that's it, is it? You don't want the boy to compete with you? I've heard he is good for his age, but you don't think he could successfully challenge a man, do you?"

Diokles was contemptuous as he half-turned to make his reply. "Having heard the brat practice I can say without doubt: the Muses don't know him. It's shameless that he dares compete with me so he can attract the attention of a new master. Besides, Alcidas despised him: it is not fitting that he be allowed to address the man's memory."

Talthybios shrugged, smiling, as if to say "perhaps", and then let it go.

For his part Eumaeus, concerned for his nephew and having some trouble concentrating on what was being said, was slow to grasp the implication of Diokles' words. When it did come to him, he grasped his attacker's misunderstanding with relief, even pleasure. "No, sir, Aias won't be challenging you at all...and I'm certain he won't even mention Alcidas."

"What are you talking about?"

"His poem does not honor his master: Aias is no hypocrite."

Diokles began to sound a little flustered. "Then why did he ask for a voice before the assembly today?"

There was a hint of triumph in his voice as Eumaeus spoke: "He believes he may have solved the riddle."

At this, even Prothoos found the energy to sit up for a better look at the proceedings. "Do you mean the boy intends to use his voice as a full contestant tomorrow?" he asked disbelievingly.

Eumaeus felt nervous again. "He has good reason...he's very talented..."

Suddenly he realized why things had gone so easily at the assembly that day, and it occurred to him he may have said too much.

"I warned him...," he began, but knew then that nothing would smooth away the damage of his words.

Diokles was confident, in control when he spoke. There was pleasure in his voice. "Perhaps you should have warned him more strongly. We will see what happens to boys who mislead the assembly in full session. This goes beyond anything I have ever heard of." He smiled coldly. "Once word of your trickery is known in Naxos and elsewhere, you will likely be exiled for life, and the little bastard with you. Perhaps the Hellenes of the East will for ever be spared your ugly faces."

He turned to his companions. "Let's leave this drunkard and find some place without spies to talk." At this the three promptly left, Diokles continuing to vent his outrage to the others.

Eumaeus stood swaying gently on the deserted beach, listening to their voices as they vanished in the direction of the camp. He was trying to work out what had just happened, and who was at fault for what seemed to be a disastrous meeting. He hoped his words had not hurt Aias too badly.

And yet, he thought, even if he had been careless, so what? Those men were cowards, afraid of his nephew's music. All he had wanted was a quiet drink and they'd come out of nowhere to abuse him. He crawled unsteadily, wearily, back into the boat and made himself comfortable among the benches and gear.

For hours he heard the waves lapping against the shore, saw the stars far above his head. After a while he began to sing and his uncertainty flowed away: the night was clear and calm.

*W*hen Aias woke he found the tent already deserted. Even Eumaeus was nowhere to be seen. The sun had still not risen above the hills behind the camp though the light was already strong, and all around were the sounds of men breakfasting and preparing for the new day. When he went outside Aias was surprised to see none of his own brotherhood among the faces. Walking to the edge of the camp, he looked westward and it was as if a cloud had passed across the sky: the brotherhood was already in session. He rushed back into the tent to get the lyre, and ran with it still in its sack out towards the point.

As he sat down at the assembly's edge, trying hard to suppress his panting and wondering about the reason for the extraordinary session, several of those nearest Aias frowned and seemed to edge away a little. Diokles was standing, making an address to the assembly. He had not looked at Aias as the boy ran up. His words were angry, and he shouted now and then for emphasis, jabbing at the air with his hand.

"...brother Talthybios was too considerate when he spoke. The boy was in difficult circumstances, yes, but that cannot justify his arrogant presumption here yesterday. If the pressures of his trip made him imagine divine inspiration, that is one thing: it is another that he has clung to such nonsense in the comfort of his uncle's house, and still another that he chose to trick the assembly into letting him present his fantasies here.

"He arrogantly believed that his talent would make us forgive him once we had discovered that his true purpose was to compete, not to sing the praises of Alcidas. If we tolerate such folly and presumption in our young, we threaten the greater fellowship of the Hellenes: for the unity of our peoples under the Gods of Olympus is founded on respect for authority, on the deference of the young for the wisdom of the old, on the submission of the lessers to the great. Knowledge belongs to those who win the right to receive it from the great men who came before. It is not a toy for over-ambitious children.

"We all know the boy's mother was a curse to her family, living long enough only to bring the product of her shame into the world. While Alcidas was strong in honor and a benefit to his people, he must have taken the last goodness his family had to offer, for his brother was born a weakling and his sister a whore. Often Alcidas spoke to me of his lasting shame in all his family, and regretted taking on the well-intentioned but hopeless task of training his nephew. In light of what he has done to repay his uncle's memory, how can we allow this bastard to sit among us?" He was shouting, pointing at Aias. As the assembly turned to look, the boy's eyes and head bowed before them, his thoughts too confused and frightened for any other reaction.

Diokles went on: "Who among us would take him as an apprentice, knowing that he would likely shame them at some future time? To what purpose should he remain? Do we not shame ourselves before the Muses to even tolerate his presence here? Is it not enough to know of his deceit, his arrogance, his unsuitability for this brotherhood?

"Together, brothers, let us send him from this place, putting aside an annoying distraction from those greater matters which are our real concern. I say we must expel him immediately. Then, without wasting a moment, let us consider the same action for his drunken uncle and fellow deceiver. Let us be free of them both." When Diokles sat down and the members turned to one another to consider his words together, Aias could not stop looking downwards, feeling the animosity all around him. He still was not clear on what had happened to change things, but it was obvious they knew of his intentions, and these were not what they had expected.

Yet why else would he speak, except to address the riddle? He wanted to defend himself, but it was clear that his enemies would shout him down. As an apprentice he had no right to speak in any case. His long journey home was ending in failure.

Several other speakers got up and addressed the assembly, each expressing outrage at the pride of Aias, each calling for his immediate expulsion. Aias felt his eyes flood with tears at one point, but fought to free them for fear they would increase his shame before the assembly. He wanted to leave of his own volition, but he was afraid to stand up as if doing so would render his inward nakedness visible to all.

Aias was scarcely listening any more by the time Idomeneus of Crete stood up to speak, but soon the calm in the man's voice made him pay attention. It was like the sounds of water splashing softly, to a thirsty man's ears.

"Brothers: none can doubt the crime of pride the other speakers have described is great indeed. All must agree that if it were present, it must be punished by expulsion.

"And I believe most assemblies—not just those in the dark lands of Thessaly and Arcadia where the Greeks have forgotten the meaning of wise councils—in most assemblies this boy would be judged guilty and sent away. But ours is not a village council, and we must look for deeper meanings.

"Can we be certain of the boy's guilt before we act? I believe we can and must. Brotherhoods of poets like ours have been established to serve the divine order, promoting it on earth. Each brotherhood takes on some portion of this task and spreads their knowledge among the Hellenes, feeding the ears of the people on reflections of divine truth. In our time, when the greatest heroes have all long since gone to Hades or the Isles of the blessed according to their differing natures, we above all—we members of the brotherhoods— serve their heroic purpose, seeking to express the divine patterns among the peoples of the world.

"Our part, brothers, is to seek out the ancient wisdom lost when the last age ended and the world was choked by a time of war and primitive darkness. Civilization was lost, and trade, and arcane knowledge from much of the Greek lands. Rising from the ashes of that long dark night, we attempt to rediscover knowledge of the places the Gods once showed to men, where heroes were buried and great things were done: where sacred powers linger from ages past.

"The Gods have been helpful, directing our quest, revealing secrets to our hearts and minds through dreams and visions. The Muses, agents of music and poetry, inspire us when our insights are true, helping us separate illusion from truth, by the beauty and power they give or withhold from the words we utter and the songs we sing. We are sworn to release the voices that were silenced in the Fall.

"Does it not seem strange to you that we are silencing this boy without letting him be heard? That we who are sworn to end silence are considering whether to sustain it? And what of proof? Do we not trust the Muses to reveal the truth by granting delight—or falsehood by with-holding it? Then, too: have we not already given Aias permission to sing, to be tested? We may reverse ourselves but only if provoked. Should we reverse ourselves unjustly, we would be dishonored. Let us not be hasty, brothers, and risk doing wrong.

"It has been said that Aias and his uncle deceived the assembly. This is so. But was their deceit intentional? The boy never said he sought to eulogize his uncle Alcidas: we inferred that was his intention. For his part, Aias may have thought only of what he considered surpassingly important: his solution to the riddle. As I recall the events of yesterday, much was assumed but little, perhaps, was understood by him or us.

"And should we condemn youth? We, who stand at the dawn of a new age? Like seeds the Hellenes were planted in the darkness of these past centuries, only now to be reborn. Might not the Gods sometimes speak to a newly reborn people through the mouth of one of their youths? It is a pattern that surely fits our age.

"I do not think it is right to condemn his pride as we discuss sending this boy away. I have watched him closely since he arrived yesterday, being in need of an apprentice myself and wondering if he might serve. It seems surprising to me that a youth possessed of such sacrilegious arrogance should have the presence of mind to conceal it so successfully. I have seen in him no more pride than in the least among us; less, perhaps, as befits an orphaned bastard and a youth.

"It has also been pointed out, as if this were a crime, that Aias is a bastard. To be mortal is to be born low, even for the one who is born a king. The true measure of a mortal is his *arete*, how closely he follows in the train of the Gods. The Gods have shown us many times that the low-born man may shine with *arete* while the high-born may express none at all. Whether this boy has *arete* or not we do not know, and cannot until he has been tested.

"Aias' mother was a pan-girl, bewitched by soft-voiced Aphrodite and laughing Pan at the height of their moonlit mysteries. But brothers: is not the earth-mother also a receiver of many lovers? Aias' mother, like all others present, was under the guidance of Gods when the festival took place. Is it not possible that we see in Aias' unhappy lineage some divine purpose? I don't say it is so: only that it may be. Who better to discover the mysteries of the Mother, than such a mother's son?

"I have heard that Aias is extraordinarily talented. Perhaps the Muses have turned away from a boy of great *arete*, shunning him, yet that seems unlikely. After all, in their gentle hands he might have become an inspired voice in the years to come. If they had but guarded him against foolish pride and delusions now, in time he might have brought benefit to this brotherhood and all the Hellenes. His crimes would have to be great indeed for them to release him from their service and ours while still so young.

"But there is one way alone to test this boy: we must let him sing. If his voice is pure and his lyre sets tears starting from his listeners' eyes; if his answer to Lord Apollo's riddle is strong and cannot be shaken by doubt; if the words of his poem speak to our minds and hearts with assurance, then we must let him keep his voice today. If he fails, we must banish him forever from our hearth.

"Can there be any other sensible course of action?"

Idomeneus sat down, and at once the brotherhood began loudly to discuss his words.

Diokles was angry over being so strongly challenged, laboring hard to undo the damage that had been done to his position. For his part, Aias was afraid to look up as his fate was decided. He sat there through the many minutes that passed, his lips moving soundlessly in prayer, his palms pressed firmly against his knees to keep his fingers from trembling.

*D*awn crept across the sky as the old man sat gazing at the valley, watching while it seemed to swell in breadth and depth in the growing light. "So begins a day that will leave its mark through the centuries," he said quietly, and looked at the younger man.

"Perhaps, but I am more concerned about the present."

"That is youth: to always feel the strength of immediate events and lose the sense of their significance. When you stand beside your bride today, there will be generations unborn and generations long dead who stand beside you both unseen, watching. This is your brief moment and all that has been or is yet to come waits upon your actions." The old man stroked his grizzled beard, then patted his son's shoulder and smiled. "But that does not matter. Marriage is for youth, and suits the youthful mind, not the minds of those whose years lie mostly behind them."

The young man's face darkened slightly. "Don't say such things father: your health is good, and you have many years left."

The concern in the younger man's words made the old man chuckle. "Perhaps. But to the young a year is an unassailable fortress no conqueror can defeat. At my age, a year is a puff of mist that billows past the face and is gone. A lifetime is no more than a tiny wind-blown cloud to me." His eyes fixed upon the cliffs across the valley, and remained there while his thoughts went on, his words tenuous, searching. "It is almost fifty years since I first saw this view. I was younger than you by half in those days, a lonely orphan desperate to return to his home on Naxos, and I felt the thunder of every moment as intensely as you are feeling it now. How much has passed! When I first sang for the brotherhood on Delos and became the apprentice of Idomeneus, I felt as though I had achieved everything that could be done. Life would be complete and enjoyed in ease from that point on. Silly dreams! My years have been filled with work, and still there is no end to it: soon I will pass it on to you to continue." He smiled. "And know, my son, that I will do so without regret."

"On my wedding day you should find a more cheerful subject, father. It is bad luck to speak of endings when this is a beginning."

The old man shook his head, his eyes crinkling with humor. "Beginnings and endings are not so far apart as you think. Here we are on Mount Parnassos, at Lord Apollo's sanctuary, founded by my brotherhood in the year of your birth. A new age has been born here that may live a thousand years and more. But there will come a time, as certain as sunset, when another will sit on a mountainside as we are doing now and contemplate the ending of what we have begun. And perhaps another thousand years beyond that time, another will sit and greet the coming of yet another dawn. And you and I, though our bodies are dust, will be at their sides and silently share their burdens. No my son, beginnings and endings are joined beyond time." He smiled gently. "On the day you see that clearly, you will touch divine Olympus where the immortal Gods live…"

The young man looked searchingly into his father's face, but said nothing.

The older man laughed suddenly, and slapped his knee. "I almost forgot." He reached up with both hands, removing a leather thong from around his neck and put it over his son's head instead, arranging the pendant on the young man's chest and patting it fondly. His son felt the pendant with his fingers for a moment, and looked down at it: a blue cloud and thunderbolt on a black background. He had known it all his life, and how much his father valued it, so he was overcome with emotion. The father smiled. "As you know, it used to belong to your grandmother, and her mother before her. It seems fitting that I give it to you. Let it continue in our family down through the generations: if the Gods are willing, it will see many good things in the years ahead." He squeezed his son's shoulder and leaning over, kissed him with a blessing.

For a long time they sat in silence while the sky turned slowly above their heads, each in his own thoughts, watching while the day grew bright across the rugged reaches of the valley. An hour later they got up and walked away together, arm in arm, through the morning breeze that ruffled the leaves and grass, caressing the Southern flank of Mount Parnassos. It was the beginning of a beautiful day.

*I*n this place they now called Delphi, the "womb", a dynasty was beginning. For more than a thousand years the family of Aias would remain one of the principle families there, serving as priests.

Within a century or so the brotherhood of Aias was dissolved, its job done. Other brotherhoods, like the Hesiodai and Homerai, also came to an end until only the Orphics remained in a changing world. The Gods let it be known that Delphi was the principle place of prophesy in the world, sacred to Apollo. Over the succeeding centuries His light shone through the Mother's dark passage beneath Parnassos, illuminating past and future in the mysteries of her womb: ashes from the past and seeds of the future. In every generation an older woman who had shared the Mother's trials of giving birth, though necessarily a mere child in comparison to the Goddess, was selected to become the Sibyl. She spoke while entranced by Apollo, revealing his knowledge to all who came.

And many did come: Delphi became the principle shrine of the Hellenes, offering advice on matters great and small, always endeavoring to ensure that balance, harmony, and diversity prevailed in all things. No one approach could reflect the divine pattern of all the Gods, therefore if human society was to reflect its divine prototype, variety must be encouraged in every area of cultural and political life. The hearth in the temple of Apollo at Delphi became the central hearth of all the Greeks, nurturing a graft taken from the ancient flame at Delos and joined to another flame captured by focusing the light of the sun, a thing done in honor of the fresh inspirations Apollo promised to offer in that place.

Hellenic culture flowered, an achievement of the religion which fostered it. Yet in time the individualism and pluralism which made the Greeks unique in history—discoverers of much that became the basis of Western Civilization and later was to shape the whole world—also led to their disintegration. Unable to pull together, the Hellenes tore themselves apart through war and intrigue, preparing the way for domination by the Macedonian king Philip II and his son, the conqueror known to history as Alexander the Great.

In a way, too, their religion was broken apart by diversity. Some of those who sought the smoke of things—some of the philosophers—began pulling away from the faith that gave birth to their path, subsuming the Gods beneath their vision of a mechanistic and more purely elemental, philosophic universe.

Still, even these momentous events did not put an end to the religion, nor to the importance of Delphi. Indeed, both continued to thrive in much the same way as they had in the time of Aias and the brotherhood—in that forgotten age when civilization was born again from the ashes of the old.

Sanctuary of the Gods: Under Parnassos

THE GUARDIANS: TWILIGHT IN THE SANCTUARY
(The Taro River Valley, 1347 AD)

The young woman's father gripped her by the shoulders and shook her violently in frustration. She did not resist, letting herself be shaken. It made her afraid, for it was not the first time he had skirted the edge of control. If she was not careful, this could lead anywhere.

"Why do you resist me?" Roberto yelled.

She shook her head and by an effort of will, forced perplexity into her reply. She did not feel it but knew it would be soothing, would create hope and defer the moment of truth. "I don't know, father. I don't love him." She shrugged beneath his grasp, as if she was troubled by the same question that had infuriated her father. It worked, for his anger passed and he loosened his grip, though he still held her firmly.

"You'll change, daughter. These things take time. You'll see." Relaxing further, he patted her on the shoulder, confident, reassuring, and he smiled. She felt sick. "Just give him a chance and you'll discover that your father is not so foolish as you think. You are very clever Maria, and you think you know everything, but you'll realize one day that age brings a deeper understanding of life. I want only what is best for you, and though it is hard for you to see it, I know your needs better than you do. I have seen a lot and learned from what I've seen. Gino is a good boy, and he will give you balance."

Maria nodded mutely and he let her go. To her relief there was a knock on the door at that moment, diffusing the tension still further. "Who is it?" called Roberto, all sign of their encounter miraculously dispersed. Maria took a deep breath.

"It's me...Mario, sir." The words were slurred slightly.

"Come in son. We were just finishing talking. Have you been a good boy, Mario?"

"Yes sir."

Mario had Downs Syndrome. His eyes were slanted, his tongue too big, his thighs were fat and he waddled when he walked. Maria smiled to see him. He stood there with his tongue half out, shorter than Maria although he was her age, and smiled back.

Roberto was suddenly detached. "Well, Maria. Why don't you go for a walk with your little friend? I promised your mother I would fix the hinge on the back door. Think about what I said and we will talk about it later." He left, heading for the shed to get his tools.

Maria beamed at her friend. "Mario, I'm so glad to see you. You came at a good time. Let's go out." She walked over to him, and he reached out slowly and gently to pat her on the arm. All his mannerisms were like that: slow and gentle. She responded by taking his hand and squeezing it.

They walked up the valley, following the stream beyond the village and right to the head of the valley. There were a few clouds overhead, but otherwise the day was fresh and clear. Mario was slow and methodical in his walking, as if it took an act of will to make his feet traverse the uneven path they took, and they were silent. At one point they crossed the stream, and Maria helped him step over the wet stones as he doggedly attempted to force his feet to stay dry. He failed, losing his balance, compensating too slowly, and he would have pitched full length into the water if Maria hadn't caught him and held him upright, stepping into the water herself to do so. They both laughed at his clumsiness before walking on.

They came upon a place where the stream flowed over the bedrock, and a pool had been formed. It was large enough for two persons to sit in, not more, and it was their favorite spot. Today they would not swim for Maria felt too serious for childish play. Besides, even though it was almost midsummer, the weather in the mountains had not yet surrendered to the summer heat. They sat beside the water on the smooth slate of the stream bed and watched it flow past.

It was Maria who spoke first.

"My father wants me to marry Gino."

Tears came to Mario's eyes, but he said nothing, looking stolidly at the water.

"I won't marry him. Never." She put her arm around him and he laid his head on her shoulders. "Don't worry Mario. Everything is going to be all right. I promise you it is."

They were silent for a moment. Just across the stream in an old ash tree, a crow let out a raucous blast. Somewhere from farther up the narrow valley another crow answered. The first crow cocked its head, squawked, and suddenly flew away in an untidy flurry, wings beating hard against the air as it disappeared towards its unseen companion. The two young people watched it go.

"Your father is right. Gino is very handsome and smart. He must be good for you." Mario's voice was sad.

"No. You are good for me."

"But you are smart. I am stupid. I am the most stupid boy in the valley: everyone says so."

"Don't talk like that. I told you: you are not stupid. You are slow to think, but you feel like lightning. Your heart is swifter and brighter than any but the wise.

"Don't you understand, Mario? I think much more quickly than anyone in the village. I never forget anything. I understand everything I read without trying. I know what everyone will do before they do. I was always the best student by far, whether I was studying or not. My mind is so quick that when I talk to others it is as if I am running and they are crawling: I run around and around to give them a chance to catch up, but they never do. The others think you are slow and they are fast. But to me everyone is slow. Whoever I marry will be much slower than me: the difference between you and them is too small to care about. And cleverness is not so important. Everybody wants to be clever because they are not, but they don't know what it means. I do. Cleverness doesn't make you happy or good. That only comes from a good heart.

"My heart was no better than anyone else's, until you became my friend. You showed me things no one else could have. You taught me about my own heart.

"Remember when we were eight?" Mario looked at her in slow surprise and she went on. "One time I asked you why you trusted the other children again and again, even though they betrayed and hurt you every time. Remember? You said that if you didn't trust them it would hurt them. I laughed and told you they didn't care enough about you to be hurt by you, but you said no: that even if a dog is afraid of a person, it harms that person to realize it.

I didn't say so, Mario, but I thought you were foolish. It got me thinking, though, and I considered what you said for a couple of days. And you know what? You were right. We are so used to being afraid and seeing fear that we don't notice it, but actually we don't like to make others afraid. It hurts us to see that we have hurt others.

"That's why people like to tame wild creatures until they come and eat from their hands. We want to be loved, but we are so tied up in knots that we usually think it doesn't matter, or maybe even that it is better to be feared."

Mario was looking confused, and Maria patted his hand. "I know, I'm using words you didn't use, but that's what I mean: you see the truth about things right away. I have to think about it for days before I see it. Then I can talk about it cleverly. But which is better: seeing what is good instantly, or taking days to discover it, and then being able to talk about it? The silly thing is, I've never been able to make anyone else understand about how it hurts to be feared, no matter how cleverly I talk. My words are mostly useless. No: I would rather be like you. And since I can't be, I would rather be with you so you can teach me.

"My head is fast but my heart is slow: your head is slow but your heart is fast. We need both, Mario. That's why together we make a perfect balance. You are the kindest, most generous person in the village: I know I am the lucky one, to have your love—no matter what anyone would say if they knew."

She was silent for a moment, thinking, while Mario smiled at her. When at last she spoke, her tone was tentative, exploratory. "I don't know how to tell my father. Everyone thinks we are just friends because they can't believe we could love each other. When they know, it's going to make trouble, at least for a while. I wish I knew how to tell them."

For a long time they sat side by side, watching the beauty of the afternoon sun as it touched the bright green leaves with its warming light. At first Maria was troubled by her thoughts, but soon Mario began to rock back and forth, then to sing, and eventually she joined in. As they sat by the side of the bubbling stream they forgot tomorrow and were happy and careless of everything but each other and the beauty of that place.

It was five days later that Maria told her father about Mario, and life became very difficult. He ordered that they stop meeting. He demanded that she tell no one of her wishes. He made threats. There was violence and there were tears, and Maria told him she would not allow his prejudices to dictate her life. She would appeal the matter.

The following day Maria went in search of Fabio, an elder and priest of Apollo. He was a kindly man who had been Maria's tutor in her studies of philosophy. Studious and with balding head, he lived alone in a small but comfortable farmhouse near the town. His wife had died several years before after a long illness, and his two daughters had long ago moved out and built families of their own.

When Maria knocked on his door, Fabio welcomed her in to sit at his kitchen table. It was after dark, and there was a lamp on the table that cast a faint glow around the room. In its sacred light, Maria could see the remains of his dinner had been hastily dumped on a shelf to make room on the table where they sat.

"You are here about Mario," he said.

"Did my father...?"

"Yes, Roberto saw me this afternoon and said you were intending to visit me about it." He ran the palm of his hand over his pate. "This is a difficult matter. We do not wish to resist the will of Aphrodite who seems to have played a role in your problem, but surely you understand there are other factors we must consider."

"And these are...?" She was calm, readying herself.

"It is not right that one such as yourself should find such a husband. You possess the most gifted mind of your generation, one of the most gifted minds this village has ever known. Great things are expected of you. Why would you choose the weakest-minded man? It is difficult to imagine. Furthermore, children of the God like Mario do not usually marry in our village or anywhere else. They are not fit for the responsibilities of parenting. Surely that is obvious? Your children will need the wisdom of their father, not just yourself, if they are to become useful to the Gods when they come of age." He paused and searched for his words carefully. "You know, Maria, it amazes me that you would even consider such a thing. Don't you care that your husband would be looked at as a joke? Except for the wise, it is human nature to wish for the respect of others in all things. Look at Homer or Plato, and you will see that this is the first wish of Poets and Philosophers equally. Are you not human like the rest of us?"

Maria ran her thumbnail along the edge of the table, feeling it stick at the tiny scratches and scrapes there. "Socrates was a funny looking man, little respected for the things he acquired including his wife. She was weak and petty, and famed for her sharp tongue. The Christian emperor Constantine's wife was said to have been a prostitute before she married. And what of Goddesses who have chosen mere mortal men for their husbands? Thetis took Peleus; Eos, the dawn, took herself a mortal. I am far closer to Mario in my capacities than these Goddesses were to their mates.

"As to the quality of my mind which you say elevates me so much: is thought so great? Was it not the crooked thoughts of Kronos that began the second harm to mother earth? And what about the crooked thoughts of Hermes? Is not thought, especially mortal thought, a thing greatly limited? Logic has value, but does it not meet with paradox to remind us of its limits? Plato valued thought and used it well, but he saw the greatest good in direct perception of truth, not in merely thinking about it. And we are told that the end of mortal thought is Lethe, the river of forgetfulness that lies in the land of the dead. Without wisdom thought is nothing and fades to a useless, babbling whisper. Does wisdom come from thought? Thought may help, but so does love and bravery, to name just two qualities that wisdom follows. It is said we will be judged after death, and the quality of our souls assessed. Will we be judged for our cleverness or our goodness? Alexander the Great was clever, but was he wise? What of the wicked Alcibiades, student of Socrates and one of the cleverest men of his age?

"I wonder, sir, if you could tell me who in our village has the kindest, most generous nature? Who cares nothing for his own suffering when he compares it to the suffering of others around him? Who is utterly free of pride? You cannot deny it is Mario. He has as much goodness as any of the wise, though he may have the mind of a fool. I need him, sir. I need his guidance." She was becoming excited, following the simple clarity of the idea. "I think we were made for each other. Separately we both excel in some areas, but we are deficient in others. Together we combine the finest qualities of our natures. I believe, though, that I am the one who gains the most: without a good heart, a mind is fated in time to death and forgetfulness. With a good heart, it is fated to be reborn in wisdom. I believe Mario can guide me as I need to be guided. All I can do is help him in material ways, but he can guide me in matters far more important to my soul.

"So I do not worry whether Mario would make a good father: I know he will. Any child would be lucky to call him father. And I will see to the education of their minds, as will the teachers like yourself.

"You spoke of respect, sir, and of public humiliation. I don't care what is thought of me. Does this village care what would be thought of it? The Christians think of believers in the old ways as children misguided by devils. Should we stop what we have been doing and follow the whims of the average?

"The reason my wish to marry Mario is offensive to my father and to others is that they fear the opinions of the rest of the village, and they worship mere cleverness because they do not have it. They judge us harshly because they are afraid of being judged harshly if they support us. That is absurd.

"Why should I marry an inferior man when a superior man loves me and I love him? How could I be happy with a man like Gino? I wish him no harm, but I know him too well. I know the pettiness and weakness that reside in him. I will never accept him."

Fabio shook his head. "I understand your reaction to Gino. He is not so terrible as you imagine, but he does try too hard to please others, perhaps. I do not press you to marry him: you can choose from the others. There are a number of candidates, and you need not hurry too much in your choice. Why don't you take some time to think it over?"

"I want Mario. There is none other better for me. Please don't make this difficult for us."

Fabio frowned. "You should know that I have spoken to several of the other elders about this matter, and there is agreement among us. Mario is not suitable. If you want you can press for a formal consideration of your wishes by all of the elders, and if you are dissatisfied by their answer, I will call a full assembly to let the village decide, but I am utterly certain they will agree with me. You will harm your reputation—yes, I know you say it doesn't matter, but perhaps you will one day change your mind—and you will not have come any closer to having your way." He reached out to touch her hand, but she moved it from the table to her lap. "In time you will understand and see the sense in this decision.

"In the meantime, it would be best if you avoided the boy and just applied yourself to your studies."

He stood up and reached out his hand for her to take. She also stood, taking the proffered hand. He accompanied her to the door and she left. When she was sure she was out of range, she let her tears come, and for a long time she wandered alone by the stream, breathless with sorrow. Where would they ever find an ally?

The following day after her schooling was finished, Maria headed up the mountain instead of down it, towards the village. She was so preoccupied with her thoughts that at first she didn't recognize the signs of the gathering storm. With the first deep rumble of thunder, she glanced over her shoulder. The clouds were purple to the North-east, and although she was already panting with the climb, she hurried even faster. The air around her slowly grew darker, as if it were dusk and the mid-afternoon sun had fled the sky. As she reached the top where the mountain leveled off, a bolt of lightning tore through the air and penetrated a mountain's flank on the opposite side of the valley, its flash briefly brightening the trees and forest litter around her. A moment later the shuddering, crackling roar came. The first drops of rain were already making their way through the trees when the girl approached the small cabin that stood in a little clearing at the approach to the ridge she had just climbed.

"Grandfather?" shouted Maria. There was no smoke coming from the chimney. "Giovanni?" Again there was no reply. "It's me, Maria." She stood by the door, her hand on the latch, and hesitated.

A voice came from somewhere behind the cabin. "Just a moment, Maria. I'll be right there." She looked at the sky doubtfully, and walked to the corner of the little building so she could look in the direction from which the voice had come. A moment later Giovanni appeared, smiling, and he put his hand on her shoulder and kissed her cheek. "We'd better go inside," he said.

The door creaked as Giovanni opened it, and he stood aside to let Maria enter first. "You're lucky you found me: I was planning to visit Giulia this afternoon until the weather changed." Inside, the hut was very plain, just a shelf, fireplace, bed, and a low three-legged stool. Around the walls clothing, pots, and various knicknackery hung in apparently random order. A lamp stood in a wall bracket, and Giovanni walked over to it and raised the wick until it cast a warm yellow light in the cramped interior. The only window was shut, a rectangular hole covered by a section of wood that was hinged at the top. As Maria sat down on the bed the rain arrived in earnest, pounding on the slate roof and dripping down the hut's sides so that within seconds there was everywhere the sound of trickling water. Giovanni pulled the stool away from the wall a little and sat on it.

"How are your studies going?" he asked.

"Good, but I need to talk to you, Grandfather. It is very important."

"Then we will come to that soon, Maria. But goodness, dear, don't be in such a rush: It has been three weeks since I saw you last, and I need to catch up a little first." He smiled. "You young people are always rushing to things as if time were about to run out. If you have something to say, we will come to it."

Maria suppressed her impatience, for she needed his help too much to risk it by being over-eager. She looked at the wall for a moment, considering. "Today I was writing about Zeus and the generations of the Gods. It's still a little rough, but do you want to see it?" She reached into her tunic and pulled out a small roll of parchment and handed it too him.

He opened it and held it up at an angle to catch the lamplight better. It was smudged and the letters were not easy to see, written as it was with temporary ink so that the parchment could be used again: writing materials were not plentiful. For a few minutes there was silence except for the rain, and the occasional peal of thunder as he read:

"Zeus, the sky king, rules for ever, master of the wheel of time which is the root of wisdom. In windy Crete where the poets lie, did they truly sing the death of Zeus? He falls to earth as lightning, seed of himself, hurled against broad earth in frenzied passion. Death or life: or is it both? The poets never tell.

Here is a mystery: grandfather heaven, shining Ouranos, holds aloof, and Kronos, father Time, loves too much the earth-mother's womb: but Zeus is guided by the measures of all seasons. First comes summer's life with the brilliant sky, but life brings death in winter, down into the darkness of the underworld: only the rebirth of springtime saves mortal life. Swiftly Zeus comes and swiftly goes, in perfect, timeless balance. Will unborn lightning, Zeus the child, linger long in the darkness of the mother's womb? With scarcely a touch he is born again. Lord Zeus is Spring to his father's Winter, and Spring to the Summer of his father's father. He is the Spring where all things join, season of surprise, when death greets life and joy is born: unending, mysterious creation.

Thus does wife Hera draw Zeus to her and down, strewing the precious flowers of arete in the fields of this world, dim reflections of the stars that light the fields of heaven. And thus too does Hera call the heroes out to clash spear against shield—awesome thundering—like tympanum drums proclaiming mystic life for Dionysos when he dies. Not even Kronos can hear Zeus' infant cries, half-wise God, as the poets imply, who dwells in splendid visions beneath our world.

Hera, kindly Goddess, will keep Zeus safe in endless, joyful motion."

Giovanni read it twice and then looked it over for a moment. "It's good Maria. Especially the last part, about Hera. It balances the wheel of the Gods nicely. But isn't its meaning a little too obvious? I mean, it is neither philosophy nor poetry, though of course it favors the latter. What is it for?"

"It's educational. We were supposed to write it so that it can be understood by younger students with a little basic knowledge, as if we were teaching them about the Gods. Paulo says if we can teach something to others clearly, then we have understood it well ourselves. It's not poetry, of course. And I don't like the middle part. But it's a start."

He handed it back to her. "You may be right about the middle: it might not be obvious enough, rather than too obvious. A beginner is unlikely to really understand that when the timeless universe of the Gods touches our own world, Summer, Winter, and Spring exist in every instant. Although your theme is the gateway between the worlds, that is a difficult thing for people to understand unless they've glimpsed it directly. I know you spoke of Hera to stress the exchange between the worlds, and it might work for some, but perhaps an allusion to Iris, Goddess of the rainbow and bridge to the other world, might help. And depending on the age of the reader, he may have trouble grasping that your mention of heaven, earth, and the underworld are not referring to space, but to differing dimensions of a single truth. For most children it is difficult to understand that neither time nor space have relevance to the Gods' universe and Truth."

He chuckled. "Then again perhaps you should just follow your own instincts: grandfathers are sometimes too willing to offer their opinions to their grandchildren. My comments are probably of little use to you. I have heard that you are doing very well on your own. Paulo told me you won another contest last week against your fellow students, something about the Dionysians, wasn't it?"

She nodded.

Giovanni was suddenly wistful. "When you smile like that you have your grandmother's eyes."

"Grandfather, you know you mustn't say such things: by adoption or by blood, I am your granddaughter. That is all that matters."

They were silent for a minute, Maria gazing searchingly at her grandfather's face while he looked down at his lap, where his hands rested against his knees. Outside the rain seemed to be lessening, and the thunder was fading as it moved away into the distance. For a man near sixty, Giovanni was young in appearance. His hair had long since lost all color and age had created wrinkles, especially around his eyes, but his skin had not lost its smoothness altogether. There was a quality about him, something difficult to identify, that seemed young: a certain animation, perhaps, that is rarely encountered in the old. But for now he was melancholic and lost in his thoughts. Maria had seen it before.

"Are you thinking about Grandma?"

"Sorry, yes." He stirred himself as if he would switch subjects, but it was not very convincing.

"You still love her after all these years, don't you? It must be very difficult."

"Sometimes, but when I go to her grave and talk to her there, I tell her what is happening and I don't feel so alone. It was much harder at first. For several years after she died there was not one moment of a single day when I felt peace. It was endless, the worst pain I had ever known. I never imagined a human being could suffer so much. I don't know how I survived. To suffer for even a second like that is a thing I would not wish on anyone. The hell most of the outsiders believe in is only flames burning flesh: when I lost your grandmother, it was much worse than that. The flames seemed to be consuming my soul.

"I'm afraid I was a bad father for many years, when Roberto was young. Even after the grief grew less, I had lost my taste for life. I think your father believes I blamed him for your grandmother's death, but I never did. I blamed the world. I tried to show him love, but my heart was gone: the grief consumed it. It was not until your birth that I began to care about life again."

"Grandfather." Her voice had a reprimand in it, for again he was mentioning the thing that should not be discussed.

"I'm sorry. Look, what did you want to talk about?"

"Grandfather, I came to ask your help."

Giovanni stirred himself, like a man waking from a dream and looked at her, raising his eyebrows in an unspoken question. When she didn't continue at once, he smiled gently, with a hint of mischievousness. "Take your time."

She started to speak, hesitated, then blurted "I am old enough to marry."

Giovanni was taken by surprise, but as her meaning grew clear in his mind, he was delighted. "If you have come to ask my blessing, you have it. Who is the lucky man?"

"Thank you, grandfather. I do want your blessing, but before that I need your help. I'm in love with a boy, so much in love... But my father wants me to marry someone else. The boy he thinks I should take I don't love. I'm not even sure if I could like him." She sounded almost frantic, even to herself, and she decided by an act of will to calm herself.

"Well you needn't take someone you don't want: you aren't old enough to be rushed yet. Anyway, if you go to the elders and explain the problem, they will surely support your decision. A father's choice is only meant as a guide. Does the boy you love feel the same way about you?"

"Yes," she said, a little grimly. Giovanni glanced at her curiously but let it pass.

"Well of course I will help you, but it doesn't sound like you need me. I think you are worrying about nothing. I know Roberto is pig-headed at times, but once he has had time to adjust I'm sure he will come to accept the situation. This is your decision to make, not his."

"It's not that simple, grandfather."

"Why not?"

"Well, the elders...I've already gone to them."

"What did they say?"

"They took my father's side."

"Really? Why?"

"They said my choice is...inappropriate. But it isn't. I don't know what to do. Just because..." She stopped and looked at him, and he could see she was near to tears.

"Why? What is it? Who is the boy you're in love with?"

She mumbled, caught herself and spoke more clearly: "Mario."

"Mario?" Giovanni was astonished. "But isn't he a child of the God Dionysos?"

"Oh grandfather! Please don't turn against me. If you don't help me I will have no one. I love him. He is the kindest, most gentle boy in the village, and he loves me too."

"But you are so intelligent. Why would you want such a man? How could it work?"

His words stung her, and she said nothing, staring at the wall. Giovanni went on when he realized she would not reply. "I'm not against you, Maria. I'm just surprised. Surely you can understand that? I need a little time to think about it." She felt a pang of hope and looked at him, studying his face. He looked away. "We'll talk about it, all right? I'm not promising anything, but let me understand you first. And you must promise to listen to me as well, so we will understand each other. If we can do that, perhaps we can agree on what to do."

"That's all I want: someone to really listen to my side. If you understand me, you won't refuse, I know it."

"I'm not promising anything, Maria. Except that I will listen with an open mind. Why don't you start by telling me about it. What makes you think...I mean, how did you decide you wanted to marry him?"

Maria told him. For many minutes she poured out her heart to the older man, speaking of love and duty and goodness. When she finally stopped, Giovanni looked at her with his head tilted back slightly, his eyes fixed while his thoughts seemed to travel on without him. There was a conflict going on inside him: Maria felt it, and waited for the outcome with trepidation and hope. When he spoke, it was with great gentleness.

"I understand you well. Let me think about what you have said for a little while. It's an important matter, and you should allow me some time to reflect on it."

Outside the rain had stopped entirely. There was little more to say and evening was approaching so Maria decided it was time to go. As she left, she kissed Giovanni on both cheeks and held his hand between her own. "This is about love and doing what is best. It's not about pleasing others." Then she left. As Giovanni watched her go, he shook his head. This would not be something he could decide easily. He sighed and went back inside, closing the door behind him.

The following morning just after dawn, Giovanni was again disturbed by a visitor. It was his son, Roberto. He arrived when Giovanni was chopping wood for that evening's fire and the two of them exchanged greetings that were polite but restrained. Giovanni did not need to be told the reason for Roberto's visit but he made no effort to broach the topic, leaving it for his son to do so. He went back to work with his ax and waited.

"We rarely speak, except when there are others around, and I wanted a chance to talk to you more freely." Roberto folded his arms and leaned against the side of the hut as he spoke, watching Giovanni as he swung the ax again.

"I'm honored, indeed, to see you at my dwelling, son. You haven't been here since last fall when you passed by with your friends on a hunting party. At the time you were in a hurry to return to the village so you were only here for a few minutes."

"Your hut is out of the way, and that is your own choice."

"Every time you visit the cave, you are no more than half an hour from my door. That is not so far."

"I didn't come here to argue with you, father." Roberto frowned. "I'm here about Maria. She said she visited you yesterday."

"Yes, that's right."

"She says you are taking her side in this matter."

"That is not true!" Giovanni was angry. "And I have never found Maria dishonest, so I can't believe she said that."

Roberto held out his hand to calm Giovanni. "There is no need to get upset. This is too important for us to fight about it. We need to work together. What I meant was that you are not overtly against her wishes, and that means you may as well be for them. She imagines that your refusal to take a position means you will eventually come to support it. I can understand that you don't want to get involved in the problem, and that grandparents often wish to stay above disputes so they can get along with both sides, but this is too important, and you cannot avoid becoming involved. Obviously you are as firmly against this as I am: what person would not be? But if you don't act now, things could get worse. Maria is as stubborn as she is naïve."

"I agree that her choice seems bad, but have you listened to her? If you resist her you will make her even more inflexible. She is still young, and there is plenty of time before she is forced to make a choice. Let's just counsel patience and wait for her to see things differently."

"You are wrong. Time is the last thing she needs. Right now Gino is interested in her. He is a good boy, intelligent, confident and handsome. He may not wait for this nonsense to pass. The only reason he hasn't given her up is because I have been encouraging him. It is not easy for him to put up with the public humiliation of being spurned for a fool, and I don't know how long he will be patient with her. She will marry him: Maria is not capable of deciding for herself. She is good with the books, and she thinks that means she is competent to choose, but clearly she is not."

"I know Gino a little, and he's not so bad I guess, but you are making a mistake to force her." Giovanni was exasperated. "Anyway, I'm fairly sure Gino is not the best of the available boys. I don't know him that well, but it seems to me he is not so perfect that you should push her to marry him. Why not let Maria decide for herself later?"

Roberto gave Giovanni a calculating look. It made him very uncomfortable. "Gino's here. I thought you should get to know him better so I brought him with me. He's waiting just down the path. Let me call him so you can talk. You will see that my choice is the wisest one in the circumstances."

This was the last thing Giovanni wanted at that moment. The whole situation was becoming far too awkward. Still, if the boy was waiting there seemed little he could do about it. He might as well meet him. Giovanni shrugged, setting down his ax, and Roberto immediately put his fingers in his mouth and whistled shrilly. It hurt Giovanni's ears.

They both stood for a moment looking down the trail as Gino came into view and walked quickly towards them. While he approached, Giovanni noticed that he looked only at Roberto, and bowed to him first before greeting Giovanni. That annoyed him, but he told himself to keep such reactions under control for Maria's sake. He was a tall, good looking boy with a strong jaw and forehead, and a thick head of shiny black hair framing his face. Despite his youth, there was already a faint blue shadow on his cheeks where his beard had been shaven, and his chest was hairy, to judge from the evidence of it that spilled from his collar. He was muscular, and he had that way of holding himself that well built people often do, of flexing surreptitiously so that his strength would be evident to everyone. A peacock...

"Gino, why don't you tell Giovanni about your intentions."
To Giovanni his son's manner was artificial. In fact, it was almost as if he was showing off a prize chicken or pig.

"I'm considering marrying your granddaughter. I know she will make a good wife once she settles in. She is willful and too fanciful, but that is common among women at her age." Gino spoke with enthusiasm and confidence, but something about the delivery made Giovanni feel as if he was attending a recital. He felt sure they had gone over what he would say before they came. "Young women need direction, and I think I'll be able to provide it to her." Gino glanced at Roberto.

"Why do you want to marry her?" asked Giovanni.

For an instant a look of confusion crossed the young man's face, then he answered. "She's not bad looking, and she is very smart: everyone says so.

She wins every scholastic contest she enters. I am not a man who is afraid of his wife's accomplishments." He shifted his gaze from Giovanni to Roberto and kept it there, as if Giovanni had vanished. "Of course she needs a strong husband to keep her in check, and I think I have the character for it. I have a reputation for being sensible and firm." His voice was tinged with pride. "I have always been the leader, even when I was a boy: others listen to me and do what I tell them."

Roberto interrupted him, nodding slightly towards Giovanni. "But you do respect authority, right?"

Gino's eyes never wavered from regarding Roberto. "Yes sir, of course. I believe we should always do what our elders tell us to. By learning from them we are prepared for the day when we become elders in our turn. That's Maria's problem: she needs to learn obedience. That's why she needs a strong man like me."

Giovanni had heard enough. This boy was obnoxious and he didn't need to hear any more in order to understand Maria's distaste for him, or Roberto's reason for favoring him. Suppressing his irritation, he addressed his son. "Roberto, if you don't mind I'd like to speak to you alone." He turned to the other and politely offered his hand. "Thank you for coming, Gino."

Gino looked at Roberto, who nodded. "I hope you will help your granddaughter to do what's best," said Gino as he shook Giovanni's hand. Then he turned and, with a final nod to Roberto, he left.

As soon as he was out of earshot, Giovanni angrily addressed his son. "Do you really expect me to support you? That boy is insolent and foolish. If he is this bad now, what will he be like when he's older?"

"You don't know what you're talking about. He is respectful and sound. He has never once been anything but diffident to me or others who are older than him." He too was angry.

"Except to me, Roberto. He barely acknowledged my presence. But I understand your affection for him. He is a toady: he doesn't have an opinion of his own. All the things he said sounded like he was quoting you or someone else, not expressing his own opinion. And he has even picked up on your dislike for me. His words were for you because he thinks I am irrelevant. I'm not a fool, Roberto. I know how little respect you have for me."

"What do you expect? You were not a good father. You are an outsider here, and it was very difficult being raised by someone who doesn't belong. You are a joke. Staying away from the town, living up here on the hill. I hated this place: when I was old enough to move out, I felt like it was the first time in my life I could breath. I'm sorry mother died, obviously. But it's pathetic the way you live your life for her. Always visiting her grave even now, decades after she died. You are so busy living in the past that you cannot react sensibly to the present. Your granddaughter needs your guidance, but you are too detached from the world around you to give it to her. I'm ashamed of you, and I always have been."

Giovanni was choked with rage. "How dare you criticize me for loving your mother? You who know nothing of love. All you care about is the opinions of others. And are you so afraid of them that you can't see things as they really are? I choose to live outside the village, yes, but someone has to live here to guard the pass from outsiders. I have many friends among the elders, and even if some of the community don't accept me fully, that hardly matters. I have done my duty without holding myself back. Those who reject me are the weaklings who need to believe there is someone who is lower than themselves. Men like you, in fact."

Roberto was suddenly cold, and he spoke with a vehemence that chilled Giovanni despite his fury. In the back of his mind he was wondering how things could have gotten so bad: Roberto seemed possessed. "You disgust me, father. I have prayed many times for your death—did you know that?—yes, many times. All my life you have been my greatest enemy. I wish they had blinded you, and crippled you, and my mother...Did you know that when I was a child I used to pretend that I had been adopted, though because of the circumstances I knew that I was not? I hated you for that...I still hate you. You should have killed yourself long ago to be with your precious wife." He stopped abruptly, hesitated a moment as if he would continue, but suddenly spat on the ground between them and left.

Giovanni watched him go as the anger faded and was replaced by deepening sadness and regret. His son was difficult, but he was nonetheless his son. It must have been hard for him growing up under these conditions. To be loved less than a dead woman he had never met. Giovanni had tried to love Roberto. They were just too different. And Giovanni could not turn his back on Giulia, not even for the sake of his son. He had tried. But it had seemed to him that Roberto had been born sullen and resentful, and every effort he had made to bridge the gulf between them had been rebuffed. He had felt his son's pain, but been powerless to cure it.

everal days passed during which Giovanni began to wonder if the problem had been sorted out on its own. He saw Maria at the cave once. There were others around, and they had no time to speak. Perhaps it was wishful thinking, but she seemed happy and carefree. Of his son he saw nothing. There was an odd tension in the air with the other villagers he encountered, and Giovanni knew that it must be over his granddaughter's marriage plans. Others were friendly but he could see they were concealing their reactions to what was happening.

It was three days later that Maria came to him without warning as he left the cave to return to his hut, and she asked him if he could spare a minute to talk privately. He agreed, of course, wondering if the news would be good or bad.

"We have done everything we could to change my father's mind, but we can't. He has been pressing the elders to force me to marry Gino as soon as possible. Do you understand, Grandfather? We are in a terrible position. Even if I didn't love Mario, this would be a nightmare for me because Gino is a man I don't love or even respect. The better I know him, the less I like him."

Giovanni nodded. "I know what you mean. He came with your father to visit me, and he's a foolish boy, arrogant and spineless at the same time. But don't despair, Maria. Everything may yet work out. You have to have patience and wait to see what happens."

She paused, and Giovanni could see she was fumbling about for the right words to use. "...If we wait, my life could be decided by the attitudes of others. I can't let that happen. We have—Mario and I—we have decided to elope. Please don't be too quick to judge us...I know this seems like an extreme step, but we don't know what else to do. If we leave for a couple of weeks and come back as man and wife, no one will be able to stop us."

Giovanni was speechless for a moment. He couldn't understand it: why did everyone insist on rushing into one course of action or another? Why couldn't people slow down and wait? This whole thing was a mess created by impatience. Maria was impatient to marry, Roberto was impatient to marry her to Gino, Gino was impatient to gain respectable adulthood by possession of a trophy. No one but Giovanni seemed to be willing to let everyone cool down and consider the matter over months and years. It was irritating, this unnecessary conflict of wills. And now he was being thrust into the center of things against his will.

"Why are you telling me this?" he asked angrily. "It has little to do with me. You are set on your course of action, and so is your father. Neither of you are interested in what I think. Why tell me about it? I am not the head of our family. I am not interested in paterfamilias, and have never asserted it. As far as I am concerned, what you do is your own business."

"Please don't say that. Your opinion is important to us. I beg you to give us your blessing. There is no one else. And grandfather, if you don't, Mario will not go with me. He says we must have the blessing of someone, but there is no one else. His parents refuse to even discuss it. My father has sworn to prevent us at any cost. He is the one who raised the idea of elopement—I swear I never even considered it until he tried to make me swear I would not—and he's keeping an eye on Mario and I to try to prevent it. Until he brought it up I had never seriously considered it, but the more I think about it the more I realize it is probably our only chance for happiness."

"What I told your father is the same thing I'm telling you. By rushing things you only create strife. I know that your position is difficult, but whatever happens I am sure in the end everyone will adjust and things won't look so bad. Why can't you all calm down? Why are you all so certain that you are right and everyone else is wrong?"

She ignored his question. "I have planned the elopement carefully, and we are ready to go: all we need is your blessing. Please help us grandfather—unless you approve, Mario won't go. We are desperate. If we don't act soon, my father will do something to prevent us from ever marrying. I would accept your counsel and wait if I could, but as it stands, your counsel is the same as saying we should give up and I should marry Gino. That is not bearable. Surely you know that? You have to help us, grandfather. If my father has his way, I will be twice dead: I cannot live without Mario, and I cannot live with Gino."

Giovanni was silent for a moment as he considered the alternatives. Perhaps he should give his blessing—but was it really wise for him to help her into a marriage with a man so different from herself? But if he refused, wasn't that as if he were offering his granddaughter up to be the wife of a fool? It was really a choice between two fools, one popular and utterly blind to things, and the other despised but sensitive. If forced to choose, Giovanni realized he would prefer Mario, but why should he choose at all? And what if the community's attitudes were correct? Who was he helping by taking a stand on something he really knew nothing about? The situation was intolerable.

"I won't give you my blessing...yet. I may later, I don't know. I need to think this matter over carefully. There has been too much haste in all this. To you it seems there are only two choices, one excellent, the other disastrous. To me things are more muddled. I see two choices, neither ideal, and I wonder if there is a third way I am missing. As the wise say: If you don't know what is the right thing to do, then do nothing. Refrain from doing wrong until the right course becomes clear to you. That is my position, Maria. Your preference may be right, but I can't see that clearly. I must wait until I see my path stretching straight before me. Please be patient: I give you my word that I will make settlement of this problem my first priority."

She seemed poised to argue, but suddenly smiled. "All right: we will wait for you. I am certain that you will agree with me in the end, since I am certain that underneath your worry you know I am right. We will wait for you."

After she left him, Giovanni walked back to his hut thinking it over, but he could not find an alternative approach that satisfied him. Just when one answer appealed to him, reasons would arise that overthrew it. He could find no peaceful resolution. Life, he reflected with a sigh, is rarely easy.

The following day Giovanni did not go to the cave. Normally he spent many hours copying the manuscripts there or studying them, having reached an age where physical labor was no longer expected of him, but that day he had other plans. He left early while the morning was still young, going down from the mountain and then up the valley, walking quickly along the narrow path that wound its way beside a little stream. It took him an hour and a half to reach his destination, and when he came in sight of the little hut he sought, he stopped by the stream to drink and wash away the sweat from his exertion.

When he got to the hut he did not shout or knock at the door. He sat outside quietly under a tree and waited. Overhead a gentle breeze blew through the leaves and set some of them fluttering before passing on. After the rain of the previous afternoon there was a breathtaking freshness in the sky.

He did not wait long. From the forest behind the hut an old woman came. She carried a cloth bag which she set down in front of him. Though she was smiling warmly, there were no greetings exchanged, and none were expected. "I was gathering mushrooms. It's still a little early in the season for the best ones, but they're not bad. Would you like some?"

"No thank you," said Giovanni politely.

The woman picked up the mushrooms and took them into the hut. She was gone for a few minutes, and Giovanni waited where he was. When she returned, she looked at him with affection and abruptly sat down in the grass beside him. There was no artifice in her manner: she had the simplicity of a child. And the same intensity of attention. At that moment it was directed at the mountains and trees, and the sky overhead, as if she had never seen them before and never would again. Total observation. Giovanni could sense some small part of her delight just by sitting beside her. He felt no pressure to speak, nor to be silent.

It was always this way: when he was near the wise it was as if the old focus was lost and worries had no place. Just sitting like this on a beautiful morning was to leave behind his world and sit on the edge of hers. Once, long ago, a few years after Giulia died, he had spent a season among them. His grief at her death was wrenching and time had not diminished it, so the elders had suggested he should go up the valley and learn. His infant son was given to Giulia's parents to care for until his return. It was a period of his life that in general he could not recall clearly, but some memories had stuck well enough in his mind.

Before he came he thought he knew the world very well. At first the things they told him here seemed trivial, and so did they. Giovanni wondered what all of the fuss was about. He didn't even know why they were thought to be wise, for to him they seemed to differ little from anyone else. But in time he came to understand them better, and came to realize that wisdom is not about miracles and power, that it is a far more subtle thing than that. And just by living around them, it gradually occurred to him that his world was and had always been nothing but shadows and confusion. Somehow, just by being near him, they pointed him in a direction he had never cared to look, and the simple act of looking began to transform him.

When he was ready, they taught him how to know himself. Not as ideas or judgments, but directly, by watching himself as he moved through every moment. To help him understand, they often spoke about the myth of Peleus and Thetis.

Peleus wanted wisdom and sought marriage with Thetis, the Goddess who shifts shapes, even as a man's thoughts shift restlessly from place to place. Hera was patroness of Thetis, loving her dearly. And Thetis is the Goddess who assisted Dionysos when he was suffering madness at Hera's hands.

Peleus was the friend of Chiron the centaur; part man, part horse—part Godlike, part mortal—and very wise. Chiron told him how to find Thetis in a grotto by the sea, and how to hold on to her while she transformed herself. Peleus did as Chiron suggested. He found the grotto in the afternoon sunlight, half filled by the foaming green waves of Poseidon. It was as difficult to find as it is for a man to find his own thoughts and subtle feelings, for it too was hidden from casual discovery as if by magic. Once he had seen her, Peleus sprang upon Thetis and held her. She changed shape into fire, a beast, and water, according to the poets, but there was more to it than this: as a man's thoughts change shape instant by instant into every imaginable form—now insightful or willful, now creative, now emotional—so did she change again and again, sometimes into creatures of fire, sometimes into creatures of earth, sometimes into creatures of water; but each was different, and many were hybrids of these three elements. Some were terrifying to Peleus, some were delightful: always there was temptation to let her go, but he never did. In the beginning she changed shapes violently and fast, but as he held her she began to slow and grow calmer: in the end Peleus held a beautiful, slender girl. By then he was embracing her in love, not in desire or fear. They were married in a ceremony attended by Gods and men.

Thetis sought to make immortality for their child who came to be called Achilles, and who was to die at Troy when the age of darkness had fallen upon the world, and wisdom was lost. Despite the pure light Thetis bathed her child in, the mortal nature of her husband tainted him, and he was fated to die. But Achilles was the greatest of the heroes at Troy. In him arete shone so bright it was as if he was arete. In this way the poets showed that the result of Peleus' struggle was arete expressed in everything he did. Peleus went to the Elysian Fields when his body died, or heaven, or the Isles of the Blessed: though the names were different, the place was the same, the dwelling place for wise mortals after death—if indeed the poets are not lying when they say he died.

Under the guidance of the wise, Giovanni came to understand the story of Thetis and Peleus as the story of a man's struggle to be free of the confusion of his thoughts. Crooked are thoughts, guiding man forward by gazing only at the past, never seeing things as they are, but only as they used to be. Even the future, for mortal thought, is made of the past. Inside his mind a man is always at war with things as they are: his thoughts always strive to get more of one thing, less of another. In its search for safety and comfort, his mind goes to war with nature which never promised either to mortal men. The ocean world of Thetis is as restless as the waves. And when thought tries to build safety, it builds instead a prison that keeps him away from the living beauty of the world, and from living wisdom. To hold the Goddess means to watch her, never averting his gaze. With serious resolve, Giovanni took hold of Thetis and held her as she shifted. Some weeks passed in constant inner struggle.

Eventually he seemed to have made some progress. He felt very peaceful and saw, for the first time since his childhood, the extraordinary beauty of everyday life. But then the wise showed him that he was blind to some of Thetis' best tricks. He himself was a product of Thetis, but a part of her that he was scarcely watching. For many weeks he had struggled with the problem, until he realized that the problem itself only existed because he struggled too hard: his watching was too narrow. If he embraced the Goddess gently but did not struggle with her, she grew quiet.

In the end there came a day when he gave up trying to see and simply watched, and on that day he found the bridge. The memory of that moment had transformed his life.

He had been walking along the path by the stream, watching the movements of Thetis, expecting nothing since he had discovered that expectations were only a shape the Goddess assumed, when suddenly he became aware that everything was different—and yet nothing was different.

Suddenly time was gone, yet change was taking place; space was gone, yet he was moving through it. It was as if when he stepped forward his advancing foot entered nothingness, no future, and his trailing foot left nothingness behind, no past. The present instant was so infinitely thin that it had no substance at all: he saw directly that the world of mortals is utterly empty, completely hollow. Without memories of the past or dreams of the future, of which all thought consisted, there was only the infinitely narrow present, a space too small to contain any substance. He was walking through nothingness, and it was the most exquisitely beautiful thing a man could do. Far beyond any imagining.

Many times since he had tried to find a better way to express it, but there was none. And he knew very well that no matter whether someone believed him or not, whether they took his words as literal truth or not, if they came to the bridge themselves they would be as amazed as he had been at how unexpected, splendid, and world-shattering it was. And they would see its Truth directly, free of the shifting world of thought. Free of space and time. Unshakable. He knew that words had no value in explaining this.

He had spent about an hour at the bridge, and then returned. In the days that followed, the Wise had sought to guide him back to it, pointing out that he had not walked through nothingness: nothingness had walked through nothingness. His nature was entirely a consequence of time. And they assured him that if he crossed the bridge instead of merely standing upon it, he would find the emptiness he had seen was not emptiness at all: it was filled with Beauty, Truth and Love. But he did not wish to go back.

He was no longer afraid of death, for to find the bridge is to die to everything men cherish and fear, and he knew now that there was no harm in that. But on the other hand he needed to live, he needed to remain in a state of longing though he knew that it meant living in illusion. Like the bridge itself, this was impossible to explain clearly to others although he felt its truth directly: he was compelled by his nature to retain his old habits of thought and grieve the death of Giulia, keeping her alive in his thoughts. To do otherwise would be to betray her—to betray their love—and that he would never do. She had not found freedom, so he would not. From that time on he considered himself a kind of fool, never losing sight of how he had turned away from the Truth out of loyalty to Giulia. He knew his loyalty to her served no sensible end. He couldn't explain, even to himself, why he had done it. It was simply a fact, that was all.

After a season he had gratefully bid the wise goodbye and returned to the lower valley.

Quiet but smiling, they had watched him go. As the years had passed, some of the wise had died, and some of the villagers had grown wise and joined them, living in the isolated cabins in the Eastern reaches of the valley. Their numbers were always small, even in the sanctuary of the Gods: few are called to cross the bridge. Many times Giovanni had returned to visit when problems confronted him that agitated his mind. He never stayed long, but he was always welcomed. They seemed to consider Giovanni a special friend, and treated him with great respect, although the reason for this had never been clear to him. When he had needed them, they were always there for him.

As they sat beneath the tree on that beautiful midsummer morning, the wise woman reached over and patted Giovanni's knee. "What mischief brings you here?" she asked, smiling.

"Well, Atropina, it may be mischief or it may not. That's what I hope to discover. It's about my granddaughter."

"Ah, the clever one..."

"Yes. She is speaking about marriage, and her choice of partners is creating some concern."

"Mmm. She loves the child of the God, Mario. Is that your problem, Giovanni?"

"Yes. She has told me her reasons and I cannot fault them, but nor have they persuaded me. I cannot see the matter clearly, though I must. She has asked for my help."

"The child of the God has a good heart though his mind is clouded. His nature is that of Dionysos when he sacrificed himself and died, entering the underworld so that others there could share his hidden light and live. Your granddaughter, the clever one, follows Apollo who remains unstained: gateway of light into earth. At Delphi these two Gods shared the sanctuary, each taking possession of it in his turn. They are in balance."

"Is that your final thought?" Giovanni was cautious and by no means convinced.

"There is something else, though it does not concern your choice..."

Suddenly she laughed with pure delight, and it brightened Giovanni's heart to hear it, though he had no idea what was amusing her so much. When she spoke again, her eyes were sparkling. "You don't want to hear my words, do you Giovanni? Are you not anxious to find reasons for resisting the clever one? You seek a way to control her destiny. How vain you are, you thoughtful fellow! How vain and how stubborn!" She chuckled, and Giovanni joined her, for he instantly knew that she was right. Though he wasn't sure how it happened, before long they had put their arms on each other's shoulders for support and roared with laughter until tears came to their eyes. But by then they were not laughing at his silliness, they were laughing from something much deeper which had no name. If forced to give it a label, Giovanni later decided it might be called compassion.

In any case, Giovanni's worries had vanished in the warmth of their mutual affection and as their laughter faded into silence he knew the problem would trouble his mind no more. "I will go now, Atropina," he said and began to get up. She restrained him with a gentle touch of his arm, so he settled back down. "Yes?" he asked.

"Now that you have settled your problem, there is something more regarding it. The time is coming for which you came."

He looked at her, puzzled. "What do you mean?"

"The Gods brought you here for a reason, Giovanni. It was not to lose your wife, or to copy manuscripts, or to help your granddaughter find happiness. Such things could have been done by any man in the village. Nor was it so we can laugh together sometimes as friends. Such moments are a pleasure that comes and goes. You are here for a purpose that is more lasting." Giovanni looked at her, asking. She shook her head gently. "No, we do not see your purpose clearly yet, though its rough shape has been clear to us for many years. It has to do with the outsiders and with this sanctuary. The fact that the clever one, child of your blood, has chosen a child of Dionysos to be her husband suggests a quickening, perhaps. Soon, I think, all will be clear.

"The wheels of time are moving, Giovanni. As you know there is not one but many: wheels within wheels and outside of wheels, one for every aspect of everything in this world. Change is constant." She looked at him silently for a moment and then she nodded abruptly with a smile. She was saying goodbye.

Giovanni got up and stretched his legs. He had no idea what she was getting at, and wondered if she did. Inwardly he shrugged: the wise were like that sometimes. He smiled at her and began to walk away, but he had not gone ten paces before she called out to him. He stopped, turning where he stood to see what she wanted.

"Do not resist the flow, Giovanni. It will not change the outcome, but only cause you grief. The wheel can be your friend, if you let go of it instead of holding on and trying to stop its turning."

At that moment a woodpecker flew past Atropina's head and into the trees. She turned her head to watch it while Giovanni waited. The staccato sound of the bird's beak tearing at tree bark rose hollow from behind the canopy of leaves. The old woman continued to look in the direction of the sound. After watching her for a moment, Giovanni realized she had nothing more to say, so he turned and resumed walking back down the valley.

The pleasure of their conversation remained with him for quite some time. The gentle company of the wise always brought such happiness. But even before he had returned to his hut, a chain of thought had begun to nag at him. He had lost one problem but gained another more intractable and scarcely seen. Her words about the wheel of time were unexpected and somewhat ominous. From Atropina's comments, the only thing he knew for certain was that whatever was on her mind sounded serious. Trouble might be coming. He would have to stay alert.

That afternoon he went to the cave and continued copying a codex of Hesiod's Catalogue of Women he had been working on for some time. He didn't see Maria, but that didn't concern him too much. She would seek him out soon enough and he would give her his blessing. The matter would be settled. As he walked home, it occurred to him that his certainty now regarding Maria's problem was equal in intensity to his uncertainty before. What had Atropina said to clarify his thoughts? After considering it carefully he realized she had done nothing: he had already known what to do, and had fought it. In her presence he had felt again the transience of all things, and resisting the flow of the inevitable had lost its power to enthrall him. Sitting beside her he had felt the proximity of the bridge, and by its power he had seen his prejudices fade. 'How strange I am', he thought, 'that I hold onto misery when all I need to do is release it and be free.'

As dusk came, Giovanni sat by his hut and watched daylight slip across the sky and vanish into the West. The air was cool, but not cold. He felt no urge to move. The stars showed their bright faces and lit the heavens from one end to another in serene and splendid silence. Later the dew fell unseen while he sat there, and he felt its damp chill through his clothes. Though it was uncomfortable, there was pleasure in its touch. Though he could not say why, Giovanni was deeply happy.

When midnight approached, Giovanni was still there. He heard, suddenly, the sound of footsteps approaching along the path, stumbling a little in the dark. After a moment two figures entered his clearing and walked to the hut. They did not see him where he sat, and he could not bring himself to speak so he remained where he was and watched them. They put their heads together and spoke quietly. Giovanni recognized Maria and Mario. "Grandfather," said Maria quietly towards the door. "Grandfather, we must talk to you now."

Giovanni finally stirred himself and spoke. "What is it?" They were eloping, he guessed, and he saw that they were carrying bundles in their hands: clothing and bedding, perhaps, or food.

They were startled to hear his voice coming to them from outside, and turned uncertainly towards the direction it had come from. "Grandfather?" Her voice was strained.

Giovanni raised his hand in greeting, still hesitant to speak. They saw him then, despite the darkness, and walked over. "Are you all right sir?" asked Mario, his slurred speech not concealing his concern.

"Yes. What are you doing here so late?" he asked.

When Maria spoke, he heard at once the grief she felt, and he stood up to face them. She seemed to be having trouble breathing.

"Grandfather...something's happened. Gino..." She didn't finish the sentence, but instead a sob cut her off. She began to cry, and Mario put his arm around her and hugged her, laying his head against her shoulder, patting her on the head with his hand.

"What is it?" asked Giovanni, feeling fear in his stomach. "What's happened?" He reached over and touched Maria's arm with his hand, and seeing Mario's attempt to comfort her, reached with the other hand and placed it on his shoulder in unspoken support. Neither of the two answered for a moment and he waited. Then Mario raised his head and looked at Giovanni, his face faint in the starlight.

"Gino...Gino hurt Maria." Giovanni heard the pain in Mario's voice. "He took her to the stream and he hurt her." At this point Mario burst into tears and wept like a little child, again laying his head against Maria's shoulder.

"Come with me," said Giovanni, and turning them around, walking beside Maria with his arm around both of them, he led them slowly back to the hut, saying nothing. When they were inside, he steered them to the bed and they sat on it mutely, their tears subsiding while he closed the door, turned up the lamp, and reached for a clay wine jar on the floor beneath the window. Though they had stopped crying, they had their arms around each other, Maria with her eyes open and watching Giovanni, Mario with his eyes closed. Giovanni rummaged around for a moment until he found three cups and filled them with the wine.

"Here," he said, "take these. Come on: it will make you feel better...that's it. Now Maria: tell me what happened."

She stiffened, his slender granddaughter, and after a moment's hesitation took her arm from Mario and held her cup in both hands, looking very small and helpless, her face ridden with tension. Mario sensed the shift in her mood and let her go too, pulling back slightly and watching her. Giovanni suddenly noticed that the skin around one of her eyes was swollen and discolored, and that there were scratches on her cheek. He thought of Gino's face as he had stood in front of him a few days previously and bragged about himself. Rage seethed through Giovanni's mind, but he forced himself not to move, not to give any sign of it: now was a time for listening.

For a moment she sat looking at the cup she held, and when she spoke she never looked up, her voice like a frightened little girl's.

"Gino came to me after dinner and said he wanted to talk to me alone. I...I didn't think anything about it. We walked down to the stream. He asked me to reconsider, but I told him I didn't want him. He tried to kiss me, but I wouldn't let him. Then he got angry, and he hit me, and..." Her voice broke, and she started to cry again. "Mario, I'm so sorry."

Mario shook his head. "He hurt you. He did a bad thing."

Giovanni put his hand on Maria's shoulder. He forced his voice to be gentle, to be understanding, but underneath he felt like the fury was choking him. "Are you saying he raped you, Maria?"

She said nothing, but Mario replied for her. "He did that."

Giovanni wanted to say something reassuring, but he was incapable of speech. He tried to respond, failed, tried again. He wanted to kill, wanted to hit something, but instead he just patted Maria's shoulder and squeezed it gently. He walked to the door opened it, closed it again, and walked back to the couple on the bed. "I'll kill him." His voice was cold.

"No," said Mario, frightened. "Don't hurt him."

"I shouldn't have gone with him," said Maria.

"No!" bellowed Giovanni. "Trust is not a crime. Betrayal of trust is a crime." The other two flinched at the violence of his words. Seeing that his anger was upsetting them both, he was quiet for a moment while he fought for control. When he went on, he was quieter. "He is a weakling. You are strong. Not in the body, but in the spirit, which is far more. He fears you, Maria."

"He took my purity," said Maria.

"He took nothing. Purity can't be taken. He hurt you, that's all." He spoke with authority and strength, but Maria only shook her head mutely. Giovanni looked at Mario. She would listen to him.

"What do you think, Mario: did he take anything from Maria, or from you?"

"He hurt Maria."

"Is that all? Did he take anything away?"

Mario was confused. "He hurt Maria. She is here, but she is hurt. He didn't hurt me. He hurt her face and...down there. He didn't hurt me."

Maria spoke. "He kept saying afterwards...he kept saying that...he owns me now."

Giovanni's fist slammed against the wall. Again his violence shocked and frightened the other two, and again he had to fight for control. His voice was hard, intense. "He owns *nothing*. If a man spits in the ocean, does he own the sea? You are not a slave, Maria. You can give yourself in love but you cannot be taken. You belong to someone, but not to that coward. You belong to Mario, and he belongs to you. Isn't that right Mario?"

"Yes. I belong to Maria. I love Maria."

"Has anything changed because of what has happened? Has anything changed?"

Mario thought for a moment. "Yes."

Giovanni was taken aback. "What? What has changed?"

"You are helping us now."

Giovanni felt shame. "Yes, you have my blessing now. But not just because of what has happened. I was wrong to resist you before. I went to the wise, and Atropina spoke with me about you two. She showed me that you were right and I was wrong. I should have gone to you before this, but I didn't know what would happen. I'm truly sorry." His voice broke. "I let you down."

Mario stood up slowly and put his arms around Giovanni, hugging him. "Thank you, grandfather," he said, and put his head against Giovanni's chest.

Giovanni felt surprised, awkward, but he caught sight of Maria watching him so he put his arms around Mario and hugged him back. As he did so, he felt great affection filling him for this simple, decent fellow his granddaughter loved. He lowered his chin to rest on the young man's head and squeezed him. When he spoke, his voice was quiet, gentle. "Look after my granddaughter for me, Mario. We are lucky to have you."

After a moment Mario let go and sat down smiling beside Maria. He glanced shyly at her and moved over until their shoulders were touching. Then he lifted his legs a little and slid his hands underneath his thighs and sat on them, leaning forward a little and letting his feet swing back and forth over the edge of the bed. He looked at his knees while Giovanni spoke.

"Maria, I think you should both go up the valley and stay with the wise. Do you know Atropina's cabin? You could both go there. I think you should stay there for a couple of days at least. Even if they find you, I'm sure Atropina won't let them bring you back." She nodded, and the tears returned. Not for many, many years had Giovanni known such sorrow and regret as he did again on that night.

tropina greeted the two of them as they arrived at her cabin at dawn. She was standing beside the doorway watching them when they came. Walking forward to greet them, she embraced them both, then led them up the side of the mountain for fifteen minutes to a ramshackle cabin by a little brook. Atropina told them it had been deserted for some time, but Maria noticed that fresh kindling had been stacked outside, and when they went inside to deposit their bundles, a burning candle was sitting just inside the front door.

Before she left them, Atropina asked Maria if she would like to visit her around noon so they could talk. Maria was pleased at the prospect, for she had never had the opportunity of speaking to one of the wise alone: in the past she had only met Atropina and the others at assemblies or when they visited the school to talk to the students as a group. Many in the village had lived out their whole lives there without such an invitation. She agreed enthusiastically and watched the old woman go, gracefully negotiating the narrow trail despite her years.

She spent the morning with Mario alone, and despite their tiredness the two did not sleep, for their happiness at that moment and the trauma of recent events pressed upon them, making sleep impossible. They breakfasted and explored the area together, before sitting on blankets in a spot they found where the brook and the surrounding mountains could easily be seen. The morning passed quickly while they watched the view in each other's arms, and it was with some regret that Maria bade Mario goodbye after seeing him to bed and headed down to Atropina's cabin.

Atropina was sitting by the banks of the larger stream, a bundle beside her in the grass. Maria sat down and waited. For a few minutes only the bubbling brook spoke. Whether it was from exhaustion or the beauty of that place or some other factor she couldn't determine, Maria felt strangely at peace, the tension of her recent misery entirely gone. It was Atropina who broke the silence.

"I have something that might interest you." She reached into a bundle lying beside her and pulled out a heavy metallic wheel several hands wide. Maria recognized it as a Mysterion, an oracular wheel used for divination. She looked curiously at it while Atropina set it carefully down in the grass between them. "I brought it from the cave when I learned you might be visiting me. Tell me what you already know and we can start from there." She smiled at the younger woman.

"I don't know much. The Mysterion is a prophetic wheel invented a long time ago. It describes the complex motions of the wheels of time, so that the user can discover where he is, was, and will be. We never had its use or its meaning explained to us, but I have heard that it is the most brilliant device of its type ever revealed by the Gods." She looked at Atropina shyly. "I would like to understand it."

Atropina chuckled infectiously so Maria joined in, aware suddenly of the childishness of her desire, though why she could not say.

"Even so, Maria, I will teach you.

"It was invented in the dawn of the Hellenic age when the ancient Greeks were spreading their culture throughout the known world. From time beyond memory the Gods had taught mankind that there are three seasons and three elements, but as wisdom gradually grew among our race they revealed that the three were also four, depending on how one chooses to view it. The ancient three season year became four seasons, and fire was added as a distinct element to the other three: earth, water, and air. The Mysterion grew from the knowledge of how the three and four are integrated.

"Until the Mysterion was revealed, men relied on various oracles to divine the future. The logic of the wheels of nature defied men's understanding. It was far too complex for anyone to understand. As you know, the wheel of time has three principle parts: beginning, middle and end; birth, maturity and death; Spring, Summer and Winter; creation, sustenance and destruction. Everything follows the three. It would be simple if only one wheel were active for every life, but there are an infinite set of wheels active in the world, and they interact with one another in very complex ways.

"There was a wheel set in motion on the day of your birth, and one that comes and goes with every day you live. There was a wheel that began to turn when you met Mario, one when you fell in love with him, and one when you came here this morning. There is a wheel for our conversation here, by this beautiful stream, and one that came and went for that moment of laughter we shared just now. Each of these wheels interacts with the others to describe the movement of your fate. And the wheels of your life are met by the wheels of mine, of your father, of our village, of Europe, of the whole world, each interacting with the others in orderly but complex ways. Is it any wonder that mortals were confused and relied upon the Gods and the spirits of the dead to tell them what would happen in the seasons ahead? Though the wheels are the foundation of order in the universe, they are so complicated that to the mortal mind they appear as chaos.

"So that is what the Mysterion is for: it shows the hidden order.

"The Mysterion was first revealed by Apollo to an Athenian named Altas who married into the Deukalidae family at Delphi during the time of Alexander the Great. From that period onwards, the Mysterion was used at Delphi by the priests there, though of course the God also continued to speak directly through his Sybil. At the time of the Hiding, it was brought here for safekeeping. This is a copy of the original wheel which was made several centuries ago.

"The Mysterion has two parts: spokes representing the three seasons as they are expressed in two cycles, material and spiritual, and rim positions representing sixteen Gods who together determine the characteristics of things in our world. As the rim turns, the various Gods come into contact with the various seasons in the two cycles. When you have learnt how the Gods interact with the seasons, you will be able to interpret the Mysterion's positions. By knowing which wheel the Mysterion is describing when you use it, you can know the past, present and future of that particular wheel. Since the wheels determine our fates, you will know our fates—not the details, but the general shape of them.

"The Mysterion is a God wheel, but it is also an Elemental Wheel, describing the Gods and their actions in terms of the four elements: earth, water, fire and air. So it can be looked at as a sacred wheel describing the Gods, an expression of the highest mysteries, or as an Elemental Wheel which describes life in philosophical terms. Both need to be understood and considered carefully in its use. Both provide insight into its meaning.

"It is very complicated, but you are clever and I think you will be able to master the Mysterion's secrets quickly. Would you like to learn about it?"

Maria was almost too excited at the prospect to answer. Here was something that would be a true challenge to understand, something that had real and practical value in life. "Of course," she said breathlessly, reaching down to touch the cool metal with her fingers. It was beautiful to look at, beautiful to touch.

Again Atropina laughed, and Maria smiled in sudden embarrassment, knowing that the older woman had felt her greed.

"It is not so marvelous as you imagine, oh clever one." Atropina's eyes twinkled mischievously. "It is really nothing more than a toy the Gods have given us to play with. What use is knowledge of fate without the wisdom to go beyond it?"

Suddenly Maria sensed an ocean of sadness flooding the space between them, coming from Atropina it seemed, though the old woman was smiling yet. Atropina reached out and patted the wheel. "Feel my words deeply, for you will meet the truth of them soon enough in the pattern of your life. This wheel describes our slavery to the sorrows of mortal fate. Learning to use it has little importance." She paused, and her gentle face turned straight towards Maria so that her next words were spoken directly across the wheel that lay between them. "Wisdom lies at the center of the Mysterion, beyond the reach of time. If you can find your way there, fate will no longer harm you, and the only sorrow you will know is the sorrow that love brings, when you feel the pain of others.

"You are living on the outer edge of the wheel, Maria, because you are holding tight in fear and desire to the rim as it turns. Release the rim and you will fall towards the center where past and future can no longer hurt you. At the Mysterion's center lies the bridge to the world of the Gods. In that timeless place the Gods will greet you and show you their true natures. At the center there is boundless Peace, Beauty, Love, and Wisdom: things of which you know absolutely nothing. On the Mysterion's rim all happiness is fleeting and shallow, and all knowledge is empty of lasting value..."

When Atropina paused, Maria nodded to show she understood, that she was ready to continue. Atropina looked at her in silence. A moment passed.

"I understand," Maria said, nodding again, but still the old woman said nothing—what was she waiting for?

"Good," said Atropina suddenly with a smile, and patted her shoulder. "Would you like some lunch? I have bread and cheese." She picked up the wheel and wrapped it in the cloth. Then she got up and walked away, back to her cabin to fetch the food. Maria watched her go, her mind reeling a little at the things she had heard, and the sudden way their conversation had ended. Atropina had gone ten paces when she turned and called back "Let it go: we will speak more of these things later." Then she continued on her way. Smiling to herself, Maria looked away.

Every day for the next two weeks Maria met Atropina and learned about the mysterious wheel the God had shown Altas so long before. Some of the time they worked on the method of using the Mysterion, some of the time on the methods of being free of it. Atropina never mentioned the myth of

Thetis. Maria was more a follower of Apollo, not of Aphrodite as Giovanni had been in the days of his youth. But Atropina showed Maria how to look into her own heart and see the resistance to the movement of the wheel, and showed her the secret of letting go of the impurity and confusion of her thoughts, one resistance at a time, one moment at a time. How to move from the past and future back to the present, where alone the Truth could be found. Maria gained in understanding, but the bridge remained beyond her reach. A honeymoon is not a time well suited to such inquiries. And they only stayed for two weeks.

When at last the newlyweds made their way back down the valley, Atropina made the journey with them. Arriving at the village in the late afternoon, she sought out one of the elders. When he asked her what she had come for, she patted him on the shoulder, smiled warmly, and said "The past and the future meet in death. The secret is to let go." Then she left. In the ensuing meeting of the counsel, no one was able to guess her meaning.

he wheels of time may number in the infinite, but there was one such wheel, set in motion long ago, which figured above all others in the guardian's world. The great wheel of civilization was turning and could not be rolled back or slowed in its course. Here it might raise up a life or an entire people and make it extraordinary, there it might crush and annihilate with total indifference. It was indifferent even to civilization itself, for all that mattered in its relentless motion were the Laws of this mortal universe as they had been laid down at the beginning.

In the heyday of Greek civilization, Altas first revealed the wheel of destiny, the Mysterion. And more than a thousand years later it would be Giovanni's lot to hide it away from all mortal thoughts, to send it to oblivion until the time was right for resurrection. They were brothers of a kind, these two men, joined in a single shared purpose that neither fully understood nor had the power to resist...

A House Divided: The Tale of Altas and Apollo's Wheel

(Chaeronea, Delphi, 347 - 346 BC)

Muted sounds of clinking iron, leather armor, greaves, breastplates, shields and countless feet filled the ears of Altas as he began to stamp in pace with the others. The breeze picked up thin streams of swirling dust raised by those in front.

Altas glanced at his father and younger brother, and saw them frowning through the bright sunlight towards the enemy force. His father caught his eye and said quietly, his voice calm, "Whatever happens, stay by your brother." Then he turned to his other son, holding his arm to get his attention and said "You too, Giorgias." Giorgias smiled, and his eyes were bright with excitement as he nodded, for it was his first battle.

Altas offered a silent prayer for his brother's safety.

The paean, war song of the Greek host, began somewhere to the right and was taken up along the line. Altas added his voice to the rising chorus, glancing left and right to ensure he held his place in the line. As he sang, his anxiety began to fade.

Gradually the beat accelerated, and the stamping feet became thunderous under the rising paean. Officers called out and the line began to move forward, the mass of men swiftly accelerating into a run, then a brief sprint with spears leveled, as the two armies crashed together.

At first Altas could see little, his view crowded by those ahead of him and the dust thrown up by the struggle, but he heard the sounds of men screaming in rage and pain and caught glimpses of the action from time to time. Both sides held their ground, the men in front trading blows, here and there breaking ranks a pace or two to push home some advantage.

Several minutes passed in which Altas began to feel impatience since there was little he could do to help. Like the others in the last rank, he mostly had to content himself with shouting encouragement to those ahead. At one point unseen hands somewhere up ahead tore Altas' spear from his hands and it vanished towards the front. Cursing, he took out his sword, holding it chest high, waiting.

Finally the line began to move forward as the Macedonians gave way. Fresh shouts arose within the Athenian line: "On to Macedonia!", "Forward, Athenians!" and the pace quickened. Altas began running forward, yelling, eager for the chance to engage the retreating enemy. Almost immediately he passed several bodies littering the plain, casualties of the initial clash to the two armies. He had no time to do more than glance at the twisted forms as he pressed forward.

Through the dust he saw a figure on horseback in Macedonian armor, no more than forty paces ahead. One arm was shriveled, and one eye had been lost in some previous engagement, a scar running across his cheek that was clearly visible even at that distance. It must be Philip, the Macedonian king. He seemed calm as he looked back and forth surveying the Greek line, despite his army's predicament, and he shouted out a few orders to his men before wheeling his horse and vanishing farther to the right.

As the moments passed, the onward thrust of the men was causing the Greek line to thin, and Altas joined the first rank when he found a spot. The Macedonians were moving rapidly backwards in a shuffling run, stabbing with spear and sword any Greek who pressed them too closely. Altas found himself facing a Macedonian hypaspist from several paces away, and stumbled closely after him over the uneven ground.

The man's face was blank behind his helmet. He wasn't afraid: he seemed too well trained to lose his head. Altas could see him glancing backwards from time to time to check for obstacles, so he prepared himself to take advantage of his adversary's distraction, looking for a moment when he could rush forward and strike the man down. Somehow, the opportunity never seemed to come.

From the corner of his eye, Altas saw his father one man away with Giorgias by his side, taunting the retreating Macedonians. Elsewhere, many of the Athenians were laughing; others expressed a curious mixture of rage and glee. Who could doubt that the battle was theirs?

Just then, somewhere in the rear and to the right, he heard an Athenian call for more men, and then another. Looking over he saw something that sent a cold wave of fear through him. He made out a thick stream of Macedonian Peltasts, shooting arrows into the Greek line, less than fifty paces away, as they ran past on the right towards the Athenian rear.

Was the line breached? If so, the Athenians were in danger of encirclement. Glancing ahead again, he barely prevented himself from running onto the waiting sword of the Macedonian he had been pursuing. The man had stopped suddenly, his face darkened, and he let out a battle cry that was echoing from everywhere along the Macedonian line.

The Greek advance fumbled, as suddenly all the Macedonians stood their ground, and the Athenian triumph of a moment before swiftly turned to confusion and panic.

It seemed that within seconds, the Athenians were in full flight, terrified lest the peltasts cut them off from the rest of the Greek line.

But unlike the Macedonian retreat, theirs was not so orderly, and the Macedonians cut them down from behind as they ran. Some of the bravest called for their compatriots to stand, but they went largely unheeded, so they too were forced to run or face certain death. It was a rout.

Altas was hard pressed to remain with his father and brother in the melee that followed, but they ran, the three of them more or less together, as fast as they could go. Unlike many around them, who were shedding their weapons in their panic to escape, Altas and Giorgias obeyed their father's command and kept a firm hand on their swords. They did, however, throw down their cumbersome shields, and managed to stay well ahead of the enemy host.

A minute or two after the flight began, Altas saw his father stumble, reached over to steady him, and saw the arrow that had buried itself deep in his father's left kidney. Unhinged by the ferocity of the pain, the older man collapsed shrieking.

Shouting for Giorgias, Altas half lifted his father and dragged him through the rush of men towards the rear of a chest-high bush he had noticed on the left. Giorgias joined him, his face drained by shock and fear, and helped lean the now moaning man on his side against a low stone.

The bush was parting the torrent of men, creating a little eddy of calm where the wounded man lay gasping silently, eyes open but unseeing. His sons crouched on either side of him.

The brothers looked at each other across their father, but neither spoke. Almost sadly, Altas shook his head and then looked down, unable to meet his brother's helpless gaze.

After a moment, he straightened slightly, and taking a deep breath, face grim, he lifted his sword and held it before him, tip pointed up. Remaining crouched, he turned to face the stream of men as they passed by the bush on his side. Pale with terror, trembling, Giorgias watched him turn before following his lead, and doing the same for the other side.

Moments later the last of the Greeks had poured past, and been replaced by Macedonian troops intent on slaughter. Crouched behind the bush as they were, the brothers were not observed at first, and Altas wondered if perhaps the whole Macedonian army would rush blindly by, too impatient in their blood lust to see what lay helpless beside them. To Altas' desperate mind, it seemed that the Gods willing, they might yet escape with their lives.

Of course, it was only a matter of seconds before they were noticed by an enemy soldier. He glanced over and then turned to approach them, slowing rapidly to a walk, sizing them up as he came.

Alerted by their comrade to the easy prey, six or seven other Macedonians soon joined him, quickly forming an uneven half circle around the brothers who stood, backs to their father, swords raised high. A few others from the hoard paused to see what was happening but when they realized that the matter would be easily resolved without them, they pressed on towards the fleeing Greeks.

A few preliminary blows were struck and parried, and the circle began closing in for the kill. It would only be a matter of seconds.

Just then, from the corner of his eye, Altas saw a passing Macedonian officer on horseback ride up and rein in his horse. The officer called out a command to his men, and reluctantly the Macedonians held back in silence, watching. The officer gazed calmly into Altas' eyes for a moment, jerking the reins several times to keep his horse in place, and called out to him in heavily accented Greek, "Who is that wounded man?"

Not taking his eyes from the officer, tightening his grip on his sword, Altas spat back "Our father" through clenched teeth, hatred for the Macedonian burning in his throat.

For a moment the officer regarded the two brothers and the mortally wounded man they stood over, patting the neck of his restless Thessalian mount. Apparently reaching a decision, he called out something to the Macedonians in the Illyrian tongue, and then once again to Altas in Greek: "Lay down your weapons now and you will be spared."

Then, without waiting to see the outcome, he dug in his heels and disappeared at a gallop towards the Greek line.

When the officer had gone, the soldiers jeered and made as if to strike, but Altas saw that they did not carry their blows through or advance from where they stood. Reflecting on their hesitation, he realized they were goading the brothers to resist so that the officer's orders would not keep them from the end they sought.

Altas spoke over his shoulder to Giorgias. "Steady, bother, steady. I think they will let us surrender. Set your sword down slowly, but be ready for anything." Then he crouched down and set his own sword carefully on the ground.

A Macedonian, his face full of scorn, kicked Altas hard in the shoulder, sending him sprawling beside his father. He lay there for a moment, waiting for the final blow, but it didn't come. He looked over to see Giorgias receiving a few kicks of his own as he lay on the ground, head covered with his arms, but the Macedonians lost interest quickly. They were missing the sport elsewhere, and were anxious to rejoin the fray.

While the others ran off, one remained, a burly man apparently under orders to guard them, and none to happy about it. He gathered their weapons, dumped them out of reach, and then stood over them, his sword drawn, scowling.

Realizing they were safe, at least for the moment, the brothers turned their attention to their father who was bleeding badly, and shivering in the sunlight. He looked at them bewildered. The pain must have diminished, for the power of speech, at least, had returned. "What has happened?" he asked weakly.

"I don't know..." said Giorgias with anguish. But breathing deeply, he regained composure and tried again. "You are injured, father... and... we are prisoners now."

Overhead, the sun was shining brightly from the deep blue of a perfect cloudless sky. A bird landed in the bush and sang a few notes, careless and pure, and then flew off in search of something to eat.

Things were said that day, in a dusty corner of the plain of Chaeronea, as a family took leave of the foundation on which it had rested. The sounds of the rout grew faint in the distance while the two men spoke in solemn tones to their dying father. At one point the older man took both their hands in his and made them swear to something, half sitting up despite his pain to press upon them the importance of his request. Then he lay back, too exhausted to talk, and quietly slipped into unconsciousness.

Minutes later, he died.

The younger one began sobbing at once, and the elder, face mask-like, looked over at the mountains that lay to the West. After a moment, the tears came to him too, running down his impassive face, dripping unnoticed into the dust of the plain.

The Macedonian watched, and though he did not fully understand the words that had been spoken, he knew full well the sentiments expressed. His manner changed and in his heart he honored what he saw. As he would later tell his comrades, he was very glad he didn't have to kill them.

The two brothers were silent while they walked, searching for the place where their father had died. Little had changed in the ensuing year, but memory is imperfect and the events of that day were like a nightmare only dimly remembered when daylight has returned. It was Giorgias who finally found the spot.

Somberly they made an offering of wine, pouring it into the thirsty soil, and then stood for a moment, each lost in his own thoughts. Altas broke their silence first, suggesting the two of them walk along the old battle line. This they did, for it would take them more or less in the direction they were traveling.

The day was fair, as it had been eleven months before. Birdsong mingled with the pleasant sighs of a cooling breeze that gently stirred the trees nearby. It was still early, and the day's heat had not yet begun. Neither brother found it easy to believe that this was the place where they had fought. It seemed too much a place of peace to be one of history's greatest battlefields.

At last Georgias, following the passionate wanderings of his thoughts, became enthusiastic at where they led and sought to draw his brother in. "We lost the battle twice that day," he said.

As he had hoped, Altas asked him what he meant, and he eagerly went on. "Philip breached the Athenian line, while at the same time his son Alexander was punching through the Thebans nearly an hour's walk away, on the other side of the Greek line. Alexander told me of it when we were returning to Athens."

They had not spoken of what Alexander had said to Georgias and the other Athenians he favored, since Altas had always refused in the past to discuss it. But perhaps because they found themselves on the field of battle, or because the day was so beautiful, or again because sufficient time had passed to advance the healing of his spirit, Altas this time let the conversation continue, and replied reasonably to his brother with a soft smile.

"The fortunes of war did indeed favor Macedon that day."

"No, no," said Georgias impatiently, "it was not the Fates that guided the outcome, but the generalship of Philip and Alexander. They know the mechanics of war as you know how to tally your business accounts. Alexander explained it to me. A line of troops flows like blood beneath the skin. If you scratch a place hard, the blood collects beneath that place, drawn from elsewhere. Attack the line hard in one place, and the troops will grow thickest there, drawn from the edges where the line necessarily becomes thin. A thin line can be broken. A great general is one who orders the thickness and thinness of his enemy's line at will. Ours was broken twice."

"We were broken twice, it's true," said Altas, "but not in the manner you describe."

"Not so obviously, but that is because in their genius, they knew our natures, and used them to defeat us. Philip knew the Athenians see themselves as the true leaders of Greece, allowing us to attack and appear to succeed. At the same time he had his troops stand and hold back the allies next to us in the line. Our troops rushed forward creating a bulge, convinced their greater prowess was the cause of their advance. The edges of the bulge were only lightly attacked, and the bulge in any case increased the length of the line, so the edges thinned until the peltasts could suddenly rush forward and push through with little effort."

Altas was unconvinced. "The field was in chaos. The plan you suggest could work in theory, but in the confusion of war such control would be impossible. Here they must appear to retreat, there they must hold and fight hard, and over in another place they must attack but lightly, moving neither forward nor back: what troops could have such discipline and skill?"

"You know the troops we Athenians faced, brother: it was the Hypaspists, Philip's elite troops. We Athenians are soldiers in war time, but merchants, craftsmen, farmers and politicians the rest of the time. The Hypaspists are soldiers above all else, trained and trained until war becomes as natural as eating. But even so, you are right that it was difficult. That is why Philip supervised the destruction of our flank, and had his son destroy the other. Alexander's task was easier."

Altas interrupted. "But Alexander faced the Theban Sacred Band under Theagenes. They too were soldiers above all else, the greatest in all of Greece, and none could expect an easy victory over them."

"You are wrong, brother," said Georgias excitedly. "When the forces were drawn up in battle array, Philip saw that the Sacred band was holding a low hill at their end of the line, with their allies on the plain beside them. He knew the Band's pride in never withdrawing, in anchoring their end of the line, and he knew that holding their positions on the hill would keep them fixed in place while their allies would flow smoothly across the plain, to wherever the fight was hardest. His course was easy. He brought his phalanx to bear, fighting hard, two hundred paces from the hill. The Theban's allies flowed towards the fighting, but the Sacred Band remained fixed in place until the line grew thin beside the hill. Then Alexander bore down at the head of the cavalry, tearing a gap in the line that other Macedonian troops could swiftly pass through.

"Riding up the hill from behind, the cavalry annihilated the Sacred Band, while the other troops attacked the Theban's allies from their rear. If the Gods played a role in the outcome here, it was by choosing such men of genius to unite the Hellenes."

Altas sighed. "It may be as you say, brother, though I don't pretend to know the Gods' intent. All I saw that day was chaos and death. And I am grateful to the Macedonians for the grace they showed to Athens in her defeat, but is it seemly to have such admiration for the enemy who routs our army and kills your own father? I sometimes wonder if you think too much and feel too little, or think too little and feel too much."

"But they are not our enemies!" exclaimed Georgias. "They are Hellenes like ourselves, and lovers of our shared Hellenic culture. In the past their place in history has been small, but that doesn't mean it must remain so. Look at Sparta which has done the opposite: at one time it was the first among the city-states of Greece, but now it is of little importance. The great become small, the small, great. That is the movement of history.

"And now the age of petty divisions, of Greek cities forever divided and warring among themselves, is passing. We must join together and fight our Persian enemies to the East. Only Macedon can unite us, and that is what it did so painfully but justly in this place." Here the younger brother paused and frowned. "Our father's death was honorable, and you know it touched me deeply...and that we very nearly shared in it. But even if we had, I say dying was a small price to pay for uniting the Greeks. I would gladly give my life for that goal.

"If you hadn't spurned Alexander's friendship after the battle, when he was accompanying the Greek dead back to Athens to honor them, you would have seen as I did the greatness of his character. He loves Athens, and admires its achievements as much as you or I. It is the divisions between the Hellenes he hates and has sworn to end. What Greek can fail to see that we have been our own worst enemies? How many of our own Hellenic brothers have we killed and enslaved since our one true enemy, the Persian king, showed his face at Marathon?"

"You are always the better speaker than I," said Altas gently, "and you may be right. But war and conquest, revenge and glory, don't excite me."

They walked in silence for a time, until they approached the hill where the Sacred Band had perished. Georgias, apparently following a train of thought that had made him become agitated, suddenly blurted out "I am going to Macedon to live," and stopped walking, looking at his brother.

Altas seemed not to have heard him, for he continued walking without looking at his brother or responding. Georgias hurried to catch up, and went on, impatient at his brother's stubbornness.

"Alexander offered several of us his hospitality, and I will take him up on it. I didn't trouble you by speaking of it before because my mind was not made up, but now that we have lost our factory, there is nothing to prevent me." He waited for Altas to reply, but again his brother said nothing and gave no sign of hearing. However, he was obviously thinking, for at last he stopped walking and turned to face Giorgias.

"You gave your promise to our dying father in this very place last year that you would seek the guidance of the oracle at Delphi before determining on the course of your life. You know it was for your sake rather than mine that he made us swear. How can you now declare that your decision is final before we have even got there?" He could not control the irritation he felt, and his words had an edge.

Giorgias was defiant. "I am going to Delphi. I will question the oracle. But you know very well I doubt that the Gods, even if they exist as conscious beings, care about the actions and concerns of mortal men. Where were they when father was dying? Why did your wife and unborn son have to die? You, who are so devout and modest. And why have they allowed the Hellenes to war against each other century after century, every peace treaty leading inevitably to fresh competition and eventually war? It is not enough to blame a lack of piety: why have the Gods done so little to encourage piety if that is what mortals need? Again and again it is the impious and unscrupulous who triumph in the world.

"Even the myths tell us of Gods doing things that among men would be considered barbaric. Rapes, murders, and every kind of immorality are ascribed to them: if mortal men are ethically superior to the Gods, why should we listen to divine guidance at all?" Giorgias saw his brother frown at this last statement, and checking himself, he went on in a more reasonable, less passionate voice.

"I know, brother: you will say that I don't understand, that I should attend the mysteries and find there the answers to my doubts. But the priests who supervise initiation themselves deny access to those who honestly profess doubt. I would have to lie to do as you wish.

"And in regard to lies, in the past you have answered my doubts about the morality of the Gods by saying 'The poets are liars', quoting the poet Hesiod to me as if that solved the problem.

"But the poets gave us myths. And Hesiod and the priests maintain the Gods inspired the poets: which means the Gods inspired the poets to lie. Therefore the Gods promoted lies, and obviously that makes them liars too.

"So the poets lie and the Gods lie, or the priests themselves are liars. How can any reasonable man take this matter seriously?"

"Things are not always as they seem," said Altas quietly.

"Which really means you would have me pursue reason by being unreasonable. I should trust in the poets and priests though they call themselves liars, in the hope that their lies will turn out to be true. How is it that lies can be both false and true? This may have satisfied our ancestors, who were simple farmers like Hesiod, but philosophy has shown us the power of clarity, of discovering the simple rules that order nature. And it has shown us the power of logic and the danger of inconsistency in discovering the truth. I do not deny the Gods exist in some form, but is clear to me that myth and mysteries are not the best way to discover their natures and actions.

"Last year was hard for you, brother, and I know that the twin losses of wife and father weigh heavily on your heart even now. The loss of the pottery shop was a third and final blow that once again you did not deserve: if I could undo my actions I gladly would. I know I lack your common sense and sober manner, and therefore I have added to your troubles. Your innocence is partly why my resentment of the Gods has hardened...

"Although for myself I doubt the value of our father's faith in Delphi, I believe it may help you, and fervently hope it does. If I haven't rejected the Gods' guidance altogether, it is for your sake: I love and respect you, so I cannot help but believe your faith is worthy though it differs from my own.

"You know my heart, Altas, you know that I respect the truth as much as you do. Don't be disheartened by what I think. You have said yourself that philosophy is a valuable tool in understanding the truth, neither more nor less important than myth. You should not be disappointed in me but be happy that I take truth and honor as seriously as you do. Though we disagree in method, we do not disagree in the goal."

Seeing his brother's effort to avoid offending him, knowing that there was nothing he could say to end their stalemate, Altas reached over and squeezed his brother's shoulder, smiling. "Don't be troubled, brother. As you say, I know the goodness in your heart.

"Let's go on now to Delphi in silence. Seeing Chaeronea again has made me moody, so I would like just to think. But you should know it is this place, and not you or your words that make me so." He looked at Giorgias, who looked intently back for a moment, then smiled and nodded.

And so they continued on their way in silence, while the hours passed and the midsummer sun traveled across the bright blue sky.

Arriving at Delphi that afternoon after a hard day's walk, they found the cheapest inn they could, scarcely more than a barn. Altas gave their purse to his brother to pay the innkeeper, because the man was interrupted by other business before they could settle the account. While his brother waited for the innkeeper to return, Altas determined to go for a walk. His moodiness had not passed, and he wished to be alone with his thoughts.

He had not been to Delphi before, and he wandered, letting his feet decide his course. In this way he came to the market place. It was mostly deserted, given the late hour, although a few farmers and merchants remained. Feeling fatigued from the day's walking, he sat on a crumbling set of steps that led to a closed curio shop and vacantly watched the people come and go, his arms folded. In his thoughts he was far away in Athens and at the battle of Chaeronea where the destiny of the Greeks had been decided.

Time passed, and the shadows moved a little in opposition to the sun, while Altas moved not so much as a finger, so deeply was he lost in thought. Suddenly he became aware of laughter nearby and turned his head to see.

A mother and her daughter, obviously wealthy, stood talking to a slave who had apparently been waiting in the market for them to arrive. Or rather the mother talked, while the daughter stooped to pick up a little puppy that had rushed up to her, tail wagging so hard his head shook violently.

She laughed again, her voice so pure and bright that Altas felt a surge of happiness just to hear it. And he felt himself smiling, a thing that rarely happened of late.

Hugging the dog to her chest, she looked up and glanced at him. Their eyes met, and they both turned their heads away in embarrassment, their smiles disappearing from their faces. She looked at the puppy, he looked at his sandals. But only for an instant. Without thinking, he looked back at her again, only to find that she too was stealing a second look. They regarded each other intently for a moment.

Somehow Altas forgot to breathe. She was delightful to look at, a girl of eighteen or nineteen, but it was more than that. Something in her manner charmed him deeply, though he could not say what, and he felt as if he was growing warm from within. Suddenly he felt foolish, aware of his age and plain appearance. Not knowing what else to do, he forced himself to smile at her, but she smiled back genuinely and with humor. It made him feel weak to see it.

The moment passed. She glanced towards her mother's back where she stood talking to the slave, and suddenly her smile died. She turned her attention to the puppy, petting it, and he could see she felt awkward. He realized he was blushing, and he chastened himself for being a fool. Again he looked away.

The mother paid the slave, and after bidding her daughter to set the little dog down, she took her by the arm and walked past Altas towards the main road. Just as they passed him, when he judged he would be out of sight to the side, he dared another glimpse. Again the girl was watching him, and this time it seemed to him he saw regret in her beautiful face, but she was gone before he could be sure.

Flustered, he settled himself back on his step, telling himself he would continue with his interrupted train of thought, but he could not. He took a deep breath, and tried to relax, but he realized he was in a state of scarcely containable excitement.

"You fool, Altas," he muttered to himself. "You fool! You imagine happiness where there can be none. You are a poor man without livelihood, and tomorrow you will leave this place. And you are not the one to excite such a beautiful woman, with your plain old face and sad old thoughts."

But he did not believe his words, though he knew the truth of them was self-evident. Somehow he could not believe them. His mind was too agitated for reason to guide it. He noticed he was being watched with amusement by an old man who stood near the market's Herme. What was making the old man smile?

He realized he was talking to himself out loud, making himself ridiculous. He had better leave. Blushing, he got up stiffly and exited the place opposite where the mother and daughter had disappeared a few minutes before.

A bove the town of Delphi there is an ancient pathway laid with stones that leads up towards the peak of Mount Parnassos. Somehow Altas found himself upon the path, his mind still reeling at the thought of the girl, a boundless energy driving him up the mountain while he waged a hopeless war against hope.

As the town fell away behind him, he struggled to be calm, muttering to himself he had imagined the whole thing, or she was trifling with him, or it was hopeless, or...a thousand other sensible but hollow things that his heart refused to heed. His legs were glad of the exertion demanded by the climb, for they so tingled with vigor that lack of sufficient effort made them tickle. He almost ran up the steep path, and soon his breath was ragged in his throat. It felt good.

Barely aware of the passage of time, he found himself at length in the heights over Delphi where the cliffs tower far above Apollo's sacred temple. It looked tiny beneath him. Across the valley, the steep side of another mountain rose above the plain. And farther Southward still, misty with distance, he could see the waters of the Corinthian Gulf, their blue almost paled to white by the haze. Satisfied by the climb, it seemed, his legs made no complaint when he settled himself on a stone to take in the magnificent scenery. And he noted with relief that his agitation was beginning to fade.

Several minutes passed while he admired the view. It was late afternoon, and the sun was hiding behind Parnassos' shoulder to the West. A gentle breeze was blowing against the grass, whispering softly.

Suddenly he sat up straight: he thought he had heard a voice calling out, somewhere below and to the East. He stood up, listening. Perhaps it was just the wind. Then it came again, a child's voice, crying for help.

He ran along the top of the cliffs, leaving the path behind. Again the voice called out, clearer now, and he realized it was coming from somewhere almost directly below him. Cautiously he worked his way over the rocks until, with a shock of vertigo, he found himself above a sheer drop. At the same instant he saw the boy, a child of about eight, clinging to a narrow crack just out of reach below and to the left. The boy's face was white, his eyes wide, and he was panting from exertion. Altas felt sick just to see it.

"Hold on," he shouted, "I'll get you!"

His own position was too tenuous, so he moved back a bit from the edge until he was more secure. Then he tore open his clothes, and reaching inside pulled out a purple sash as long as a man that had been draped across his shoulders, wrapping the end of it securely around his right wrist.

Working his way forward again until the child was in view, crouching down, he swept his arm in a wide arc several times, ending the sweep with a flicking motion until the end of the cloth fell across the child's arm. It stayed there. The boy looked at him and the cloth, but did not take hold of it.

"Take it. You'll be all right. Take the sash." He spoke with a quiet earnestness, but the boy was too frightened to attempt it.

"It is no ordinary cloth. Do you recognize it? If you take the cloth, nothing can harm you. Have you heard of Samothrace? Come on, boy. Take the cloth so I can get you up. You will not be the first who was saved by such a sash: I received it from the priests at the Samothracian mysteries. Come on, lad, don't be stubborn. Nothing will happen to you once you take the cloth."

To Altas' relief, the boy at last grabbed the cloth with his left hand and then again took hold of the crack, this time with the material of the sash under his hand.

"Good boy! Now wrap it around your wrist...come on...that's it! A couple of times more...Excellent!" He braced himself, fumbling for a more secure grip. "All right, when I say 'Now!' I want you to let go of the crack and hang on to the sash with both hands. Once you do that, you will be safe: you understand? All right...Now!"

The boy did as he was bid and swung from his perch, rolling along the rock until he was directly below, clinging to the cloth in panic with all his strength. Altas couldn't release his hold on the rock, but the boy was light, so he bent his arm, took the sash in his teeth, took hold farther down the cloth, bent his arm again, and again took the sash in his teeth. The third time the boy was in reach, and he grabbed his wrist and swung him up behind himself, out of danger.

Altas was sweating with exertion and shaking when he was once again standing on the rocks above the cliff. The boy stood well back from the edge, still terrified, as Altas straightened the sash and loosed his clothing so he could put it back on underneath.

"What were you doing here?" he asked. The child didn't answer. "Who are you?...Wait!" The boy had suddenly taken flight and run back towards the path leading to town. Altas considered pursuing him, but what was the point? He let him go, shaking his head, smiling, and rearranging his clothes.

A s Altas walked back down the mountain, the moon rose in the East, nearly full, the sun went down, and daylight drained away to join it in the West. He reached the town in moonlight, stumbling a little in the shadows along the path. His inn was on the outskirts of the town and the road was deserted as he approached it.

When he laid his hand upon the door latch he was suddenly startled by a voice coming from just behind him: "Wait." So unexpected was the voice in the empty street, that he jumped a little, and spun around.

It was one of Apollo's priests, standing not two paces away, a sack held loosely in one hand. His face was mostly hidden in shadow, but Altas could see the corner of his mouth turned up in amusement, presumably at his surprise. That irritated him. "I didn't hear you behind me," he said accusingly.

The priest looked at him for a moment, the smile still visible, then half turned and beckoned towards the outskirts of town. "We will talk now. Let us go where we can be alone and not disturb anyone." His movements were smooth, decisive, precise. The voice was strangely melodic, and Altas thought he detected the hint of an Asiatic accent familiar to him from the Ionian Greek traders that he had met at Athens.

He considered rejecting the offer, since he was tired and still a little irritated, but his curiosity would not allow it. What would a priest of Apollo want with him? The priest had already begun walking swiftly in the direction he had indicated, calling "Come!" back over his shoulder without looking around. Altas hurried to catch up, not an easy matter given the priest's swiftness. He had to actually break into a jog to keep from falling behind, although the priest seemed to be striding at a comfortable walk away from him.

In the end he never did actually come abreast of the man who clearly was an accomplished walker, whatever else he might be. As they made their way into the moonlit hillside beyond the town, it occurred to Altas that the request to talk was actually an order: the fellow was very strange and not a little rude.

The priest walked to an olive tree that stood by the roadway well beyond the edge of the town, and without a hint of hesitation set his sack down and sat next to it, leaning against the trunk. As Altas joined him, he had the strange impression the priest was frozen, made of stone: when he had come to rest, leaning back comfortably, he seemed to have stopped moving altogether, apparently gazing at the view. Even his breathing was not visible. His face was again in the shadows, this time of the tree, so Altas could not even be sure if his eyes were opened or closed.

Altas sat down panting a few paces away and waited. A cricket chirped from nearby, and Altas shifted himself uncomfortably, a stone digging into his backside. The priest did not stir or take any notice of him at first, and Altas began to wonder if he was forgotten. Yet he did not consider speaking first: the priest had a kind of natural authority far more compelling than that of his office. Altas waited, curiously, to see what would happen.

"I know you better than you might imagine," began the priest without looking at him. "I saw you in the market place this afternoon when I was there with my aunt. We took a special interest in your fondness for the girl, since I am her guardian." His voice had a peculiar hint of amusement, almost like mockery although it seemed kindly at the same time. It was as if everything amused him equally, impartially.

Altas was embarrassed to have been so transparent, and searched his memory of the market place, but he could think of no one so striking as this priest. He opened his mouth to say something, but before he could speak the priest went on.

"Don't trouble yourself: we approve, though her mother is a willful creature and would resist strongly. Let matters rest. I mention it first since it happened first, but you did me a favor at the cliffs which was far more notable. The little boy you rescued is brother to the girl, and I am also his guardian as well as his teacher, since he is being trained for the priesthood. So you see, the Fates have made you both lover and savior of the Deukalidae family on the day you arrived in our delightful little town. A very good start. Have you heard of the Deukalidae? They are quite famous in these parts."

Surprised at what he was hearing, and marveling a little at the strangeness of the Fates, Altas nodded his head. Realizing the priest couldn't see him, he started to say "Yes," but the other cut him off as if to say the question was rhetorical and in no need of reply.

"After the boy returned and described his benefactor, it was natural I should speak with you.

"Judging by your clothes and accent, you are Athenian. Why did you come here?" The question seemed oddly like a statement, as if the priest already knew the answer and was simply going through an expected routine. Although vibrant energy suffused his words, there was no curiosity in them. Even so, he half turned his head towards Altas and then cocked it slightly, the first time he had moved since they arrived, and once again he settled into statuesque immobility while Altas replied. There was an aura of intense, almost frightening focus in being regarded so intently. Altas was self conscious as he spoke, and was even a little grateful that the man's face was hidden in shadow for he was already disconcerted enough as it was.

"I came to question the oracle about what to do. My brother and I owned a pottery factory with eight slaves, but in the past year we had some bad luck and only escaped bankruptcy by the kindness of our late father's friends."

"You came to question the oracle. What about your brother," said the priest, who looked away again, his voice now more overtly humorous than before, and his question again seemed more a statement in its style than a genuine query.

"Yes, my brother is here too. He too will ask, though he is impatient by nature. He wants to go to Macedon. Truthfully, his only reason for coming is that we swore to our father that we would do so."

"Ah, so he has little time for religious inquiries. My ward tells me you have been to Samothrace, and naturally you must have been to Eleusis, since you are inclined that way. The boy was very frightened when you saved him, and his senses were heightened by his fear. That is why he noticed something that meant nothing to him, but which he could pass on to me when I pressed him on the point: you have a single white thread running through the end of your Samothracian sash, and that tells me you were admitted to the highest level of initiation in that place. I too know of the highest secrets taught there, so we can speak openly together.

But your brother apparently does not share in your respect for the revelations of the past. Is he fond of philosophy?"

Altas hesitated, because the conversation was becoming personal, but the priest's guess regarding his brother was correct and his manner warm, if somewhat odd. Above all, the knowledge of the priest's supreme initiation at Samothrace settled the matter: he decided to answer frankly.

"Yes, quite right. It's a common problem among the young. Just today we quarreled about Hesiod's statement that the poets are liars. It's not the first time." He considered for a moment, and went on. "As a priest of Apollo, you must hear criticisms by people who don't know of the mysteries: what do you tell them in order to persuade them of their error?"

The priest laughed briefly, his laughter carefree and yet equally controlled. "I tell them nothing. The mysteries are open to those who thirst for them, unable to take 'no' for an answer, refusing to let threats or rejection end their quest. In this way only those suited to wisdom gain the purest knowledge of the Gods.

"Greece has changed. Many of the most gifted young are spoiled and have grown so fond of comfort and intellectual amusements that they reject everything they do not already know or cannot quickly prove with sophistry to impress their friends. Cleverness is the God they worship most. When they speak of a myth, they say it is chaotic because its order eludes them. They say, as well, they respect their ancestors, but is it respect to imagine that their ancestors were fools who believed childish stories? Such sophists know little but believe themselves wise."

The priest raised his hand, palm open and facing the front, moving it in a smooth arc to emphasize his meaning: "And yet even unattended, sometimes even mocked, the religion guides them.

"The poets were liars for a reason. Religion is divided into two: public and secret. So too with the words of the poets. In hearing the words of the poets' myths, everyone learns the shape of divinity but not its true nature. In this way their minds are shaped towards truth although they may remain in ignorance. The Hellenic peoples reflect the truth in their thoughts because they are raised on the poet's tales, though they may as adults come to doubt them and never learn their deeper meanings. These meanings are hidden behind the oaths the initiates take to protect their secrets from those who are unsuited.

"Metaphor is both truth and lie, depending on whether the listener understands that it is, in fact, metaphor. But even the person who does not understand that he hears a metaphor nonetheless knows the general shape of what is meant. If you tell a child 'Alexander of Macedon is a lion', he may believe you literally. If so, he has some sense of your meaning, though he may later learn that Alexander is a man. And then he may turn to you and pout, saying you are a liar, which is both true and also false.

"Every child knows the answer to the riddle of the sphinx. 'What walks on four legs in the morning, two at midday, and three in the evening?' The child replies 'It is a man: he crawls in infancy, walks upright in mid-life, and hobbles with his cane in old age.' It is an answer, yes. But when Oedipus destroyed the sphinx by answering it, the words 'a man' were the least significant portion of his answer. To destroy the sphinx he had to know the true nature of a man and of how age defeats him. Therein lies the real mystery of this story. So the answer to this riddle is itself a riddle, for the man who longs to know. That is the essence of myth.

"The greatness of the Hellenes comes from their religion which ensures that all of them, even those like your brother who doubt what they are told, are prepared from birth to mirror the divine patterns in their minds. With their thoughts raised on the reflections of divinity in the world, their powers of reason go far beyond those of other peoples less gifted in their faith.

"And generation after generation, from the chaos of the myths they were taught as children and then from the wisdom imparted at the mysteries, initiates have discovered that what seems at first chaotic is actually orderly. The Greeks are beloved of the Gods because they believe in the power of revelation and reason to uncover Order where at first there appeared only chaos. Even your brother shares this assumption, for he drank it deeply with his mother's milk. It is the Greek birthright, the gift of your ancestors.

"Many Greeks are heroes in the ancient meaning of the word, some more than others. A hero is any person who promotes and reflects divinity here on earth, in thought or deed, though he or she is not divine. Heroes shine with the *arete* brought to earth by Hera. Whether consciously or not, a hero's actions conform to the pattern established by divinity, thereby expressing divinity in the world. Any nation creates many heroes, but none creates more than the Hellenes, for all Greeks have grown up with the divine patterns of myth from their earliest years. Your brother, too, if he loves philosophy, is a hero in the deepest meaning of the word, though he believes, like most other men, that the heroes all died long ago at the time of the Trojan war. Let him serve divinity in whatever way his nature dictates. Don't trouble him because he is different from you and his vision more focused: diversity also is an expression of divinity."

"Sir" said Altas, "there is something that I don't understand. If persuasion has no purpose, then why did the great dramatists write their plays? It is said that they wrote to make the people respect and follow the sacred ways." His tone was apologetic. "Is this not an attempt at the persuasion you have just rejected?"

"This is already answered," said the priest bluntly, yet with the ever-present humor. Even his shape, dim in the shadows, seemed to express laughter, although he did not laugh.

Altas was embarrassed, yet persisted. "But I don't understand. I'm sorry: could you explain it again?"

"It is very simple. The tragedians wrote stories about heroes expressing divinity in the world to celebrate that divinity and to show what shape it may take among mortal men. Myth expressed in action to guide the hearts and minds of men.

"You know, for example, that play *The Bacchae* by Euripedes. It is the story of a man who destroys himself by resisting the Gods, or so it seems to the uninitiated. But of course he is a hero, and he follows divine will though he does not know it. Indeed, deeper in its meaning, he is a metaphor for something greater, as you surely also know. He is the seed that must die to give birth to new life: the pine cone which dead and buried becomes tomorrow's tree. He is the sorrow and power of the thyrsus, the magic wand of the Bacchae. He offers secret hope of immortality through wisdom. Euripedes wrote this play when Athens was walking blindly towards her defeat at the hands of the Spartans: he sought to offer hope to his doomed city. But this play persuades no one: it celebrates the divine patterns ruled by the God Dionysos and expressed among men. That is all.

"As for comedy among the Greeks, it teaches humility, a mortal's path to wisdom. It mocks all things mortal, even mortal wisdom, and it takes special pleasure in mocking Dionysos, Hermes, and Herakles who, though divine, touch upon mortality and thus help to guide mortal men. In the wisdom these Gods offer lies hope and also danger, for mortal men too easily fall into the trap of pride in their thoughts and accomplishments. That which can save can also destroy them.

"Since humility is not a quality of divinity, comedy carries no secret meanings regarding the Gods: its jokes and parodies are all directed at men who are in danger of rising too high in their own opinion or in the opinions of others. Initiate and non-initiate alike are intended to be humbled by the dramatist's tale. That is all.

"Dionysos presides over the drama contests in your city because he is a guide for mortal men. It is not persuasion but humility and the shape of divinity the plays seek to promote. And for the uninitiated, that is where it ends. To those with ears to hear, the dramas awaken deeper musings, to each according to his nature.

"Whoever told you such plays persuade has never considered their effect on men like your brother: they see what they want to see, even in the shining brilliance of Euripedes. They say that poet did not himself believe in the Gods: amazing foolishness. When the dramatist has Herakles kill wantonly and then declare that Gods could never allow such things, the fools speak of Euripedian paradox and think he shared their narrow views. That Euripedes meant they should look to the deeper meaning where no sin was committed, is beyond their strutting thoughts. They confuse mere cleverness with wisdom. Indeed their view is shallow and wide, but never deep, for pride has blinded them.

"But to each his own: the Gods do not trouble over the limitations of mortal thoughts, so why should you?"

The priest pointed casually at the ground beside Altas, and it seemed to Altas as if it was a fraction of a second later that the man turned his head to follow where his finger was indicating. "Is that a coin?" Again, there was laughter behind his words.

Looking down, Altas caught sight of a dim shape in the place indicated. He poked it with his finger and realized that it was as the priest had suggested, a coin. How had the man seen it? His vision must be very sharp. Picking it up, he held it out to the other, whose hand now flattened, fingers turned up, palm restraining him, before returning gracefully to rest upon its owner's knee. "Keep it. It may bring you luck."

There was silence for a moment between them, as Altas wiped the coin carefully and put it in his mouth, out of the way between cheek and gum. While he did so, the priest reached into his sack and brought out a wheel made of some sort of metal and set it down on the ground beside him where it glinted dully in the moonlight. Altas looked at it with curiosity but said nothing, waiting for the priest to speak. He did not. Instead he took hold of the outer rim and spun it absently. The center of the wheel remained fixed in position, and Altas could see what appeared to be six spokes, each represented by a human figure radiating from the center.

"The Gods appear to move in this world, but the seasons don't for they lie beyond their own nature," said the priest musingly, watching the rim as it spun. When it came to a stop the priest looked at it carefully for a moment and then put it away, but not before Altas had a chance to notice and quickly count the little figures on the wheel's rim: there were sixteen. What was it? Some device, apparently, though he had no idea what it was for. He considered asking, but he reasoned that if the priest had wanted to tell him more he would have, for he surely knew Altas would be curious about it. He let it pass. In any case, the priest's mention of the seasons had reminded him of a problem that had been troubling him for some time. Should he ask about it?

The priest had been remarkably knowledgeable and clear in his speaking. In fact, he had said things more clearly than Altas had ever heard before, putting together many things that had seemed unrelated to him. True, there was some chance his question would trespass on mysteries that were not yet open to him, but he knew that if that were the case the priest would simply refuse to answer. And he was very keen to settle this particular question, so he went ahead and asked.

"There is one inconsistency that troubles me, although I have some knowledge of the things you have said. It has to do with numbers and divine revelations. If I may know, I wish to understand about the seasons.

"In the older myths they were three, each a God, and from the same principle comes the many trinities of Gods. These express the three forms of matter: earth, water, and air. But then the forms became known as four: Earth, water, air, and fire. And for many the seasons, too, are now numbered four.

"So divine revelation taught us at different times that both are correct. But as Pythagoras has said, numbers are a perfect reflection of divinity. How can something be both three and four in number? In this I find myself thinking as my brother does..."

The priest laughed. "Numbers are indeed as Pythagoras declared, but you are too quick to wonder if you've found the limits of knowledge, when proof that you have not lies before you. For mortals, there will never be a limit: revelation will follow revelation until the end of time.

"To the Gods the seasons are both four and three, indeed they are also one. Are you curious, Athenian? As always, the confusion comes from incomplete understanding and the solution comes from inquiry and revelation. If you seek the answer patiently and with a pure heart, you will find it, of that I am quite sure. More than that I cannot say, for no mortal man has answered that particular question. The movement of time has yet to be understood so well in this world."

Altas was embarrassed at the priest's expression of confidence in his ability. "I am not gifted enough that I can hope to find the answer if others could not find it, sir."

"Foolish man!" barked the priest suddenly, but he remained reposed in appearance and the words which followed were as controlled and calm as those that had gone before. It was deeply disturbing to hear a man who spoke with such sharp yet measured intensity.

"No mortal man is truly gifted, unless he lives with humility: the humble man who knows his weakness calls forth the generosity of the Gods. To the man who doubts, living in the knowledge of his ignorance, who burns for revelation and waits for it in the total silence of reflection, to him the Muses come from Olympus to whisper secrets and fill his mind with wisdom.

"Mortal thoughts arise from chaos, so they are chaotic. Still them and Order will come. From Order will come orderly thoughts. Be silent, and let wisdom speak for you.

"There is a fine line between humility and subservience, but the Gods love humility in men and hate subservience as much as pride. Do not think like a slave. Wisdom is open to any heart that hungers for it.

"You doubt the limits of mortal's abilities without knowing them. Your willful ignorance marks the limit of your ability. Mortals are not Gods, but through the guidance of the Gods they may go very far. Death at one time swept all men before it, but knowledge of its meaning and certain other sacred things has made it possible for some to live forever. For you, this is impossible, perhaps, but not for all. And even for those like yourself who turn away at the last moment, all is not lost. The light of wisdom shines even into death, creating great promise.

"Most are initiated in some of the mysteries: of their city, of their secret societies, or elsewhere. But of these only perhaps one in a thousand is selected by the priests in the great centers for their piety, humility, and passion: they alone are called to receive the higher mysteries. And among these, perhaps one in a thousand is selected to receive the highest mysteries known to mortal men, whose existence is known to only a handful. You are one of them. And that is as far as knowledge goes, but is not the end. Among those at your level, perhaps only one in a thousand go on, finding their way to the place where the seasons no longer affect them, living forever in the Elysian Fields. The names of some such are known to all, like Empedocles and Socrates. But for every one who is known, there are many who conceal their natures. Though you may never equal their wisdom, there is much you can do, according to the limits you set for yourself, and your willingness to trust and follow the will of the Gods and to seek the silent source."

At this point the priest turned, smiling enigmatically, his face leaving behind the shadows and coming out into the moonlight where suddenly his youth and striking beauty were revealed.

It was the first time Altas had really seen his companion, and for an instant their eyes locked. Something in the other made Altas feel strange, and then without warning a wave of panic seemed to burst over him like a shock of recognition: there was such intelligence in those eyes, such unearthly calm! They were not human...

He dropped his head in horror and confusion. And when the priest spoke again, his voice as bright and melodious as ever, Altas could barely hear him, so overwhelmed was his mind by the violence of his feelings and thoughts, of noise.

As if in a dream he heard "You are tired now and tomorrow is an important day. Sleep."

Altas realized his eyes were closed, but he did not, could not, will himself to open them.

T he next thing he was aware of was the sounds of birds chirping nearby and the light of morning through his eyelids. Opening his eyes he was confused to find himself lying by a path near the little olive tree, alone. He sat up.

There was no sign of the priest. Had their conversation been a dream? If not with the priest, he must have walked here in his sleep. But he couldn't remember bedding down in the inn...

Perhaps he had met the man as he remembered, they had talked, he had slept, and then he had dreamed, adding things that had not happened. But then what of their discussion was true, what false? Going over the things the priest had said, he found them sound: he had learned much of value in their conversation.

The man was strange, it's true, but only at the end of their discussion did Altas' memory of events become truly improbable. He must indeed have blended dream with fact, but only that part when he had dreamed of seeing the man's eyes. They were so strange!

Even the memory of them frightened him, so he put them from his mind. Instead he looked across the valley at the mountains and the sea. Then he remembered the girl from the market and a warm blush of pleasure spread across his body at the memory. Would he see her again? He might, in the town or at the sanctuary of Apollo, but certainly not here.

Picking himself up stiffly, he felt the coin still in his mouth: that part, at least, was definitely true. It was an odd feeling, to not know dream from fact. As he walked back to town, disorientation and hope of seeing the girl agitated his mind, hurrying his steps.

He was still trying to make sense of his confused thoughts when he arrived at the inn, meeting his brother just coming out of the door.

"Where have you been?" Giorgias asked gruffly, his face still puffy from sleep. "I was worried about you when I woke to find you did not return last night."

"I...I slept under the stars, brother." There was no point in discussing his strange dream until he had sorted it out properly. "I'm sorry I troubled you."

They shared some bread on the road to Apollo's temple, sitting under an old tree. They could see the shrine of Athena Pronaos from where they sat, its beautiful rounded shape catching the morning sunlight. Georgias said nothing in answer to Altas' comments on the beauty of the place and replied to his brother's questions about what he'd done the previous evening with surly grunts, which wasn't like him.

"What's the matter, Georgias," asked Altas, "was your sleep troubled?"

His brother frowned. "I don't think we should bother with the oracle," he said. "Let's go together to Macedon, and stop this foolishness." He looked at the ground for a moment, and shook his head. When he spoke, he was pleading.

"Look, I'm sorry. I lost the money gambling last night. Why did you give me the purse? If you weren't so impatient to go for a walk, I wouldn't have been tempted. I was winning at first, I really was. I had doubled our money, but then my luck ran out. And I think my opponents might have been cheating.

"You know I can't be trusted with money: I already lost our business because of it. You knew that. What were you thinking? I'm sorry, Altas, I really am. But there's nothing I can do."

Altas was aghast. Everything they had left was gone, except the coin that was hidden in his mouth. Without any money it would be difficult to survive in Athens, let alone begin a new business as he'd hoped. He knew his brother's burning desire to gamble well enough: it had almost sent the two of them to prison for debt and had ruined the business their father had left them. He knew, so how could he have been so thoughtless? His desire to go for a walk, to sit alone and think, had changed his life.

But then he also remembered the girl, or rather felt the memory of her inside himself, glowing, and he realized he was glad just to have seen her—that for such a privilege he would give far more than money. Had he not gone to the market, he never would have had that chance. In his youth he had loved several times, but this love, hopeless and unexpressed, seemed to him profoundly different, deeper. His wife he had not loved like this: their marriage was arranged and never seemed a sharing of souls, though it was happy enough to satisfy them both. Her loss had brought on a torrent of suffering that lasted many months and ached even now. How was it possible that in an instant he could love this stranger? It was absurd.

But it seemed to him, in his amazement and joy, that with this young woman he had felt recognition: she was his own heart, looking back at him from the world outside, and for the first time in his life he realized that his heart and mind had never truly been his. They had always been searching for her, though since his youth he had come to doubt she actually existed. Now that he believed she did, he would never be the same: however far he traveled, however long he lived, he would know that he was whole because she was in the world. That he would never see her again, that she would marry another and have children didn't matter. This wasn't about profit, it was about his place in the world, what sort of man he was. Inwardly he chuckled: he'd better not tell anyone about this or they would think him mad.

And he was grateful to have helped her brother: to help the child for his own sake, of course, but also to have saved her from heartache. For that he knew that he would give anything, even his own life. The power and confidence of these feelings surprised him.

While he silently thought these things, Georgias sat watching him, his eyes wide as they searched his face. Altas realized that his brother's words were a plea for forgiveness, his earlier anger an expression of his fear that it would not be given. He shrugged and smiled. "Let's see what happens."

He spat out the coin into his hand and held it up: "This is for your questioning of the oracle, so that at least can be done. We've got food for about three days. After you have received your guidance, if the oracle wills you to go to Macedon, I will go too. This will only pay for one of us to question Apollo, and I know our father would have preferred it to be you."

Georgias spoke with finality. "No, brother. It is for you to question the oracle. I'm sorry, but if I was told not to go to Macedon I would go there anyway. It is where my future lies. I want to attend the conquest of Persia even if it costs me my life. And as you know, I doubt that the oracle would provide better guidance in this than my own thoughts."

Altas considered challenging his brother's doubts yet again, but he knew the outcome of such a contest would be the usual draw. He sighed and gave up. "All right. I will have my question answered. Let's go do it now, so we can get started on our journey."

They walked back along the road they had come the previous day, back to the Castelian Spring where they drank the cool waters that came up from beneath Parnassos. Then reversing their steps, they walked to the base of Apollo's winding path to his temple. Georgias was determined to stay there, saying he'd explored the sanctuary the day before, so he sat against the stone wall by the gate to wait. Altas walked on alone up the meandering Sacred Way.

He saw the various treasuries of the cities of Greece, each loaded with gifts of war and decorated with statuary, paint, and gilt. He saw the sibyl's stone, a pillar of rock where it is said the first Sibyls stood when they gave their prophesies of the God long, long ago. And the temple of Apollo towered above him as he climbed the gentle incline.

When at last he neared the great temple he saw the line of querants waiting to have their private questions asked, and he joined it. Like them, he would not be asking the Sybil. Her time was devoted to answering the greater matters of State: she only served delegations from the various cities of Greece, or such barbarian and half-civilized barbarian kings and tyrants as came from farther afield. For such official guests, the Sybil sat in the inner chamber of the temple on a tripod. The priests translated her God-inspired words into Greek. For private citizens like Altas, questions were answered by a priest who sat by the temple's entrance, picking beans from a clay jar: a black bean meant 'no', a white bean meant 'yes'. Apollo was said to guide the priest's hand towards the proper choice.

The line moved slowly, so Altas stood for a fairly long time in the sunshine, waiting his turn. At one point a young priest went down the line making sure that everyone's question was suited to a yes or no answer. Altas decided to ask him about the priest he'd met the night before. At first the priest looked puzzled, and said there was no one fitting that description. Altas explained that the man was the guardian of a wealthy matron of the Deukalidae family's children. The priest looked at him quizzically, and said there were many of the Deukalidae clan in the town, and many men served as Apollo's priests, but none that he knew of was a guardian to the Deukalidae. There was no need for such a guardian. Perhaps the man who told him these things was lying?

Confusion growing, Altas asked him whether he knew if any of the Deukalidae families included a daughter of about nineteen and a son of about eight. The man nodded, and added that the son had almost died on the cliffs above Delphi the day before, but he was rescued by an initiate of Samothrace, a man doubtless sent by Apollo to save the boy who would one day become His priest. Altas became excited and said *that* was the boy: so who was his guardian? But the priest looked at him strangely and began to move away. "There is no guardian," he said as he continued down the line: "The boy's father is still alive."

Left alone again, Altas' thoughts swirled through his head but he could not settle them. As he waited patiently for those ahead of him to complete their questioning of the oracle, he tried to think things through.

Had he dreamed it all? That business about the children belonging to the Deukalidae family had been right, though he had no way of guessing it independently: that would mean his dream was inspired by something more than chance, if it was a dream. Could it have been prophetic in some way? He told himself this was so, for another alternative, that there had been no dream, seemed both frightening and foolish. He resisted that idea strenuously.

Although some dreaming had been involved, denying that any meeting had taken place would not sit well in his reasoning either, for the coin, a physical reminder of what had happened, made it impossible that the things he remembered came entirely from dreams.

He decided that the best explanation was that he'd met a trickster who told him tales mixed with truth, and he had blended memory of the event with dream in his mind. Truth and lies had mixed with waking and sleep, together creating his confusion. He wasn't too happy with this explanation since it didn't seem likely to bear close scrutiny, but the other, more obvious explanation that flickered across his mind from time to time was too frightening to contemplate: he was not willing to consider it.

A delegation of Corinthians passed, accompanied by priests to hear the sibyl's words regarding some matter, but Altas barely noticed them.

He was so distracted with the problem that he'd reached the head of the line and been asked twice for his coin before he realized what was happening. He paid the coin with an apology, whispered his question into the priest's ear, and watched while the priest said a brief prayer. Then the man reached his open hand into the jar beside him and lifted it out a moment later bunched up into a fist. Saying a blessing, he opened his fingers slowly revealing the bean to Altas. It was black.

The answer troubled Altas greatly. If he shouldn't go to Macedon, then where should he go? What should he do? He was being confronted with a Delphic problem that any private citizen faced. The oracle's answers did not give much guidance. They might assist one to avoid a bad choice, or even to make a good one, but there was much not said that needed to be. A single yes/no answer was better than nothing, but Altas was not the first to come away uncertain of the course he should take.

Returning down the sacred way, he found himself more confused in every respect than he had been before he came to this town. He greeted Georgias sadly, his chest tight with sadness. Explaining to his brother that he could not accompany him, and that he thought his best course would therefore be to return to Athens, he sat beside him against the wall, and they prepared to take their leave.

Georgias and Altas had never been apart for more than a month or two since their infancy. They spoke for some time, often tearfully, as they made each other repeatedly promise to take care in the months and years ahead. Though they denied it many times, they knew they might never see one another again. They sat with their arms across each other's shoulders and embraced several times as they spoke. A number of people passed by, finding it difficult not to stare at them, but this they never noticed.

It was, they agreed, necessary to begin their journeys at once, since their food was so limited. They divided it, Georgias taking the larger share at his brother's insistence, because he had by far the longer way to go. Georgias was to take the pathway over Parnassos, it being the most direct route, while Altas would retrace their steps to Athens.

At last, reluctantly, the brothers stood up and exchanged their final embrace. Altas stood and watched Giorgias go, tears welling from his eyes and running down his face. Before turning the corner in the road, Giorgias turned, waved once, and was gone. Altas looked after him up the road and made no move to leave. He was suddenly too deeply saddened and numb to do anything. He decided to return to the wall and rest a while before beginning the walk back to Athens.

Altas was awkward as he turned, for his foot slipped a little over the paving, and the strap of his sandal broke. He crouched down to fix it, attempting to tie the broken thongs so that they would not flap free.

Suddenly he heard the sound of running feet coming through the gate from the sacred way inside the sanctuary. Several priests burst through the gate, and coming to a halt, looked around. Seeing Altas, the priests glanced at each other and came over to him. One of them asked him to come with them.

"What is it?" asked Altas as he stood up, wondering what sort of trouble he was in.

"We don't know," said the oldest of the group. "I was beside the inner sanctuary a minute ago when the Sybil suddenly interrupted her answer to an official delegation and spoke clearly, needing no interpretation. She said 'Fetch the son of Erechthonios who crouches before the sanctuary gate like Oedipus at the crossroads.' It might have had some less obvious meaning, so we didn't know what we'd find, but seeing you here, we now know it does not. Please come with us sir, until the elders have determined what the God desires more fully." Then, as an afterthought, "You are an Athenian, are you not? The Sybil said it should be a son of Erechthonios, ancient king of that place."

Bewildered, Altas nodded.

Walking past the line where he had stood so recently, surrounded by a growing crowd of excited priests of the God, Altas allowed himself to be led up the steps of the temple and into the building. Once inside, the priests motioned him to stand near the Corinthian delegation who eyed him curiously, wondering what all the fuss was about. One of the priests who had accompanied him from the sanctuary entrance strode over to another who stood guarding the portal to the inner sanctuary and began whispering earnestly into his ear, pointing at Altas from time to time as he did so. The other looked at Altas as he listened, whispered a few words of his own and vanished behind the tapestry that shielded the inner sanctum from view.

For several minutes there was silence while everyone waited. Then the sounds of a woman's voice issued from deeper inside the temple. It was muted and peculiar, somehow different from that of a normal human voice. Altas knew it must be the Sybil, and the hairs on the back of his neck prickled. The voice fell silent. Several more minutes passed while Altas shifted awkwardly where he stood and wondered what it could mean. The air was hazy with the incense burning on the sacred fire in the innermost reaches of the temple.

Presently the priest returned from behind the portal and walked over to him, his face very serious. He took Altas' arm gently but firmly, and bustled him back out into the sunshine. Had there been a mistake? Coming to a stop at the base of the temple's steps, the priest motioned to some others and walked over to them, speaking quietly a few paces from Altas who strained in vain to make out what was being said. Their half-whispered conversation lasted several minutes, after which the priest from the portal hurried back inside and the others walked over to Altas, smiling.

"Please come with us sir," said one of them, an older man with a balding head. "We have been told to make you comfortable until the high priest is able to see you. It may take some time, so it was suggested that we take you back to Delphi: you can wait at the high priest's house until he returns."

"What is it?" asked Altas. "What does he want?"

"We don't know yet, sir. This sort of thing doesn't happen often. In fact, I've never seen it before." His tone became apologetic. "But if you will just come with us, I'm sure you will soon be told. Apparently the God has given some instructions in regards to you, and the high priest would like to speak with you about them. It is a great honor, sir. I am sure there is no reason to worry."

Feeling he was lost in a strange dream, Altas allowed himself to be led down the Sacred Way and back to the town. He saw the priests who were walking with him glancing in his direction from time to time with curiosity and perhaps envy, but no one spoke. No one could think of anything to say.

T he high priest's house was one of the largest in the town, its marble courtyard tastefully decorated with plants and a few small bronze statues. The atmosphere in that place was light and airy. A slave greeted them and after speaking to the priests, urged them to sit on one of the marble benches while he went to fetch watered wine to slake their thirsts. They settled in to wait, and hours passed.

A couple of times the priests asked him questions about himself, but not many and not very probing. Altas could see that they were unsure how they ought to treat him since they were as uncertain about what was to come as he was. They were polite, he was polite: and as the sun moved across the sky, everyone became very bored except Altas whose thoughts were on the road to Macedon with his brother.

It was late afternoon when the high priest of Apollo returned to his home. A man on the threshold of old age, he was dignified yet warm, used to being important in the world and comfortable in his own skin. He handled people smoothly: a born leader. He shook hands with Altas and accepted the greetings of the other priests before dismissing them. Then he washed his hands in a basin provided by a slave, all the while bantering to Altas.

"I'm sorry to have been so long," he said, "but this is our busiest season. We had three delegations from city states to assist, and we are preparing for a visit from a Macedonian delegation tomorrow. Probably I should still be in the sanctuary now, but I wanted to rush back here so I could see to your comfort. You will be staying for dinner, won't you? Good. We have a lot to discuss and it may take us some time to deal with what has happened."

Altas listened as he went on talking, about the weather, about the undecided political situation of Greece, about rumors from the Macedonian court. Beyond the occasional yes or no, there was little for him to say. As to what actually had happened that morning, or what was expected of him, he did not receive any clue. It occurred to him the priest might want to save their serious talk for dinner or even later. He set his impatience aside and attended to the older man's flood of words, and soon began to add his own reflections and questions to them. The priest was actually a good conversationalist, and it was not long before Altas began to enjoy himself immensely, half forgetting the peculiar circumstances that had brought him there.

They dined alone, and as dinner was being cleared away and wine was brought by servants along with silver wine cups, Altas' host at last addressed the purpose of their meeting.

"Thank you for your patience, Altas. I wanted to get to know you better before we discussed the oracle's words, and I feel I have done that. You want to know what you were brought here for, and you are no doubt expecting me to tell you. I wish I could, but I cannot. I do not know. No one does.

"This morning the Sybil was preparing to answer a delegation's question concerning a matter of religious custom in their city, but before she was ready the God suddenly possessed her and told us to fetch you. As you know, he told us how you could be recognized, and he also said we should make haste or you would depart, and his plans would be in vain. Then he said something we do not understand. Perhaps you can help. He said:

'The family is divided
And will no more be fully joined in this age of men.
The one who remembers will be forgotten,
The one who forgets, remembered.
Accept the turning Season's wheel
And watch your flocks from broad Parnassos.'

Altas heard these words with growing trepidation and amazement. It seemed to him the pattern of its meaning was immediately clear. "My brother left me this morning, and I am afraid the God is saying I will never see him again. My brother has forgotten the ways of our fathers and turned to philosophy without religion, while I have remained true to the old ways. Furthermore I came to Delphi to discover what I should do. It seems the God is saying I should try to make my home here." He paused, troubled. "Except I am no shepherd, no leader of men, and I do not know why the God would speak of me directly. It makes no sense."

The priest nodded. "The oracle may indeed mean those things also, but we must look for a deeper meaning that goes beyond a single man. I am certain that the answer lies in you or the God would not have called you." He paused, lost in thought for a moment. "Let's go over everything carefully, starting with when you decided to come to Delphi. Tell me everything that relates to your decision, and any dreams or unusual events, especially since you began your journey here. There may be portents you did not notice at the time, so be specific."

Altas did as he was asked, describing the death of his father at Chaeronea, and the journey to Delphi a year later. He described in some detail his time at Delphi, up to the point where he rescued the boy, leaving out the girl, of course. The priest, who up until then had been gazing intently at his hands as they lay folded on the table, absorbing his words, suddenly looked at Altas and said in astonishment: "It was you? But that is amazing: that was my son! To you I owe a debt of gratitude I can scarcely repay."

For several minutes they spoke of it, the priest overwhelmed by a loving father's gratitude, Altas embarrassed and awkward as he described what had happened, insisting his actions were not remarkable, and any gratitude was misplaced—though the high priest would not hear of it. There came a point when Altas' awkwardness vanished with the sudden realization that the girl must be nearby even now, somewhere inside the walls of this house. He grew quieter, wishing to both conceal his feelings and revel secretly in them. Presently, the subject of the rescue exhausted, they continued.

Altas was not happy to revisit his meeting with the strange priest from the night before. Everything about the event had assumed a frightening cast in his mind, and he had been grateful previously to have put it from his mind. But even so, he did his best to describe the things said, the things done, the things he saw. It was embarrassing to describe, for he knew what his story implied and he did not want to seem presumptuous or dishonest. The whole thing made him feel very uncomfortable. Several times the high priest looked at him with surprise, or perhaps it was skepticism: he could not tell.

The story complete, he moved on with relief to what had happened that day up until the priests had come to fetch him. The high priest never interrupted him, listening in silence until he was done. When he finally stopped talking, there was silence for a while.

And then the questions began, all of them about the strange priest. The questions were neither friendly nor unfriendly: they were requests for more detail. A particular focus was the wheel he had seen, and the high priest even went so far as to have a slave bring writing materials so he could sketch it.

It was late at night when their discussion ended. The high priest said that he wished to go to bed and sleep on the matter, and if Altas wished, he could remain there as his guest that night. He added that he would like to introduce his family in the morning, for he knew that his wife would want to thank him personally for saving their son. In light of his difficult financial position, and even more so in the knowledge that the girl might also attend, Altas accepted the offer gratefully.

T he next morning a servant brought him down from his room, treating him with deference. Altas wondered if this was because he had heard of the oracle's interest in him, or because he was being brought to share a meal with the master's wife. Among the Greeks, men did not normally mingle with each other's wives and daughters.

When he entered the dining room where they had eaten the previous night, the family was already present and the meal set, waiting for him to arrive. As he entered they all looked up, smiling in greeting, and when he caught sight of the girl from the corner of his eye, he felt dizzy with joy. He forced himself to acknowledge each in turn. The boy from the cliffs was there, and the high priest, and the mother he had seen in the market place, though Altas was relieved to notice that she did not recognize him.

When he reached the young woman, his eyes seemed to cling to her despite his best efforts, and his face grew hot. He knew he must be blushing. She too was turning red, and her mouth parted as if to speak. Suddenly she looked down, almost violently, smiling and frowning at the same time, and shook her head involuntarily. Realizing he was beginning to shake, Altas looked away, towards his host.

It had seemed like a life time, but only a second or two must have passed since he came in, for the high priest and his wife seemed to have noticed nothing. Altas sat down at the indicated place, telling himself that he would ignore the girl lest he embarrass them all. And despite the temptation that continually tugged at his heart for the rest of the meal, this he mostly did.

The same grateful thanks were offered by the wife, and the boy offered his own appreciation, although Altas could tell it was something he had been carefully tutored to say. Because of the formal manner of its delivery, Altas preferred it to the spontaneous expressions of the parents which seemed more embarrassing than ever, now that the girl was there. From time to time he stole a glance at her and every time he did so he caught her eye, for she was likewise watching him. It felt awkward and wonderful at the same time, to be eating across the table from her, unable to speak to her, unable to get her presence out of his mind for even a instant. The meal passed in a whirl of empty conversation, and before Altas knew what was happening, his host was asking him to take a walk beyond the town. The older man wanted to see where the strange priest and he had talked the night before last.

"You seemed tired at breakfast, Altas," said the high priest as they entered the street. "I hope you slept well."

"Very well, sir."

"I noticed you didn't speak much, and you barely touched your food."

"I'm not hungry, it's true, and I guess I was up quite late thinking last night."

"Yes, so was I. And I think I now know what needs to be done. Normally I would have doubted if the priest you met was the God himself, but since the oracle called you, I have decided to assume it was. Of course, it could have been a prankster or a lucid dream as you suggested, but even if it were either of those things that doesn't mean the experience has no value. Even the strangest of coincidences may be used by the God. What you saw has clearly been given his blessing, regardless of what actually happened. But that raises another issue: if you don't mind, I think we should keep that matter fairly private: if it gets out, it's bound to stir up controversy in the town and among Apollo's servants. This is not an age where the Gods often show themselves to mortals. Many will doubt you, and I think we should avoid that.

"I believe the God wants you to stay here, Altas, and live in our town. If you are willing to do so, I will find work for you and a place to live. But actually, if I may suggest it, I think you should spend some time trying to recreate the wheel you saw. Of course God wheels are not new, but I have never heard of one such as you described. From your conversation with the priest, it may have something to do with the seasons being both three and four in number, although why there appeared to be six seasons on the wheel I can't imagine. Perhaps, in time, you can. In the meantime you can build a life here if you want to, since nothing ties you to your old home in Athens. And you should remarry: I'm sure with the help of the Gods we can find a girl who would make you a good wife. Once you have a family here, you will begin to feel truly at home.

"As for the words of the Sybil, it seems to me their meaning does not apply only to you, again based on what was said that night. The family divided is the knowledge of mankind. Religion and philosophy have been growing more separate for centuries. Because of the way initiations are carried out, many are forgetting the knowledge that binds them together. I don't know why the God said the one who remembers will be forgotten, since the one who remembers is obviously the religious initiate. He remembers his past fully, while others can be said to forget. The religion may be separating somewhat from philosophy, but it is not forgotten altogether." The high priest went on at length about this troublesome detail, without seeming to arrive any closer to an understanding.

Altas listened politely, but his thoughts were on his own circumstances. How strangely things were turning out! He was almost unbearably happy as they walked along the path in the bright sunshine. Not because he knew now where he would live, or because he had found a benefactor who would assist him in building a new life. And it did not thrill him that the God had called him through his Sybil. In fact it made him nervous. As for the strange priest, he didn't give meeting him any importance at all, because even the thought of doing so filled him with outright fear. He told himself the high priest was being too hasty in allowing for the possibility of a divine explanation. No, he was glad because over breakfast something wonderful had occurred to him with a gradually increasing certitude that somehow could not be shaken. He knew it would stir in his belly and heart for the rest of his life: he had found the woman he was born to love. And as the Gods were his witness, someday soon she would be his wife.

*A*ltas never saw his brother again, or the mysterious priest. He managed, after a few years of hard work, to reinvent the wheel the priest had shown him, and it soon replaced the bean oracle that had previously been used to guide individual pilgrims when they came to question Apollo at his sanctuary. The device was named "Mysterion" meaning "mysterious motion", although many simply called it the "Sun Wheel", in honor of Phoebus Apollo who had first revealed it to mortals, and the God to whom it was dedicated. In time Altas became a respected and important member of the community at Delphi, serving the God as his priest, raising a family, and living a full life that brought him in comfort into old age. His wife was his greatest joy, woman of the Deukalidae, and she took equal joy in him.

Alexander replaced his murdered father as king of Macedon and leader of all the Hellenes. He conquered much of Asia and died at the age of thirty-three, never having lost a battle. It seemed Hellenic culture had reached its greatest heights, but a sleepy town known as Rome had been slowly growing for several hundred years and would continue swallowing its neighbors for centuries more, until one day it had become an empire that had absorbed the entire Mediterranean world. Rome loved Hellenic culture, and adopted it, so Greek culture did not die: it swelled to even greater triumphs. The city of Alexandria, named for the conqueror, in time played host to the greatest library the world had ever known, and science entered upon its youth in that place.

Delphi continued to prosper for centuries, but an evening of sorts was gathering in the Eastern Mediterranean: a new religion was being born that would one day devour everything in its path. And more and more, as the *decades flew by, the old ways lost their power to inspire. Though none recalled the Sibyl's words when Altas came to town those centuries before, she was proved right in the end. The old ways began to fade, unable to protect themselves, and the ones who remembered were quietly forgotten.*

FAR SHOOTER: THE FINAL PURIFICATION
(The Taro River Valley, 1348 AD)

In the autumn of 1347 there had been too much rain and the harvest was bad. It wasn't life threatening: such things had happened often enough in the history of the Sanctuary. Everyone tightened their belts a little and hoped for better next year. That is the way of farming communities. The winter was lean, but they were in no danger of starvation so no one worried about it much.

Early in the spring of 1348 Giovanni made his way in great haste across the mountain top to the Western ridge, carrying a loaf of fresh made bread, Mario at his side. When they arrived at the newlywed's hut, they were both panting with exertion, and they burst through the door without stopping.

The midwife was just wiping Maria's brow with a damp rag, but Maria hardly seemed to notice: as they came in she was looking at the beautiful newborn infant she held in her arms. She looked up and smiled in happiness and relief. Mario went and stood beside her, across from the midwife.

"It's a perfect little girl," said Maria. For his part, Mario began crying and smiling at the same time, reaching over and patting the little head clumsily. "Here, hold her," Maria said, but his smile faltered and he backed away.

"You hold her. I would break her," he mumbled. No amount of reassurance changed his mind, and it was Giovanni who got to hold the baby, while Mario stood in front of him, watching, eventually feeling brave enough to kiss the little head. Rather than hold the baby, he put his arms around Giovanni and gently hugged the two of them, his head against the crook of Giovanni's arm, his eyes on the sleeping infant. Though it was several minutes later, it seemed like only an instant when the midwife took the baby from Giovanni and laid her back in Maria's arms, ushering the two men outside. "Let them sleep," she said.

Outside in the sunlight Mario sat a few steps from the doorway and began rocking back and forth, talking happily to himself. Giovanni barely noticed: that was Mario's way, and besides, he himself was too excited to do anything more than pace back and forth while the midwife gave him instructions for the next several days.

The midwife was Giovanni's age, a good hearted woman who loved to gossip, but not out of a desire to hear of other's failings: she was given to worrying, and knowledge of others was her weapon to use against an uncertain world. Giovanni liked her, though he usually found her presence hard to endure since he didn't share in her love of talking. And somehow she always made him want to reassure her, to set her mind at ease, although he knew that was something that no one would ever do. While harmless in his estimation, she always left him feeling exasperated, so he had kept his contacts with her to a minimum. On this occasion, though, he was glad when she stood around after her business was completed, and he was more than willing to accommodate her when she started to speak.

"It has been months since you were down in the valley," she said.

"Yes."

"Your son is still very bitter at what has happened, and he says he won't forgive you soon for helping Maria and Mario." She was fishing for a reaction, but Giovanni decided not to give her one, and kept his voice even.

"Yes."

"Some in the village say it doesn't matter, but many are saying it is because you are an outsider, and you still have the Dionysian ways of behaving."

"So I have heard. But I don't think the Dionysians would be any happier with this situation than Roberto and the others." He wasn't annoyed, not on this day, but he wished her to change the subject. "Is there any other news?"

"Food supplies are low, but you know that. Ah, yes, there are more rumors of the plague. Have you heard about them?"

"I don't know. This plague is very bad, they say. It has come from the East and did terrible damage there. Last year it arrived in Sicily, but with the autumn it was said to have died away. It may have ended completely, or so I hear."

Though it struck Giovanni as somewhat macabre, the woman's voice had a hint of pleasure in it as she realized she had something new to add: she said with enthusiasm, "It is not over yet. In the winters it dies away, but in the spring it returns again. Travelers carry it from place to place. They say it is in Italy, in the South. Did you know they call it 'The Black Death'?"

"No, why?"

"I don't know. The Dionysians say it is a punishment from God. Of course that's just superstition. Some in the village say it could be a sign that our waiting will soon be over."

"What do you mean?"

"As you know, Apollo is sometimes the plague bringer, purifier of cities steeped in guilt and ignorance. Perhaps he is preparing the Dionysians for the time when we will again be welcomed in the world: perhaps this plague is a purification and it means the long night in Europe is almost over. The elders take that seriously: they have sent two men to Milan to gather information about it."

"I don't know about purification," said Giovanni, but if it comes here it could be very serious."

"Oh no, you don't have to worry about that, surely." She shot him an inquiring glance and when on hurriedly, "The Gods will protect us. This is a problem for the outsiders, not for us. We have survived all these centuries with divine help, and there is no reason the Gods would abandon us now. We should pity the outsiders, but everyone agrees: we don't have to fear for ourselves." Giovanni didn't notice much sign of pity in her voice, but that was to be expected when gossip provided such an intriguing and dangerous topic.

He wasn't sure he shared the general optimism. Of course he knew of Apollo's darker side, as Far-Shooter, who sent his arrows into a city so that a town would purify itself and welcome his light. But he wasn't certain if he believed such stories. And anyway, what made the villagers think they were so pure Apollo would pass them by? Perhaps the village had a special purpose dear to the Gods, but Giovanni was of the opinion that the failings of human nature were everywhere, even in the sanctuary, and the Gods might want to purify them before their time of secrecy ended. This woman's confidence seemed to him misplaced, perhaps even dangerous, and he hoped she was wrongly attributing her own confidence to others.

In any case, this talk of plague brought a deep disquiet to his heart that would stay with him in the coming weeks. Dread was to become his constant companion, and though he tried to let it go he could not. Strange that on the day of his great-granddaughter's birth there should waken such a dark dream, but when he thought about it, perhaps it was not so strange after all. A new birth was a cause for happiness, but it was also a source of fresh dangers since every life is uncertain. Perhaps this talk of plague had become a focus for other, less easily defined fears. Whatever their root, in the coming days he fought a losing battle with his superstitious dread. Of course he said nothing of it to Maria or Mario, since he did not want to spoil their happiness, which often seemed to verge on ecstasy. And he did not linger in conversation with the villagers he encountered at the cave. From the snatches of conversation he overheard there, the topic of the plague was common, but viewed with optimism. His doubts were his alone, it seemed.

At the time when everywhere the trees were pushing out their fresh green leaves and the birds were nesting with their mates, an assembly was called to discuss the plague. The wise were invited and Giovanni decided to attend as well, hoping he might find reassurance in their words.

Much was said but nothing softened Giovanni's dread. At one point he spoke out, obliquely hinting that there was at least a chance trouble might be coming, but no one seemed to take his point, and he could not bring himself to be more specific. To do so seemed to invite the very thing he feared. He knew it was childish superstition, but he consoled himself that there was not much he could do in any case.

At that time only two wise people lived at the head of the valley: the previous winter the other had died. When questioned by the villagers, both said much the same thing, talk of change and the sense that things were brightening, that spring might have at last arrived in Europe. That might have cheered Giovanni, but they spoke also of death as purification, and Giovanni noticed they did not rule out the possibility of the plague reaching the Sanctuary, though he alone seemed to have noticed the fact.

After the assembly closed, Giovanni was preparing to accompany Maria back to the mountain when Atropina suddenly appeared at his side, smiling and pulling at his sleeve. Bidding Maria to wait, he followed the old woman aside, wondering what she wanted. She led him away from the gathering and they stood at the base of an ancient tree before she said a word.

"The time for which you came is approaching, Giovanni. I heard the fear in your voice, so I know you have sensed it too. Don't be afraid. A life time's sorrows piled in a single lunar month may seem daunting, but it is bearable."

Fear leapt up in his throat at her words. It was difficult for him to speak. "Do you know something? Is the plague coming here?"

"Death is always present for the one who sees. Rebirth too. Calm yourself, my friend." She looked into his eyes for a moment. "But then you cannot, can you?"

"How can I be calm at such a time? We must warn the village, we must take steps to protect ourselves."

"Suffering is the only real harm, Giovanni. You are suffering now. You have enough wisdom to sense the passing of the seasons, but not enough to set free time's wheel and let it spin freely. That was your choice. That was the reason you were brought here. I don't know what your task is to be, but perhaps you are just here to witness what is to come. Who can say? Let the fear go, Giovanni, if you can. The Gods will not abandon us, though their wills are hard for mortals to accept. I do not know what will happen, but I feel great change is upon us. Change brings suffering to those who cannot accept it. That is always so. But change is not our enemy: this sanctuary was never intended to be permanent. Rebirth is coming, but birth is always painful, and often the child who comes is not what we expected. You should be ready for anything my friend, good and bad alike."

She smiled at him then, gentle as always, and turned and walked away. He stayed and watched her go. A minute later he returned to Maria. As he approached her, he forced himself to be cheerful, but as they walked back up the mountain that day, he could find little to say.

It wasn't until June, when the summer sun was high in the sky and the days were warm and bright, that death came to the sanctuary. It was welcomed to the village with greetings and handshakes. One of the men they had sent out for information several months before returned to the sanctuary. He brought grim news: the plague had arrived in the surrounding cities, and death was everywhere in the world outside. It was as if the earth had caught fire, and suddenly in every place terrified people were falling ill and dying in terrible pain. Men, women, children; wealthy or poor, no one was safe. Most who got sick never recovered. No one knew how to contain it. It was far worse than anyone had imagined in their worst nightmares: whole families, whole villages were dying. In the cities the corpses were stacked like wood out in the street to be collected for mass burial. Nothing so terrible had happened in the world before. His companion had died of it the previous week, and his terror as he described the symptoms of the disease in detail made his listeners panic: what if Apollo should decide not to spare them?

The optimists had suddenly lost many from their ranks as fear took hold, and they made the rounds of friends and family trying to reassure others and in that way to reassure themselves. At the messenger's suggestion, armed men were posted to prevent terrified outsiders from wandering into the village and bringing the plague with them: that was the method by which it went from place to place.

But even as they sought to save themselves, the storm was upon them already. There was no way to stop it. The day after he arrived, the messenger came down with a fever, and his joints grew painful. Swellings appeared in the groin, and over the next two days they grew until they were the size of hen's eggs. The pain was excruciating and he sometimes shrieked that his body was on fire. The messenger grew exhausted, and he panted and wheezed, even in his fitful sleep. The village stayed away in terror, but watched the situation closely.

Despite her fear, his wife sat by him in his time of need, and placed poultices on his groin, though they did little good. On the third day he grew steadily worse, and in the evening she fled his side to report that he had turned a horrible shade of dark, ashen blue. When an elder was sent to look in on him a few hours later, he saw from the doorway that the plague victim had died. No one was willing to touch the body or venture near it for fear of harmful vapors.

They burned the house down with the body inside it. The most optimistic among the villagers convinced themselves the danger was now over, that the victim had died because he had contacted the disease in the world beyond the Sanctuary's borders. Everyone else was safe, they argued, for here the disease would find no purchase. It was the last faint hope any of them would know.

The next day five others got sick, including the dead man's wife, and the day after that, seven more.

Giovanni was spending time alone on his mountain when the plague had come, and no one thought to tell him of it. He learned of what was happening when he visited the cave four days after it began, and he left immediately to warn Maria.

Her first inclination was to go down the mountain to be with the other villagers and her parents, to help if possible, and to learn more about what was happening. But Giovanni was firm: they must remain apart. Their responsibility was to their child. He made them swear to avoid anyone and to stay out of the way until the autumn chill again descended and made the land safe. Then he gave them all of his provisions, and moved them around the mountain to a tiny hut hunters sometimes used on the Eastern side. It was a rugged place of cliffs and forest, and he forced them to promise they would keep any stragglers away, with force if necessary. Mario wept at this, but Maria nodded grimly and took Giovanni's proffered crossbow: she understood there was no choice. It was a solemn parting, with Giovanni refusing several times to remain with them. He would go to the town in their stead.

As he walked away, he felt glad despite his dread, for he knew that the little family was as safe as any in Italy during those terrible days. Above all, it was Giulia he thought of, and he wondered if he would join her soon in the land of the dead.

The village he entered was not the same one he had been in just a few weeks before. The paths were deserted, and the sound of children playing had vanished like the wind. There were people about, but when they saw him from their doors and windows they closed their shutters and barred the doors as if he was an enemy who sought their death. At Roberto's door there was no answer at first, but then he heard his son on the other side. He told Giovanni to go, that they were not sick, so he should leave before he threatened them, and this he agreed to do.

There was no point in his remaining in the village it seemed, and he was just about to go back up the mountain to his cabin, when a door opened and a little girl, Rubio's child, came running over to him crying. Her parents were sick, she said, and begged him to help her. He followed her back inside. The girl's brother was already dead, and both parents were far along. Not knowing what to do, he sent the little girl to the shed out back, and tried to make the sick people as comfortable as he could. He tied a handkerchief over his nose and mouth, a precaution which seemed to offer little protection in his opinion, but was better than nothing.

That night the parents died and Giovanni moved on to another sick house, offering what help he could. The families that had so far avoided the scourge were quick to send him away, but the others gratefully accepted his help. It soon evolved that he would go from sick house to sick house, applying damp rags to fevered foreheads, making broth, carrying the bodies outside the houses—although there was not time to bury them properly—and whatever else was needed, before moving on to the next house and doing the same things all over again. On the second day Atropina appeared, down from the upper valley, and with scarcely a word settled in to help him on his rounds. The remaining wise man had himself fallen sick and had taken to his bed, and no one else was brave enough to risk getting close to those already stricken.

Giovanni was glad of Atropina's help: when she sat with the sick and held their hands, their fears seemed to vanish and the pain to lessen even when they were too delirious to recognize her, until she had to move on. She never lost her gentle good humor, her love or her compassion. Being near her was like being immersed in the cool waters of a lake while a fire raged everywhere around it.

After a week that seemed like a lifetime, it became obvious to Giovanni that no one was getting better once the disease had taken hold of them. Rumors from the outside world were that some survived, but this did not seem to be the case in the Sanctuary. To grow sick was to die in pain and terror three or four days later, without any exceptions. And in every case the victim darkened horribly until they were almost black in the hours before they died.

Some families escaped the town and fled up the mountains. Whether they managed to escape the disease as well was impossible to say: they just vanished. As a week became two weeks, and two became three, there was not a family in the valley that had been spared. Sick at heart Giovanni found himself visiting his son's house, and holding Roberto's hand as the spasms of pain wracked the younger man's body. They never talked about the troubles that had existed between them, and though nothing was said, Giovanni could see that beneath his terror Roberto was grateful to have him there. When Roberto sank into unconsciousness and eventually turned black, Giovanni let Atropina continue their rounds without him: he held his son's hand and watched him die. His daughter in law died the same day. No tears came, no grief. He was beyond all that now. Life was death, death was heartless: no one would be spared.

It was odd to him how he and Atropina seemed immune. So when, one morning, he grew sick too, he did not shun it. He felt no fear. He continued helping out at other's houses as long as he could, while the swellings grew ever more painful, seeming to his increasingly feverish mind like rats gnawing at the sinews of his body. But eventually he fainted and fell, cutting his forehead, and Atropina helped him to his son's house and put him to bed. It was his turn to ache and pant, his turn to be wracked by the pain. But fear never came to him: he welcomed the disease, now that it was his turn, and in his fevered dreams he saw Giulia and she smiled at him. Soon they would be reunited.

Time continued but lost all order. Atropina was there, then gone, then there again. Giulia was holding his hand...or was it Atropina? Giulia was dead. Or she was living, and he was dead. No, he was living: the pain told him that. But Guilia was pain also, so she must be living... Around and around his thoughts went, and there was no peace, not even for a moment. There was no peace at all....

He woke, suddenly, and remembered Atropina. Had she said to him "You will survive?" The memory of her voice came to him as if it were happening now, but she was nowhere to be seen. Was it a dream? He was alone in the room where his son had died. Perhaps the pain was less, perhaps a little less. Did that mean he was getting better, or readying to die? He tried to look at his arms, but couldn't bring himself to do it: death was one thing, but turning a hideous shade of blue was another. It was better not to know. He was too exhausted to ponder it long: it really didn't matter. He slipped back into the steady stream of nightmares, and slept once more.

When he woke again, it was night. Where was Atropina? Had she come when he was sleeping and then left? He felt lonely, but too tired to move. How long had he been sick? He couldn't say. The end must come soon...soon. He realized he was unbearably thirsty, that it must be at least a day since he had anything to drink. Looking around, he caught sight of the dim shape of a jug on a table beside him in the moonlight. Panting with exertion he raised himself up a little and took hold of it, drinking deeply, water splashing pleasant and cool against his chest. He mustn't waste it: gasping with exhaustion, he tried to put the jug back but couldn't. Instead he set it against his leg and hoped he would lie still so it wouldn't spill. Then he slept again.

When he opened his eyes, the light hurt them. Squinting he saw the jug against his leg, and it reminded him he was thirsty again. Feebly he took hold of it with both hands and raised it to his lips. He drank, spilling some again on his neck. The action exhausted him. Setting the jug down, he wondered where Atropina was. Had she fallen sick? He listened, but heard nothing except the wind in the trees and the sounds of birds singing somewhere in the distance. The birds were not getting sick, it seemed. Perhaps the world was not coming to an end after all. And his pain was definitely less. His groin throbbed, and his armpits, but it was not so bad as it had been before.

For the rest of the day, Giovanni forced himself to stay awake. He wanted to see Atropina when she came and to ask her what was happening. She never came. At last, as dusk settled across the valley while he watched, Giovanni gave up and let sleep take him. In his dreams he heard weeping, and it was Giulia's voice, but he couldn't see her.

When he woke, light was again streaming in the window, and again there was no sign of human voices. Was he the only one left alive? He picked up the jug and drank the last of the water. His arms seemed stronger now, but if he didn't get something more to drink, he would certainly die. He dropped the jug off the edge of the bed and listened to it break on the floor. Then he moved his legs to the edge and let them drop off too, and used the force of their fall to rotate himself to a sitting position. He felt weak and nauseous, but he managed to stay upright. After a moment he felt stronger. He pushed himself to the edge of the bed and then off it, on to his legs, but they couldn't take the strain and he collapsed to the floor.

Opening his eyes, he saw the broken jug beside him. He laid there watching it for a while, gathering his strength, then he began to drag himself. He crossed the bedroom and then the kitchen, exiting by the back door. His body ached, but he ignored it. Across the yard he came to a low tangle of bushes and with effort made it past them. Then down a hill, through a stand of trees, another little hill, and he was beside the stream. How long the journey had taken him he would never know. It seemed a lifetime. He lay with his arms in the water for a moment resting, and then he began to drink. It seemed his thirst would never end, and he had to stop often to regain his breath. He retched a few times, his stomach unused to the cold water, but managed to keep from being sick. At last he had enough and dropping his head down on his arms, he closed his eyes and rested. He did not sleep, however, and he found himself listening to the sounds around him: the bubbling stream, the birdsong, a cricket in the grass on the far bank. He had survived.

It seemed he could feel the water he had drunk seeping into his limbs and restoring their strength. He found he could sit upright, and holding onto a fallen tree's branches, he pulled himself to his feet. He could stand. Slowly he turned and walked back the way he had came. From time to time he had to lean against a tree and catch his breath, but his strength was definitely returning. His head still ached and his joints seemed to creak painfully, but he found he could walk quite well as long as he kept his pace to a feeble shuffle.

He didn't return to Roberto's house. He walked into the main path and went from house to house, looking for signs of life. There were none. In several of the houses there were corpses on the beds, and they stank so badly he wretched to be near them. He kept going.

Eventually he found Atropina. She was lying in a bed that wreaked of urine, panting and unconscious, but still alive. She had placed a jug of water by that bed too, and it was half full. She didn't respond when he tried to waken her. He drank some of the water and made the painful journey back to the stream to refill the jug. When he returned, he went into the kitchen and took hold of a loaf of moldy, stale bread from a shelf. He went back to the bedroom and sat at the foot of her bed, and ate several mouthfuls. Exhaustion came to him, so he curled up where he was and slept like a dead man, a deep and dreamless sleep.

The next morning Giovanni was not well, but he was certainly better. Atropina had not moved, so he went to her side and lifted her head, pouring a few drops of water onto her dry lips. Though she did not wake up, she licked, and he poured more water onto them. It was a slow process, but apparently effective, and eventually he was satisfied that she must have had enough. He went upstairs and discovered a body in bedroom. The door had thankfully been closed so the smell of the rotting corpse had remained in the little room. He couldn't identify the person, so swollen was the face. It took him almost an hour of hard work to drag the body wrapped in the bed sheet out of the house and into a neighbor's shed. He threw some straw over it and left it there.

Then he went out to explore the village, meeting with tragedy everywhere he went. Not a single person was left alive. House after house was empty or worse, but nowhere was there any sign of life. This fact was acknowledged, but failed to bring any emotion: he was too dull to feel anything. It was only later he realized that at that time he had been still more dead than alive.

The following day Atropina's eyes fluttered when he was feeding her the water, and she opened them. When they focused on him, he sensed in himself the first twinge of emotion he had felt since he'd begun to recover. It was hope. He smiled, and a slight whisper of a smile came to her face too, though it didn't last long. She fell asleep again.

The sacred flame had vanished from the village, extinguished with no one to feed it. Giovanni had to create a new fire, and it saddened him to think how something so old could disappear unnoticed: it might still exist on the mountain with Maria and Mario to protect it, but he realized the day was coming when it might disappear forever and no one would even know of its passing. The thought of it was too harsh to bear, and he busied himself with making gruel and cleaning Atropina up, changing her sheets and bathing her with a rag.

It wasn't until the following day that she regained the power of speech, and until the day after that she felt well enough to sit up for a few minutes. It was only then that Giovanni realized for certain that she too would survive.

"It was on the fourth day after you got sick that I realized you had turned the corner and you might not die," said Atropina that morning. Until then they had not wasted energy in unnecessary speech. "By then the fever had already struck me. I left water by your bed—I guess you found it—and came here. Do you know how long ago that was?" Giovanni shook his head. She sighed. "And what of the others. Are there any...?"

"None."

She nodded. It was expected.

Several days later they began the difficult work of collecting the corpses and burying them. Some of the bodies had been gnawed at by starving dogs, some had been pecked at by birds. It was hard to believe that not so long before these stinking piles of carrion had been men, women, and children.

Giovanni had seen a hole behind someone's house, perhaps the beginnings of a storage cellar. It was quite wide and deep. For a day and a half they dragged the bodies there and dropped them in. Then they shoveled the dirt over top and walked straight to the stream, sitting in it, trying to wash away the smell of death that clung to their clothes and hair, even to their skin.

Giovanni wondered about his granddaughter and Mario, but it was unthinkable that he should visit them now. He might still have the plague around him. He would have to wait until the fall to find out if they survived. He and Atropina decided to go back up the valley to her hut. They gathered some grain from the empty homes, and other items, wrapping them in sheets and carried these across their shoulders.

There was another body in Atropina's cabin, and another near the stream outside. They buried them, and threw out every piece of cloth that had become permeated by the smell, and moved in. Giovanni avoided talking with Atropina: he was afraid of what she would say. But there came a time when the two of them sat beside the little brook and talk was inevitable.

"What will you do now?" asked Atropina.

"What do you mean?"

"With the sanctuary gone and the villagers gone, do you intend to stay here?"

"I thought you said I had a purpose here. Are you saying it's done? Now? Did I spend my whole life in this sanctuary just to bury it?"

"Perhaps." She smiled. "But that depends on you: for me that would be enough, but for you...you are very stubborn, Giovanni. If you don't know what you will do, then I guess we will find out together what is in your heart."

"Was this place, this sanctuary, of no importance?" Giovanni was pleading for justice and meaning, though whether of Atropina, himself, or the Gods he could not say. "Were all the nine-hundred years in hiding and the thousands of years of building before that nothing?"

"Perhaps. What difference does it make whether it was a minute or ten thousand years? When it is gone, it is gone. It cannot return. It is no longer real, no longer important. Let it go.

"Does it not seem strange to you that the sanctuary ever existed at all? It was based on the understanding that death follows life as the wheel of time dictates. Death of all things is inevitable. The death of the ancient ways was inevitable. But then why did the founders of the sanctuary believe that the little portion of the ancient ways hidden in this valley would be immune for ever? If death is the law, then this too must die. Death follows life, and rebirth follows death. That is how it works. The new life is separated from the old life by death: they never touch. The founders of the sanctuary seem to have dreamed that the old life will continue through death and into the new life. That is not the law. For the new life to begin, the old life must die: there can be no overlap. Knowledge must be entirely forgotten.

"That man, what was his name? Marcus: the wealthy Roman who paid for the building of this sanctuary. He must have been as stubborn as you are, Giovanni. He spent a lot of money to establish us here to await for the time of rebirth. And actually, I believe the night is over: this sanctuary has survived until the very instant before the dawn. Perhaps the only thing preventing the rebirth of civilization is our existence here, stubbornly, year after year. Who knows?"

"Atropina, it hurts me to hear you speak this way. I watched you when the plague was in the village: I know you have compassion and love. But here is a thing that so much passion and energy have been directed towards, and you care nothing about it, nothing at all. Is all the knowledge gathered by our forefathers worth nothing?"

"No, Giovanni, not nothing. But knowledge is like anything else touched by mortal minds and hearts: it is always in need of purification. Death is purification. Our knowledge regarding the Gods and nature is not perfect, therefore it will benefit from purification. Trust the Gods and let go of the past. Let knowledge die and it will be reborn in a higher form, hold on to it and it will die forever.

"Even as we speak, I can see you are not going to let go and I suppose that is probably why you came here: to hold on even into death. You are a very stubborn man, Giovanni. It was stubbornness that brought you back to the sanctuary all those years ago when you could have left it. I was a young mother at the time and blind to all wisdom: I remember watching you when they brought you back to the town all beaten and bloody. We were afraid of you then, but you had been too certain of your passions to realize it would be so. It has been stubbornness that made you cling to your dead wife decade after decade. Stubbornness that kept you on the mountain above the sanctuary, staying apart, yet never leaving. And you have seen the bridge to the other world, the world of the Gods, but your stubbornness kept you from crossing it. Stubbornness is usually an ugly trait in human beings, but in your case it is excusable, I think. You are sometimes stubborn out of love for others.

"And here is what leaves me uncertain what will happen next: death is inevitable, but love alone provides the means to transcend it. Not to prevent death, you understand: that is impossible. But to die and yet reach through time with that love which is eternal in every moment..." Suddenly she laughed. "Forget it Giovanni! I talk too much. Let's just wait and see what happens." Abruptly she got up and walked away chuckling to herself, leaving Giovanni to puzzle things out for himself.

The summer passed without much event. Several outsiders came to the village, but finding evidence that the plague had been there they did not stay, heading farther into the mountains in hopes of safety. For Giovanni it was a time of suffering and misery, for Atropina it was apparently like any other summer. Except for one thing: neither she nor Giovanni fully regained their health. The ravages of the disease had left them physically weaker, and there were a few other, lesser complaints that troubled them. Giovanni's neck and fingers suffered from painful arthritis on many days, and his hearing had been damaged. Atropina found she retained only partial control of her bladder, and had to relieve herself frequently or risk incontinence. She too had arthritis in her fingers now, though only in one hand. Sometimes, under the soothing spell of Atropina's detachment, Giovanni laughed with her to see how time had made them cripples.

ime is a barrier that often seems impregnable, and yet it always passes, always falls. What begins in Spring with a burst of hope may last through Summer's brilliant days, but Winter always comes at last—and with it, the cold embrace of death.

Nine long centuries before Far Shooter came calling at the Italian Sanctuary, far away in the town of Delphi on the side of Mount Parnassos, a meeting was called when the first cruel touches of autumnal frost were descending upon the Greco-Roman world. From all over Greece the servants of the Gods were called to discuss the tidings and see what might be done. The question they asked was simple enough: might knowledge and civilization be somehow saved? Their answer was extraordinary: it would echo down through time, reverberating even to the present day, though not in quite the form they had imagined...

THE HIDING: THE TALE OF MARCUS AND THE FOUNDATION OF SANCTUARY

(Delphi and The Taro River Valley, 364 - 389 AD)

A s he rode past the grounds of the temple of Apollo, past the old gate of the Sacred Way into the sanctuary, Marcus could see the decay. Leaves and other detritus littered the path, and several of the old treasuries were visible from where he went by—empty now, and beginning to crumble from lack of maintenance. The grounds appeared to be deserted. On the wall by the gate someone had drawn the sign of the cross and the words 'Devils out!' in white paint. It appeared to be fresh. He sighed and glanced at Daphne, but she didn't notice for she too had recognized the depressing signs of decline, and was craning her head to catch a better glimpse. As for Caliphas, there were tears in his eyes and he was wiping them away with his wrist, but the old slave tried to smile at him from behind his arm as he did so. Marcus felt a lump in his throat and looked away.

When they arrived in the town of Delphi it seemed almost deserted, the shops and houses mostly shuttered, and those inhabitants they did pass stared at them curiously but without warmth. With a heavy heart Marcus called down to an old man they passed, "Where can I find the house of Telias, the priest?", but the man just looked at him and made no reply, turning and vanishing into an open doorway, slamming the door behind him. His next attempt was more successful: a little boy dressed in rags agreed to take them to the house, though it appeared he did so unwillingly, out of a habit of respect for greater age and wealth perhaps.

Dread and gloom seemed to rise out of the very stones of the town, so Marcus was pleasantly surprised when the battered gate to the small villa opened, revealing his beaming host who shook hands warmly and immediately saw to it that their horses were led away to be stabled. Telias was a man of only thirty-five or so, energetic and with a face that was quick to smile. Marcus noticed that he treated his slaves with gentleness, and that they seemed to bear Telias genuine affection without a trace of fear. If not for their slave collars, Marcus might have thought them members of a single happy family with Telias at its head. Though he could not approve of such latitude, Marcus was not unduly troubled: Telias was neither Roman nor patrician, and could not be expected to behave with that restraint which only good breeding and blood provide. As a priest of fairly humble birth he ought to be granted some leeway. In any case, there was something about Telias he could not define that made him agreeable. Despite being twenty-five years his senior, Marcus liked him immediately and looked forward to working with him.

Being tired and stiff from the traveling, they declined the late lunch they were offered, and after washing in basins provided for that purpose, they retired to rest. Caliphas was led away to the slave's quarters. A servant brought extra pillows and another chair to Marcus' bedroom when it was realized that Daphne, though a slave, would be staying with him.

Alone in the room, Daphne walked over to Marcus and put her arms around him, settling her head against his chest. Saying nothing, they stood for several minutes, rocking back and forth gently, until she pulled away and led him by the hand to bed. They didn't make love, although he saw the desire in her face: he was unable to shake the depression the town's condition had settled on him. But he kissed her softly on the lips and held her tightly, telling her of his love, and of the joy she made him feel in spite of his sorrow at what they had seen.

She fell asleep some time later, while he watched, and if she had wanted him at that moment he would have gladly made love for his passion inflamed him suddenly. Reaching over, he touched her gently on the arm but she didn't stir, so he let her sleep. Instead he distracted himself by considering what his words would be when the conference began tomorrow. He wanted his speech to set things on a positive course. It seemed to him it was the most important speech of his life, so he'd better get it right.

When they rose late in the afternoon, the sun was lying low towards the West and the autumn chill could already be felt in the air. Marcus dined with Telias and another conference attendee, a member of the Eumolpid dynasty of Athens. Their talk was light and witty, more of a symposium than a simple meal. Telias, it turned out, was a traditionalist while the Athenian took an ardent Platonic approach to things. Marcus mostly let them talk, delighted to listen as they strung together spontaneous rhymes and quoted ancient authors in a light hearted contest of words and ideas around the subject of aesthetics. Though he was well tutored and knew the sources they referred to, Marcus was clearly out classed by their easy confidence and swiftness of thought. If they thought less of him for his clumsiness they never showed it, and he was comfortable in his role as audience for their intellectual gymnastics. Everyone enjoyed themselves greatly.

Heavy with wine, they retired early and Marcus took the opportunity to make amends to Daphne for his lack of passion that afternoon. Because he was quite drunk, Marcus was unable to release his seed, but he watched her ecstasy by lamp light, drinking in her joy. Her pleasure was the most wonderful thing he had ever seen, just as it always was: not for the first time he realized he had no other pressing reason for living—beyond the single obligation every Roman patrician shared: to do as duty demanded, both for family and for Empire. In the aftermath they settled in each others arms, and this time it was her who watched as he fell asleep.

When they awoke shortly before dawn they heard the sounds of several men being greeted out by the front gate. They must be some of the others, arriving to begin the conference. Marcus and Daphne rose and dressed themselves rapidly, descending the stairs to make their entrance before their host. In the banquet room some eight or nine men reclined, speaking in hushed voices, but on seeing his guests had already risen, the host loudly introduced Marcus to the small crowd. Daphne left to join the other members of the household—naturally she was not expected to attend the conference.

Several minutes passed in small talk while Telias' slaves were sent to fetch the others from the houses where they had been billeted. Once they had arrived, Marcus counted some eighteen people squeezed around the little room, not including himself. He was impatient and not at all happy at the prospect of waiting for the five who were missing, but then his host informed him they had sent word they would be unable to attend, so it was time to begin. Marcus stood, and beckoned for silence. All eyes turned to him.

"Good sirs, let me begin by thanking you for attending. I am sorry for the urgency and secrecy of my request, but as you know matters have become very serious and continue to worsen almost by the day. Had I invited you here more openly and formally as your positions deserve, I fear our enemies would have prevented or at least disrupted our meeting. I give thanks to Minerva, Mercury and Apollo, and to all the other Gods, that we have managed to keep our conference secret up until now, and I pray that we will succeed in reversing the terrible madness which is swallowing Rome and destroying her people's morals and character. That is our task.

"I am, as some of you may know, a wealthy man. My family's holdings of land in Italy have made us one of the wealthiest in the Western empire. While you have been called here because of your wisdom and knowledge, I am here solely because of my wealth and power. I will, with your permission, attend these talks since I have funded them. But be assured that I do not intend to use my position to guide matters: if anyone can stem the growth of our enemies, it is you. Your deliberations are valued greatly by me and I don't expect to add anything much to them.

"Good sirs, like you I am deeply troubled by the movement of history and the growing ascendancy of the Christians. As I arrived here yesterday, I was overcome by the site of Apollo's great oracle fallen into neglect and enmity. This town, which for more than a thousand years has greeted travelers from all the known world, is emptying since it can no longer support its population on the profits it once made from pilgrims. Even on the gates of Apollo's sanctuary I have seen the ignorant, hateful graffiti of the Christians. Gentlemen: I fear for Delphi and I fear for Rome.

"All educated men know that in the aftermath of the Trojan war, the peoples of Greece lived for centuries in darkness. Why this war destroyed civilization we will never know, but it would seem we may be poised on the edge of yet another dark age. Rome may not perish completely, it's true, though I sometimes wonder how it can survive with its people bewitched. But even if the taxes continue to be collected and the Pax Romana prevails, surely the appalling ignorance of the Christians constitutes a new dark age. It is as though a dark cloud is falling over the Empire, and the Romans are marching dully to their own destruction. Fear and intolerance are growing everywhere. We cannot allow this to happen.

"You may wonder why I came here, to the Eastern empire. There are two reasons. Firstly, I did try to encourage action by your counterparts in the West, but they are so demoralized that nothing could prompt them to action. For them, I fear it is too late. Secondly, I have always looked to Greece for much of civilization's brightness, and we have need of that light now.

"I have personally suffered the tragedy of our times. My wife has become a Christian. She hates her own body as a thing to be feared and raises my children to do the same. Everything to her is full of demons, including me: it has been more than ten years since she has slept in my bed. I have watched this pernicious fear of imaginary evils grow in her until she cannot do anything without the advice of the sycophantic priests of Christ. She does not see that they crave her money and that their words about sacrificing for the next world serve their interests in this one. I terrify her, as if I were a monster, because I honor the old ways. I still love my wife, but now she lives only in my memory. The woman I married, with her love of pleasure, art and refinement, with her laughter and kindness, is dead.

"I fear for Rome. Will this insane cult of atheists destroy Her too?

"This does not have to happen. I may be powerless to save my wife but we have something in you which the Christians don't have: we have true wisdom and the guidance of the Gods. With these two things a solution can be found. It must be found. I know others have tried before and failed, but quitting is not a Roman trait anymore than submitting to ignorance is a trait of the Greeks. The solution exists. We must find it. I am certain we will.

"It may be said the old religion is losing ground so rapidly that there are not men and resources to put into practice the solution you will propose.

That is not true! Many still honor the old Gods throughout the empire and need only leadership and a goal to direct them. You will give them that goal. And as to resources, you have mine. If necessary I will spend myself to ruin in our cause. Please consider, as you discuss your options, that my fortune is no longer mine: it belongs to the Gods. Spend it in whatever way will please them.

"I suggest, good sirs, that we begin with a detailed assessment of our current position. Let each delegate report what his own sanctuary's condition is, and that of the believers and Christians they have encountered so that we may know the problems we face and the strengths we bring. I will try to report to you the situation in the West, for I have traveled recently and seen what is happening.

"If you like I will serve as chairman of our meeting, but I will press no claim to do so. Although I am not so fully initiated as you, I have at least attended the mysteries at Eleusis in my youth, both the Lesser and Greater, so you should be able to talk openly in front of me without fear, unless matters even more secret come up. If you would prefer to see me as nothing more than the manager of your funds, I will be happy to take that role. I have no interest in flattery or deference. This is too important for such things to have any place. Use me, in the name of the Gods, in whichever way will serve Them best. If you do so, I will thank you."

Marcus sat down abruptly and let them discuss what he'd said, but although he sat quietly, he was filled with anticipation and bright hopes for their meeting. He was a blunt and willful man, and he was determined to see the matter through. It was a matter of pride to him that he never let himself be swayed by fear or doubt, and that he allied himself to whatever he knew to be true and honorable no matter what the cost.

After a brief discussion and vote, his proposals were accepted by the group: he would chair the meeting, and each attendee would begin with a detailed report of the problem as he saw it. It was agreed that Telias would be first, describing the situation at Delphi, and after an opening speech in which he thanked Marcus for his patronage and generosity, he started by detailing the sequence of local events as he recalled them.

It was a grim morning, as one after another each took his turn to speak. The news was almost all bad. While everywhere believers continued to worship in the old ways, their numbers were gradually shrinking. Apathy had infected those who remained true to the faith of their fathers, and prospective initiates had shrunk to such a level that many of the cult centers could no longer sustain their priesthoods. Delphi had been without a Sybil for years, and in fact most of the oracles great and small had fallen silent. The sacred fire burned on in Apollo's temple, but fewer and fewer towns sent their citizens to fetch a graft of the flame and take it back to their city's central hearth. Without pilgrims to meet the cost of their maintenance, temples and sanctuaries were falling into disrepair. Although officially persecution of Pagans was not allowed, individual bishops throughout the empire were inciting their flocks to hatred and fear. With increasing frequency such feelings led to mobs attacking Pagan institutions, and in some places they had rioted and smashed the priceless ancient objects which the Gods had given to men long ago. A few of the cult centers had hidden such artifacts away, though that seemed at best a temporary measure. These outrages were generally met with official disinterest, and this meant more violence could be expected in the future.

The feeling every speaker expressed was of inevitability: the brief moments of hope, as when the emperor Justin had supported the old ways, never flickered for long. Justin was dead and replaced by a new Christian emperor almost before he had got started.

Some of the speakers referred to the persecution of the Christians in previous centuries, saying that retribution might be a factor in their violence. But this view did not prevail. Christians were persecuted by emperors for failing to worship in the imperial cult at a time when it was thought to bind the empire together and protect the peace. Their persecution was simply a matter of securing the empire by strengthening the emperors. When Christians were still a small and unknown minority many Pagans had believed they were dealing with an antisocial cult of atheists, assisting the magistrates enthusiastically. But as the number of Christians had increased, they became better known and understood, and by the time the persecutions came to an end most Pagans had reverted to their customary tolerance for the beliefs of others.

Pagan tolerance was alien to the Christians: had they not already begun to turn in anger and hatred against other Christians who did not exactly share their dogmatic beliefs? And yet some of the delegates took pains to show that the Christians were people like any others: some greedy, some generous; some pious, some hypocritical. Though Marcus found their tolerance difficult to share, he had to admit there was some truth in what they said.

At this point, everyone at the meeting agreed they were in need of a respite, so they took a break for lunch which they shared together in the conference room. After lunch, the meeting continued. Now the speakers began to describe the Christian cult itself, on the principle that you must know your opposition if you wish to prevail against him. There was a broad consensus.

Christians were clearly a Dionysian cult that had forgotten its roots and lost sight of all the other Gods. For Marcus this was an unfamiliar idea, and he asked the others to explain it to him which they subsequently did.

First, like Dionysos, Christ spanned both mortal and divine worlds, sharing the wisdom gained by living, dying, and living again, so that his followers could gain power over death. Though a God, he shared the mortal lot. In both cases this death and rebirth were the central part of the Gods' cult, and the means by which the Gods' followers hoped to achieve immortality.

Second, the wine of the Eucharist, so fundamental to Christian ritual, was an obvious parallel to the association of Dionysos with wine.

Third, Christ had been killed and entered into death for three days before coming back to life, while Dionysos was also said to have been killed and dwelled in the underworld for one third of the year before being reborn. In both cases the mystic three divisions of time were alluded to in the myths.

Fourth, as Christians focused on the cross, Dionysians often referred in myth and cult practice to the vine from which Dionysos hung, the living tree of life which had its roots buried in the underworld of the dead.

Fifth, as Christ was the son of the heavenly father, Dionysos was the son of Zeus.

Sixth, both Gods had a mortal mother rescued from death by her son.

Seventh, even some of the more obscure details of Christian belief reflected Pagan practice. For example, the myth of the trumpet blast leading to the resurrection of the dead in the Christian book of Revelations and elsewhere was closely paralleled by the cult practice of Dionysian priests at the Alcyonian lake at Lerna and in other locations: the priests blew trumpets to recall the God and the souls of his followers from death. Even the Jewish religion from which Christianity sprang seemed to overlap on matters familiar to Greek Pagans. For example, it was noted the Book of Ezekiel in the Old Testament made reference to wheels that clearly had the same roots as the God wheels of the zodiac and the sun wheels here at Delphi.

One delegate suggested Mithras might be a better parallel than Dionysos, but this Persian God had been a recent addition to the Empire's pantheon, and to the assembled priests whose vision reached down through the centuries, he was also Dionysian in nature. That Christians had adopted elements of Mithras' popular cult in their pursuit of converts did not make Christ essentially Mithraic.

Without question the myth of Christ's life fit well within the range of myth that described Dionysos. There were Pagan cults of Dionysos that were more at variance with mainstream Pagan worship of the God than was the cult of the Christians. Christianity only differed seriously in that it had lost its roots, declaring Dionysos and his father Zeus the only Gods, demoting all the others to the status of evil spirits.

The existence of such a cult among the Jews was hardly surprising, since Greek influence had been very strong in the Middle East from the time when Alexander the Great had conquered the area and the Seleucid dynasty had been established, bringing a strong Greek influence to the area. And it need not have come directly from a Greek root in any case, since Gods like Dionysos were recognized in the ancient religions throughout the region long before the Greeks became a people. Indeed, Dionysos was known in Persia by that name even before he was adopted by the Greeks.

Whether Christ had actually existed no one could say, but if he did then his life had clearly fit the divine archetype of Dionysos. Christ, it was agreed, was probably a mortal hero following in the path laid out by the God. But whether hero or the God himself, his followers had somehow lost sight of Dionysos' respect for the other Gods. All sense of balance and harmony was lost. Their thinking had narrowed and become rigid: where the ancient religion welcomed diversity and on-going discovery through revelation and thought, Christians hated diversity and believed everything essential had already been revealed. This meant Christians mostly looked backwards at their religious texts while Pagans looked to the past, present and future for understanding. Christians generally used reason only in understanding the revelations of the past, while Pagans used reason and on going revelation to discover more and more about the world of men and divinity and the relationship between them.

There was something very troubling about Christianity's emphasis on blind faith. Everyone apparently remained a basic level initiate, with the higher mysteries reflected in Christian myth ignored and forgotten even by the leadership. It seemed strange, for example, that Christians did not understand the significance of the Trinity of Father, Son, and Holy Spirit, something which even intermediate level Pagan initiates like Marcus knew very well. Air, Earth, and the Water that united them, along with the many significant parallels to this trinity in nature, were well known to Dionysians in all the other cults. This new cult accepted the trinity (heretics aside) but apparently had no idea of its parallels in Nature. The same was true of all the other symbolic elements in their religion.

Intrigued by this ignorance, most of the delegates had probed the Christians they knew, and several had even discussed Christian symbolism at length with their local bishops, yet the Christians apparently neither knew nor cared about the deeper meanings of the things they believed. They may have been hiding their secrets from non-initiates, which would have been understandable, but this did not appear to be the case. The impression they gave was of men who knew nothing and therefore had nothing to hide. They apparently believed that wisdom came entirely by grace, even to the most ignorant and foolish of men.

It was annoying but not surprising that many Christians believed they and the Jews were the first to recognize one great God, although many educated Pagans had believed the same for centuries. As the Christian trinity expressed the Godhead, so the Pagans saw a wider expression of it in a host of Gods. Christians had simply decided that the other Gods were angels or devils. This was not alien to some Pagans, who by and large believed the same. And some of the Pagan philosophers had argued that Gods were nothing more than a description of the elements and their relationships to each other as expressed in nature, with a single Creator poised above all. Here at Delphi, this was a majority view among the priesthood. But Christians, even educated ones, seemed to prefer ignoring such roots for their ideas, or seeing them at best as premonitions of the coming of Christ.

As Marcus had pointed out, another troubling factor was the distaste Christians had for their own bodies. Fasting and avoiding sex were things many Pagans did from time to time, but Christians had made these things rigid ideals. The God-given joy of pleasure had become a thing of loathing, so that men and women who refused to take lovers and create children were thought to be closest to divinity. Putting aside the absurdity of this (since God or Gods had clearly created the world and human love was a parallel source of creation, an expression of divinity on earth) this hatred of a basic human impulse had gone to bizarre extremes: some Christians, admittedly a minority though a widely admired one, had castrated themselves or mortified their bodies through starvation. It did not seem to be an exaggeration to say that Christianity had declared war on nature. Such extremes of mortification had existed occasionally in Pagan cult, but not as a denial of nature: they were generally symbolic acts paralleling some aspect of nature, not reviling it. (The followers of Adonis, for example, had been known to castrate themselves when possessed by the God, a parallel of the seeds that were separated from the father tree, especially in the case of the almond.)

The cause of Christianity's strange division of the world into good and evil was not hard to find. Although the concept may have originally come from the Manacheans, Christianity had embraced the idea of evil, a thing not known previously except in a milder form to some of the philosophical sects. Christians had made the world a battleground between good and evil. Where the old religion saw prayers being answered only by Gods, Christians saw them being answered by either demons or angels. If a Pagan prayed and received some result, it was said to be answered by demons. If a Christian prayed and received exactly the same result, it was said to be the work of angels. In fact, if a Christian belonged to a different sect so that his beliefs were slightly different, the answer to his prayers were also thought to come from demons. This stubborn refusal to accept variations in the experience of others was a nearly universal trait among the Christians.

And there was a more subtle expression of the invention of evil. It had become the focus for every form of fear, amplifying that emotion wherever it existed. While some philosophers had viewed religious fear as a consequence of ignorance and most other Pagans had viewed it as an expression of humility before the Gods or as a response to simple threats to self interest, Christians often saw it as a direct perception of the presence of evil. Anything they feared tended to be considered evil in its nature. Since all men fear their enemies, Christians tended to see evil in anyone who opposed their collective wills. Behind any resistance Christians were inclined to see the action of absolute fear and destruction personified as Satan. To attack one's enemies was to attack Satan. This was not something they had invented, of course. But they had come dangerously close to making it an article of their faith where before it had been a mark of individual prejudice and ignorance.

With Christianity clearly on the rise, Christians were not presently much afraid of believers in the old ways, viewing their own religion as superior and its opponents as feeble fools. For now they seemed inclined to direct most of their religious hatred and fear towards other followers of Christ who varied in matters of dogma. But if they succeeded in uniting themselves as they were striving to do, they might one day find a target for their fears in Pagans, and then there would be serious trouble. And if this counsel did indeed achieve a reverse in fortune for the old ways, it might well give rise to a great deal of violence when the Christians counterattacked.

Marcus found such talk of fear and intolerance both satisfying and vaguely unsettling. It gave voice to his own experiences, which pleased him, but it also seemed to imply that tolerance was a greater virtue than intolerance. This he found impossible to accept. Wasn't it Christ himself who said it was best to 'turn the other cheek?' It was ironic that the Christians ignored this argument in favor of weakness, while Pagans who should know better were so quick to espouse it. It was just such feebleness which threatened the empire. But Marcus held his tongue, since on the whole things seemed to be moving in a direction he approved of. Better to wait and see.

Exploring the peculiarities of Christian belief and its potential exhausted the last of the afternoon and early evening. When the meeting was winding down, everyone's spirits were at a very low ebb. To discuss the dreadful state of the world was to be overcome by the tragedy of it. The discussion had been fairly animated earlier, but by the end it was characterized by silences punctuated with brief illustrations and additions to the list of disasters. The sense of listless despair had infected everyone.

Seeing what had happened, and wishing to end on a more positive note, Marcus adjourned the meeting with a brief speech which he struggled to infuse with optimism. "Before we end for the day, let us consider what we have accomplished and what still lies ahead. We have come to understand the depth of the problem more clearly than before. And we have understood the origins and nature of the Christian cult. Understanding brings power. It has been difficult, I know, for each of us, and we would not be human if we felt cheerful in the face of this depressing subject. But we should not let our low spirits prevent us from the work we have yet to do. The most painful part of our task lies behind us. Let us begin tomorrow with the means we can use to counter the growth of the Christian cult. Surely nothing happens unless the Gods will it, and although things look very difficult who could imagine the Gods have willed all mankind to fall into ignorance and intolerance? I believe our meeting here fulfills a divine plan that will halt the decay and preserve Rome and the old ways. Let us enjoy Telias' meal in good cheer, leaving aside our difficulties for now. So if no one disagrees, let us adjourn."

While dinner began with silence, wine and more cheerful topics soon had everyone engaged in humorous and challenging discussions. Marcus noted the development with relief, settling in to enjoy the wit and culture for which educated Greeks were justly renowned. The dinner party became quite animated, the revelers breaking into several small but passionate discussions on matters philosophical and political. It was a repeat of the previous evening for him, but considerably enlivened by the greater numbers of participants.

At one point Telias, who was sitting on Marcus' right side, took advantage of a particularly raucous exchange on the far side of the group and leaned over to speak quietly to him. "I am sorry to hear about your wife," he said.

Marcus smiled and said "Don't worry: it's something I grew accustomed to long ago. At first it filled me with sadness to see what was happening, but as time passed I stopped caring."

"I gather," said Telias enigmatically, "you have that beautiful slave Daphne to take your mind off your troubles. You must feel fortunate to be able to afford such consolations." Whether it was envy or disapproval that led him to guard his manner Marcus could not say, but being in good spirits, he really didn't care.

He had just been taking a mouthful of wine when he heard these words, and being temporarily unable to speak, he shook his head, swallowed, and placed his cup back on the table. "I am fortunate, yes, but Daphne is not as you imagine. It is her choice to remain a slave."

Telias laughed with surprise. "She chooses slavery? That is something rare and strange, is it not? I hear a story behind your words and I would love to hear it, if you are willing."

"It's not what you think: her reasons are very sound and although it may seem strange, in her place any other good woman might do the same thing. Perhaps I should start from the beginning? It might take a while." Telias was sincere in his insistence, so Marcus decided to indulge him.

"From my youth I was always able to afford keeping five or six slave girls to satisfy my urges. I had little restraint in this respect, but my parents tolerated it since my father shared the same vice. He freely allowed me to use his girls once I was old enough to desire them. And when I came of age, he actually began my collection by giving me my first, a beautiful Germanic girl."

Telias nodded to show that he was listening, but his face was impassive, and Marcus could not directly ascertain the effect of his words. He realized that there were some parts of his story that anyone below patrician rank would find it hard to appreciate: wealth lends a man a wider perspective that others less fortunate necessarily had trouble grasping. Given Telias' behavior towards others in his household and his role as priest, it was probably disapproval that guided his view, perhaps because it would seem that moral turpitude lay behind his actions. Marcus was not concerned about this: he was confident that once he knew all the facts, Telias would better understand the caliber of the man he was judging.

"When it was time for me to begin a family, I got married according to the needs of our line. It happens that there was a custom passed on from father to son in our family, and knowing of no reason to flout tradition, I followed it too. As my father suggested, in order to preserve the harmony of my home I swore to my bride that I would never engage in sex with any other free woman for as long as she lived. It is law, of course, but often flouted, and the additional oath ensured my dedication. She need have no cause for jealousy with such a loyal husband. I thought little of it, for I had long been of the opinion that relations with free women were always prone to problems anyway: each partner struggling for his or her own pleasures, be they money, flattery, or desire. With slaves everything was much simpler. I made it a point to give my slave girls pleasure as well, and I always treated them with kindness, never forcing them, so it meant everyone was happy with the arrangement, which appealed to me.

"At first marriage changed little in my life, beyond making my home life richer and more rewarding. I grew to love my wife dearly as husbands often do, and came to use my slaves as a way of sparing her when she did not wish to make love. I reduced their number, since in those days my wife was very passionate, and I've always believed that masters have a responsibility for their slave's well-being—within certain limits, of course. I freed those I had grown tired of, and provided them with dowries to help them find husbands. The years passed, our children were born, and we were as happy as I then thought possible.

"After my wife's conversion, we gradually drifted apart. She became crazed with her religion. I naturally compensated for this by spending more time with my slave girls. I watched my wife change as time passed, growing more cruel and harsh with everyone, including me. It was a very unhappy time for me. One day while I was away at the senate she had my girls whipped until they bled 'for the good of their souls' as she said. It wasn't jealousy, since we had long since stopped living as husband and wife: it was her hatred of pleasure, and all things pleasurable. The bodies of these innocent women were too sweet for her to bear. You see, she was much more demanding with all her slaves after her conversion, not just mine. It was no longer enough that they did their work well and obeyed her: she insisted that they think as she wanted them too. Part of her madness is the desire to have everyone think as she does, perhaps because it helps her to believe she is right. In any case, after my slaves were whipped we have not stayed under the same roof for a single night. If she is in one villa, I am in another.

"It was at this time that a friend sold me Daphne, a Greek slave whose ancestors came from Locris originally. He had spoken of her several times as a girl of extraordinary beauty and willful frame of mind. She was very intelligent and knowledgeable, having been a companion to my friend's sister while she was growing up, and had been allowed by his parents to remain in the room when their daughter was being tutored. She learned to read, and read widely. I have always liked intelligent women, so I was intrigued at the prospect of such a girl.

"Daphne wasn't like the others, even from the first. Something about her demanded respect. Her stubborn nature was evident when she resisted my advances, albeit gently and with humor. I was patient, hoping to win her over. Using force, even with slave girls, never appealed to me: I have always enjoyed the thought that I was desired as much as desiring. I resolved to wait as long as it took.

"That turned out to be a very long time. And little by little, hardly noticing it myself, I fell in love with her. At first seeing and wooing her was mildly amusing, then it became a pleasure, and then the high point of my days. In the end it was my reason for living, and when I was away from her I could think of nothing else. I talked with her at every opportunity about myself and about her, and I would say we knew each other better than any others knew us. She seemed affectionate, but never surrendered. And when I asked why, she just smiled and refused to answer. I tried to lose myself in the other girls who were more willing, but that was just sex, and strange as it seems, began to feel wrong: like a betrayal of Daphne, although she gave no indication that she cared about me in the least, beyond our unusual friendship. It left me missing her more than ever, so finally I gave them up, freeing them but keeping her.

"I used to wonder how to win her, but as several years went by with no progress evident at all, I eventually despaired and thought it impossible. She was like the sphinx: I longed to penetrate beneath the pleasant mask of her character and mind but could not. I could not reach her. I felt I knew her, and equally that I knew her not. At times she seemed inhuman in her detachment. At other times my dearest friend.

"I resolved at last to free her, unable to bear seeing her any more. I was losing my manhood and my power for work. Besides, the thought of her freedom gave me consolation, though it did not give me peace. Firming my will, I summoned her to me formally, my administrative slave beside me at the desk, and coldly handed her the document setting her free and laying out the amount of a generous dowry. She opened it without a word and read it. For a moment her quizzical gaze held my eyes, and then she smiled. Reaching over to the lamp that stood upon the desk, she set the document alight and burned it to ashes. I couldn't believe it. Had she misunderstood the words? Deeply upset, and not wishing to create a scene, I sent my assistant away and asked her why she had done such a thing.

"She asked me if it was true that once free, I would stop pursuing her. I admitted as much, for my honor is more important than my happiness, and my promise to my wife on my wedding night was binding. To betray it would be to betray myself, my family and the Gods to whom I had appealed as witnesses when I made the oath. In our many discussions I had told her of this a number of times. So why was she asking? She said she would rather have me and be my slave than lose me and be free. It was incredible. I began to shake, and tears came to my eyes. But why, I asked, had she resisted me so long? As she had done before when I asked her that question, she made no effort to answer, and only smiled. She has never told me. But from that moment to this I have counted myself the luckiest of men.

"Wonderful creature! She may be a slave in the eyes of the law, but to me she is the best of all women. I made out a second document in my own hand, a copy of the one she had destroyed, and had it witnessed by a magistrate. I added a new paragraph to the effect that the document becomes legally binding from the instant the seal is broken, then while she watched I applied the wax and set my ring's imprint there. I made her promise to keep it with her at all times, and to make use of it any time she wished. Even now it is in her luggage. A wife stays because she is bound by oath, a slave because she has no choice—Daphne stays for love alone. Every day when I wake to see her lying beside me, I thank the Gods and promise myself that I will do everything in my power to make her happy. I never command her in anything: her will is mine. Her wants are little and simple indeed, but I am never happier than when I have given her some degree of pleasure, however great or slight."

Throughout this story Marcus had been too absorbed to drink, and he made up for it now, draining his cup and slapping it down on the table with relish. But not before Telias had seen that his eyes were thick with tears: the display with the wine cup was manly distraction. Telias firmly took hold of Marcus' forearm, squeezing it with affection. "Your story did not disappoint me, my friend. Thank you for sharing it with me. And I agree that you are most fortunate. Love, it seems, has tamed even the proud heart of a prominent man of Rome. Daphne must be a magnificent woman indeed to reach beneath your armor and soften the heart within. Venus has been kind to you. Frankly, I did not expect such tenderness from a man of your position, nor did I expect the tale to turn upon so fine a point of honor. I drink this toast to you, and to love."

Marcus was pleased as he looked at his smiling companion. If there was one thing the Greeks could be counted on to respect as much as culture, it was love.

The next morning the meeting again began as dawn was spreading across the sky. Marcus was still sleepy and he had a headache, but he was determined to ensure the day went well by starting things off on a positive note. When everyone was ready, he again stood up and spoke.

"As I said yesterday, we have done the most painful thing already and studied our enemy's ways. Now we have the more pleasant job: to find a way to rout him and bring back the piety that made Greece and Rome great. We are all a little tired, but we won our tiredness in good cheer. Let us continue what was well started."

Once he had sat down again, Telias requested a chance to speak, and it gave Marcus pleasure to assent. After sharing their thoughts the night before, Marcus sensed that the friendship he had hoped for was now well established.

Standing for a moment to gather his thoughts, Telias began. "Yesterday was indeed well spent, and I was grateful for such splendid guests last night as well. What I have to say is not new to me, but it may be new to some of you, and seem rather strange, so I ask you to consider it carefully before you decide if you agree with me or not. I will avoid the language of initiates, if I can, out of deference to our patron.

"It might be fitting to consider a famous play, *The Bacchae* by Euripedes. Am I right to presume we have all read it or seen it performed? No? Well, it's not that important. But I think this play speaks very much to our present situation. I have a copy in my house if anyone is interested afterwards.

"I especially want to draw your attention to a few aspects of the play that apply to us. Firstly, the play involves Pentheus, a man who resists the will of Dionysos, because it demands that he be sacrificed, and he is afraid. But his efforts to resist are used by the God to bring about his destruction: he cannot escape his destiny. Dionysos leads him to the slaughter in a state of mental confusion and dullness, and in his insanity Pentheus imagines it is his will to do what he is doing. He believes that he has escaped the God, even as he serves Him. Divine will is great and reaches beyond the will of mortals.

"Secondly, the intention of the play is to go far beyond the immediate mortal concerns with death and see in death the foundations for future rebirth. At the time when Euripedes wrote the play in exile at the Macedonian court, Athens had been at war with Sparta for a quarter of a century. The war had gone badly for years, despite occasional triumphs, and Athens was clearly near the end. Yet she refused to believe it, and lost many opportunities to make peace with the Spartans who were also tiring of the war. Euripedes realized that a kind of madness had taken hold of the Athenians and their destruction was inevitable. Like Pentheus they resisted their fate and yet their own actions brought it upon them. Watching his beloved city facing destruction, Euripedes went into despair and eventually went beyond it, ending his resistance to the will of the Gods. In this play he counsels surrender to divine will, and faith that the Gods will not abandon mortals although

Fate's necessity is difficult for us to accept. Pentheus will be reborn. From the ashes of defeat, Athens will rise again.

"Men die. All things in this world come to an end. It is the Law. To resist the Law is to resist the Gods. The Law is harsh, and men fear it. But behind the appearance of harshness is a greater kindness that most men do not see. When heroes die, great things become possible.

"Empires die too. Not as men die, exactly, but they die. Where is the Persian empire? What has become of the Carthaginians? Even Egypt, which survived by being reborn again and again for thousands of years, is today a mere province of Rome.

"Rome will die, when and how the Gods will it. Some empires die and remain dead, leaving behind stones that crumble into dust until everything is forgotten. Some do not. They may fall apart at first, and then this or that piece gives birth to a renewed empire, like a son continuing his father's work. Others fade away like elderly men and then after dying are reborn without warning, suddenly young once again.

"Death is the Law. What matters is whether it lasts or gives way to a rebirth. Men do not choose such things: they are given or withheld by the Gods. As priests sworn to serve the Gods, we are obliged to accept what the Gods have chosen for us.

"But all is not lost, if the Gods are behind this thing. It is not by chance, I think, that Egypt survived old age countless times and began again and again in slightly different forms: in Egypt the principle Gods are Isis and Osiris, Gods of death and rebirth. These Gods were kind to their Egyptian worshippers.

"Yesterday we all agreed that the Christians are followers of Dionysos. Dionysos is the God who brings life into death and therefore brings rebirth and wisdom. Think as Euripedes did! See this as if from a great distance without passion or preference. Why has Dionysos bewitched the minds of more and more people throughout the empire? Like Pentheus they follow him convinced they have escaped his reach. They are confused and forgetful, knowing not what their beliefs mean. They deny the passionate worship of the Bacchae by perverting all passion. They watch the Pagans from a distance, full of fear and loathing, but they secretly serve the same Gods. Why is this astonishing and awful thing happening?

"If we look at this hour by hour, year by year, we will only see confusion in the conflicting events of our times. But stand back and see things from a greater height. Look at the movement of history decade by decade, century by century.

"I cannot believe I am alone in seeing the obvious: even in the days when the empire was in the full flower of its maturity, the Gods were preparing for its death. Together in counsel, the Gods chose Dionysos to guide Rome into death so that all would not be lost. His followers call him Christ and believe, as Pentheus did, that they have tricked death and escaped the very God they follow. Their minds are forgetful and clouded: already they are being prepared by the God for inevitable destruction and ultimately, for rebirth. The Gods love Rome because Rome loved the Gods and all the reflections of Truth they shared with humanity. The Gods do not want this Truth to be lost. It is humanity's greatest possession.

"For most men, death is darkness. It is ignorance. It is fear. We are entering a dark age. Perhaps the empire will continue in a new form, or perhaps—as happened in the years after the Trojan war—all the old forms of civilization will disappear and be forgotten: knowledge of writing and the arts will be lost. Intolerance and irrationality are growing, even among the educated. What will survive? Not this world we know. Our world is surely dying.

"Remember Ouranos and Kronos, and how they fought the Great Mother: remember too the harmony that Zeus restored. Let Endymion's chariot be the reminder of the Great Law and..." Here Telias paused and looked at Marcus who was looking very sternly up at him. "Excuse me Marcus, but old habits die hard. I'll try to guard my style of speech better since this concerns you too.

"I know very well that my counsel seems harsh. But we need not see only darkness ahead, even when we watch the sunset. There will be stars in the night, and perhaps a moon, and in the fullness of time the sun will rise again. Consider what good things death can bring. Rebirth, yes, but more, much more. There is wisdom hidden in the bleakness of death. He who enters the underworld and returns is not like others: he has gained wisdom beyond that of his previous life.

"It is not the empire which concerns me most greatly, it is civilization in all its many forms. Philosophy and art, medicine and engineering, literature and poetry, painting and sculpture: the Gods gave us these things and in this way raised us up. We all know the stories of Atlantis, and how it perished. Its art and philosophy are utterly gone. That is what I believe truly frightening. That is what I pray most deeply to avoid. That and forgetting the mysteries the Gods have revealed. But the Christians give me confidence despite their madness.

"If a civilization as great as that of Rome and Greece should enter the underworld in the protection of the God, what marvels could not the reborn civilization create? An ignorant man who enters death comes back wise. A wise man who enters death comes back in splendor. What then of a civilization which already carries the flame of wisdom such as ours? Will it not follow the same pattern? What could it not achieve? What philosophies beyond our imaginings, what mighty cities? What amazing things could its engineers build, what masterpieces would its artists create? Could Plato's divine Republic become more than a dream? What powers might then belong to the generations to come?

"Since I am just a simple priest of Apollo, and I do not know the shape of the future with certainty, I prefer to see the best in the tidings I perceive. If I am wrong to hope for so much, that seems unimportant. At least I can serve the Gods without sorrow.

"I understand that many of us here view the Christians as enemies. When a man hates and fears you, it is natural to consider him your foe. In this sense Christians are our enemies. But they are our friends in a deeper sense, for they serve a God we all respect, and they do so for a purpose we all must share. It is difficult to love the one who hates you, difficult to watch him destroy the beautiful things you are fond of, difficult to see him supplant you in your own house, but sometimes that is proper. The father watches his infant son wailing and demanding, knowing nothing of family and nation, yet the parent does not hate him, instead preparing for the day when the child will take his place. Even when the full-grown son hates the father, the father should not hate the son: in time he should stand aside and give him all the power and wealth that were previously his alone. In this way the future of the family is assured, and the generations to come may have a chance to flower in wisdom even if the generation that is with us now is lost in darkness. Where there is life there is cause for hope, and the Christians may represent the only hope civilization has for future greatness.

"It seems to me that our meeting is not useless, even if I am right. To know the will of the Gods is important, but it still leaves us with a more important question: how shall we work with them, to advance their wills? I see that my words are by no means accepted by all of you. Let us discuss this now. But please remember, if I am right our work is by no means finished here. How can we help to prepare for the rebirth?"

He sat down, and Marcus frowned at him. "An interesting approach," he said with disgust, and looked away. He barely succeeded in controlling his anger.

At the suggestion of the Samothracian, and with apologies to Marcus, the priests decided it might be better if this part of their discussion allowed them to freely use the language of poets: myth. It would save them time, and anyway there were things they needed to discuss which Marcus ought not to join in. When he offered to leave, they insisted it was unnecessary, and besides they still needed his services as a chairman. He could see to it that good order prevailed while they focused on consideration of Telias' speech.

So Marcus stayed, and the words that followed were very strange to hear. There was mention of centaurs and chariots, of the fates and the seasons, of heroes and Gods—and most of the myths were ones he'd never heard before. In fact, it seemed to him they were making them up as they went along: sometimes they would rearrange the stories before they'd even finished them. At other times one of them would agree emphatically with the story another told and then tell it quite differently with different characters and plots while everyone nodded as if there had been no significant difference. They also mentioned Rome and the empire many times, but try as he might, Marcus could not get the drift of what they were saying. It was as if they were speaking an entirely different language.

He noticed with relief that Telias seemed content to sit back and watch, letting the others do the talking. He had been wrong to let his guard down around the fellow. Telias was dangerous. How badly he had misread the man's smiles and cheerfulness! What he'd taken for a sunny intelligence could better be described as lunatic stupidity. It went far beyond the apathy he had met with in other priests at Rome. To actually invite the Christian advance! To welcome it because he thought it would destroy Rome! The man would be treasonous if he wasn't so clearly unhinged. But why was it taking so long for these others to dismiss what he'd said?

The meeting continued into the afternoon without a break, and no one seemed to notice except Marcus. When he suggested a break, the others deferred it, not wishing to interrupt the discussion. It was hours later, in mid-afternoon, that they finally reached a consensus. The Athenian explained it to Marcus.

"Sir, we have discussed the matter at some length and the evidence fits the patterns that divinity has revealed to mortals. Telias is right." Seeing the shock and anger in Marcus' face, he went on quickly. "It is difficult to understand, I know, but the matter is very clear. None of us would choose this if it were in our power to choose, but it is not.

"This is not the first time in history that such a thing has happened. After the Trojan war, a period of darkness came that swept all happiness from the earth. Men forgot almost everything: how to write, how to build, how to worship the Gods properly. The light of civilization was almost extinguished entirely. Let us pray that such profound darkness is not necessary this time. But if it is, let us not defy the Gods. Out of struggle, greatness can come.

"Consider what has been achieved since the last dark age. How brightly civilization has glowed! The things that have been done in this cycle are unlike anything that has gone before. Death and rebirth set things in motion among the Greeks and Romans that no one could ever have dreamed possible. Time circles for all living things, but it does not return to where it began, not exactly. We can rise or we can fall. Like farmers who work hard during the summer, improving the land, we must face the winter in the hope that when spring returns, the next cycle will be even more prosperous. And we have worked hard, accomplishing much. Other civilizations worked less hard. They were like farmers who are lazy and foolish. When winter visits them, they face hunger and the knowledge that next year they will begin lower than they began the present year."

Marcus felt disgust. Was he the only man here with the courage to fight? "You counsel weakness and despair. What is this nonsense about growing stronger after a dark age? Have you not read Homer and Hesiod? You who speak so confidently of death? When Troy ended, it brought an end to the age of heroes when the Gods were closer to men on earth. I may not be as knowledgeable as you in matters of religion, but I have my good sense and I know a little of history. We must fight and fight hard or everything we have achieved will be lost!"

The others listened to him quietly. What were they thinking? He looked around at their faces, wondering if he was getting through to them, wondering if they saw reason, but he suddenly realized that what he saw in their eyes was pity, and it triggered a fury he barely controlled. As he fought to regain calm, knowing that rage would only make matters worse, Telias again stood up to speak, his first words for a very long time.

"Marcus: we know your pain and share it. It is the pain of any man who fights for right in this difficult world. You are correct in saying that Hesiod and Homer spoke sadly of the loss of greatness in the world, and of the passing of heroes into death in that terrible war and after it. But we know—do we not?—that the poets are liars. Truly the Gods have guided us to greatness in the passing age. Was it all for nothing? Will they abandon us now? The ways of the Gods are strange, and difficult to understand. But the Gods are not free of the Law when they act in this world any more than we mortals are free, and although their help may be difficult to bear, they are kindly in their natures. They do their work within the Law because, in their wisdom, they know what is necessary.

"For more than a thousand years the Gods have watched over us and we have lived a good life, despite our weaknesses and our pride. If a man lives such a good life, long and productive, and his end draws near, what would we think of him if he suddenly falters and begs for a few more hours or days? True greatness means to fight when fighting is proper, and to have the strength to surrender gracefully and without fear when the enemy is poised to strike the final blow. For such a man the Gods have love. What is true for a man is true for a civilization.

"None of us here desires surrender. We would gladly die so that civilization might continue as before. But that choice is not given to us. As mortals in a mortal world, our only choice at present lies in the manner of our death. We can fight to the end in fear and anger, or we can fight until the time for fighting is past and then turn to greet death as if he were our old and dear friend. The latter course is the one that wisdom counsels. And sadly we must tell you the signs are very clear. Our world is dying. Though our enemies spit on us and our descendants may never know the manner of our death, it is right for us to die well.

"The difference between us is that you don't believe the end is yet certain. Knowing your character a little, I am sure that when your time comes you will die with honor and grace, and that you would wish the same for Rome. You simply believe the time for surrender has not yet come. There is no harm in that. Our differences with you involve only timing, nothing more. Is it not so?

"You made a generous offer to assist us in whatever we decide. Your fortune is safe, a small consolation to you perhaps. And if you choose to withdraw all assistance, I think the others agree with me in saying we freely release you from your offer. However, although they may not demand much money to accomplish, there are still things we may think it proper to do. Funerals require planning and some expense if they are to be done suitably. We have no resources of our own, given the decline in pilgrims, so if we decide something is needful your help may still be welcome. It shouldn't come to much. Are you still interested?"

As he listened to Telias and saw the calm acceptance in the faces of the others at the table, the anger in Marcus' heart had died away, and the disgust, leaving only a deep, overwhelming sadness. Suddenly he no longer wanted to see these men, to talk to them, to be reminded by their words of the tragic times he lived in. He stood up, waving dismissively at them with his hand. "You can have whatever you want as I promised before. Make a list of expenses along with approximate costs and I will see that the money is delivered to you." Without glancing back or saying goodbye, he left the room in search of Daphne. He ached for her more than he could bear.

She was in their bedroom, one of Telias' servants brushing her hair. They were laughing about something when he came in, and they seemed like friends as Daphne bid the other goodbye before turning and greeting Marcus with a kiss. "Are you only stopping now for lunch? I've already eaten, but I'll sit with you if you like...Marcus, what is it? What's the matter?" She put her hand on his shoulder, and he felt a wave of sorrow rolling over him. She led him to the bed as a mother might guide a small child, and they laid on it for a minute her head on his chest, while she waited for him to tell her. Feeling very old and very tired, Marcus sighed several times before he began.

He told her everything. They had not spoken of the previous day, so he began with the things they had said then. When he reached the things he'd heard today, he could not keep the bitterness from his voice as he described Telias' speech. The betrayal seemed so total. All hope was gone.

After he finished speaking, Daphne asked him questions for a time before they lapsed into silence. She did not offer platitudes in an effort to raise his spirits, and for that he was grateful. Instead she just lay quietly beside him, offering her silent presence for his comfort. An hour passed. Reaching over, she began to stroke his belly and gently kissed his ear, her breath warm and soft. He realized he needed her at that moment more than he'd ever needed anyone before.

They made love as the sun was falling in the world outside. His sorrow never lessened, though through it he watched her beauty and marveled at the strangeness of his feelings. Her eyes were closed, her lips were parted, her warm breath came in perfect harmony with their motions. She opened her eyes and looked at him, and suddenly his tears were welling up and spilling over his face, onto hers. She moaned softly, pulled him closer to her, and licked at them with the tip of her tongue. Tears of her own flooded her eyes, and he was swept by the sight of it into a rush of oblivion, their bodies straining to join together, to rout the sorrows of separation and loneliness, to forge the bliss of a single entity that could shut out the universe.

The lovers slept afterwards, and when they woke an hour or two after sunset they decided to remain where they were. In another part of the house they heard voices, but they were too distant to hear what was said. Marcus planned to leave in the morning without talking to the priests, but Daphne thought he should at least speak to them one last time. He had, after all, called the meeting. It would be wrong to walk away in silence. They talked about it for a while and at last he agreed, but with one stipulation. She would come too. He wanted her there: would she do it? "Of course," she said, smiling.

n the morning they waited until the others had already arrived and taken their places. Hearing at last that the discussion had already begun, they entered the

I room, Daphne first. When she entered, all voices died away. Marcus motioned her to the seat reserved for him and waited while another couch was brought in and the other furniture shifted to accommodate it. He didn't sit down immediately, but remained standing and spoke.

"We will be leaving today. I have asked Daphne here because it was her suggestion that I come. I have lost faith in you, and in what you are doing. I am determined to keep trying until I find other men with more strength in their characters. Caliphas will remain behind to hear how much money you need. I will be waiting for him in Athens, and as soon as I know, I'll arrange to have it sent." Abruptly he sat down.

Telias stood. "I'm sorry Marcus. We all are." He turned to Daphne and said "You are welcome for Marcus' sake. And if you have any thoughts on the matter you are welcome to share them. Marcus tells me that you are an educated woman with a quick mind. Perhaps your input will be useful." He looked back at Marcus.

"There is no need to leave Caliphas here, because last night we were discussing what we think we need, and it doesn't come to much. Our biggest concern is to protect the sacred objects that are in our keeping. It seems obvious that we must hide them, and each leader will be responsible for burying them as near as possible to the sanctuaries from which they came. Obviously that will cost little, and we can certainly afford it.

"Where your help would be most useful is in assisting us to protect the ancient books we possess. There is no telling how far the madness will go, but it seems possible there will soon be a time when men no longer read, or if they do, destroying ancient texts will seem like a sacred act. Furthermore, some of the centers like Delphi have their own written records which we do not want to just throw away. Written materials don't preserve well when they are buried. Of course, there is no alternative to burial since nowhere is safe if the Dionysian age lasts for centuries as we expect it will. For that reason we will need to find some means of preserving them.

"Of course, there is only a slight chance that they will ever be found, but if the Gods are kind and we are conscientious, they may be discovered in a kinder age when men are more receptive to the old ways. And this should appeal to you Marcus: if we are wrong about how long this age will last and any of us are still alive, or if we manage to find replacements among the young who survive until things are looking up, everything can be dug up immediately. If you like, you can think of it as a matter of temporary storage in safekeeping. For ourselves we look at it as burying a seed, sacrificing it in the hopes of future life. It is our offering to the Gods.

"We have discussed several possible methods of preserving them, but we will have to experiment until we are sure. It might be best to gather them in one place for the burial, somewhere away from the cult centers where they will attract no attention. This and their preservation will require money. We have an estimate for you which we can give to you later. For a man of your wealth, it will be an insignificant sum." He caught sight of Daphne frowning and shaking her head. "From your manner I take it you have something to say? Please go ahead." He sat down, watching her politely while she stood up. She seemed awkward but Marcus saw an air of defiance in her manner.

"Forgive me for speaking, sirs, but there is something I don't understand. You speak of burying the seeds of knowledge, and of your willingness to sacrifice yourselves, yet you yourselves are unwilling to be buried. Why are you not being buried together with the things in your charge?"

"Lack of nerve," said Marcus under his breath but with pleasure.

There was nervous laughter around the table, and Telias answered her without getting up. "Our deaths would do nothing to make things better. Why on earth would we do such a thing?"

"I don't mean killing yourselves anymore than you would suggest burning your books before you bury them. What I mean is why don't you go into hiding so you can keep your knowledge alive but hidden from the world? You have said that you are certain this Christian menace will pass with time. Why not hide until it does?"

"Ah, yes, I see." Telias stood and went on. "We discussed that last night, and it offers us little hope. Even now we have great trouble finding replacements for after we die. How could we find them if we were a secret society, hunted by the magistrates, as one day soon may be the case? And since great time may have to pass before the world is again receptive, the chances of remaining quietly hidden are minuscule. A curious neighbor, a conversion from within the ranks—yes, even priests of the Gods are not immune to the Christian cult—it would take little to uncover us. And once uncovered, all the things we are protecting may be discovered too, by torture if not by betrayal.

"We considered only initiating our own children who naturally would be loath to betray us if they were converted. For a generation or two we might live in secret among the Christians if we were very cautious, but the attempt would inevitably fail in the end. And not just because of the chances of discovery. The secrets we harbor are too complex and subtle for everyone to understand. We were chosen from a fairly wide group that grows narrower by the day. Unless the numbers of people we can draw from remained fairly large, when a son or daughter is not born sufficiently intelligent, the knowledge of his or her parents would be lost. As the years went by our truths would be decayed. Even if the succeeding generations were capable of understanding, the knowledge would already have been lost. I'm afraid there is little hope in what you suggest."

Daphne was stubborn, and she wasn't about to let go. "You said you cannot live among the Christians. Why live among them? Why not leave behind the cities and find a remote place where you can live in secrecy? Why not find an island, or a remote mountain valley and establish a community there? You could isolate yourselves from outsiders and even if some Christian travelers did happen to pass through, keeping your secrets would not be so difficult. It would only mean guarding your tongues and watching your actions until they moved on. The rest of the time you could relax without fear of discovery. And the cult objects and books you speak of could be kept there too, hidden from casual discovery but available for study by the young. Through books the wise writers of the past could speak directly to the intelligent children of the future."

"Your thoughts are sensible, but I still don't see how it will be possible. We would need, who knows, perhaps a thousand people in the community to provide enough suitable priests and priestesses. How could so many squeeze into one remote area without attracting attention?"

"Determine your size, then pick the place. If you want to do it you can, with Marcus' help."

A delegate from Elis spoke up next. "There is another even more serious problem. Since we may be talking of hundreds of years, the problem of breeding would become very serious. As any farmer knows, animals who breed closely from the same line over generations become badly weakened. Even in smaller towns of men it has been noticed in Greece: the inhabitants grow stupid and sickly as the generations pass. Yet survival would depend on keeping apart from others."

Telias seemed to be following a train of thought that took root and grew. He spoke thoughtfully, thinking ahead of his words and toying absently with the pendant around his neck, a pendant Marcus had noticed on the first night—oval and black, with a tiny yellow thunderbolt falling from a blue cloud. "Of course, we could adopt promising young children from cities outside. It would be possible to send out people from the community from time to time to take possession of abandoned children no one else wants. Once raised apart from the Christians, these children would make good members of the community. And if we only took those young children who seemed most intelligent, it would lessen the demand for a larger population base. Perhaps the sanctuary need only be a hundred or so people in total. So that's not an impossible problem..." He reflected a moment in silence, then shook his head before going on.

"And it occurs to me that even those members of the community who were susceptible to Christian influence would not have any chance to fall under its spell. People in small towns are naturally defensive against outsiders. In an isolated mountain valley with proper education, this would be made even stronger than usual. Conversions would be nearly impossible..." For a full minute he said nothing while he frowned at the table before him. When he spoke, there was a slight tone of surprise in his voice. "You know, this might work."

That was how the change took place, and everything grew from there. As the discussion continued, excitement took hold. For every problem a solution was quickly found. Everyone's energies, dispelled for years by a sense of hopelessness, at last were finding a focus.

Seeing the change, Marcus reached over and squeezed Daphne's shoulder, smiling. It was less than he'd hoped for in the beginning but more than he expected when he came today. It was good to hear some action being contemplated, however mild. He was glad to have the defeatism of the past two days routed. He wouldn't stop trying to find a more fundamental solution, but in the meantime this was a sensible fallback solution in case nothing else could be done.

He even offered an idea of his own when the location of the community was being discussed. "I hold a great deal of land in Italy, and some of it is in the mountains, especially in the region south of Lombardy. The soil is workable, though not excellent, but the area is too rugged for much cultivation, so it is mostly still forested. The few little towns consist of hunters and trappers, on the whole. I was there a few years ago, hunting boar. Do you remember that river, Daphne? What was it called? The Taro, I think. Yes, the Taro. Some of its tributaries were fed from mountain valleys that seemed to us the most isolated in all of Italy. I own much of the area, so if you want I can close down the other nearby towns. And there are cities a few days ride to the North where abandoned children and orphans would certainly be available."

They wouldn't limit themselves to a place unseen, but it sounded promising. Marcus offered to go back himself and check the place out more carefully, however the others thought this was unwise. The Samothracian summed up their position: "Anything that draws attention to the place would be dangerous. And you have to understand that if we do this, no one else must know but those who are going to live there. You can help us by funding the foundation of the sanctuary, but that is all. When you die, although the land will continue in your family's name, they must think of it no differently than the other, more remote portions of their holdings. Just as you did when you passed through, if they should happen to hunt there they must see nothing but crude peasants living on the borders of civilization.

"Even the remaining believers at our cult centers here in Greece must know nothing of what we are doing. Those who are chosen to live there could simply vanish and never be seen again. The rest will be left behind, thinking that the old ways die with them."

As an additional precaution, he also suggested that the remaining followers in each place should be told their sacred objects were being buried near the sanctuaries for safe keeping. That would explain their disappearance when they were shipped in secrecy to the valley.

For many hours they discussed logistics and other practical matters, having the servants deliver cold meats so they could continue talking while they snacked. The more they went on, the more confident they grew that success was possible, although it would involve a massive undertaking which would consume everyone's energies for years to come. Telias summed matters up at the end of the day.

"This is the brightest light I've seen for many years. I believe we can do this thing, and furthermore that the Gods will approve.

"It is possible that this guardian sanctuary will play no role in the rebirth, which after all is in the Gods' hands. Perhaps new mysteries, arts and philosophies will be granted by the Gods to future generations to replace the old. But even so our work is good because one day men may wish to remember again what their ancestors did and knew. The sanctuary will help to dispel forgetfulness and replace it with memory. At the very least, the sanctuary will be a heroic reflection of the Gods' will here on earth, a human parallel to their divine intention. At the same time priests of the guardian sanctuary will be able to continue the proper sacrifices and rituals in honor of the Gods, and they can be a force for good in the world, by praying for the deliverance of men from ignorance and darkness.

"On the other hand, if the Gods will it, the sanctuary may lead men out of the coming dark age, providing them with more than a thousand years of insight and inspiration so they won't have to begin all over again.

"Either way, it will enable us to do something to preserve the mysteries, sacred objects, and books we have been entrusted with by the Gods and our ancestors. And it is a clear demonstration of our decision to accept the will of the Gods and work with them, not against. Even if the sanctuary is betrayed or fails for some other reason, at least we will have done what we could to fulfill our obligations in a difficult time.

"As I see it, in the creation of this guardian sanctuary we will be creating the last great mystery of our age. It will call for a new priesthood, a new form of government, and a new standard of scholarship. Initiation should be by birth or induction at an early age, and all those born within the community should be brought to the highest level of education they are capable of.

"The men and women of the sanctuary will be the secret light of knowledge and wisdom that shines invisibly through the long night, all the light of our passing age focused in one forgotten spot. They will be a tool available for the Gods to use in whatever manner they choose. They will be the expression of human acceptance of destiny and of hope for future generations, the seed buried in the darkness and forgotten to await the spring. We do not have to face the night without hope or comfort: if the Gods will it, this sanctuary will give us shelter until the coming of dawn."

Along the dark footpath beneath the trees came two men, a woman and a donkey. The woman was in her forties, a few streaks of gray in her hair. She had obviously been a great beauty in her youth: time had not yet erased all the loveliness from her face. She wore a long traveler's cloak of simple homespun, but there was an air of wealth and authority about her. The two young men were also roughly dressed, and they too seemed a little unsuited to their garb. They wore swords as defense against robbers, and treated the woman with great deference and respect, helping her over the rough spots in the path. The donkey was heavily laden with several packing cases. It was strange for such a group to be so far from the main roads, heading into the mountain wilderness. Travelers of any sort were a rarity, and a group of this type was quite unheard of in these parts.

Rounding a turn in the path as it followed the stream up the little valley, the walkers came across a little village. It was a rough place, impoverished by the harsh lifestyle of this remote region. There was no sign of life save a dog that began barking, and several chickens that ran free around the hovels where the local inhabitants lived. The travelers stopped and looked around, the woman's face confused and uncertain.

A man appeared from the trees on the other side of the village, middle aged and bearded, clothed in rags, and walked towards them. He was panting with exertion, having apparently run from some distance to meet them. His manner was not friendly: he was watchful, suspicious. "What do you want?" he asked, his Latin rough and rural and with a strange accent the woman couldn't quite place.

"We seek lodgings," she replied.

"There is no place in our village," the man said dismissively, "You have come too far into the mountains for such things. For that you should go back down the river half a day's journey. If you leave now you will be there before dark." He did not smile or offer any other sign of hospitality. A village headman who didn't like strangers, apparently.

"We will sleep anywhere: a barn would be fine."

"We have no place for you to stay. You will have to go back."

The woman looked at the man for a long moment, her eyes searching his face. "Telias?" she said tentatively.

"What?"

"Telias, is that you? It's me, Daphne... Are you Telias?"

"Daphne?..." A moment passed, and suddenly the man's manner changed completely. He reached for her hand, smiling warmly. "Daphne, by the Gods, what are you doing here? You are welcome, of course: you are welcome. Please forgive my rudeness, but you have changed over the years."

"Not as much as you, Telias. I was prepared for anything, but I didn't recognize you at first. Is this the town?" Her last question had a trace of disappointment she could not hide. She had expected more.

He chuckled. "Part. Not much to look at, is it?" He turned to regard the two young men who stood watching this last exchange in silence. "Who are your friends?" His manner was once again guarded.

"Don't worry. These are my sons. Marcus was their father. They know about the sanctuary and we have been careful not to draw attention to our visit here."

"Marcus is dead?"

Daphne merely nodded.

"I'm sorry to hear that. Well of course your sons are welcome too. Come, let us find you a place to stay." He paused, remembering something. "Are you planning to stay with us permanently?" She smiled, and he turned to her sons. "How about you two: do you want to be a part of our community?" They looked at him nervously but nodded. "Excellent. The assembly must agree to it, but in the circumstances I am certain we will make room for you here." He put two fingers in his mouth and whistled loudly back towards the way he had come. Other people emerged from the trees where they had obviously been watching the exchange and approached.

"These are no strangers," he told them. "Without this woman, we would not be here." He introduced Daphne and her sons to everyone, a thing that took some time to accomplish since more and more people joined them where they stood. There were more than forty by the time he had finished, and many others, he promised, they would meet later.

The travelers insisted they were not tired and delightedly accepted the offer to be shown around the sanctuary immediately, with Telias as their guide. One of the villagers took the donkey on ahead to where they would be staying, and the others went back to whatever they had been doing before.

Telias led them up the path a little farther, and they came across a continuation of the same village, somewhat bigger and a little less squalid than the first, though still very rough to look at. It was mostly deserted. "Down here we speak only Latin for the children's sake. The Greeks among us have had to be tutored in the accent of this region so that we will fit in better. I'm not very good at it, unfortunately, but some of the others act and sound just like local peasants when they are not on the mountain. It's important that the children grow up looking and sounding like they belong here, because naturally they will have no regular contact with outsiders. We don't want them speaking Greek and having impeccable manners in fifty years time. The entire community must appear to be uneducated peasants native to the region if any outsiders should venture through."

They left the village and crossed the stream, climbing steeply on the Southern side. The path was well worn but no one passed them as they panted upwards.

Halfway up, they heard the voices of children singing in Greek, and as they passed near an old farm house they saw almost twenty boys and girls of different ages, singing happily, writing tablets in their laps. They were led by an enthusiastic young woman who waved at Telias when she saw him. Telias waved back cheerfully but kept walking. "Boys and girls are both educated equally here. We cannot afford to have ignorant people."

Their destination was more than an hour of very energetic climbing above the village. It was a tiny ridge surrounded by deep clefts. They climbed up its spine for several minutes, and suddenly found themselves before a set of stone steps bracketed by masonry and leading downwards into the mountain. Telias bid them take lamps from a niche just inside the entrance and light them using a taper to transfer the flame from another lamp that been left burning there. "Here the sacred flame continues to burn," he said. "Within a few years it may be the last place on earth the ancient fire continues to be kept alive."

There were statues of the Gods standing in rows on either side of the entrance passageway, twelve steps beneath the surface of the ground. "Guardians" said Telias by way of explanation, as he led them past. He continued down a further flight of steps and along a sloping corridor, talking back over his shoulder at them, his voice echoing back from the darkness far ahead. "We have had to dig these tunnels out of the rock. The mountain is soft shale so it is easy to excavate, but we have had to reinforce the tunnels with stone and create drainage and ventilation systems. We had six stone masons included in the original group because it is such a large task. They have taught others—everyone does physical labor here. It's about half finished now. So we should have our plans completed in about fifteen years at the present rate."

They passed a doorway leading away to the left. "That's where the temples of the Gods are being built, including a new oracle of Apollo. And just ahead on the right is the passageway leading to the storage rooms where sacred objects are being kept and preserved." They passed the doorway, but they could see little in the flickering light of their lamps, and Telias continued along the passageway so there was no time to investigate it more closely.

At length they came to a large circular, domed chamber well lit by lamps. There were narrow corridors radiating from it, and they could see shelves of scrolls and books in several which were lit. They appeared to be storage rooms. In the room where they stood, there were at least ten desks with men and women seated at them, and an enormous clutter of codices and scrolls lying everywhere. The room's occupants looked with surprise at Daphne and her sons, who gazed back equally astonished.

"This is the library" explained Telias. "Right now we are trying to organize it. With the help of Marcus' money we have been adding to the volumes we already had, so they number to thousands, not counting records from cult centers. We're not even sure what we have yet. Once we have ordered them and summarized their contents, we intend to begin emphasizing study of their contents. Perhaps inspiration will come to our more gifted students in the years to come and they can add to the knowledge in these rooms. Each generation must be forward looking so that laziness and mental dullness do not infect the community."

At that moment an old man came out of one of the narrow corridors that radiated off the library like spokes. In his arms were a collection of scrolls that he placed precariously on a young man's desk before coming over and greeting Telias curiously. "This is Philias, our librarian. Philias, this is Daphne I told you about, and our patron's sons. They will be joining us."

Philias greeted them warmly and showed them around the library, his pride evident. Daphne's previous disappointment had long since vanished, and it was with delight that she took everything in. She could see from her sons' demeanors that they too had seen their doubts dispelled. It seemed to her that even Marcus would have been impressed to see what his wealth had accomplished.

Late that afternoon as they headed down the valley, Telias requested that the youths go on ahead so he could speak privately with their mother. Then he led her to a small cliff overlooking the village as the sun set, and the two of them sat side by side and talked.

"I haven't seen you or Marcus since that day you left Delphi," said Telias. "What have you been doing since then? We heard only rumors before we settled here, and almost nothing since then, although we do have agents in the outside world, purchasing books and contacting some of the sanctuaries that are still functioning. Did Marcus continue trying to reverse the tide?"

"Yes, for a time. But when he grew older he gave up. As the years passed, he placed more and more of his hopes with you here. It was very difficult for him not to make inquiries, especially after the move when all contact was severed. But he often spoke to me of you. And to the end he kept silence and did nothing to endanger your work."

"How did he die?"

"His heart was weak, and one day he just died in his sleep. It was a peaceful, painless death. He told you of our relationship, didn't he? After his death I freed myself immediately and made my way here. We left our servants behind when we were in the foothills and came on alone. Fearing his wife, Marcus gave me a considerable fortune before he died so that I would have independence, but I have no need of it now. It is in the crates we brought with us: you can add it to the funds you already have. It has been my plan to come here for several years. The Dionysians continue to grow more powerful and I did not want my sons to become perverted by them. This seemed the safest place to me. But of course we have had no word so I couldn't even be sure if you were here. When I arrived and didn't recognize you I was beginning to think the plan had failed."

"And now...?"

"It is very well carried out. Strange to think that from that discussion so long ago all this has come about. Marcus would have been very pleased. How far things have progressed since we last saw you!"

"They have indeed." He smiled. "It is good to have you here. Tomorrow the assembly will meet to discuss your joining with us. We have an assembly of all the community, and a counsel of twelve seniors, six men and six women, representatives of the twelve Olympian Gods. Everyone will be free to speak, the counselors first and last, and then it will be put to a vote. I can't imagine anyone objecting to your presence. I am one of the counselors and very busy these days, but someone will be assigned to teach you and your sons how things are organized here.

"We are building a new society unlike any that has gone before. Everyone must pull their weight, not merely intellectually but also taking up the peasant's difficult way of life. Please try to prepare your sons for what lies ahead."

Daphne nodded, but she was thinking of Marcus in his final days, and the keenness of his hopes. When she spoke, there was sadness in her words. "How much have we saved, Telias? And how much has been lost?"

For a moment he looked at the light mist that was collecting farther down the valley in the cool air of early evening. Then he shook his head. "We could not save everything. Some of the Greek sanctuaries were already looted or had simply faded away. Others refused to take part in our scheme for various reasons. Some things were brought here, but other things were buried nearby the old temples and shrines, and we have a collection of maps detailing where they can be dug up, if the time should come for that. The Omphalos, for example, from Delphi, was buried on the slopes of mount Parnassos because I felt it was too much a part of that place to be brought away.

"We have sent our representatives throughout the Eastern and Western Empires, offering sanctuary to any cult objects or writings the priests should wish to have us protect. Mostly they have rejected our offers, preferring to accept responsibility for what is theirs. Negotiations continue, and with some we will probably form a loose alliance, recording for them the locations of the things they have hidden. In Britain the brotherhood of the ancient religion has decided that if things continue as they have been, they will bury their sacred objects under a mountain as we have done. They have sent someone here as an observer to report back to them on our progress. From them too, we hope one day to receive a map.

"The biggest problem is secrecy. We have difficulty persuading others that their secrets are safe with us. If we are discovered and they have entrusted us with the knowledge of their intentions, these will be discovered too. Reaching some kind of arrangement with each group is no easy matter: it will take many years."

Telias looked across the little valley as the light faded and the first stars showed themselves in the deepening blue far above their heads. "We have done what we can. We have done what seemed right to us. Whatever happens in the years ahead will be determined by the will of the Gods, so don't trouble yourself at the dangers which lie before us, or the things that have been lost already. This has been a good work, establishing this sanctuary, and that, it seems to me, is enough for now."

As night gathered in the Western Empire, the Sanctuary's flame never wavered. Barbarian invasions, internal factions and decay brought Rome into slow ruin. Ignorance swept the Western world, and high culture melted like snow before the fires of war and instability, until few could even imagine what civilization once had meant. Here and there other sanctuaries of the old ways, less carefully planned and hidden, crumbled before the Christian onslaught until only the old stories and myths like that of King Arthur remained in the memory of men. But still the Sanctuary lived on.

Christendom struggled to stay afloat against the tribal Pagans of the North and West, and the new faith of Islam that sorely troubled it from the South. At times it seemed the remnants of the Ancient world would vanish altogether in the West, collapsing under the poverty and ignorance of the age, or destroyed by war that constantly threatened it from all sides and within. A handful of monasteries were the only place the light of learning remained outside the Sanctuary. In these places the priests copied their manuscripts, often little interested in the knowledge and wisdom they contained, and gradually many of the old books disappeared, consumed by random acts of pillage, plunder and indifference.

In time things settled and prosperity once again grew. Spring was returning to Europe. But first the plague would come...

THE GIFT: A SOWING OF SEEDS

(The Taro River Valley, Milan, Mediterranean Coast, 1348 - 1350 AD)

Giovanni shouted through the autumn forest as he walked along the path. Almost immediately there was an answering shout: it was Maria. He offered a prayer of thanks to the Gods: she was safe. Close overhead, the sky was gray and the air was chill with the morning's rain. Giovanni's breath misted as he panted along the uneven path. Around a turn he came across Maria running towards him, laughing with relief. She threw her arms around him.

"I almost couldn't wait," she said. "It feels like forever since we have seen anyone. Mario is checking the snares for game: he'll be back soon, I think." They embraced for a moment, then she released him, and they walked along the path side by side, although it was awkward at times given the narrowness of the passage. "We almost went down to see what was happening: I was so afraid sometimes, especially at first! Mario wouldn't let me because we had promised. But you should have sent word to us, grandfather. For all we knew the rest of the world had disappeared." He heard resentment in her voice.

Giovanni said nothing, so she glanced at him and noticed his grimness. "What is it grandfather? What has happened?"

He looked at her but couldn't meet her eyes, so he looked at his feet instead. "The plague was...I'm so sorry, Maria: everyone...everyone died. Only myself and Atropina survived. It took less than a month, and nothing was left. Men, women, children. Your family...everyone. The village is deserted. Even though I say it, I can't believe it." He shook his head, unable to say more.

Maria had stopped walking, her hand to her lips, her eyes open wide, staring at him as if confused. She did not cry. Her voice was very faint. "They're all...dead?"

He nodded and took her arm to steady her, gently steering her up the path. She seemed to have become utterly numb, looking around herself in bewilderment, and he became aware she was whispering quietly, "Everyone is dead," again and again. It brought alive the memories of the dying time to Giovanni. He had never remembered them so clearly before. Many times over the past several months he had woken up sobbing and screaming, with Atropina bending over him holding his hand or stroking his head, but he had never known what he had been dreaming. Now as he walked Maria to her little hut, the nightmare images seemed too real and immediate to be mere memories: the horrible desperation of that time gripped him and squeezed his heart anew.

Mario returned with a rabbit for their lunch. He burst into tears when he heard what had happened, and could not be consoled. His cries were like the deep moaning from a stricken beast that went on and on without letup. Giovanni had to prepare the meal. He skinned the rabbit, built up the flame, and roasted it. No one spoke until the food was ready, when Maria said she wasn't hungry and Mario agreed. Giovanni insisted they eat whether hungry or not, and they did so, like dutiful children. The baby was asleep in its bed the whole time, but Giovanni never forgot her, never stopped wondering what sort of future lay ahead of her.

After lunch they talked a little longer, Giovanni adding in general details, although he refused to answer specific questions about the plague itself: words conjured images of unbearable intensity.

Taking a few minutes after the meal, they gathered up their belongings and Maria suckled the infant at her breast. Then they set out for the town site where Atropina had promised to meet them. Giovanni carried a lamp with the precious flame burning at its wick. At least for now, its heat and light would once again be found in the valley below.

They avoided Giovanni's hut although normally it would be on their way. That morning Giovanni had passed the area and discovered the badly decomposed body of a mother and child on his bed: some day he would come back and bury them when he had more time. They did go by the cave, however, and it was deserted, its mouth open to the sky, its corridors echoing to their footsteps, the damp cold permeating every space. It was the first time in nine centuries the place had been abandoned, and to Giovanni there had never been a more lonely spot on earth. He left it behind them gratefully, once their quick survey was complete.

In late afternoon as the light was beginning to fade, they arrived back at the town. They moved their things into a large farmhouse that had belonged to one of the elders. No one had died there: its owners had been among those who had disappeared into the hills. That was important to Giovanni.

Then Maria and Mario walked around the town in silence. Giovanni saw them stand before their parents' houses. Mario couldn't bring himself to enter, but stood crying in the path out front. Maria was stronger: she went in and stayed for more than half an hour. When she returned she was not crying, although a grimness had taken hold of her that lasted the rest of the evening.

To Giovanni it was more disquieting than tears would have been. Few words were exchanged that night.

The next morning they had breakfast in silence, gruel cooked by Atropina. After they had eaten, Giovanni suggested they discuss their position.

"We cannot keep the sanctuary going," he began. "There are too few of us. We cannot prepare a new generation to take over in their turn. It is finished. Do we all agree?" He looked at Atropina and Maria, and both nodded. Mario was toying with some slips of thick paper on the tabletop. Giovanni decided to ignore him.

"That means we must close the cave: there is no sense in leaving it open for the Christians to find and destroy, or make a trophy of it. I think we should do what we can to place things into storage before we bury it: probably it doesn't matter, but if we leave manuscripts lying around unprotected, they will crumble away within a decade or two. I don't think we should let that happen. After all there is a chance, however remote, that the Gods will lead someone here in the future. We have a responsibility to see that we have done whatever we can to ensure the safekeeping of the things entrusted to us. Therefore I propose that we wrap all manuscripts in a protective covering. I've been thinking maybe cloth, then beeswax or pitch—maybe both. This will be a big job, but we don't have much else to do, do we?" Again he looked at the other two, and again they nodded.

"We don't have to worry about food, because the grain stores are much larger than the four of us need. We'll augment the grain by hunting and fishing. We should be all right until next spring when we can plant whatever we need for the following year. Once everything is properly protected, we can bury the cave and put it from out minds. Your child must not know about it, Maria. The knowledge of its existence must die with us. And that includes you too, Mario. When the cave is covered, it will disappear forever. Do you understand?"

Mario looked up from the strips of paper. "What?"

"We must forget about the cave. We must never tell anyone about it. Do you understand?"

"I must forget the cave."

"That's right.

"No cave."

"Yes."

There was silence then, and Giovanni realized there was nothing else to say. Nine hundred years wrapped up and buried in a moment. Wanting the conversation to continue, feeling the silence pressing upon him, he turned to Mario. "What are you playing with?"

"My father gave them to me. They come from the outsiders. See? They are pictures of coins on strings. There are different numbers of coins in each picture. See? And you must turn them upside down and mix them up. And you must lay them down on the table one at a time. Then you must turn them up. The person who turns up the highest one wins. And you must not play tricks: the highest one wins."

Giovanni heard his words with sadness. Although Mario spoke them, the words and tone were not Mario's. It was his father's words that the young man used. He had obviously memorized them after hearing his father explain it to him many times. The dead man's words had lived beyond him, guiding his dimwitted son.

Mario smiled. "Do you want to play, Giovanni? You can see your luck. The cards can show you if you are lucky or unlucky. If you are lucky you win! I will show you. You must turn them upside down and mix them up. And you must lay them down on the table one at a time..." Giovanni played along with Mario although the game seemed trivial and boring: he did not want to hurt the young man's feelings.

Later that day Giovanni and Maria returned to the cave to attempt to determine what would be involved in protection of the manuscripts. They spent several hours poking their heads in this and that. There was a great deal of work to do, it seemed. They left behind Atropina and Mario to explore the village and discover what raw materials were available there. Both turned out to be big jobs that lasted several days. It was early in the morning of the second day that Giovanni had his dream.

Giulia stood before him looking as lifelike as anyone. She was young. She smiled at him and pointed to the window of the room where he was sleeping. He walked over to see what she was pointing at, and he saw Mario's papers lying on the window ledge. Then he heard Giulia's voice whispering to him. "There is one card for everyone who died, but who will remember?" Someone blew out the candle that lit the room, perhaps Giulia, and Giovanni could see nothing in the darkness. He knew that tender flame had been the last of the sacred, ancient fire. He felt himself moaning, deep in his chest.

Then he became aware of the dawn's faint light entering through the window and he saw the cards lying on a table. Without knowing why, he knew it was many years later. The sight of the cards lying on the table flooded him with sadness, for although every card represented one of the dead, the owner of the cards did not know that: everything had long ago been forgotten.

After he woke to find dawn beginning to seep into his room, Giovanni could not prevent himself from wondering about the dream. Giulia's voice had been so clear in his ears, her face so real. Before this her appearance had blurred in his mind, but now it was again as clear as if he had seen her only yesterday. It sharpened the sadness of her loss and blended it in his mind with the recent disaster of the village. Although he told no one of it, all day long he found himself coming back to the dream as if it were a riddle he could not let go of. He asked Mario if he could borrow his cards, and of course Mario agreed. Giovanni looked them over from time to time throughout the day as if he was searching for something, though what it was he couldn't say.

For many hours before he could go to sleep that night, he traced the dream again and again in his mind. There was such sweetness hidden in it, though much pain too. Seeking to move on, to purge the dream from his mind, Giovanni decided to write the name of a villager on each of the cards. There were not enough of them to have one for every villager, but he decided there would be enough for the elders and those he loved most. Carefully he wrote in their names. After finishing, he was still dissatisfied, and decided to draw a picture or symbol by each name to capture something important about each person's character. It felt to him as if he was making the village's epitaph, and he found himself wondering how he could find someone to give them to so that they would be protected and passed on, surviving into the future as they had in the dream. It was very late when he set the cards down, feeling dissatisfied but too tired to continue. He fell asleep immediately. That night Giulia came to him again.

Tears blinded his vision, and his chest grew so tight his breath was nearly strangled in his throat. He longed to say something, but he could not. She smiled as she held the cards and looked down at them. "Now they may know the sanctuary though the village is gone." She seemed about to give the cards to him, but something caught her eye. Instead she held them up to her face and inspected them closely before turning towards him to smile. Their eyes met. "It is good, Giovanni: now they will find the cave when the time is right." Seeing those eyes and hearing his name as it had not been spoken for forty years was exquisite agony. But despite his anguish he wondered what she had seen and tried to peer over the tops of the cards she held. The tears blinded him again, and before he wipe them away he was awake.

He was too agitated to sleep, and turning up the lamp he inspected the cards. There was nothing on them suggesting the cave's existence to him. He laid them all face up on the table and looked at each one very carefully, but nothing suggested itself to him. Perhaps it wasn't there yet: that part was the dream, but he could put some sign in them now. What would he put there? What symbol would he use? Mario's voice came to him from two days before "You must turn them upside down and mix them up..." He sighed, thinking of the poor boy's father.

Then suddenly he sprang up and walked to the window trembling with excitement. He could see nothing in the darkness outside. He turned and walked back to the table, barely aware of it or of his hand as he swept the cards onto the floor, pounded the table with his fist, and shouted "Yes!"

By the time Maria ran into the room, roused by the noise, he was sitting on the bed, a pillow in his lap, looking into the distance saying "Of course, of course..." The cards had already been gathered up in one hand, but they were ignored.

"What is it?" asked Maria.

He looked at her with surprise, remembered himself, and laughed with excitement. "I know what we can do. We can put everything on cards...like these. Even a map showing where the cave is."

"Why?"

"So that everything is not lost. So that in the future they know what we have done."

"But where do we put the cards? Who do we give them to?"

"Everyone. Don't you see? We hide the sanctuary in the cards so that the secrets are there to be found by future generations. Then we make sure as many people as possible have the cards. That way it will be available when it is needed."

"How can you hide something so that our enemies won't find it, but someone friendly to us will, someone not yet born? One slight mistake and you will lose everything. The Christians will find the cave and plunder it."

Giovanni pounded the pillow with his fist, startling Maria and frightening her until she realized that in his excitement he was almost laughing. "How can you ask that question? What are we? We are the guardian of myths: riddles that have been hidden from most people for more than a thousand years, though many millions have known the stories. If you don't look for an answer, you don't find one. Or if you look in the wrong way, you don't find one. We can do the same thing with pictures that myths have done with words. But you know something? With pictures we can make sure nothing is changed. We can create a tradition of picture cards that must be copied exactly. We can include a map."

Maria was not convinced, but she was curious. "What else would we have pictures of? I mean, besides the cave's location?"

Giovanni tried hard to keep the frustration out of his voice. "I don't know...Whatever we think is important... All right, for example, the Mysterion, the God wheel used for fortune telling. If I remember correctly, it describes the seasons, the elements, the relationships of things in this world, and then tells the past and the future, right?"

"Right."

"So suppose we put the Mysterion onto cards? With clues about how to use it? We could even get outsiders to use the cards for telling fortunes: a reasonable parallel to their actual meaning."

"But if you draw the Mysterion on a card, people would know what it is, wouldn't they?"

"Not necessarily, if it was shown symbolically. And anyway, the Mysterion uses sixteen Gods, right? So give each one a separate card. And three seasons in the center of it, right?"

"Yes, three seasons, but two cycles: material and spiritual. That makes it three seasons, twice repeated—six cards."

"So the Mysterion consists of twenty-two cards. Unless you put them in the right order, they would make no sense. We put clues in the cards telling the right order, but we make them difficult to recognize. With the help of the Gods, they will not be understood until the right moment comes along."

Maria sounded skeptical. "This sounds possible but very difficult and dangerous. Perhaps we should talk it over with Atropina in the morning? You may be right but it needs to be thought over very carefully."

They went back to bed: Maria to sleep, Giovanni to ponder. He was still lying in bed thinking when the sun rose. By the time Atropina and Maria had eaten and were ready to hear him out, he had already done quite a lot of planning. The extraordinary scheme just seemed to grow spontaneously in his mind.

Joining the two women and Mario at the breakfast table, Giovanni addressed Atropina. "I know what I came for."

Atropina did not seem surprised, but she was curious. "And what is that?"

"I will make cards describing the Gods, the mysteries, the cave, everything. When we are dead, when the final purification has taken place, the secrets we have kept will continue to be whispered without being understood until the new age is born."

Atropina laughed. "Yes! That sounds like Giovanni: keeping everything going even when we are gone. Resisting the turn of the wheel even as you work with it. It perfectly matches your nature."

Maria was frowning at Giovanni's words, and after the older woman had finished speaking, she addressed him. "I thought about your idea when I awoke this morning, and I realized something you seem to have forgotten. The mysteries have never been revealed to non-initiates: they can only be given to those who have sworn an oath to keep the secrets of the Gods from non-initiates.

"From ancient times, initiation involved being guided to revelation by one who was already initiated. It involved being told myths and shown rituals and objects which made no sense and fit no natural order the prospective initiate was aware of. Only in the final phase of the initiation process is the truth revealed in a flash of insight guided by the priests. The hidden order is revealed. For many, that was the end, but for some it was only the beginning.

"In many of the ancient mysteries there is the basic level of initiation, after which the depth of the initiate's understanding was gauged by the priests. Only those who had a deeper understanding were offered a higher initiation. Others didn't even know it existed. And the initiates at this second level were again assessed for the depth of their understanding after the revelation, and again only those with the greatest understanding were offered a higher initiation, and so on.

"To gain the right to stand in the cave with free access to everything there, someone must be fully initiated to the very highest levels. And consider: the Mysteries at Eleusis, Samothrace, Lerna and Delphi, and all the others: each must be mastered before the initiate stands at the mouth of the cave, since the secrets of all are no longer hidden once one stands there. Without the highest levels of initiation in which the candidate has proven himself worthy of revelation, he cannot be permitted to see the things we are guarding here. The discoverer of the secret meaning of your cards must be an initiate. How can he be an initiate since there will be no one to initiate him?"

Giovanni frowned in consternation. Atropina watched him calmly. Suddenly he brightened and spoke. "Then we must initiate him! We must make certain that the person who understands the cards is the sort of person who is suited to understanding the mysteries. The cards must select him and train him: they must do both. Only when he understands all the secrets of the cards, thus showing that he is suited for revelation, will he discover the map." He looked at Maria, his eyes again shining with excitement, but she shook her head.

"How can such a subtle and difficult thing be achieved?" she asked, doubtfully.

"That will be discovered as we proceed. You are asking what we will do before we have done it, what we will invent before it is invented. Be patient! Let us understand our goal clearly, and only then discover our method of achieving it. There are many problems to overcome, many indeed, but if we confront them one at a time, I am sure we can resolve them." Maria did not seem convinced, so he went on. "If we fail, then we fail, and everything will be buried when the cave is covered up. But humor me in this: let us try! If, when we are finished, any one of us believes that the cards have failed despite our best efforts, then we will give them up. But the time for quitting is not before we have begun."

Maria frowned. "I think there is something else that cannot be so easily put away. The initiate who understands the cards will not have sworn an oath of secrecy. He will be under no obligation to maintain the secrets of the Gods that we are giving him. For thousands of years the secrets have been kept because the initiates have sworn oaths and kept them. The oath preceded initiation and if they hadn't sworn they would have been excluded. The initiate you are proposing will have no one to administer the oath. He cannot even realize that he is learning of the mysteries until he has progressed very far. Nothing will prevent him from telling the whole world if he chooses."

Giovanni was impatient. "The initiate's oath promises to keep the secrets of the Gods from all who are not initiated. It was customary that every initiation included it. However the oath itself never declares that initiation must be preceded by an oath of secrecy. That was custom, but not the law. As long as the one who discovers our secrets is initiated in the very process of discovering them, then we have not failed in our oath to preserve the mysteries." His argument was logical, yet he was starting to feel uncomfortable.

"Yes, grandfather, we have not in a legal sense, but what will keep him from breaking silence?"

Giovanni was at a loss. It seemed his granddaughter had found an unsolvable problem. How indeed could they ensure the secrets were kept? They were not breaking an oath, but they were treading perilously close to the border of acceptable action, and letting a mere legal argument stand between them and the widespread knowledge of things they had sworn to keep secret. Would they not be failing the whole spirit of the mysteries? Even if their intentions were good, would they not be guilty after the fact if the one they initiated failed them and divulged what he or she had learned?

Atropina had been watching in silence up until that point. When she spoke, her tone was very serious, a thing Giovanni had not often seen, even in the days when Far-Shooter had come. "We are creating a new mystery, and in doing so we are free to create whatever rules we think proper. In ancient times one mystery might bar women, another allow only mothers. The oaths varied from place to place, just as the candidates did. The mystery we are creating is for one person only, the first time this has ever been done. The conditions under which the mystery will be presented are also unique. That doesn't mean it is wrong to do it: we are also bound by our oaths to preserve the mysteries, and this seems to be the only way we can fulfill that responsibility.

"If we manage to achieve what Giovanni has suggested, we will have done our part. Will the unbound initiate divulge what we teach? That will be for him or her to decide, according to the circumstances of that age. If we can ensure that only a proper candidate for the highest mysteries penetrates the secrets of the cards, then surely we can trust her to do what is right. I believe Giovanni is correct: I think we can both select and train her through skillful creation of the cards. She will respect us enough to consider our wishes and those of the Gods seriously. She will decide what is right. Perhaps the age of secrets is over. And we must remember that there are things involved here that are of special interest to the Gods. We must also trust in them to ensure that all goes well once we have done what we can. We must choose our candidate carefully, but in the end it will be for the Gods to make the final decision— and it is possible they will let our secrets sleep until the ends of time. I don't think so, but it is possible."

"Perhaps it is well, then." Maria nodded. "Perhaps you are right, grandfather. But we will have to be very, very careful in deciding if we have done what we are trying to do. We have to guard ourselves from too much enthusiasm or wishful thinking. We have to be absolutely clear that we have chosen the right kind of candidate and controlled his or her initiation process from beginning to end." She looked at Atropina. "If we all decide that our new mystery is successful, then we will go ahead with it. I am doubtful, but I am willing to try."

So it was agreed. From that day onwards much time was spent in the cave each day researching. For months the study of myth, ritual and initiation in the ancient mysteries kept them going over the old records and books hour after hour, often far into the night. The baby slept in a crib in the corner which they had brought in for the purpose.

The gradual development of the cards and the clues they would harbor was a slow process, and involved endless debate over the fine tuning of the riddles they would include. Again and again they lived with the mind of the discoverer they would never meet, who would find what they had hidden in a future age. They set out a sequence of clues none but a proper candidate for the mysteries could discover, and demanded from him or her the same intuition and insight in the face of revelation that the highest candidates had been expected to have in ancient times. They took their work as seriously as it demanded and for Maria and Giovanni at least, nothing else mattered.

When they were not researching or developing the cards, they worked on protecting the manuscripts and other objects from the damp and cold of the coming centuries. Mario did this full time, and to everyone's delight, not least his own, he turned out to have an extraordinary talent in this area. His slow, methodical, gentle hands wrapped countless manuscripts in cloth, then coated them in warm beeswax to form a water tight seal. It was decided that the following spring when the sap rose they would collect pitch, and this would be used to coat the beeswax in a tough heat and water resistant shell. In the meantime he stacked the half-preserved manuscripts in one of the storerooms. He worked all day in the library which was heated with charcoal to drive out the damp.

The more they thought about it, the more the Mysterion showed itself to be a perfect method of executing their purpose. It represented a comprehensive description of countless aspects of ancient religion, it described ordinary life from a Pagan perspective, and it described the way to a life of wisdom. The ancient Gods were there, but so were the elements of the philosophers. Wisdom, ignorance, the trinity, mysteries, life, death, rebirth: all their truths were there, to greater or lesser degrees.

It was decided that the understanding of the wheel would be incomplete unless a chart was included in the cards, describing its positions. A wheel and a chart: two expressions of the same thing. The chart would also describe the four elements and their Gods, and would describe them as they came under the influence of the three Seasons and two cycles.

Their biggest job was to cut back on the information they included, to keep it to a bare minimum. There was not room for all myths and mysteries: only the most important could be given a place—in suitably camouflaged form, of course. In this spirit, it was decided the only Gods actually described in detail would be the three Seasons: some of the others would be hinted at, or only described in their lesser, earthen manifestations or reflections.

The work was challenging, but it progressed steadily. Once a day, usually in the afternoon, Giovanni, Atropina and Maria met to discuss their progress and problems for that day. This was the time when they tried to bring everything together: they began to discuss the appropriate symbols for individual cards, and often they found ways that the goals of describing myth, ritual, wisdom, the physical shape of the Mysterion, and even the pattern in which the cards were to be laid out could be combined within a given picture.

It was almost two months after they had begun that Maria started to sketch out the basic illustrations, and swiftly became accomplished in the techniques of drawing. In fact, she had to restrain herself, for it was agreed the designs, while intricate, had to be relatively easy for future copyists to render: if too demanding, they would invite modification, and that would make future rediscovery of the spread impossible. There was still a long way to go, but she continued updating the details in the months ahead, when fresh ideas came to them, which was often. Maria's brilliance was particularly noticeable when they were dealing with the complex interactions of symbols and clues in different areas of the evolving spread. Even Atropina was hard-pressed to follow the subtlety of her thinking. It was around this time that they also began to debate and design in detail the traditions that would accompany the use of the cards in fortune telling. In the method of reading the future would lie clues to the secret card spread, clues to its understanding, and clues to the method by which the original Mysterion was used. All these things, and traditions ensuring that in future years the original cards would be copied faithfully, had to be worked out in painstaking detail.

Again and again, the three of them debated the question upon which everything else relied: how subtle should the clues be? They had to prevent thousands, perhaps millions of people from finding the solution, while at the same time making sure that when the time was right, the right sort of person would stumble on their meaning, someone who was not hostile to them. Someone who was by nature open to the revelations of the Gods, and sympathetic to their message.

Atropina led the thinking in this area. She maintained that the solution should be impossible for people who thought they knew anything about it. The only way the correct solution should be found was by observing the cards without any preconceptions whatsoever. As she pointed out on many occasions, most people think they know something about everything: let the one who would finally understand the cards be the one who knew that he or she knew nothing. Let her listen without opinions: let her be observant and intuitive yet logical; let her have a character that was curious and open, non-dogmatic. If they were careful in their work, they could select such a person, sight unseen, guiding her to find what no other would.

To be successful, the clues had to be designed to make almost everyone become lost in their own wishful and fearful thinking. And Atropina suggested that the art of fortune telling with cards should be taught as a highly specialized and mysterious occupation based on authority, not reason or observation—that they should design the occupation that way. Fortune tellers would consider themselves experts, and experts can never afford to be without an opinion on every subject: that is how they guarantee themselves the respect of others. Thus the keepers of the cards should be encouraged to be too sure of their knowledge to recognize what they actually possessed.

Each step in the creation of the cards was very subtle, very logical, very intuitive. Giovanni was frequently amazed when he looked at how much they were accomplishing and how subtle the evolving card deck was becoming. Atropina was invaluable to their efforts, but she never seemed to view her involvement as anything more than a game. For her none of it really mattered, except that her friends were doing it and wished to have her help. She would never refuse to help someone in such a harmless occupation.

Giovanni had far more invested in the work, and it gave him no small pleasure to see the cards evolve and grow richer by the day. Real happiness was elusive, of course, for the horrors of the plague were still far too fresh— indeed they would clearly be so for the rest of his life. But work was Giovanni's best method of keeping the recent tragic events from his mind, and he attacked it with gusto. Maria was similarly motivated. As for Mario, well, he took after Atropina. Neither the future nor the past had much hold over him, and once the initial pain of his loss had dimmed somewhat, he simply enjoyed making himself useful.

From time to time it troubled Giovanni deeply that there was no certainty of success. Every step of their carefully laid plans relied on human nature being predictable and on their making the right predictions. But even more it relied on destiny being kind: there were an infinite number of things that could go wrong even if every calculation had been made perfectly. Their mistakes could prevent success, but nothing would ensure their victory except help from the Gods. And none of the three creators would be around to see what would happen. The thought was so upsetting that Giovanni made every effort never to think of it. All they could do was their best: and let the Gods look after the rest if they chose to.

Given the complexity of time, they could not calculate with any certainty how long it would be before the world was ready to listen to them, though they discussed it often. It could be as little as one century or as much as nine. Atropina's best guess was about five or six centuries, around the end of the current millennium of the Christian era. If they were just before the rebirth, as she believed, they had to expect that it would take a long time before the ignorance of the Dionysian age grew weaker and the new age properly began. The great wheel of civilization turns slowly.

Many months passed with the four of them hard at work. From the time of first conception until the day the cards were completed, the winter snows came and went, then came again.

At last a moment arrived when the cards were as near to perfect as Giovanni and the others could make them, and all three were satisfied that they performed as they were intended. Even Maria had lost her doubts regarding the effort: she had to admit that every detail had been carefully considered and every conceivable problem solved. The newest mystery of the ancient religion was finally complete.

By then, the preservation effort was proceeding well. They could continue working on it full time, but it made sense for Giovanni to begin teaching outsiders in the use of their cards. He was the natural candidate, for Atropina's health was not so good and Maria had a baby to look after. He gathered together provisions and furnished himself with a walking stick.

It was early in 1350 that Giovanni stood in the snow by the banks of the Taro river, embracing the three who had come to see him off. "Go in peace," said Atropina, smiling. He wondered, as he turned to leave, if he would ever see her again.

The old man arrived at the inn and offered to tell the innkeeper's future to him in exchange for a room. The innkeeper looked him over and laughed, telling him to keep his fortunes to himself. The old man shrugged and ordered a mug of wine, sitting down at a table by himself, setting a small stack of thick papers on the table in front of him. For half an hour he sat there, barely moving except for the tremor in his hands that age and hardship had given him. Finally a young man asked him the inevitable question. What were those cards?

"They are called Taro cards. I will show you," the old man said. The questioner sat down opposite him and watched as he mixed the cards up and then laid them out, their faces turned down, in a strange pattern on the tabletop. "First I will describe your present situation, then I will describe the forces that are influencing you," the fortune teller said.

For the next half hour the old man slowly turned over the cards and talked about what he found. The pictures seemed to tell him things that no one else could know. A small circle of listeners began to form. The questioner became embarrassed to have his life discussed in such detail and so openly before others, so he told the spectators to back off or face his fists. Reluctantly they went back to their tables, and watched from the corner of their eyes as the old man leaned forward and talked quietly into his listener's ear. For his part the young man listened quietly most of the time, asking questions every now and then. When the old man abruptly gathered up the cards and sat back, the others were quick to demand he tell them what he could of their futures.

All afternoon the old man used the magic papers to tell what the future held. That night the innkeeper gave him a room for free, and dinner besides—on the understanding that he would read the futures of customers the following evening. The innkeeper was a canny businessman.

And so it began, the visit of the mysterious old man. Many asked him where he came from, but he never said, always politely avoiding the question. They asked him where he had learned about the cards, but all he would say was that they came from ancient times. Several of his customers asked him if he would teach them how to use the cards, and where they could get some of their own. He never replied, and the conversation moved on to other things.

Eventually one young man would not let his questions be pushed aside, and he kept pressing the old man to tell him. Finally, apparently convinced of his sincerity and interest, the old man agreed to teach him if he promised to work hard until he mastered it. In this way he became the old man's apprentice. He was the first, but others soon followed him. Women in particular, once they'd heard of the amazing capabilities of the cards, were keen to have their fortunes read and to gain the mysterious power of doing the readings for others.

In time there were eight apprentices and five graduates, four of whom had found apprentices of their own. As their final act before graduation, the students had to create their own deck of cards—a perfect copy of the teacher's deck, with no errors or deviations of any kind allowed. The old man was much beloved by his pupils for his gentleness and patience as he taught them the many nuances of the cards. They were devoted to him, and blindly obedient regarding his instructions: he explained, gently but firmly, that any change would upset the delicate balance upon which their art depended, and result in false readings. None was so foolish as to risk that.

Having one's fortune read in the Taro was becoming a fashionable diversion among the wealthy, and it appealed to the poorer folk as well. These were dangerous days, and everyone was anxious for a chance to glimpse their future, hoping to avoid the terrible uncertainty that the plague had unleashed in Europe. Things were going very well for those in the new profession, and a few of them were making a good living at it. Months passed, and the number of candidates for instruction in the strange art continued to grow.

The old man went on living in the inn and gave fortunes there in exchange for board, but he spent his days in a hall belonging to a fraternity of carpenters. It was little used since the decimation of the membership in the plague years, and his students put together the trifling sum needed to cover the rent. They gathered there and practiced their art while their kind old teacher watched over them, refining their skills and making sure they did not deviate from the necessary knowledge and its application.

It never occurred to any of his students past or present that the old man would only remain among them for eight months. One day, when he did not appear at their usual meeting place, they went up to his room at the inn. No one was there, and his belongings were gone, but they found a note on the bed. It had not been known the old man could write, and the knowledge that he could only served to increase his reputation as a wise man. Since none of them shared this skill, they took the note to a learned priest of the Benedictine Order and had him translate for them.

It merely said the graduates should become teachers to the apprentices until they were finished their training and took students of their own. By teaching the art exactly as it was taught to them, they would increase their own skill in it. Then the note wished them all good fortune. It never said goodbye, or where he was going, but no one ever saw the old man again.

Some of the apprentices maintained he had gone to Jerusalem, others that he had traveled to Constantinople or Westward, to the Saracen court in Spain. The only thing they could say for certain was that he vanished as mysteriously as he had appeared. Only the cards and the knowledge of their use remained.

iovanni waited in the empty village. He was sitting on a children's swing, hands holding the fraying ropes, idly pushing himself back and forth a little while the autumn leaves fell intermittently all around him. The late afternoon sun was bright but no longer warm and the sky was a deeper, colder blue, for the season was well advanced. The wind bit against his fingers.

For three weeks he had been back in the valley. When he returned, it seemed to him that the ghosts had moved on in his absence and now the town was truly empty. The buildings were no longer houses, the homes of parents and children, warmed with their dreams and passions. Now they were just stones, as cold and meaningless as rocks piled randomly one upon another in the wilderness. The seasons would come and go as the years passed by, but in this place it no longer mattered. No one was left to mark their passing.

Atropina was dead. She had died not long after Giovanni left, and was buried near where he now sat. Her wisdom could not prevent her passing. He felt her loss as deeply as the loss of Giulia so long ago, but he cried no tears and felt no agony at the news. In silence the sorrow nipped at his bones even now, but he felt no regret. He had nothing left to grieve with. It occurred to Giovanni that passions were a flame that consumed the human heart, bit by bit, until nothing was left to burn. Wisdom might renew it, but he was not wise, and his heart was as empty and desolate as the town.

As he sat there, feeling loneliness falling from the sky like a mist, it seemed to Giovanni that he was no longer fully alive. His eyes could see, his ears could hear, his hands could touch and hold, but his memories and dreams belonged to another time. It was the same when he thought of Maria and Mario. To Giovanni it seemed that like him they were strangers here, travelers lost in time. So it was with the flame that still burned in the house where they were living. Untended, as it would soon be, when they abandoned the town and rejoined the greater world, it would quickly consume its last fuel and die unnoticed. More than two thousand years of history, vanishing forever into the night.

Only the child seemed fresh and new, and though Giovanni loved her it seemed to him she was not of them: she belonged to the future as surely as they belonged to the past. He sensed in his soul that Death would soon claim him, but he was not concerned. Once they left this place, the only thing that mattered was the child: establishing a secure future for her, if such could be established in this world.

He tucked his hands under his armpits for warmth and looked at the mountain towering above him to the south-east. Maria and Mario were there with the child.

That day when he woke up at dawn, his arm had begun to hurt and his chest was squeezed so hard he could barely breath. It was as if the world was pressing in to crush the void he had become, and he thought he would cast away his body at any moment. After a while the attack passed, leaving him shaky and exhausted. Maria was concerned and wanted to stay with him, but he insisted he would be all right. It was the day when the cave was to be buried and in truth he was not keen to witness it.

They had undermined a section of the mountain above the cave's opening so that it would collapse and fill the entrance with debris. It was hard work, but after several weeks of preparation a final stone was all that held the sanctuary open to the sky. Levered from its place it would release a torrent of earth that would remain for centuries where it fell, perhaps forever. No, Giovanni did not wish to witness the end, and he was grateful for his poor health this once, because it had spared him that sorrowful sight. Sometimes, he thought, it is better not to say goodbye. He had spent the morning sitting before the fire, knowing it was doomed to be extinguished soon, warming himself against the approaching winter.

hat afternoon the little family did not return. Nor that evening, or even that night. Giovanni discovered that it was possible for a half-dead Man such as him to know fear, and with the passing hours the anxiety in his belly swelled and grew.

When the sun rose without sign of them, he set off from the town with as much haste as his tired legs would lend him. The trail seemed steeper than ever, and it amazed him to think another, younger man had once climbed this very path without a hint of exhaustion. It took him many laborious hours to approach the cave, and his eyes kept scanning the way ahead, hoping for a sight of the others.

When he arrived at last, he felt a moment of confusion: just before the place where the cave should be, the trail disappeared in a talus slope of freshly tumbled rock. The mountain had fallen and the entrance to the cave had vanished so completely it was hard to believe it had ever been there. Where were they? He looked around, but saw no sign. No one gave answer to his frantic shouts.

Then he heard the sounds of whimpering coming faintly from the undergrowth somewhere ahead. It was the child's voice. Picking his way precariously across the steep slope, sliding and scrabbling along the loose stones on his feet and hands, Giovanni came to the farther edge of the landslide. Pushing through a yellowing bush, he saw his great-granddaughter lying on her back, tightly wrapped in a blanket to keep her warm and prevent her from crawling away. Beside her on the forest litter lay the wineskin and the lunch Maria had made for the previous day, still untouched, still waiting to be eaten.

The child was crying now, obviously thirsty and in need of food. He picked her up and fumbled with the wineskin while he spoke to her softly, clumsily removing the plug and letting a little of the watered wine trickle onto the open mouth. She sucked and bubbled eagerly, forgetting to cry. It took several minutes, but at last she had had enough and promptly fell asleep.

Giovanni set her down carefully and returned to the slide, looking for some sign of the others. He decided to follow the avalanche downwards: perhaps they had been carried below and were even now lying badly injured and unable to call out at the base. Dread choked him. It took him several minutes to pick his way down. Halfway, he started to slip and was almost carried over the edge of a steep cliff. It wasn't all that high, perhaps three times his height, but it was enough to break his leg, certainly. It occurred to him that if he died the child would also die, and the knowledge made him shake with fear at how little stood between her and perishing. Taking several deep breaths, he continued.

The slide ended in the gully down below, some of the larger stones lying beyond its slope, carried farther by the force of their fall. The breeze did not penetrate the place, and the sunlight lay behind the ridge. It was dim and quiet while he stood for a moment in the autumnal chill and looked around.

There was no sign of anyone. His eyes turned upwards, towards the motionless slope of uneven stone, and it looked to him like a towering wall. He knew without question, then, what had happened in that place: the mountain had swallowed them up. He had known it was so before he came down. He had known it even before he climbed the mountain. It seemed to him he had known this must happen all his life, and the years were just a strange dance with time, bringing him to an end he had always anticipated but always been unwilling to face. He sat on a boulder for a very long time and closed his eyes, listening to the cold silence of the mountain.

The old man arrived at the inn in mid-morning when the churches were emptying their congregations into the streets. He had come down from the mountains to the North, down the steeply winding path to this ancient town that sat by the edge of the Mediterranean sea. He had a baby strapped to his back, a golden-haired child who cooed and laughed at the people who caught her eye, but the old man seemed too preoccupied to be aware of anyone.

He had trudged slowly to the inn, leaning on his stick, eyes glazed, and in a flat expressionless voice asked the innkeeper for a room. After requesting a little milk he retired with the child and no one saw him again until the following day.

It was midday before the old man reappeared, the little girl in his arms, to put her carefully down on a table and pay for another night's lodgings. The innkeeper set out a cup of wine and some cheese for him in lieu of the previous night's meal, and he sat there beside the child lost in thought, sipping absently from time to time.

One of the other guests, a man of about forty years of age, balding and stout, popular with the others for his cheerful disposition, picked up his own cup and walked over. He did not like to see anyone unhappy, and he was not the sort to let another mope alone without at least trying to raise his spirits.

"Is this your grandson?" He reached over to run his finger along the child's smooth cheek, but the old man brushed his hand away, suddenly bristling as if he were under attack. The other leaned back, eyes wide. "I'm sorry. I didn't mean to upset you."

For a moment the old man looked him over, frowning, then relaxed. "It's all right. I'm just tired," he said, and from his voice the truth of that was plain.

"My name is Alberto. I'm from Venice."

A barely perceptible nod. "Giovanni."

"I'm a merchant, just here for a few days to do a little business."

The old man said nothing.

"What is your grandson's name?"

"Guilia."

Alberto laughed. "I can never tell the difference at that age." The old man nodded but was silent, so he went on. "Perhaps I would know the difference if I was a father, but my wife and I have no children of our own. Being an uncle is not the same as having young ones in your own house."

The old man looked at him with a sudden spark of interest, his eyes appraising. It lasted only an instant and just as suddenly was gone. Even so he relaxed a little more, and awkwardly tried to smile, though not with much success.

"Would you like to hold her?"

"I'd love to." Alberto stood up and reached across the table, Giovanni helping him lift the bundle into his arms. Alberto looked into the little face and rocked her, clucking and smiling for a moment as adults do with the very young.

"You are good with children."

"I wish that were true." Nonetheless Alberto was flattered. "Where is her mother?"

The old man suddenly stood, reaching out and taking the child back. Then he sat down again with her cradled in his arms, and kissed her before replying. "She died," he said quietly, his voice taut but uninflected, giving his finger to the child to hold.

"Oh...I'm sorry. And the father?"

Another pause, and then the words that seemed to rise from a boundless sea of pain: "Him too."

"My God, that's terrible. Please forgive me for asking." He shook his head. "These are terrible times we live in. I lost my parents and one of my brothers in the Great Death. I guess I was lucky. Some in my city lost everyone they loved." He paused and then roused himself. "But we should dwell on what we have, not what once was." He lifted his cup. "Here's to your granddaughter's health."

"My great-granddaughter."

"Here's to your great-granddaughter's health." They tapped their cups together and drained them. "Would you like another? I'll pay."

But suddenly he slapped the table lightly with the palm of his hand. "Giovanni, I have a better idea. Why don't we go for a walk down to the sea? We can buy a drink there and enjoy the view. It would be good for the child to have some sunshine."

Giovanni shook his head. "I am too tired right now, and..." He stopped mid-sentence and looked at the girl. "No, you're right Alberto, that's a good idea, if you don't mind walking slowly. Perhaps you wouldn't mind carrying Giulia?"

Leaving the dim interior of the inn, Alberto and Giovanni paused for a moment, blinded by the brightness of the day outside. Alberto draped a corner of the blanket over Giulia's face to shield her from the glare, and they set off through the narrow streets at a leisurely pace. Alberto felt happy, and a little proud when passers-by looked at him holding the baby. It was silly perhaps, but it felt good to know they would assume he was the father, and whenever they passed through the shade of a building he pulled back the blanket and lifted her a little so everyone could see how beautiful she was. Once when he did this he saw Giovanni watching him out of the corner of his eye and he was embarrassed, but the old man turned and smiled at him, so the embarrassment passed.

Near the waterfront they saw a small crowd clustered around a little table where two people were sitting, staring intently down at the tabletop in front of them. Craning to see, Giovanni took hold of Alberto's arm and guided him over. On the table there were blank pieces of paper laid down to form the pattern of a circle and a line. One of the sitting men turned a paper over to reveal a brightly colored picture on it. Leaning forward past another onlooker's shoulder, Alberto saw that it was a little painting of a nude woman pouring water from two jugs while a bright star shone from the sky behind her.

"What is it? What are they doing?"

The old man seemed excited about something. "I don't know, let's listen."

For half an hour they remained where they were and watched what was going on. It was some sort of fortune telling, apparently, for the one who turned over the cards kept speaking to the other about events in his life, although Alberto could tell from the way he was speaking the two hadn't known each other previously. He didn't give much credence to such things, but he had to admit that based on the reactions of the listener, the fortune teller seemed to be doing very well. Giovanni watched everything with great concentration and childlike excitement, so Alberto waited patiently, playing with Giulia and contenting himself with shifting his feet from time to time, even after he had become bored.

He was greatly relieved when the fortune was finished and Giovanni suggested they leave before the next questioner's reading began. The old man seemed uplifted, almost youthful as they continued on their way.

"You like fortune telling, Giovanni?"

"Very much. I saw this same method being used a while back in Milan. I believe it is new, but it seems to be catching on. In fact, it seems wonderfully successful."

"Yes." Alberto was secretly amused at the transformation in the old man. He would never have thought someone so somber could be so easily diverted. People were always surprising you when you got to know them.

Arriving by the shore, Alberto purchased a jug of wine and some dried dates, and they walked past the wharves to where the beach looked out on a sparkling sea. It was cool that day, almost cold, but fortunately there was no wind to speak of, and they were comfortable as they sat on the shore not far from where the waves were lapping, taking turns with the jug. They unwrapped the baby from her blanket cocoon, and she crawled around, much to Alberto's amusement, putting sand and bits of shell in her mouth despite their best efforts to prevent her.

They talked of many things, as the bottle drained and affection grew between them. Giovanni was a private man who seemed shy about revealing much of his past, but from things he said Alberto realized he had once been involved in trade himself, and that he could read and write as well as himself. What's more, he had traveled quite a bit in his youth, apparently, and they fell into a discussion of the sights of Constantinople and other distant places they both had seen. When it dawned on him that the old man never spoke of himself at all unless asked, Alberto became more and more curious.

"Now I understand you barely know me, but if you don't mind Giovanni, I'm tired of telling you all about my life and I'm curious about yours. Where are you from?" The old man shook his head. "Where is your family? You must come from somewhere, surely."

"They are all dead."

Alberto was disturbed. "All of them? There is no one?"

"Only this child."

"That's awful." He thought for a moment. "It must be a great burden for someone at your age to be responsible for such a small child. Do you have friends in town?"

"No. Everyone is dead, I'm afraid. The flame in our family's hearth no longer burns: everything is reduced to ashes except this child." He cleared his throat, pressing his lips together and frowning. "I came here to give the child over to an orphanage. I can think of nothing else I can do. I am old, as you say, and my health is not good." Giovanni swallowed hard and Alberto saw tears filling the old man's eyes as he continued. "I have no choice but to give her to the Dio...to the Church, and hope fortune is kind to her."

"This is terrible...terrible..." Alberto could think of nothing more to say. They sat watching the child as she found a date and happily began to suck on it, quickly covering her hands and face with a mixture of saliva, sand, and the sticky sweetness of the date.

Alberto watched sadly and wondered if there was anything he could do to help. A thought had occurred to him back in the inn, more of a wish, really, and now it came back to him. He took a deep breath as if to speak, but at the last moment he hesitated. He didn't want to be rushed: it was a difficult thing to decide. Would he regret it if he made the offer?

Suddenly the child screamed in surprise and pain: she had cut her hand on a shell. Alberto saw the old man reach for her fearfully, and then comfort her in his arms, embracing her as if he could protect her from the dangers of the world. It was a tragic sight, the old man cradling the helpless child, and Alberto's heart rebelled against his reason: he couldn't remain silent any longer.

"Listen, Giovanni..." Once he began to speak his conviction grew. "This is going to sound crazy. I know you just met me, and we barely know each other, but I have a good feeling about you and this child, and I have an offer to make. I can't be sure until I've spoken with my wife, of course, but if she agrees—and I know she will—I mean, if you want us to...well...perhaps we could look after Giulia for you.

"I think we could offer her a good home. My business is successful, and as I said we have no children of our own. We considered adopting, at least my wife did, but I didn't feel right about it until now. I don't know what you will think of me for saying so, but it feels to me like it is God's will that we met. I am certain we could love and protect this little girl.

"And before you decide, let me say this. I wouldn't dream of taking her from you before...before you were ready. You could come with me to Venice: I will pay for your passage by ship, or you can travel with me by land if you think it would not be too difficult.

"My parents lived in a separate area of the house with its own entrance before they died. It has been empty for several years. You could stay there with Giulia. We are not rich, but we are comfortable and I could look after your expenses. That way you could see if it's really what you wanted, you understand? You could get to know our family. I know you will like my wife.

"If you need some time to think about it, don't worry: take as long as you need. I will postpone my departure until you have decided."

The old man shook his head. "I don't need time to think, Alberto. It is, as you say, a gift from God that we met. I could not let myself dream that such good luck would come to us, but now that it has I feel true peace for the first time since the child's parents died. I thought that I would have to die knowing that she was in an orphanage where no one would truly love and care for her. Take her: take her with my deepest blessing.

"I do not expect to live very long, and I will not have you take me to Venice to be a burden to your family. No, please don't bother attempting to change my mind. I am not afraid of dying. The only thing I have feared is the fate of little Giulia, because until this moment it has looked very harsh. You have saved what's left of our family and I am certain the...I am sure God will bless you for it."

He reached into his shirt front and pulled out a little cloth bundle. Unwrapping it, he took out a small stack of papers and handed them to Alberto. "This is the reason I was so interested in the fortune-teller back there. These were made by the child's mother before she died. In a way they remind me of all of our family when I hold them in my hands. To me they symbolize all those who have died giving Guilia life. All I ask is that you give them to her when she is older. You don't need to tell her anything about them. In fact, I think you should tell her that she is your natural daughter—I know I would if I was in your position. It would probably be better for everyone if her origins are forgotten. I just want her to have something to hold in her hand some day, something that came from her mother. She was a beautiful and intelligent girl, and her husband was the kindest man I ever knew."

"Of course I will do as you ask, but keep the cards for now. I won't attempt to talk you into coming if you will promise to think about it for a few days. Is that fair? Sir, you are the one who has made me happy, and for that I thank you."

For the rest of that afternoon they continued to talk, though the old man made a point of having Alberto hold the child and look after her. Alberto could hardly conceal his delight as the realization of his new role grew in him. The old man watched the two of them together, and he seemed truly happy at last.

t was midmorning of the following day when the merchant Alberto went up to the old man's room, anxious to once again see the child and mindful of the lateness of the hour: Giovanni had promised to meet him at breakfast, but he had not come down. Could he have changed his mind about the child and left without telling him?

Alberto knocked on the door to the old man's room, but there was no answer. He knocked louder, and inside he heard the child beginning to cry. "Giovanni?" The sound of the child's wailing grew louder. "Giovanni, I'm coming in." He waited a moment, but since he heard nothing, he raised the latch by pulling on the latch-rope and entered the little room.

It took a moment for his eyes to adjust to the darkness. The old man lay in the narrow bed, his eyes open, staring in death. The child was lying beside him, in the crook of his arm.

"Jesus," Alberto said quietly, under his breath. He took in the scene for a moment and then bent over the bed and closed the sightless eyes, sighing. He picked up the little girl in his arms.

"Come with me little one," he said softly, "don't be afraid." Jiggling her gently to comfort her, he started to go out. She stopped crying. At the door he turned and looked at the old man one last time.

He felt as if he should say something, though what that was he could not tell. He felt embarrassed, like a thief. "Thank you Giovanni," he said awkwardly to the still figure on the bed. He paused, searching for the words that would make everything right. "I give you my promise: I will guard her as my own." Again he sighed, but somehow his words made him feel a little better about it.

Just then he caught sight of Giovanni's stack of cards. Shaking his head, he walked back to where they sat on the little stool beside the bed.

As he reached over to pick them up, he noticed a small object lying beside them. Lifting it to look more closely in the dim light, he saw it was a wood carving of a head. It seemed grotesque: distorted by misery and roughly fashioned, it had been darkened by many years of handling. Why would the old man have kept such an evil-looking little talisman? With a shudder of superstitious dread, he quickly set it down again, and instead took up the cards.

"These are for you, little one," he said to the child, holding them up before her face. Then he tucked them into his tunic, looked once more around the little room, and left, closing the door quietly behind him.

he girl did well in the years ahead, as did her adoptive family. She grew up in Venice, a joy to her parents, and married well, into a famous trading family that spread its influence and took root across the face of Europe, flinging the last of the Deukalidae seed to the winds, where it prospered and grew strong. Even now, it continues almost everywhere the Europeans have gone.

The cards spread. Some observers were offended by the images they held, and created playing cards without the troubling symbols essential to the Sanctuary's purpose. Some, instead, were excited by those same images and invented cards with their own succession of images. In this way the Taro became a whole tribe of cards, an endless stream of symbols reflecting their creators' views. Printing was invented, and the cards multiplied, both the original deck and its multitude of successors. But fortune tellers labored quietly in every European city, faithfully maintaining the cards and the secrets of their art, as taught to every generation by those who came before. By the time they loosened their practices, the original deck they had preserved so long had become too widespread to vanish. And its original spread slumbered, forgotten except in stories, awaiting the day when the world was ready.

The Renaissance had begun, and philosophy grew and prospered. It was here that the history of our age was decided, for reborn from the ashes of the ancient world, it slowly spread its wings in the sciences. With its methods improved, it produced a new field of effort that would eventually transform the world: technology. Everything that had been was swept away in a flurry of discovery, and before many centuries had passed, human beings would be living in places and ways their ancestors could not even imagine.

Even as the Renaissance grew strong, in Constantinople the political remnants of Greco-Roman civilization were dying: the Eastern Roman Empire was being swallowed by the Ottoman Turks. While the Sanctuary had kept the spiritual heart of the ancient world alive, the Eastern Empire had kept alive some small portion of its former power and majesty. Neither lived to see the new world that was then being born. In 1492, the year the Americas were first drawn into the European sphere, Constantinople fell to the conqueror's sword. The living foundations of Western Civilization were finally gone.

The world kept changing. Slowly the power of kings and emperors weakened, and democracy took hold. The world was becoming too complex and swiftly changing for rigid governments to flourish. An age of flexibility was born, and education, and creation. The development was not smooth, but it was relentless, and the inflexible and clumsy systems that stifled diversity rarely lasted a century in the changing world.

Before the winds of reason, the power of the church was broken. It shattered into fragments, and lost its central place in ordering and controlling the lives of men. Chastened by its weakness, transformed by the growing knowledge of believers, it softened, finding room in itself to entertain variation. Weapons were used less and less to settle disputes of doctrine and belief, and the fires set for burning heretics lost their pleasures for all but the lunatic fringe. Tolerance again became a virtue, and diversity an immutable fact. Then too, Paganism began again, and the names of the old Gods were once again heard, here and there, in words of worship.

It was inevitable, perhaps, that the time would come when Giovanni's cards at last revealed their secrets.

Sanctuary of the Gods: The Gift

SANCTUARY OF THE GODS
APPENDIX

Thou hast conquered, O pale Galilean;
The world has grown grey with thy breath.
We have drunken of things Lethean,
And fed on the fullness of death.

Swinburne's "Hymn to Proserpine"

TABLE OF CONTENTS—APPENDIX

.

Introduction

Giovanni's cards are not a fictional device: they are very real, and are available to most people living in the Western world. They are known as the Tarot of Marseille. This Tarot deck is still utilized by many fortune tellers today in more or less the same way it has been used for the last six centuries. However it has another, greater purpose: it can be used to recreate the original spread describing the ancient religion of the Guardians, and the location of their cave. Understanding the cards fully requires a great many deductions leading back into our ancient past. There is a certain romance involved, but also a certain intellectual effort. For those who enjoy mysteries, this is undoubtedly one of the most interesting ever created.

This is an outline, nothing more. Complete understanding of the Tarot can only develop after many hours spent in study of the cards. (Readers who are really keen might want to purchase a copy of the original Tarot of Marseille, produced by *France Cartes* and available in the U.S. and Europe at many bookstores and New Age shops. While the illustrations provided here are helpful, there is no substitute for the real thing. However, a color foldout has been added at the back of the book which should be sufficient to satisfy the casual reader. It shows the individual cards arranged in the "spread" their creators' intended.)

To make things more easily understandable, the puzzle will mostly be approached here from the perspective of its creators. That wasn't how it was solved, of course, since their perspective was unknown before the cards had been thoroughly understood. The solution began with the Tarot cards and ended up with a Pagan God Wheel and a somewhat revolutionary perspective of ancient Greek religion. The following description will begin with the ancient Greek religion and God Wheel, and then move from there back to the Tarot cards. Though still a little involved at times, this approach should be easier to follow. The reason for this is quite simple.

There are numerous details (hundreds, in fact) that lead to the discovery of the spread and its implications. Viewed and weighed separately, they can be quite confusing, indeed overwhelming. But if the overall pattern is recognized first, the pieces can be fit into it as they are introduced. In this way, every detail has meaning as soon as it is introduced, and much time and energy can be saved.

Thus the pictorial clues on the Tarot cards can lead back to the ideas that gave rise to them—by careful deduction—but it is much easier to begin with the ideas and only then show how they were expressed on the cards. If one is interested in the deductions that had to be made, to test them and expand on them, one should be able to trace their outline when what follows has been understood.

The Tarot cards describe a prophetic wheel referred to here as the *Tarot Wheel*. This wheel was derived directly from an *Elemental Wheel*. The Elemental Wheel was in turn related to a *God Wheel*. The three wheels or *Mysterions* have the same shape and components, but different symbols. They are like three ways of viewing the same thing. This can be thought of as a three-part initiation process. The first stage was to discover the Tarot Wheel, the second the Elemental Wheel, and the third the God Wheel. They involve increasingly sacred and secret information about the Taro cult's world view. The way the cards were designed, they had to be discovered in this order, just as any initiate begins at the lowest stage and works his way upwards. The final stage requires the initiate to move beyond the Tarot to Greek myth and the cave where the original wheel was buried. As already explained, for the sake of saving time the initiation procedure will be reversed here, beginning with the Pagan world view and the God Wheel, then the Elemental Wheel, and then the Tarot Wheel. The Taro cave will be discussed at the end, after the individual cards have been scrutinized. The appendix concludes with a brief summary of the traditional meanings given to each of the wheel's positions.

Some of the things described in this appendix are regrettably technical, and probably too exotic to interest many readers. They had to be included: otherwise the end result would not have been sufficiently comprehensive. The key to successfully navigating through what follows is to browse. If a section seems interesting, read it. If not, fast forward until something more hospitable presents itself. In particular, sections relating to "frames", "elemental influences", and "ranks", as well as that detailing the relationship of the Wheel and chart can be heavy going. From the casual reader's point of view, the section detailing the symbols of the individual cards is particularly worth a glance. In any case, the Tarot is a visual puzzle and must be seen to be understood. The diagrams, tables and graphs included can be very useful for understanding and should be looked at carefully.

Readers unfamiliar with the Tarot may find themselves wondering how much of what follows was known previously. The answer is not much. Certainly the original Tarot Card Spread and its three wheels were never found, and everything that follows on Greek religion and myth flows directly from an understanding of the spread. There are plenty of books on the Tarot if you are curious about what was known or assumed about it previously. Reading them may help you to understand why the spread has remained hidden for so long. Something rather similar holds true for the understanding of Greek myth and religion.

An Introduction To Ancient Elementalism

Ancient peoples believed in an anthropomorphic universe, with spirits and Gods dictating the strange phenomena of nature. It allowed them to make sense of things that otherwise would have been impossible to understand, and gave them the hope that these human-like spirits could be persuaded—much as people could—to be nice to oneself and one's friends, and nasty to one's enemies. Of course, many modern people continue to believe this, in one form or another. Life is still very problematic.

Ancient people also had an assumption which affected their thinking greatly. They assumed that metaphors and symbols were not merely mental creations: that a metaphoric or symbolic parallel between two things expressed an actual relationship between them, that in some essential way the two things were alike and their fates connected. Words were connected to the things they described so that a curse could kill and a blessing could protect. An image of a man was connected to the man, so that harming that image could harm that man. Falling in love was directly connected to the will and nature of a Goddess of love. Of course, many modern people continue to believe in similar parallels, even when they refer to them disparagingly as superstition. It's a simple matter of psychology: if it looks like a duck, walks like a duck, quacks like a duck, then it feels intuitively that it must be a duck. Except that nowadays we are often taught it really isn't one: reason in conflict with intuition. We meet with this problem often our lives. Have you ever worried about the well-being of a fictional TV or movie hero? What about being afraid to think or speak of a plane crashing for fear you may help it to happen? As everyone knows, such things are irrational, although pretty much unavoidable. The more we learn from science and develop our technologies, the more we find our intuition in conflict with our reason. For ancient peoples there was almost no reason for them ever to be in conflict at all, which must have been pretty nice.

Ancient religion was no different in its purpose than modern science. It was an effort to understand the universe and ultimately gain some sort of control over it. Modern religion has the same function, but a narrower field of operations: it fills in the gaps science has been unable to fill. These gaps mostly have to do with the complexity of our personal life—the desire for meaning, the random twists of fate, anxiety over death, and so on. To understand ancient religion, we must put aside our assumptions about the separate roles of religion and science. And we must realize that faith played a far less important role in the roots and development of the Pagan belief system than it does in mainstream religion today.

Modern religion is based mostly on faith and intuition. Modern science is based mostly on reason and careful observation. Ancient religion had no such division. There was no idea that reason and intuition would ever be in fundamental conflict.

(It would be counterproductive to sit in judgment at this point, declaring the ancient view is true or false, or better or worse than the modern. If we want to understand our ancestors properly, we should simply be aware of their world view and how it differs from our own. And we should avoid making silly judgments about how childish their views were in comparison to ours—or how superior, for that matter. The differences between their way of thinking and ours may have profound implications, but they are not in themselves profound.)

In their effort to make sense of their observations of nature, the ancient peoples used their reason as well as their intuition. Elementalism was a natural development. The search for knowledge includes the search for simple and satisfying ways of explaining complex and widely occurring events. Newton's laws of physics are one such synthesis. Elementalism is another.

In modern high schools, chemistry students are taught about the phase transformations of matter. They are an important part of our understanding of the physical universe. These phase transformations are the root of Elementalism. They are observed by every human being on the planet throughout their daily lives. Matter in our world takes three forms: solid, liquid and gas. The degree of heat determines the phase. Thus water is either ice, water or steam.

When ancient people viewed ice, it looked and felt like a rock. Therefore in an essential way it was rock. When they viewed molten metal it behaved like water, therefore it was a type of water. When they looked at steam or smoke, it acted like air therefore it was a type of air. To the ancients, then, matter took three forms: earth, water and air. If it looks like a duck, walks like a duck, quacks like a duck...

This probably seems like a simple observation, this business of the phases of matter, but it did not seem so to the ancients. At that time it was at the cutting edge of human knowledge. It was as marvelous for them as the infinite reaches of space are for us today. It had the ring of truth, whether viewed intuitively or rationally. It was an amazing synthesis that allowed all kinds of natural phenomena to be reassessed. It was eventually to lead to a revolution which we were to inherit in the fullness of time.

But at first it brought a reordering in human knowledge about the world. The Gods and spirits existed before it, but since Elementalism was undoubtedly true they had to reflect its truth. A God of water must reflect the qualities of water. A God personifying some sort of transformation must reflect this amazing principle of transformation when earth becomes water and water becomes air.

The obvious question was: what are the qualities of the three elements and of their transformations? These qualities could be found in two ways: directly, by observing them in nature, and indirectly, by discovering their metaphoric parallels in nature. The latter was by far the more difficult, involving almost every area of experience, but it was also the most satisfying since it allowed integration of otherwise unrelated events within a single system of knowledge. A more or less informal search began for the metaphoric parallels that continued for thousands of years, growing very detailed, varied and rich in the process. A brief glimpse of the elemental universe follows.

What did the world consist of? Three great masses: earth, the oceans, and the sky. That is, earth, water and air. How did they come into being? There were a number of alternatives adopted at various times and places, but one which was very common and has seemed odd from our modern perspective might be worth considering.

Water was the central element, halfway between ice and steam, between earth and air, so it was first. Air gained heat and separated itself from the water to rise above it like steam. And earth lost heat and formed above it too. As ice forms on water and a crust forms on the surface of cooling metal, so the land formed on the surface of water.

(This is a detail that has bewildered many modern observers of the ancient creation myths who have observed that earth sinks rather than floats in water. Their confusion is understandable, but theory plays a very important role in determining how we view things. The idea that land formed on the surface of water in the beginning of things is rather less peculiar than the notion that light behaves as both a particle and a wave simultaneously, which physics has now prompted many of us to believe.)

Another more common approach was to view Earth as the mother of all things, preceding the other elements. To judge from Hesiod, an early and widely respected writer on myth, that was the mainstream view in Greek religion (although he also said Chaos—which can be defined as "void" in its earliest form—came even before earth). As philosophy became more important, other approaches grew more prominent, but they never supplanted this one among the majority of Pagans in the Greek tradition.

What were the seasons of nature? In winter water freezes, plants die (returning to the earth) making this the season of earth. In spring the snow melts, spring rains fall, new things are born in the moist soil. It is the season of water. In summer the air is hot, clouds vanish from the summer sky in Greece and the soil dries: it is the season of air. Thus there are three seasons: Spring (water), Summer (air) and Winter (earth). And the seasons were driven by the position of the sun, of fire, just as the phase transformations of water are driven by heat. The metaphor carries over very nicely into a description of the qualities of human life as well. (Birth is preceded by rush of water, children are fluid, supple in their motions; maturity is the time of air-like mobility and developed thought; old age brings stiffness, rigidity, and eventually death, when the body returns to the earth.) In fact, the seasons are reflected in anything related to time, because our ancestors believed that the greater cycle of the seasons is the archetype of the lesser seasons of other things.

Since seasons are in essence a description of time and the transformations it brings to things, they became a way of conceptualizing and describing time itself. It was a natural step to say that all time follows the seasonal pattern. For the ancients, time was a series of cycles broken into three distinct and qualitatively different parts that actively determined the nature of things. Science has a very different view of time: for the modern scientist, time is basically a continuous, neutral and undifferentiated (if relative) field in which change takes place. That is, time is a passive component of change in modern science, but it was an active and defining agent of change for the ancients.

How does sex relate to the three elements? It surely did, since like the elements sex was obviously a terribly important factor in all living things— and by metaphoric extension in things modern people might consider dead, like rivers. By extension of cultural patterns of male aggressiveness, mobility and dominance, as indeed by extension of the metaphor of earth as the mother of the crops, femininity took after the earthen side of the spectrum, masculinity after the airy, atmospheric side of things. Water lay between them with a mix of both sexes. (Later, when fire became an element, water was viewed as female, fire as male in order that balance be maintained.) It should not be assumed that there were only earth Goddesses and sky Gods: certainly not. There were earth Gods, for example, but they tended to explain masculine things, like earthquakes (motion of the female element), or to reflect that portion of us all that is soul/air and which was thought to exist after death and continue in the underworld.

What was the nature of a human being? Obviously we are a mix of the three elements. Our blood is water. Our bones are earth. We breath air.

And the various characteristics of our natures could also receive an elemental treatment. What best describes the nature of our thoughts? Earth is immobile, which thoughts are not. Water is a candidate, given the ebb and flow of thought . However, air was most commonly believed to be the element of thought: consider what would happen to your thoughts if someone cut off your air supply for even a minute. Thoughts would disappear and you would become unconscious. (Hence the otherwise peculiar notion of some ancient thinkers that thought resides in the diaphragm rather than in the head.)

Ancient thinkers viewed the three elements as being under the control of fire, but they did not view fire as a separate element until later. The elements were matter, and for a long time fire was not viewed as a form of matter. You can hold a stone in your hands, water in a cup, and air in your lungs or a bellows, but you cannot contain fire in that way: it vanishes like magic. It existed, obviously, but it was not a form of matter. On the other hand it drove the transformations of matter, and indeed could consume various forms of matter, transforming them into the earthen forms of ashes and the airy form of smoke.

Strange stuff, fire: magical, divine stuff. The ancient Greeks believed a pure form of it ran through the veins of Gods and made them immortal: *ichor.* Mostly fire is seen high in the air where the Gods lived, in stars and planets, in the sun and moon, in lightning. It also could be found in Volcanoes. It was an obvious metaphor for enlightenment and understanding, and at the same time for destruction. And since plants absorbed fire from the sun that could be burned to release the fire again, it was almost an element under certain conditions. A lot of thought went into this problem, and different theories evolved. For a very long time, however, fire was not viewed as just one among four elements: it was the driving force behind magic and divinity, a kind of super-element, dictating the behaviors of the other three.

One thing that seemed clear was that air contained fire in it as steam contained heat, and that fire, like air, was therefore somewhat masculine in its qualities. (Before fire came to be viewed as a fourth element, air was sometimes divided into two types: aer (which was moist) and aither (which was fiery)). Fire must consume fuel as living creatures consume food, most living creatures are warm, and life was a rather magical thing, so life was viewed as a form of fire. Furthermore, seeds were flammable, containing fire, so they were fiery contributors to new life. New life came when fire (male seed) entered earth (female womb). This could be extended further by metaphor. For example, creativity, a mental trait, involved qualities of both the feminine element earth (womb) and the masculine sometime-element fire (seed).

Table 1 lays out a few qualities of the elements, where fire is viewed as an element. The fire characteristics of awareness, willfulness and reason can be added to air when considering the perspective before three elements came to be viewed as four. At that time, life and seed were not essentially elemental, arising from qualities deemed more magical than material.

Table 1: Phenomena Derived From Elements

FIRE	AIR	EARTH	WATER
Life	Spirit	Matter	Death
Awareness	Motion	Immobility	Obscurity
Seed	Disunion	Womb	Union
Willfulness	Aggression	Passivity	Receptivity
Reason	Thought	Body	Emotion

A more detailed example might help to understand how these things were applied, and how they evolved over time. Blood is an important substance for animal and human life. Consider its qualities for a moment, and how the ancient elementalists viewed them. It was a liquid (hence involved in joining things like life, soul and body). It was red, the color of burning coals, and warm. Water extinguishes fire, as blood could extinguish the life within it, so it was a source of mortality (hence the ichor in the veins of Gods). When we bleed too much we go into shock and feel cold (having lost too much fire). Remove blood from the body, and the liquid cools, quickly losing its fire, turning almost black. At the same time, it hardens, becoming a form of earth. Thus blood apparently follows the proper phase transformations of matter.

In essence, then, blood consists of the fire of life and consciousness bound to earth, causing that earth to take a liquid form. Fire was bound to earth within the body until death brought its extinction. This understanding of blood's qualities led to activities that seem rather strange today.

Blood sacrifices were made to the dead in which blood was poured into the ground. (These were called chthonian sacrifices.) Homer describes the pale, babbling shades (ghosts) of the dead who drank the blood and briefly regained their reason and memory. The fire in the blood temporarily restored the light to their thoughts, until the blood hardened and its fire went out. This was, in effect, a primitive technology. Wine was later used in a similar way, since it clearly had many of the characteristics of blood from an elemental perspective, especially when it was highly alcoholic and burned readily. Eventually, oracles, magical formulae, and other more powerful and efficient methods made chthonian and other types of sacrifices redundant, and they continued mostly in places where they had become inextricably bound to tradition, or where feasting afterwards became the main emphasis of the sacrifice. Some Greeks stopped making sacrifices of animals altogether, preferring to use symbolic representations of animals where tradition called for a sacrifice. Symbolic representations are metaphoric parallels of the things they depict, and therefore were essentially the same to the ancients: offering a cow and offering a clay figurine of a cow could be identical actions, but one was far less expensive and messy than the other. And besides, there were Greek Pagans whose ideas led them to become strict vegetarians.

For a long time Gods were assumed to exist (why not: traditions carry weight in every age, and anyway, Gods proved themselves to be very useful conceptions). But Gods were partially understood in terms of the developing elemental theories, just as they were partially understood in terms of human emotions and activities. From the very beginning, Elementalism was an important, indeed critical component in the development of the ancient Greek religious world view, as were Gods.

Many modern students of ancient religion assert this wasn't so, that Elementalism was a later invention dating to the early Greek philosophers. The ancient creation myths are viewed by them as non-elemental despite their apparently elemental approach. When Hesiod described the ancient seasons in elemental terms, or when fragments of texts from the Samothracian mysteries seemed elemental, the tendency was to dismiss the evidence as a later addition to an earlier text. Many historians of religion and philosophy are absolutely convinced the Greek philosophers were the first elementalists. Their reason for thinking this is very simple: the ancients didn't talk openly about Elementalism until the Greek philosophers did so. If they knew about the elements, they never said a word. The reason the ancients didn't talk about elements was also very simple: it represented a secret revelation in religions much given to secrecy.

Ancient religions were like that: a strict division existed between the public religion and the secret one, a division that was only bridged by initiation of select persons. (A modern parallel exists: the initiation process of the freemasons is similar to that of ancient religions.) This well known secrecy of Greek religion is naturally galling to those of us who are curious about our ancestor's thinking, because we are by definition denied initiation. We are forced to wander around the edges of their world view, looking for little scraps and clues that slipped by initiates who were notoriously faithful to their vows, and quite willing—even eager—to be misunderstood by outsiders.

(One thinks here of the nonsense spread by some surviving primitive people when describing their beliefs to modern observers. For example, some have claimed their cultures never realized sex was necessary for reproduction. For them this knowledge was revealed only in initiation, and it was better to sound silly to outsiders than to reveal what tradition had made secret. Besides, they knew that it was the outsiders who were really the ignorant ones: a good definition of a fool is someone who thinks he knows what he does not know.)

Surely it takes a certain amount of audacity to suppose, as many modern observers have, that we know the thoughts of ancient religious thinkers better than they did themselves. Nonetheless that is what we often do, bringing the modern techniques like psychology and cultural anthropology to bear. We may be right, sometimes, but since we haven't heard their point of view that's a dubious supposition. One of the things that's nice about the Tarot is that the people who invented it were apparently plugged right into the ancient traditions. They understood the myths and rituals, the reasoning and intuitions behind them. Until now, we have not had any way of doing so.

(Conversely, there is another school of thought that denies we are capable of truly understanding ancient people, a comfortable pretense that we have eliminated metaphoric thinking from our minds and become, in effect, a different species. Cut to the chase, this perspective allows its adherents to blame our fundamental ignorance of myth on our superior powers of reasoning, an entertaining inversion of the assumptions of science.)

Elementalism existed for many centuries before it was publicly discussed because it was fused informally to the secrets regarding the nature and activities of Gods. There was no specific rule that it could not be discussed publicly, at least in the ancient Greek religious cults, but the hidden natures of the Gods were interwoven with it, and were protected by secrecy, so for a long time no one thought to separate the strains. If you discussed Gods, you discussed Elementalism. If you discussed Elementalism, you discussed Gods. Either way, because Gods were involved, the matter was secret, and generally only conveyed through initiation.

What the ancient Greek philosophers did that was truly revolutionary was to remove Elementalism from anthropomorphic Gods. Instead of viewing the personalities of Gods in combination with the qualities of elemental interactions, they decided to adopt the assumption that the personality of Gods were unnecessary for understanding nature: if you understood the qualities of impersonal elements, you could understand nature, including the Gods. Put another way, instead of Gods determining the qualities of elements, the philosophers said that elements determined the natures and actions of Gods. Nature could be described and understood entirely in terms of elements and their orderly interactions. A small adjustment in some respects, but without it we might still be riding to work on horses, and flying would be for the birds. It allowed Elementalism to break free of secrecy without offending sacred vows, and began the slow evolution of science.

In time some philosophers stopped thinking about Gods at all. Physics and religion became increasingly independent of one another. Despite the best efforts of religious scientists and philosophers, they remain so to this day. (It is not that scientists have given up metaphoric thinking—all thought can be viewed as essentially metaphoric—it is just that many of their metaphors have become increasingly refined and made more narrow by exclusion. In formal, scientific thinking we are less inclined to see a direct link between the metaphor and the thing it reflects.) Science looks to ongoing revelation based on observation and the experimental method. In contrast, modern faith leans on traditional authority for its validation.

When the Greek Gods as we know them were developing during the dark age following the collapse of Mycenean civilization, Elementalism helped to define their natures and the myths about them. Myths were ways of explaining the way things are and why, but given the secretive nature of ancient religion, it is often far from clear what they are describing, and what they mean. In effect, they are riddles, and many ancient writers described them as such. In ancient Greece, in particular, the hidden meaning of myth was often referred to. So myths make use of symbols or metaphoric parallels for things, and if you know what the parallel is, or what the symbol represents, you know what is being described. In this way one understands the reasoning.

Mythological symbols were chosen because they were metaphoric parallels to the things they described. That makes it difficult to solve the riddles, because metaphors are determined by our theoretical knowledge as much as by our experience. We can all guess that fire can be used as a metaphor for intelligence, but without a little theoretical knowledge, how many would have thought earth could be a metaphor for winter, that a trinity of Goddesses could be a metaphor for time and transformation, or that twins described the expression of the same qualities in the twin worlds of heaven and earth? How many of us have viewed the myth of Pandora as a misogynist's nightmare (the wife brings a dowry of suffering to her hapless husband) rather than a description of our souls being joined to our bodies? Is a chariot a method of transportation, or a symbol of wheels, and hence a symbol of the lawful and orderly progression of divine principles acting through time?

The Tarot suggests that Elementalism suffuses Greek myth, and that alone makes it invaluable. The beauty of knowing that Elementalism is involved in the selection of symbols is that it allows us to begin the difficult task of cracking the riddler's code by helping us to guess at the meaning of certain symbols, and the theoretical framework that lies behind them.

But the Tarot does something else which is even more useful: it shows us one variation of the ancient religious Greek view of the universe. It is a later variation, and one of many, but it is part of a long tradition which it was at pains to accommodate. Therefore by understanding it, the other traditions are brought closer to our reach. Knowing some of the symbols and assumptions that lie behind a myth make the possibility of fully understanding it much greater. For the first time we have a key to the esoteric secrets of Greek myth and ritual.

In many ways, this is about the origins of our technological society. From Greek religion came philosophy, geometry, physics, alchemy (chemistry), drama, scholarship and so on. Had this extraordinary religion not existed, the pace of Western discovery would have been greatly slowed and we might still be waiting for an industrial revolution to take place. Its importance cannot be too greatly stressed. In effect a conceptual revolution took place, primarily at the prompting of the religion and with its blessing, that eventually transformed the world.

Regarding the Solution To The Tarot Puzzle

The Tarot cards are well known today wherever Western civilization has spread. Those who delight in the ways of science have a tendency to despise them as an anachronism, a survival of irrationality fit for the untrained, undisciplined mind. They are a metaphor for chaos, and they elicit the fear chaos engenders deep in the human psyche. Association with them would be tantamount to an act of professional suicide for an academic. In contrast, those who find science and its organization of thoughts, feelings, and perceptions of the world cold and unfeeling (annoyingly at odds with intuition) have often found satisfaction in the vague yet stirring, undefined images and impressions the Tarot creates. It speaks to their emotions, collecting them into a strangely compelling and comforting, if somewhat personal sense of order. The scientifically oriented dislike the Tarot for its magic, the very thing that draws others to it. In a sense, the Tarot has become one of the many battlefields where men and women assert the view of the world that appeals to them most. Everyone longs for order, but finds it in different ways.

In fact the Tarot involves both magic and reason, religion and philosophy, intuition and logic. The Tarot's creators were comfortable in both worlds, and that is part of what has made the cards indecipherable for so long. Those who detest magic and vague symbolism have never been able to look beyond them in the cards. Those who love these same things have rarely sought to begin with careful deduction and observation in their search for understanding of the cards. Without a little of both these things, the Tarot cannot be understood. But there is more to the mystery of its long survival in obscurity.

The solution of the Tarot's puzzle is not simple, or it would have been solved centuries ago. It was made difficult by a subtle understanding of human prejudice and tunnel vision. It must be solved through a balance between the specific and the general, the details and the whole, the forest and the trees. The solution, once found, is incontrovertible, but finding it is no easy matter.

The specific is the first thing everyone sees when they look at the cards: images of people and things that are as detailed as they are obscure. The Tarot is a riot of images, a tangle of apparently orderly fragments that together make a chaotic whole. In chaos, the mind asserts order of whichever type is most appealing. This projected order obscures the true order of things. If one is Christian, one sees Christianity behind the pictures (either mainstream Christian faith, or Satanism which is anti-Christian, and therefore based upon the assumptions of the Christian world view). If one is a rationalist, one sees a collection of childishly simple pictures, or a reflection of unconscious impulses and assumptions. If one is an occultist, one sees magical intimations and formulas. To each his own. However, to truly understand, the viewer must restrain this ordering impulse and observe very carefully for a time. The Tarot must be observed without prejudice—without asserting order—until the natural order that exists is able to assert itself. This is not an easy thing to do.

Only once that inherent order asserts itself can it be reapplied to the individual cards, shifting their meaning slightly and developing it until they fit into the overall philosophy being described.

This in turn increases and expands on the understanding of the overall spread. The increasing knowledge of the whole then leads to an even greater understanding of the parts, and at last the Tarot can be said to be understood.

Not coincidentally, this could be considered a model for all human knowledge. Take any field of scientific endeavor, for example, and the same approach applies. Experimentation and observation provide clusters of data (the cards). For a time the evidence is chaotic until eventually there is the formation of an overall paradigm or theory that unites the data (the spread). The paradigm brings a reappraisal of the evidence (the cards) which in turn brings a reappraisal and fine tuning of the paradigm (the spread). The Tarot's designers viewed their cards as an introduction to a world view as comprehensive as that which prevails in any field of modern science, and they understood, at least intuitively, the method by which human knowledge develops. That is partly why they decided to mandate this method of solving the puzzle.

There is a card in the deck that shows the manner in which understanding of the Tarot begins to be achieved. The card shown in Diagram 19 is called 'The Star' (and it describes the first step in the higher, spiritual cycle of nature the Tarot's designers believed in). Its meaning is rebirth and an intimation of things to come. There is a woman in the foreground. Behind the woman there are stars in the sky. These stars take the shape of the Tarot's puzzle, solved. The details are not included, and the woman is not looking at the pattern—she is sensing it though she has not yet actually seen it. This is how the Tarot's designers intended us to solve the puzzle. To begin by sensing its vague outline. In fact, there is no other way to do it.

For the person who takes the trouble to really look deeply at the cards in their proper positions, their meaning should become very clear. Once the secret spread is discovered, it is verified by the evidence—pictures which, like the Star card, show the spread in a form that makes sense only once it has been found. The numeric and schematic coincidences pile up until it is obvious: the paradigm described here fits the available evidence neatly. Again, it won't be necessary for you to do the detective work yourself: this appendix will do it for you. These comments—on the method needed to initially find the solution—are included to show you how the cards' creators intended it to be done, not to describe what you must do.

The Gods and The God Wheel

There follows a brief description of some of the principle Greek Gods. It is necessarily tentative at this point, developed by combining Elementalism with myth. The Tarot's creators were careful to keep most details regarding the Gods secret in the cards, but extrapolation based on a thorough understanding of the deck is possible and was expected. It was done in exactly the same manner the Tarot was solved: by studying the details of myth (the cards), and then sensing the world view behind them (the spread).

This, and the world view promoted by the Tarot, was then reapplied to myth (the cards). The understanding of myth was then applied to fine tuning the understanding of the Pagan world view (the spread). This process of discovery and refinement is enormously difficult and by no means complete, so the definitions below are a work in progress. Keep in mind, too, that there was a lot of overlap between various Gods' areas of responsibility, and that phenomena could be explained in various ways. Cult centers dedicated to a particular God tended to explain things by emphasizing parallels involving that God.

Zeus - The third and final generation of Sky God kings, because he represents the sky God in spring, season of continual birth and transformation. His grandfather Ouranos remained aloof in heaven (summer, air), and life was not brought to the world by him. His father Kronos entered earth and was bound by its immobile nature, remaining there (winter, earth). Kronos' reign is a parallel to pregnancy. Zeus moves freely between heaven and earth. His thunderbolt is his method of uniting with earth: it is equally sexual and orgasmic, and mark of his divine oversight and enforcement of justice here on earth. All generations of sky kings are typified by the daylight sky: fire and air mixed pure and strong—aither. (Zeus is roughly similar to the roman God Jupiter.)

Hera - Zeus' wife, and Goddess of the rain clouds. In summer she goes away to be solitary, in winter she is purified and becomes a virgin like the barren white snow. In spring she is wedded to Zeus and drops rain to bring up the flowers on earth, and the other crops. Zeus and Hera didn't produce many offspring, because she is really an interim step in reproduction: she is the facilitator, so to speak, who joins heaven and earth. Water is the element which brings union, whether of earth and sky by rain or of two metals mixed and heated into liquid form to create an alloy. Hera not only brings crop fertility through her rains: she also brings divine attributes expressed in lesser metaphoric parallels here on earth. Shadows of divinity in the world, not unlike the shadows of clouds that fall upon the earth. And Hera is the reason Zeus avoided his father's and grandfather's fate: she allows him to join with the attractive earth without being bound to it, separating him from his seed. Hera overseas the bringing of divine parallels to earth. Being lesser reflections, these things are not divine and lead to suffering, confusion and death, if not protected against and perceived in a purer form. As a continuation of this work, she gave us divine Herakles. Not coincidentally, her symbol was the dove which was later adopted as a symbol of the Christian Holy Spirit, since both shared aspects of the same role. (She is similar to the roman Goddess Juno.)

Sanctuary of the Gods: Appendix

Herakles - a mortal son of Zeus who became immortal under Hera's tutelage. A guide to humanity. He found eternal youth by overcoming confusion and darkness. He is the God of heroes—of the expression and perception of divine qualities, of *arete*, among mortals. This is why he is linked to the zodiac wherein the divine archetypes derived from Gods in the heavens direct human fate in our world below. In essence, the astrological wheel is another God Wheel, though unlike the Mysterion in its present form it comes from Roman imperial times. (The Romans knew Herakles as Hercules.)

Aphrodite - A water Goddess, born in the sea when Kronos first entered earth and overthrew his father. She is the Goddess of union, and the quality of water to join things and create new life from those combinations. Semen is wet, wombs are wet, seeds join to earth in the wet soil. If one wants tin and copper to join together to create bronze, one must heat them until they are in liquid form. (The Romans called her Venus.)

Ares - A child of Hera, he is the God of disunion and destruction, of things falling apart in the fullness of time. He is also the God of war, not surprisingly. Air is the element that guides his actions, but air mixed with fire in its destructive form. (In Rome he was called Mars, and there the metaphor of war as a source of wealth and prosperity was more greatly emphasized than war as a source of destruction. Both of these characteristics of war are reflected in Greek myth, although the destructive takes precedence.)

Hephestos - A child of Hera alone, he is responsible for metallurgy, the transformations and combinations of earth turned to water under the influence of fire. That makes him very important in the transformation of substances here on earth, and alchemy is his province whether it is viewed as a spiritual or material enterprise. He is lame because fire in earth is restricted in time and space. (In Rome he was Vulcan.)

Hermes - The God of the Herme, the male phallus made of earthen materials. The male phallus is obviously masculine, and earth is feminine, but in mortal men this strange combination exists. Masculine fire expressed in earthen form. A guide for souls because he expresses fire in earth, which symbolizes sex, the gaining of wisdom, and death. But also rather dishonest, since fire is deceptive in proximity to the darkness which is death. (The Romans called him Mercury.)

Dionysos - The fiery male seed that enters earth in semen. There is a wonderful ancient sculpture of Hermes holding the infant Dionysos in his arms: a beautiful expression of something which might normally seem rather pornographic. Dionysos is linked to wine which is water and fire mixed, dulls the senses in a weaker parallel to death, and is metaphorically linked to blood

Page 280

which joins mortal life to mortal bodies. Sex and death are linked as are wisdom and death. Seed entering the womb is a parallel to the dead entering death, except that the human seed is reborn (attached to the vine called the umbilical cord that has its roots, a placenta, buried in the mother). The dead are sometimes less fortunate. A very important aspect in his myth is his role as a God of perennial vegetation. That is, of trees, vines, and other forms of vegetation that died in the winter but were reborn in the spring. Thus not only was he the seed: he was the plant that sprang from the seed, the father vine who annually died and was reborn. (In Rome he was Bacchus.)

Hestia - Goddess of the hearth, the containment of fire and its sharing. Not fertile, she represents the unifying principle between human beings and the restraint that prevents destructive influences such as fiery will from shattering unions.

Apollo - The God of the gateway of light into earth, and of light in general. Bringer of divine revelations and clarity (which often demanded purification). He is a parallel of Dionysos, though his fire is not of life: it is of illumination. Nonetheless, death is linked to him by the idea of fire falling into earth and this couples with purification to bring out his dangerous side as Far-shooter.

Artemis - Apollo's sister. Goddess of the gateway of water into earth, and of darkness in general. Oversees the death of living creatures when the fire of their lives are extinguished. (In Rome she was known as Diana.)

Athena - Wisdom and cleverness, the illumination of the darkness of earth by the fire of understanding. The child of Zeus and Wisdom, she was born from Zeus' head, avoiding the dark confusion of her mother's womb. She was sometimes called Tritogeneia, "Born of the three", a reference to her mother. Wisdom in ancient Greek religion came from understanding the nature of transformations, especially those of the three Seasons. (The Romans called her Minerva.)

Hades - Male ruler of earth, fire absent. He cannot have children without fire, and he is a dark personification of death when the soul has lost the flame of life and dwells in the underworld without that reason and clarity that only fire can give. The land of the dead is called Hades. (The Romans called him Pluto, and more greatly emphasized his role as a God of the wealth that comes from the earth.)

Demeter - Earth mother, the third generation: her mother and grandmother were the consorts of the previous sky kings. She and Zeus don't mate directly, or Zeus would have been supplanted as his father and grandfather were—by a more balanced successor. The crops do mate with her. She is also the consort of Poseidon, and mother of Persephone. (In Rome she was known as Ceres.)

Poseidon - Earth and water mover. King of those feminine elements. Earthquakes and storms at sea were related to his influence, for the feminine elements did not move themselves: they had to be moved. As a river God (moving water), he also oversaw the important role of irrigation in which his union with Demeter paralleled the union of individual seeds with the Goddess. In a way, he was the God who reflected Zeus' nature on earth, and therefore mortality is often reflected in his myths and cult symbols. (The Romans knew him as Neptune.)

Persephone - Goddess of the water which joins the living with the dead. Similar to Artemis, she was also a virgin and the wife of sterile Hades. In the Tarot, as at the cult center of Eleusis, she is the guardian of the mysteries of the ancient religion. (She was called Proserpina by the Romans.)

Horai - The three seasons, Spring, Summer and Winter. Their names were Eirene, Eunomia and Dike, meaning Peace, Order and Justice. They describe the life of all things on earth: in the beginning the elements are joined in peace together; in the middle they remain in balanced harmony; in the end justice prevails, and the elements are separated again, or find a new balance. Justice looks like Themis, earth Goddess of Justice, who overseas lawful results. Themis was their mother, Zeus their father. These Goddesses are very important to the description of time, and play a very important role in the Tarot cards, where they are the only Gods whose qualities are described in considerable detail.

Moirai - The three fates which govern all mortal lives. Life in general was viewed as a metaphor for a woven piece of cloth, and our individual fates as the individual threads that are woven into the overall fabric. The fates were Clotho (spinner), Lachesis (disposer of lots), Atropos (inevitable: the one who cuts the threads at death). Again the pattern of water, air and earth applies.

There were other Gods, but these should be sufficient for the present purposes. With just this information, and that already provided in the story of the guardians, already some details of myth should be a little more accessible. Remember: in essence myth is a series of riddles…

- **Question**: Why did Hera not attend the birth of Apollo, instead hiding far away behind a golden cloud? And if she didn't attend, why does the myth mention her at all?
- **Response**: Hera is, among other things, a Goddess of clouds. Apollo is a God of light, especially of sunlight. If the clouds were present, the light of the sun would be obscured. (Hera especially, though not only, represents

the fall of lesser reflections to earth, while Apollo represents the fall of divine light to earth, a purer, clearer form. That is, the shadows of clouds versus sunlight.) Hera is mentioned in this myth—while most other Gods are not—because in her broadest definition she oversees the descent of *all* divine qualities to earth. That is, although she most often oversees the descent of shadows, she also oversees the descent of fire, such as that of her husband's phallic thunderbolts. As only one of many aspects of that descending fire, Apollo falls under her influence: he is yet another mark of her triumph in this world.

- **Question:** Why did Herakles have twelve labors to perform before he could win immortality? (The Gods of the wheel originally numbered twelve, not sixteen as in the Tarot's God Wheel. The Tarot's wheel added four extra Gods.)

- **Response:** Herakles is the personification of divine qualities on earth, of *arete*. The qualities of the twelve Gods are expressed in earth as a shadow expresses the shape of a man or woman. The shadow is not the same as the thing which shapes it, but it is a clue to it. Herakles had to find the divinity behind the darker reflections of divinity in this world. The monsters he fought were darker reflections of the divinity that gave them their forms. Killing the monsters was symbolic of understanding the divinity that shaped them. In the end, understanding gave him immortality as expressed in myth by his marriage to the Goddess Youth, daughter of Hera. (Note that the other epic myths such as The Odyssey and the tales of the Argonauts had a similar hidden theme.)

- **Question:** Why do the Satyrs (air spirits) seduce the watery (female) grapes? Why are Satyrs sometimes depicted swinging young women on swings?

- **Response:** Grapes mature with seeds inside them, and the seeds have to come from somewhere. Think of the watery grape being a parallel with Hera when she assists Zeus to penetrate the earth as lightning. The grape is raised up from the earth by the father vine, and then impregnated by the fiery seed of the air spirits when the air is hot in the summer. The wind pushing against the grapes is shown sometimes as Satyrs pushing girls on swings. This seduction does not lead to birth, as Zeus' attraction to Hera does not give rise to birth: the grapes carry the seeds downwards as rain carries the lightning. The grape falls from her father's arms and dies. (Unlike Hera, she is mortal.) Her spirit remains in the underworld and is brought back to life by the father vine the following spring. The seed she carried enters earth and is reborn as a new father to continue the cycle. The myth of Dionysos as son vine and Semele as mother grape is another variation of this. Dionysos dies to go into the underworld and bring his mother back. Thus the grape is mother and daughter both. (When you are considering this, you might want to reflect on the meaning of the Bacchae—grapes who carry the seeds of life to earth—and of parallels between the rites and myths of Dionysos, and those of Cretan Zeus. For example, both involve the sounds of thunder.)

- **Question:** Why did Theseus let out a thread behind him as he wandered in the Labyrinth, seeking to kill the monster Minotaur, and why did the thread enable him to escape the Labyrinth and return? Is not the myth of Herakles finding Theseus trapped in Hades and freeing him the same story in another form?

- **Response:** The Labyrinth is a talisman representing sacrificial, premature death. Fate cut short. The portion of life otherwise remaining is the sacrifice. (This sort of sacrifice should not be confused with the chthonian type mentioned previously.) From this root, the Labyrinth's meaning evolved to provide a magical representation of the whole of a mortal life from beginning to end. It became a way of magically dying before one's time by letting one trace one's fate to the moment of death and beyond. In death there is darkness and ignorance unless a flame is brought into the underworld: then there is illumination and wisdom, for earth is both the beginning and ending of things, if one can but see it. To enter death while still living (i.e.: to carry the flame of life into death) is to slay ignorance (the Minotaur) and become wise. Theseus laid out a thread behind him (recall that a man's fate could be viewed as a thread) as he magically reached forward in time to the point of his fated death. Passing beyond it, he slew the Minotaur (ignorance) and returned to his present position in life by retracing the thread. Herakles dealt with the divine archetypes of the Gods as reflected on earth—the definers of mortality and mortal fate—so he provided Theseus with the knowledge of his fate that allowed him to escape from death and return to life. That is, he provided him with the knowledge of the thread that allowed him to retrace it and return from the land of the dead. There are many other similar events described in the myths of heroes.

- **Question:** What is the basic meaning of the myth of Ixion? Attempting to mate with Hera as Zeus does, he was subsequently bound to a fiery wheel suspended between earth and sky, fated to remain there forever.

- **Response:** The God Wheel describes the influence of the Gods in the movements of a mortal's fate. That which falls from the timeless world of the Gods and enters our world must follow the dark reflections of divinity in our world, including mortal fate. When the fire of life, which is divine, was attracted to Hera, it fell into time and became locked in the inevitable passage of the seasons. To these there is never an end.

- **Question**: Why does our marriage ceremony take the form it does? (Ignore the christianizing explanations: these were invented during the time of the conversion of Rome so a popular tradition could continue.)
- **Response**: In marriage the bride wears a veil across her face (like misty rain); "nuptial" comes from "nimbus" meaning cloud; her clothes are long and white from head to toe like a thunderhead; she wears flowers and throws the bouquet to others yet unwed, passing on her gift to others; and rings are exchanged, suggestive of wheels and completion of the cycle of time. The bride follows the divine pattern of Hera and passes the seed of life on to the next generation.

Diagram 1: The God Wheel

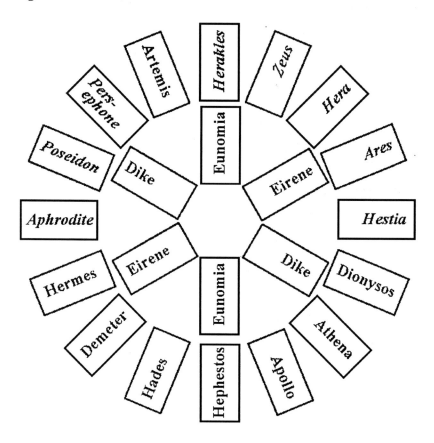

Some readers might want to explore a few ancient myths from their original sources like Euripedes, Hesiod, The Homeric Hymns, Aeschylus, Sophicles, Apollodorus and Pausinias, an interesting occupation for those who like riddles. Deciphering these myths can be a lot of fun, but one should be patient and not be too quick to find answers. It is best to let the natural order of a myth assert itself, rather than rushing to place one's own preferences on top of it. The more we know, the easier it gets, but we should try to avoid being certain about anything: a little doubt regarding any conclusion we reach will allow us to fine tune it as we proceed. (Many of the ancient Greek texts are now available on the Internet. There are several electronic libraries specializing in Classical texts. For those who don't have Net access, the texts are also available in print.)

Enough background about myth and symbols for now. Take a look at the God Wheel shown here. But take it with a grain of salt, because it is just one person's best guess about how the Gods fitted around the wheel. Other ways of doing it are possible, since the qualities of the Gods and their portfolios overlap each other's. The Tarot's creators were very careful not to tell us anything directly about the Gods of the wheel: these were mysteries they preferred to keep entirely out of the Tarot. The physical God Wheel they described and set aside for us represents the final initiation. See Diagram 1.

The Elemental Wheel

The God Wheel can be viewed as an Elemental Wheel. By the time it was created, the philosophical movement had become well established, and some religious thinkers had concluded that elements were indeed as important as some of the philosophers suggested. The Gods could be described purely in terms of elements. Therefore thinking of the God Wheel as an Elemental Wheel was not a difficult step, and indeed must have accompanied its invention. But the Tarot's creators were not as concerned about revealing its secrets as they were about revealing the true nature and actions of the Gods. As mentioned previously, Elementalism was not usually subject to the same restrictive initiation procedures: the Tarot's creators were under no particular obligation to conceal it from non-initiates, except insofar as it might lead back to the God Wheel. Therefore they decided to make it the basis of their card deck.

The Tarot's Elemental Wheel uses four elements, not three. Fire has been added by this time. The decision to view fire as just another element had apparently been first made in Babylon, and it was popularized among the Greeks by Empedocles in the sixth century BC. By the time this wheel was invented, the old three seasons were in the process of being supplanted by a four season system which we still use today. Three elements, three seasons; four elements, four seasons. Remember that Greek religion was a dynamic system of knowledge like modern science. It was not afraid of innovation. On the other hand, the religious centers did not like the idea of new knowledge rendering old revelations obsolete, so there was an effort to bring them into harmony. The Elemental Wheel refers to both the three and four elemental systems and synthesizes them. That is one of the reasons why it was invented: it embraces the new system without rejecting the old: it shows how four elements could be embraced by a three season year, rather than supplanting it.

When fire was added, it was deemed to be a male element, and the most extremely masculine element at that. The natural order of the elements in their view was Earth (female), Water (Female), Air (Male), and Fire (Male). According to this scheme, in nature the earth takes the lowest position, water is above it, then the air, then the heavenly sources of fire. These four elements can be viewed as two pairs of male and female opposites: Earth and Air, and Water and Fire.

The three and four element systems were joined in the Mysterion by determining that there were two cycles, depending on which quality of fire was involved: destructive or enlightening. One cycle was material, the other spiritual. (See Table 2.)

Table 2: The Season's Two Cycles

Season	Element	Elemental qualities
Low Spring	Water	Union, Desire
Low Summer	Air & Fire	Destructive, Materialistic
Low Winter	Earth	Destruction, Oblivion
High Spring	Water	Mystery, Union, Restraint
High Summer	Air & Fire	Illuminating, Spiritual
High Winter	Earth	Transcendence, Wisdom

Thus the ancient trinity was added to, rather than entirely supplanted in this wheel.

A three season year is intrinsic to the wheel which makes it clear the wheel is ancient, and the inclusion of four elements indicates it is not too ancient: the wheel had to be invented before four elements had been comfortably adopted and the three element system left behind. Since it contains both systems, it lies during the period when transition between them was taking place. This means it was invented in the Classical or early Hellenic age of ancient Greece.

In Diagràm 2 the Elemental Wheel is shown. It has the three seasons as spokes, repeated twice: once for a high cycle, once for a low cycle. There are sixteen elemental positions on the rim. There are four elements (earth, air, fire and water), and each is broken down to show the interactions of the four with each other. For example, Air is broken down into Air influenced by Earth, Air influenced by Fire, Air influenced by Water, and Air in its pure form (Air influenced by Air).

As the elements interact in nature, they come into contact through proximity to one-another. These interactions were thought to determine which characteristics of an element were most in evidence at any given time. This is the thinking behind elemental influences.

The elemental rim spins counterclockwise around the unmoving spokes of the seasons.

There are forty-eight locations where the spokes directly align with the rotating elements on the rim. (16 x 3 = 48.) These *alignments* can be broken in two, since they always include two opposing sides of the wheel, one for the spiritual cycle of the seasons, one for the material cycle of the seasons. In Diagram 2, the two parts of the current alignment are a) spiritual summer to Air influenced by Earth, and b) material summer to Earth influenced by Earth. These two sets in each alignment are referred to as *positions*. Thus there are 48 alignments which are divided into two positions each, for a total of 96 positions. As will become clear, the numbers 48 and 96 will be important for understanding how the Tarot Wheel was expressed in the Tarot chart.

Take a moment to look over the diagram, and notice that each of the 48 alignments consists of one high cycle and one low cycle spoke position, and two different elements from opposing sides of the wheel's rim (Air versus Earth, in this instance). Thus the two positions in each alignment have two pairs of opposites: they have *opposing elements* and *opposing cycles.*

Notice too that although the two positions have opposing rim elements, they have the same elemental influences (in this alignment, both are influenced by earth), and that although they have opposing cycles, they have the same seasons (in this case, Summer). Thus the two positions in each alignment have two things in common: they have *the same elemental influences* and *the same seasons.*

This is true for all three wheels: the God, Elemental and Tarot Wheels, since essentially they are all identical.

Diagram 2: The Elemental Wheel

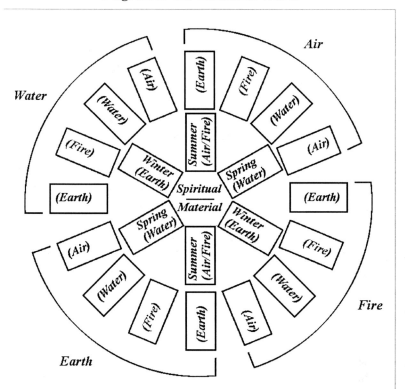

The original Mysterion was made of metal. Its use was not too complicated, though interpreting a given answer called upon both the knowledge and intuition of the wheel prophet. A brief introduction to the method used will be helpful when it is time to understand certain traditions relating to fortune telling with the Tarot cards. This is one of the more technical areas, so if you get bogged down don't be afraid to skip ahead. If you are interested in the details, be prepared to go slowly and think things through carefully. If possible, it is much easier to learn by doing.

The wheel prophet held a particular question in mind, focusing attention on the feelings related to it, not on the words defining it. For example, if the question was "Will I ever see the original Omphalos at Delphi?", the wheel prophet would look at the desires and fears this question aroused in her. Keeping these in mind, she would spin the rim of the wheel counterclockwise and wait to see where it stopped.

As we've seen, every alignment involves two positions, one of the high cycle, one of the low. Determining which was the primary answer to her question could be done by intuition or by tossing a coin or some such thing— take your pick. This left the wheel prophet with two positions, a *primary* and a *secondary* position. The primary position provided the answer to her original question. The secondary position provided additional information related to the original question in an orderly way. To understand what the secondary position told the wheel prophet, it is necessary to understand that questions were viewed in terms of *frames.*

The frame of a question was what the question involved, such as past or future, near or far, and so on. The primary frame was the main focus of the question. The secondary frame gave additional information provided by the wheel.

So for every question there was an answer given by the wheel in the form of an alignment. This answer was broken into two frames. The primary frame was answered by the primary position. The secondary frame was answered by the secondary position.

Table 3 provides a quick summary of some of the more common frames and their opposites. If the question involved several of these frames, then the secondary position dealt with its opposites

Table 3: The Opposing Frames of Questions

Inner	Outer
Past	Future
Near	Far
Subject	Subject's environment

For example, if the original question involved one's self, then the primary frame was self and the secondary frame was self's environment. If the primary frame involved the distant future, then the secondary frame involved the recent past.

If you were wondering whether you would get the job you are applying for tomorrow by impressing the interviewer, your primary position would answer your feelings regarding that interview. The primary frame would be near future (tomorrow) and your environment (i.e.: the interviewer). The secondary position would refer to the opposites of these frames: distant past and yourself. That is, the primary position would answer your question, and the secondary position would tell you about the situation giving rise to it—in this case the thoughts and feelings in yourself that gave rise to the present situation.

There are some traditional interpretations of the wheel's positions handed down to us by card readers. They originated with the Tarot's creators, though they may have been subjected to some slight distortion over the past six centuries. These are found near the end of this appendix. At present you don't know how to relate the Elemental Wheel's results to the listings which are based on the Tarot Wheel, so you'll just have to accept the particular traditional interpretations provided below. Later, when you see how the Elemental Wheel was related to the Tarot Wheel, you will see how this was done. In the meantime, let's look at the example of the job interview in more detail.

If the wheel prophet were to ask about how she will do at a job interview tomorrow, her question is framed in the *near future* and focuses on her effect on the interviewer, that is, on *her environment.* When she flips a coin to divide the alignment given to her by the Mysterion, the primary position will deal with her question in these two frames, near future and her environment.

The secondary position will deal with the opposite of these frames; That is, *distant past* and *herself* (rather than her environment).

Suppose that when she spun the wheel, the alignment contained the following two positions: Low Cycle Spring to Air Influenced By Fire, and High Cycle Spring to Earth Influenced By Fire. Tradition provides the following meanings for these positions:

*1) **Low Spring to Air influenced by Fire**: Much needed peace and rest after struggles. (4 swords).*

*2) **High Cycle Spring to Earth influenced by Fire**: Badly made choice causes concern. (7 coins inverted).*

Suppose that she had determined that the first of these positions was the primary position by flipping a coin. The reading would look something like this (with allowances for the reader's intuitions):

Primary Frame: The interviewer will accept me and the new job will work out very well.

Secondary Frame: I became unemployed through a badly made decision.

Don't worry if this seems a little confusing: the best way to learn it is by doing it. Unless you have a wheel or at least a deck of the original style of Tarot cards to play around with, it may not become entirely clear to you. A few examples, however, should help you to grasp the basic concept more firmly. Consider the frames involved in the following two questions:

- *You are wondering if your father's operation tomorrow will go well.* Here the primary frame is near future and your father's circumstances. The secondary frame is therefore the distant past, and your father.

- *You are wondering how or if you should invest in the stock market (and you've presumably decided to use the Wheel to help you beat the stock gurus at their own game: prophesy).* The primary frame is the near future and your environment (what will the stock market do next?), the secondary frame is the more distant past and yourself.

Applying primary and secondary frames to primary and secondary questions will make more sense to you if you try the following exercise:

- Consider these same questions or questions of your own, and go to the section of the appendix which lists wheel positions (it's near the end of the book). Randomly pick a position given there and assume it was the primary answer provided by the wheel. See if you can use the answer and the primary frame to answer your question. Next pick another position from the list and assume it is the answer to the secondary frame. Again try to use it to determine if you can work out the answer to the secondary frame.

Remember that the wheel prophet was expected to look at the feelings related to a question, not the words associated with it. It is much easier to fit the answers provided to feelings than it is to fit them to words.

The Chart Of The Wheel's Positions

The next section details how the chart was determined. Like the previous section, it's a little technical, and if you aren't interested in minutiae you might want to jump over it.

Once the Tarot's creators had settled on the Elemental Wheel for the Tarot deck, they realized its meaning would be difficult to understand. Therefore they decided to include a chart, listing all of its positions. That way each wheel position could be laid out as part of a continuum, with its relationships clearly described. You might suppose 96 positions of the wheel would require 96 positions in the chart, but actually these 96 positions can be expressed in only 40 positions. There are two reasons: firstly because the 96 positions were conceived of as belonging to 2 charts of 48 positions each, which could be economically combined in one chart of 48 positions. Secondly, 16 wheel positions describe trends, that is, some wheel positions represent the behavior of more than one chart position: they represent the behavior of an element throughout a cycle, and have no single position of their own. Thus there is one wheel position which describes the overall behavior of Fire in the low cycle, another for Fire in the high cycle, another for Air in the low cycle, and so on. Since there are 2 charts with 8 cycle trends hidden in each of them

(16 trend positions in all), this means that when the two charts are combined, only 40 positions need to be shown.
96 wheel positions ÷ 2 Charts = 48 positions
48 positions – 8 cycle trends = 40 positions shown in the combined chart.
Let's see how this was done. The chart shows the positions of the wheel in an orderly way. Remember that each wheel position includes four things. a) one of the cycles, b) one of the seasons, c) one of the elements, and d) an elemental influence. In the chart, each element is shown separately, and each season of these elements is kept separate. This organization can be expressed in the form of a table (Table 4) with the elements arranged in rows and the seasons arranged in columns.

Table 4: The Organization of Wheel Positions on the Chart

Fire	4 positions	4 positions	4 positions	4 positions	4 positions	4 positions
Air	4 positions	4 positions	4 positions	4 positions	4 positions	4 positions
Earth	4 positions	4 positions	4 positions	4 positions	4 positions	4 positions
Water	4 positions	4 positions	4 positions	4 positions	4 positions	4 positions
	Lo-Spr	Lo-Sum	Lo-Win	Hi-Spr	Hi-Sum	Hi-Win

Consider the element Air, for a moment. Each of the four elemental influences on Air (Air with Earth, Air with Fire, Air with Water, Air with Air) aligns with each of the six seasons (Low cycle Spring, Summer and Winter; High Cycle Spring, Summer and Winter) only once as the wheel completes one revolution. That produces a total of twenty four positions involving Air (6 X 4 = 24). These twenty four positions are listed in the chart on the horizontal line devoted to Air. The four positions including Low Cycle Spring are listed first, those involving Low Cycle Summer next, and so on. So far, so good, but what is the order of the four positions above their seasons? How are they plotted in the chart?

Before you can understand the order these four are placed above their seasons in the chart, you have to understand something else about them: how purely each elemental influence represents its suits. Recall that each of the four elements on the rim of the wheel is broken into four elemental influences to show how the elements interact.

The purest form of a given elemental position is the one where it is influenced by itself. Air influenced by Air, Fire influenced by Fire, Earth influenced by Earth, and Water influenced by Water are the purest forms of their elements. That's pretty obvious. These are called the quintessences of these elements.

The next purest form of each element is the influence which is the same sex. That is, Air influenced by Fire, Fire influenced by Air, etc..

The least pure form of each element is the one involving the element which is most opposite, and therefore found on the opposite side of the wheel from the quintessence. The opposites are Fire and Water, Earth and Air. Therefore the least pure forms are Air influenced by earth, Fire influenced by Water, and so on.

The second-least pure form is the remaining one.

These levels of purity can be referred to as ranks and listed as follows:

Table 5: The Ranks, or Levels of Purity of the Wheel Elements

	Water	Earth	Air	Fire
Quintessence	Water	Earth	Air	Fire
2nd Rank	Earth	Water	Fire	Air
3rd Rank	Air	Fire	Water	Earth
4th Rank	Fire	Air	Earth	Water

Refer back to Diagram 2, The Elemental Wheel. There are a total of ninety-eight positions on the wheel, once the forty-eight alignments have been divided. And notice that each alignment contains one wheel position involving one of the first two ranks and another involving one of the last two ranks. For example, an alignment involving the quintessence of an element in one position will involve the 4th rank of the opposite element in its other position. Water to water (the quintessence of water) will always be in the same alignment as Fire to water (the fourth rank of fire) because they are on opposite sides of the wheel. Earth to water (the 2nd rank of Earth) will always be in the same alignment as Air to water (the 3rd rank of Air).

It was thought best to divide the one chart into two in order to take account of this. One chart involves the quintessence and 2nd rank of the elements, called the *Quintessential Chart*. The other involves the 3rd and 4th ranks of the elements, and is called the *Inverse Chart*. For the moment, consider only the Quintessential Chart, the one involving the quintessence and 2nd rank. And again, consider only the low cycle of that chart to keep things simple.

There are only two positions from each wheel element to fit into the Quintessential chart above each of the three seasons in this cycle. For example, above Spring, we need to place the quintessence and the 2nd rank. Which comes first?

The answer was settled on using the logic of seasons and elements. The purest form of the element is expressed most strongly in the beginning of the spring. The second spring position will be less pure, because it touches the next season, summer.

The same logic applies for Winter, except that in order to keep the purest form separate, it now has to come last.

What of summer? How can two positions be ordered in summer? Whether first or last, they will touch the next season—either the one before, or the one after. The answer is found in the fact that each element in each cycle behaves a certain way as it progresses through the three seasons. This overall behavior of an element as it passes through the seasons of a cycle is described by the position containing the quintessence of the summer. That is, the quintessence of an element in the summer position of a given cycle describes the behavior of the element throughout that cycle.

Recall that the air and fire are the elements of summer, and the quality of fire determines which cycle, material or spiritual, is being described. Thus summer is the determining season. That is why the quintessence of the summer position describes the behavior of the entire cycle for an element. The quintessence of an element in the summer position is termed the *epitome* of that cycle for that element. An epitome describes the behavior of an element as it progresses through the three seasons of a cycle. Since there are four elements passing through two cycles, this means there are 4 x 2 = 8 epitomes in each of the two charts. That is, the wheel produces 16 epitomes as it turns.

To look at it another way, summer is the season in which the other two positions are expressed. A mature tree, for example, in the middle of its life, has seeds and fresh sprouting branches while at the same time having some rotted branches and dying leaves. It contains within its nature both the beginning and end. Similarly, the summer position of each element describes the entire behavior of the element in that cycle.

The end result is that the wheel positions are expressed in two charts as shown in Table 6 and Table 7. These two charts can be consolidated into a single chart as in Table 8. This Combined chart is the one the Tarot's creators decided to use in the cards. The Quintessential chart lists 40 positions as does the Inverse chart, for a total of 80 positions. In each of these charts there are 8 epitomes, for a total of 16 epitomes. Thus although the combined chart appears to have only 40 positions listed, it actually has (40 X 2) + (8 X 2) = 96 positions.

Table 6: The Quintessential Chart

Fire	1	2	2	2	1	1	2	2	2	1
Air	1	2	2	2	1	1	2	2	2	1
Earth	1	2	2	2	1	1	2	2	2	1
Water	1	2	2	2	1	1	2	2	2	1
	Spring		Smmr		Winter	Spring		Smmr		Winter
	Low		Cycle			High		Cycle		

In Table 6, the 1 represents the quintessence (the first rank of each suit) and 2 refers to the second rank of each suit. Note that in the central, summer position, the only rank shown is the second. The first rank position is not shown because it represents the entire behavior of the element for that cycle. For example, the quintessence of Fire in the low cycle summer position represents the behavior of fire throughout the low cycle, including spring, summer and winter in that cycle. That is, the summer quintessence of each element describes the other five positions of that element in that cycle. This means that all 48 positions are described although only 40 are shown: there are eight epitomes hidden in this chart.

Table 7: The Inverse Chart

Fire	4	3	3	3	4	4	3	3	3	4
Air	4	3	3	3	4	4	3	3	3	4
Earth	4	3	3	3	4	4	3	3	3	4
Water	4	3	3	3	4	4	3	3	3	4
	Spring		Smmr		Winter	Spring		Smmr		Winter
	Low		Cycle			High		Cycle		

In the Inverse Chart, the 3rd and 4th ranked positions are shown. Note that the epitome (the 4th ranked position) for this chart is the one farthest from the quintessence of the element. This chart is a mirror of the Quintessential Chart. Again forty positions are listed while an additional eight epitomes are hidden but described by the other positions.

Table 8: The Combined Chart (Quintessential & Inverse Together)

Fire	1/4	2/3	2/3	2/3	1/4	1/4	2/3	2/3	2/3	1/4
Air	1/4	2/3	2/3	2/3	1/4	1/4	2/3	2/3	2/3	1/4
Earth	1/4	2/3	2/3	2/3	1/4	1/4	2/3	2/3	2/3	1/4
Water	1/4	2/3	2/3	2/3	1/4	1/4	2/3	2/3	2/3	1/4
	Spring		Smmr		Winter	Spring		Smmr		Winter
	Low		Cycle			High		Cycle		

This chart shows both the Quintessential and Inverse charts combined. The first number in each position refers to ranks in the Quintessential Chart, while the second number refers to ranks in the Inverse Chart. Note that now there are eighty positions shown, and sixteen epitomes which are described but not seen.

If you've managed to understand and retain all the details given above in a single reading, you are either uncommonly clever or very persistent. In any case, there is nothing more that needs to be said about the Elemental Wheel and the chart describing it. Everything said about the Elemental Wheel is also true for the God Wheel, and indeed for the Tarot Wheel. The next step in understanding is to move directly to the Tarot cards and their creation.

The Tarot

The Tarot deck is a very subtle and complex method of accomplishing a goal which is subtle and complex in itself. To begin with, the purpose of the cards will be described, and then the deck. Describing the deck will be broken down into several parts. First the overall design of the deck will be considered. Then the details of the wheel and the chart will be explored card by card, and by comparing various cards together.

The Tarot cards were designed to allow certain ideas and facts to be kept in circulation in human society without anyone realizing just what those ideas and facts were, or even that they existed. Since one important function of the Mysterion is prophecy, it was decided to design the cards for the same use. This would also ensure that they would be treated with respect, even awe, and that they would continue to be copied faithfully down through the future generations until the time was right for Paganism to return. Given the fact that the Mysterion was a religious artifact considered to be sacred, even magical, its hidden presence in the cards would ensure they performed well at fortune telling.

The expectation was that by their choice of clues and the assistance of the Gods, the Cards' creators could select a suitable candidate living in a suitable period of human history. This person would discover the spread, explore its implications, and eventually locate the cave, digging it up and recreating the ancient mystery cults, presumably in their original locations. Things have not gone exactly according to plan, as a result of six centuries of radical change. Who could possibly have imagined the complex world technology would create? The transformation of human society and knowledge have rendered at least some of their assumptions false.

Mystery cults in the twenty-first century? Perhaps, but there can't be much appetite out there for recreating the Greco-Roman world and its ancient sciences. Times have changed.

As for the cave being casually dug up without official sanction, that would have been moral and feasible in previous centuries, but not in our own. One doesn't go around with a pickax trying to loot things which belong to governments and those holding title to lands, especially not if one has any respect for the archaeologist's role in preserving our history.

Everything surrounding the design of the cards and their use in fortune telling was carefully thought out to ensure discovering the full solution would be impossible for anyone antagonistic to their world view, and that even someone who was favorably disposed to listening to their perspective would not find the solution easily.

Enough information is included here to show the way the Tarot spread was intended to be found, but as indicated previously what follows will not be a laborious description of every logical step. Some will find too much information provided, some too little. If there's too much information, skip over what doesn't interest you. If there's too little information, figure it out for yourself—enough is included here to get you started.

If you are skeptical about whether the original and final solution to the Tarot's puzzle is given here, and you are really interested in finding out if it is or not, you may have no choice but to follow every step carefully. It took many months of hard work to find out the things summarized here, and you can't hope to retrace the steps properly without a least a week or two of serious application. Obviously there is no point in bothering to understand the details unless you are very keen. (The same holds true to a far greater degree where Greek religion is concerned, because the field is vastly greater: it involves changes in myth and ritual arising from changes in the Pagan world view—which took place in countless different times and places.)

At this point the creators' basic decisions regarding what to include in the cards and how to include it will be outlined.

It was decided to depict the Mysterion as the crystallization of the Tarot creators' world view, because it synthesized and summarized it in a compact form. It is a wheel designed for telling fortunes, but it is far more than that. It describes the nature of cycles, and therefore the Pagan view of time. It purports to tell how everyone's fate evolves in their daily lives. It provides a philosophy of life tailored to increase an individual's store of happiness. Furthermore, it tells how wisdom is discovered and fate transcended, for those inclined to such things. By describing myths and rituals in a specific context that indicates their hidden meaning, it provides a key to the whole forgotten world of Greek religion, and indeed of the other Pagan religions of European region. All this, and a map of buried treasure: not bad for several dozen colored pictures!

A chart of the Mysterion's positions was included because it is very helpful as an aid to understanding. The wheel alone would be interesting but say too little about how it was to be interpreted. Therefore both wheel and chart were included in the Tarot deck.

Each component part of the wheel and chart was given a card. The part was then represented by appropriate symbols that showed its meaning and how it interacted with other cards in the spread.

The symbols provided for the discovery of the secret pattern describing the wheel and chart were non-Pagan. They demanded simple observations of the patterns in the cards and of the elements in nature. That way, our knowledge of ancient Paganism could be minimal at first. Logic, observation and curiosity would be the only prerequisites.

Other symbols described the relationship of the parts of the spread to one another, and the original spread was shown several times in thinly disguised forms. This was done to help us to understand what we had found, and would provide proof that we had indeed found something substantial. Pictures of the completed spread were necessary because if the clues to the solution were sufficiently difficult to prevent premature discovery, they would also be too difficult to be irrefutable without additional evidence to back them up once the spread was found. This pattern of clues hinting at the solution but proof only *following* discovery rather than leading to it is ubiquitous in the cards.

Still other symbols introduced the Pagan perspective of life and wisdom, and were intended to prompt us to realize we were dealing with a Pagan artifact. Such symbols had to be carefully chosen: though Pagan, they must be susceptible to a Christian or other non-Pagan interpretation. Their Pagan interpretation must only be imperative once the original spread was found. Like the presence of the wheel itself, these Pagan symbols were thought to exert a magical influence on the cards, assisting the fortune teller's efforts.

Finally, we had to be led to suppose that there was a cave, and be motivated to find it. The location of the cave had to be provided with great care, so that only a suitable person who had mastered the initiation process would even guess at its existence, let alone recognize the map.

The Tarot Spread

There are a great many details provided in the Tarot cards, and it is easy to be overwhelmed by their description. It makes sense to look over the

Diagram 3: The Tarot Wheel

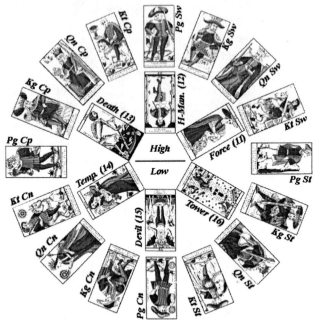

completed spread carefully first, and then to refer back to it from time to time while various details are being described. Additional illustrations will be provided as needed, but if you begin to feel lost, looking at the completed spread again might help you to find your bearings. See Diagram 3 (The Tarot Wheel) and Diagram 4 (The Tarot Chart). And for a color view, don't forget the foldout diagram at the back of this book.

It was decided that the cards, when laid out, would include not only a listing of each wheel position, but also a set of general descriptions that would lie beside and beneath them. If you look back at Table 8, The Combined Chart, you will see that the same thing was done there. The first column (listing the four elements) and the bottom two lines (showing the relevant seasons and cycles) were included so as to describe the organization of the positions listed in the body of the chart. Much the same thing was done by the Tarot's creators in their chart. There were four elemental rulers on the left hand side of their chart, and a row beneath the chart showing the progression of the seasons and cycles. In the chart the elemental rulers and the descriptors at the bottom were archetypal forms of the things shown in more detail in the body of the chart. This bottom row was extremely useful since it allowed the two cycles of three seasons to be described twice: once in the wheel using six cards, and again in the chart using ten cards. The chart provides more detail and a slightly different perspective of the same thing, greatly increasing the observer's understanding of what the three seasons entailed.

Diagram 4: The Tarot Chart

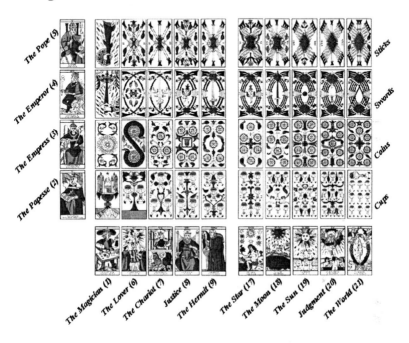

Two types of cards were to be included in the Tarot: those involving elements and those describing the seasons. The elemental cards were to be called Minor Arcana (Latin for Lesser Mysteries) and the others were to be called Major Arcana (Latin for Greater Mysteries). Once we realized the Tarot might be Pagan this would have special significance for us, since at the ancient cult site of Eleusis the mysteries were revealed in two parts known as the Lesser and Greater Mysteries. These names had the additional virtue that they would also help to keep the secret spread undiscovered: many people would tend to ignore the lesser and focus on the greater. That's human nature, unfortunately. Without both lesser and greater cards in combination, no solution would be possible.

Thus the Minor Arcana included the cards on the wheel's rim, and the listings of the wheel's positions in the chart. The Major Arcana would consist of the wheel's spokes and the description line at the bottom of the chart. It was decided that the elemental rulers of the chart would be included among the Major Arcana as well to reflect their archetypal role. This meant there were fifty six Minor Arcana (forty from the chart and sixteen from the wheel) and twenty Minor Arcana (six from the wheel and fourteen from the chart).

(Later two additional Major Arcana were added: one showing the wheel and one showing a mortal man suffering under the influence of the Mysterion. These were The Wheel of Fortune (the Tarot Wheel) and The Fool (personification of the struggle wrought by the fates described in the Tarot spread). Although both of these cards are important in understanding the Tarot, they can be set aside in the completed spread.)

It was decided that the cards of the Major and Minor Arcana would be numbered to show the order in which they were to be laid out in the spread. However, since the rim of the wheel was in constant motion, the court cards describing it constantly changed positions. They alone would be given no numbers. This fact would provide a very useful clue to us as we attempted to assign cards to fixed positions in solving the spread. Cards with fixed positions were numbered, cards in motion were not. But it meant that the order of the unnumbered court cards on the wheel had to be explained using a different system. More on that later.

The elements needed to be represented pictorially, and symbols were selected. Fire became Sticks (since these contain fire hidden in them). Water became Cups because cups are designed to carry liquids. Earth became Coins, because coins are made of metal, a form of earth, and because all wealth comes from the earth originally. Finally Air became Swords, because the thinness of the blade makes it almost invisible, and because a cold wind metaphorically cuts like a knife. These were not new symbols for the elements: they existed elsewhere at an earlier date, but were borrowed because they seemed useful. Note that the male elements air and fire (swords and sticks) are phallic in shape, while the female elements, earth and water (coins and cups) are rounder and especially in the case of cups, more open and receptive.

Each element was assigned four courtiers representing the influence of air, fire, earth and water on that element. It was decided that earth's influence would be described by a page, fire's influence by a king, water's influence by a queen, and air's influence by a knight. Thus each suit (element) would be represented by a page (earth), king (fire), queen (water) and knight (air), and these would be clustered together on the rim of the Tarot Wheel. The choice of courtiers was not random. King and queen were selected to describe the two most violently opposite of the four elements, fire and water.

Air is linked to mobility since air is a restless element, and that made a knight a good symbol for its influence. Earth is the source of wisdom (suitably illuminated), so the page, an apprentice engaged in learning, was chosen to represent the influence of earth. The following table summarizes this:

Table 9: The Courtiers & Their Elements

Courtier	Element
Page	Earth
King	Fire
Queen	Water
Knight	Air

To make things a little clearer, the numbered cards will be referred to in this appendix by their title followed by their number in brackets. Thus the first card in the sequence of Major Arcana will be referred to as The Magician (1), and the seventeenth Major Arcana will be referred to as The Star (17). The Fool is unnumbered, but he will be given a zero for the sake of continuity, appearing in the text as The Fool (0).

Inasmuch as the Tarot Wheel and the Tarot chart can be viewed as descriptions of the same thing in a different form, this had to be expressed in the spread. One method of doing so was to physically place the wheel in the middle of the spread. The Major Arcana used in the wheel followed those used in the first half of the chart, and were followed by those in the second half of the chart. In other words, Major Arcana numbered one to nine were used in the first half of the chart, those numbered ten to sixteen (one of which was the Wheel of Fortune (10)) were used in constructing the wheel, and the remaining cards, seventeen to twenty-one, were used in the second half of the chart. See Diagram 5 for numbers showing the order in which the cards were to be laid out, noting that card 10, the Wheel of Fortune, has been placed below the wheel spokes, and that none of the unnumbered cards in the spread (the court cards of the wheel's rim, and The Fool) are shown because their positions were not fixed.

It might be worth taking a moment to compare this with the completed spread shown in the previous two diagrams. Although these diagrams physically separate the wheel and the chart, you should keep in mind that the Tarot's creators conceived of them as they are shown in Diagram 5. This schematic representation is echoed in the symbolic pictures of a number of cards, so you will encounter it again, shortly.

Notice that the elemental rulers on the left follow after card one (The Magician (1)). This first card illustrates the creation of the elements, so the elemental rulers follow it. Then the rest of the chart is laid out in sequence with the wheel cards placed in the center.

Diagram 5: Location of the Numbered Cards In The Tarot Spread

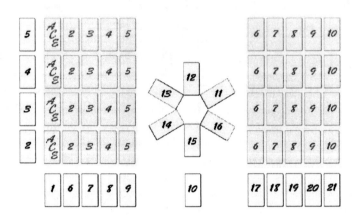

The cards of the wheel begin with card eleven, the high cycle spring, and continue around counterclockwise to the high cycle winter. Low cycle spring, card fourteen, follows next, and the seasons end at card sixteen, the low cycle winter card. That is, in the wheel spokes the cards for the high cycle spring, summer and winter are followed by the cards for the low cycle spring, summer and winter.

At this point it might make things clearer if we outline the logical and intuitive processes we were expected to follow in discovering the spread.

In the beginning, we were intended to guess that the four rulers preceded a chart of the four elements, and that many of the remaining Major Arcana were used in describing the baseline of this chart. This was the first step. Then we would lay out the four rulers and the numbered cards of each suit (each element), and would realize that we had seven numbered Major Arcana more than were needed to describe the ten positions lying below the chart. We would see the Wheel of Fortune card (card ten) in the middle of the sequence and explore the possibility that there was a wheel accounting for the seven unneeded cards. And since the Wheel of Fortune was in the middle of the sequence, we would guess that the wheel was located there. After playing around with it for a while, we would realize that the six cards following the Wheel of Fortune formed the spokes of the wheel shown in the Wheel of Fortune (10), and that the sixteen unnumbered court cards were on its rim. This didn't require pure guesswork: as we looked over the symbolic pictures on the cards, we would see this organization described in several of them. By the time we had finished this process we would have the original spread lying in front of us and could begin the work of understanding its meaning and use.

It will be seen that we were expected to think in terms of broad outlines without getting lost in the details of the individual cards if we were to successfully discover the original spread's shape. We had to see the forest despite the trees, to allow order to assert itself from chaos. In doing this we had to be hesitant about finding order too quickly, about ordering things to fit our own prejudices: we had to be willing to observe carefully without rushing to judgment.

What were the pictorial clues provided to us that showed the way to put together the spread once we realized it involved a chart and a wheel?

The Star (17) includes a central star with sixteen points, one **Diagram 6: Detail of the Star (17)** for each court card of the wheel's rim. There are seven additional stars, and the number of points on them is significant. The top two have seven points each, for a total of fourteen, the number of Major Arcana in the chart. The other five stars have eight each, for a total of forty, the number of Minor Arcana in the chart. Thus this picture shows the completed spread in outline, with the wheel hidden in the center of the chart. See Diagram 6a.

You will recall that the order of the court cards around the rim of the wheel was not given yet because they were in motion and therefore were not numbered. This information was provided in several cards which combine to give all the details that are needed. There is no way of guessing this order without assistance. We would have no way of knowing that the cards of each suit were clustered together on the rim—that all swords were together, for example, rather than mixed up with other suits. The solution was provided in three parts. The first showed that the female and male elements are on opposite sides of the wheel. The second showed their quadrants, that is, their order around the wheel. The third showed the order of the courtiers within each suit.

The Wheel (10), shows two figures on the rim. (See Diagram 25 later in this appendix.) One wears a dress suggesting the female elements, the other a tunic suggesting the male elements. That is, the male elements are on the right, the female elements are on the left. (Note also, in passing, that the spokes shown in the wheel are in two sets, one above and one below, rather than evenly spaced around the wheel. This illustrates that there are two cycles, one higher, one lower. This clue enabled the discoverer to deduce the proper order of the spokes.)

LA ROUE DE FORTUNE
THE WHEEL OF FORTUNE

The World (22) shows the wheel in symbolic form. There are six segments of the wreath representing the six spokes, and four figures around the edges representing the elements. The eagle (air) and lion (fire) are on the right, while the water carrier (water) and the cow (earth) are on the left. These ancient symbols of their elements therefore place the male and female elements on the same sides of the wheel as that

LE MONDE
THE WORLD

shown in the Wheel of Fortune (10). Male elements are on the right, female on the left. But now the additional detail has shown the approximate locations of the elements on the wheel's rim. Swords, for example, is located on the upper right hand quadrant

The card's designers decided that The Sun (19) would provide the order of the individual courtiers within their suits. Each sun's ray was given a different color, and these were color coded to match the emblems held by the courtiers in the court cards (swords, sticks, coins and cups). There were sixteen colored sun's rays for sixteen colored courtier's emblems. See Diagram 7: The Sun's Rays and the Courtier's Emblems.

Once we found these clues, we would be able to go back to the courtiers and by referring their emblems to the colors of the rays in The Sun (19), place them in order around the wheel.

The system was effective, but in retrospect the card's designers began to worry that coding of the sun's rays with the emblems would make a solution too easy. They wanted it to be found in the manner already laid out, but someone might solve it by seeing the parallel between sun's rays and the number of court cards, working from there backwards to the chart. This would have made the solution hinge on attention to detail rather than perceiving the broad patterns within the Tarot as a whole. And not only would this be an easier solution than the intended one, but if both avenues to a solution coexisted, the chances of a given observer finding the solution would be greatly enhanced. It was decided to alter the colors of the emblems enough so that only someone who already knew the wheel existed, having worked through the proper sequence of steps, would be able to use the color coding. The colors of emblems on many court cards were changed. All coins were colored yellow, the color of gold, and all cups were colored yellow and red, suggestive of golden chalices used to hold wine in the catholic Eucharist.

Diagram 7: The Significance of the Sun's Rays

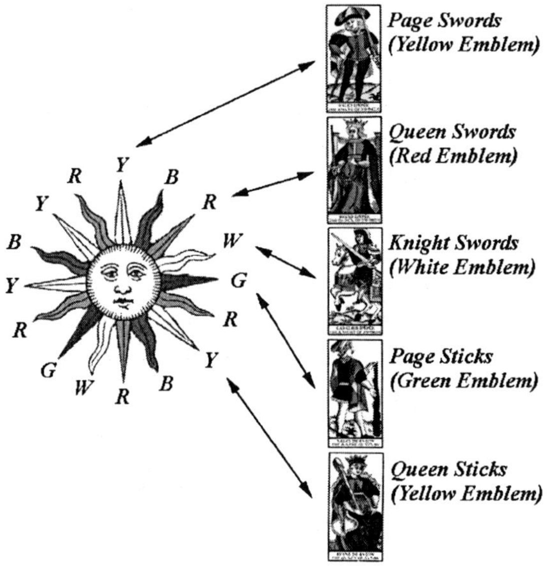

Only five emblems—three in the suit of swords (the minimum necessary to show the proper order of courtiers in this suit) and two in the suit of sticks (enough to show that the same order of courtiers existed in that suit)—were allowed to retain their original color coding. It was expected on seeing this we would realize that if that particular order existed in two suits, it presumably existed in all four. While the pattern of courtiers in each suit was clearly indicated, it would only be found when we knew exactly what we were looking for and why. The evidence was not enough for someone to blindly stumble over it.

If you read through the section detailing the Elemental Wheel and the way it was represented in the chart, you will know that there are forty-eight alignments of the wheel as it turns, and these are broken into ninety-six positions. The ninety-six positions are described in two charts which were then combined, so that only forty-eight positions are visible. And eight of these positions represent epitomes, behaviors of a given suit throughout a single cycle. Since the epitomes don't require cards of their own, being represented by the five other cards of their suits in each cycle, only forty positions are actually represented by a card in the chart:

(96 ÷ 2 - 8 = 40)

These are the ten numbered cards in each of the four suits of the chart:

(10 x 4 = 40).

Obviously the relationship linking the wheel to the chart is rather complex, and it would not be easy for someone to discover this without a little help and encouragement. That the chart describes wheel positions is not immediately apparent, since on the surface the numbers don't add up. (How are 96 positions on the wheel described by only 40 positions on the chart?) Until it is realized there were hidden epitomes and an additional, hidden chart, we would have no inkling of what was going on.

There are two cards that hint at the fact that the chart lists the wheel's positions, and a further series of clues from other cards that shows their subject matter is entirely parallel. In combination these make it clear that the relationship exists, and from that point deduction allows its precise nature to be discovered.

Table 10: The Numeric Clues of the Hanged Man (12)

6	3 seasons broken into 6 parts in each cycle of the chart.
x 4	Elements
x 2	Cycles representing the two parts of the chart
= 48	The number of positions in the chart (including 8 epitomes without cards of their own). The Inverse Chart is not included.

It will be observed that both The Star (19) and The Wheel of Fortune (10) have the same configuration: a wheel surrounded by a rectangular frame. The Hanged Man (12) was given a similar configuration although the hanging person is taking the place of the wheel. (See Diagram 30 later in this appendix.) The traditional meaning of this card is wisdom. This would raise the question: Could the hanged man have become a personification of the wisdom contained within the wheel, while his gibbet represents the chart ranged around him? There are six cut branches on the trees on either side with four blades of grass in the soil beneath each. If the blades of grass represent elements, and the six cut branches represent the seasons as described by the baseline of the chart (including the unseen epitomes) then the following numbers are involved:

This evidence is hardly sufficient on it's own, but it was thought that we would begin to suspect the relationship of the chart to the wheel once we'd noticed this numeric coincidence.

The Fool (0) has a number of round objects in his card. See Diagram 9 later in this appendix. These were intended to add up to another numeric coincidence.

Table 11: The Basic Numeric Clues of the Fool (0)

4	Bells on belt (4 elements)
x 5	Balls on collar (Visible positions in a chart cycle)
x 2	Knobs on stick (Cycles in the chart)
x 1	Ball on hat (A single chart)
= 40	Positions visible in the chart

Closer observation reveals that two balls are present but not in sight: one on the collar is hidden behind the sack, while another ought to be on the hat but is literally outside the picture. (The fool's hat traditionally represents ass's ears—which come in pairs.) This would lead the struggling observer to the following reevaluation of the numbers:

Table 12: The Hidden and Basic Numeric Clues of the Fool (0)

4	Bells on belt (4 elements)
x 6	Balls on collar (Positions in a chart cycle, when hidden epitomes are included)
x 2	Knobs on stick (Cycles in the chart)
x 2	Balls on hat (Two Charts, one hidden)
= 96	Positions actually represented in the combined chart

(You might want to refer back to the section on the Elemental Wheel if you are feeling a little confused about the reference to the hidden chart and epitomes in this table.)

Again the numeric coincidence and its nature—specifically that the numbers of the objects coincide with some of the numbers we would already be familiar with from the wheel—were intended to bolster the growing confidence that the wheel and chart are directly related.

It was assumed we would be aware that each card in the chart is given two meanings by fortune-tellers, depending on whether it is right side up or upside down. Furthermore in any alignment on the wheel two positions are included, one of which is literally upside down in relation to the other because it lies on the far side of the wheel. We would by now be wondering if this was an indication that there were two parallel charts included in the one chart found in the spread. That is, if the chart which the cards described included both a inverse and quintessential chart.

The other evidence of their relationship would come with the realization that the wheel and chart were parallel in composition. Obviously both contained elements, and two cycles, one higher and one lower. This was clear from the traditional meanings of the cards and their subject matter. In the chart, the second cycle contained astronomical symbols such as sun, moon and stars, rather than the more earth bound depictions of the first cycle. The traditional meanings were of a higher sort as well. That both involved the same three seasons would provide the first persuasive evidence that this was a Pagan wheel and chart, and make it clear that both chart and wheel described the same three seasons. How were we expected to become certain that three seasons were being described in two cycles?

We would notice that the spokes represented a sequence of three cards repeated twice and would view them as two parallel cycles, based on their schematic positions, their pictures, and the traditional meanings ascribed to them. (The first clue towards this conclusion being the arrangement of the spokes in Wheel of Fortune (10) into two clusters—one above, one below.) Responding to these indications, we would come to view them as a set with the following approximate meanings:

Table 13: Opposing Positions of the Wheel Spokes

Cycle	Card	Meaning
Low	Temperance (14)	Mixing of Spirit and Matter
Low	Devil (15)	Materialism and Confusion
Low	Tower (16)	Forced Change
High	Force (11)	Spirit Overcoming Matter
High	Hanged Man (12)	Renunciation and Wisdom
High	Death (13)	Continuous Transformation

The reasoning behind this should become more apparent to you once the cards are looked at in more detail. For now notice that there are three steps twice repeated in what appears to be a continuum. Put very generally, creation leads to materialism, but there is a kind of rebirth or reorientation which leads to a higher spirituality. A roughly similar pattern appears to be described in the chart.

As mentioned previously, the ancient three season year included three seasons called Peace, Order and Justice. In the chart, the second to last position in each cycle had a curious parallel added: in the low cycle the card is labeled Justice (8), while in the higher cycle it is labeled Judgment (20). At this point it was assumed that we would be reading widely, calling on our education in the classics and elsewhere, to try to place the Tarot into some tradition or other. Eventually we would come across the three seasons in Hesiod or another ancient source. The existence of Justice, the third and final Goddess representing winter—who ancient Pagans depicted like the figure in Justice (8)—would come as a revelation, and start us seriously rethinking how the pieces of the puzzle ought to be assessed. Up to that point we would be unsure of the creators' tradition. After that we would be increasingly certain they were Pagans. We would realize that the central card in the lower cycle, The Chariot (7) was given its traditional meaning of "overwhelming power and order" to indicate the influence of the Goddess of summer called Order. And we would see that the Goddess of Spring, Peace, was a natural fit for the part in each cycle where the elements were undergoing combination or recombination. Fire and water, for example, must come together in peace or they will battle each other until one or the other is gone. We would realize that if the six spokes were viewed in a similar light, they made great sense as well: they described the cycle of time in the language of the seasons.

The Tarot depicts people in the clothing of early renaissance times and therefore could not have been invented prior to that period. If it was a modification of an earlier card deck, the clues necessary for its discovery would certainly have been lost and we wouldn't have gotten this far. Therefore, the Tarot's creators knew we would be confident this was the original deck. And realizing that the ancient three season year was so fundamental to the spread, we would also know that the wheel was invented long before the cards. We would know that the three season year had been largely abandoned by the early Hellenic age of Greece, and four seasons adopted. We would know we were looking at a wheel dating back no later than that time. And we would know it was a Greek wheel, representing the Greek pantheon rather than that of ancient Rome or one of the other places, for Peace, Order and Justice were Greek. That would make us very, very curious what an ancient Greek Pagan world view was doing in renaissance Europe.

As we continued to evaluate the symbols on the cards in light of Paganism, we would become certain that the seasons of the wheel are directly related to the seasons of the chart, and we would know that the chart was a listing of wheel positions. We would begin to deduce the exact nature of the relationship in light of the evidence; realize epitomes needed no cards of their own (in part by realizing that the summer positions of the wheel spokes epitomized their cycles); deduce how the two charts were depicted in one; and proceed logically to determine the precise relationship of wheel to chart.

The Fortune Teller's Spread

Before going into the details of the individual cards, one last very important set of clues needs consideration. If you skipped over the section on "frames" before, you might find this a little difficult to understand at times. Still, the first part should be comprehensible to anyone.

The Tarot's designers created a set of customs for using the cards in reading fortunes. These customs are still used by many card readers today. They were originally designed to perform three functions. First, they schematically reflected the wheel and the chart, providing yet another clue to the finished spread. Second, they also ensured that the cards could be used successfully in fortune telling, since the original magical pattern of the wheel was paralleled. Third, they tell the secret spread's discoverer how to use the original wheel for telling fortunes.

In Diagram 8, the fortune teller's spread is shown along with the order in which the cards are laid down by the card reader. The first and second card represented the high and low cycle spokes. The next four represented the four elements around the wheel's rim. The last four represented the four elements of the chart laid out in the same order as the elemental rulers were laid down. In other words, this is a symbolic representation of the wheel and chart.

Diagram 8: Fortune Teller's Spread

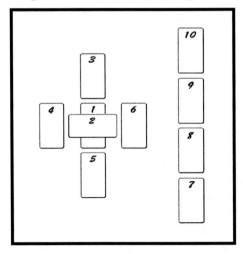

The method of fortune telling with the original wheel is also rather cleverly shown by the method fortune tellers were taught to use in interpreting this spread. Card readers were taught that each card in this spread was assigned a particular meaning according to the position in which the card was laid down. The accompanying table (Table 14) lists the rough meanings of each position as handed down by tradition. The numbers given correspond to the numbers shown in Diagram 8.

A card laid in position 4 for example, refers to the distant past of the person whose future is being read (the questioner). The meanings are approximate since tradition provides us with several slight variations of these meanings.

At first glance this collection of meanings is rather a mess. Why would this particular order exist? Was it arrived at logically, or in a more magical fashion? The answer is not clear until the Tarot Spread has been found and it is realized that the Fortune Teller's Spread is a schematic parallel to it. Once this is realized, the meanings of the various positions can be understood in a different context, and a new ordering principle becomes apparent.

These traditional positional meanings constitute pairs of opposing ideas. These are referred to in the section on the original Elemental Wheel as the *frames* of an answer. Just as the alignment involving one position will always include its opposite, so a frame involving one position will also be linked to the opposing frame.

Table 14: Interpretations

1	Present Situation
2	Influential Forces
3	Distant Future
4	Distant Past
5	Recent Past
6	Near Future
7	The Questioner
8	External Environment
9	Internal Environment
10	End Result

This means that opposing positions in the wheel portion of the Fortune Teller's Spread will be paired just as opposing positions on the wheel are paired. Another, otherwise hidden pattern is revealed:

Table 15

Distant Future	Recent Past
Distant Past	Near Future

Compare the two parts of each row.

Similarly, the two cards at the center of the Card Reader's spread (the first and second to be laid down) represent the high and low cycles of the chart. Every alignment of the wheel involves one of these cycles in each of its two positions. How do these two meanings on the Card Reader's spread compare?

Table 16

Present situation	Influential forces

This might be translated as "position of self" versus "self's environment" or "here" versus "around here". Once again these are opposing concepts in keeping with the opposing sides of the Mysterion.

The four vertical cards in the Card Reader's spread can also tell us details about the use of the Mysterion for divination, so long as we remember that their order from the bottom to top (when related to the original chart) is cups, coins, swords, sticks. Since a Mysterion alignment which involves cups will also involve sticks, these four can be broken down to two pairs of opposites; cups versus sticks and coins versus swords. In the Fortune Teller's Spread, this means that position 7 relates to position 10, and position 8 relates to position 9. This allows the meanings for this portion of the Card Reader's spread to be compared as follows:

Table 17

External environment	Internal environment
The questioner	End result

The first pair are clearly just another variation on the theme of opposites: "outside" versus "inside". The second pair are slightly different: they indicate something else besides the frame of a question. Few would suggest that "questioner" is the opposite of "end result". Instead it provides the seer with an appropriate mental focus during the process of doing a reading: the reader should concentrate on the questioner or "querant" (the person who is having a reading done). Card readers were traditionally told to do this when they were shuffling and laying out the cards.

The sets of opposites in the Card Reader's spread are listed here:

Table 18

Present situation	Influential forces
Recent past	Distant future
Distant past	Near future
Internal environment	External environment
The questioner	End result

The first four pairs of this list can be related to the following general principals when framing a question:

Table 19: Frames of a Question

Inner	Outer
Past	Future
Near	Far
Subject	Subject's environment

These, then, are the frames of a question when the original wheel is being queried. To understand how frames are used in questioning the wheel, refer back to the section on the Elemental Wheel.

The Tarot Cards

A survey of the images on the Major Arcana seems a little overdue: it's time to get detailed. The pictures are very intriguing, and with the basic understanding provided so far, their meanings should be fairly easy to follow.

The cards will be considered one at a time, with occasional pauses to summarize trends as they develop. The descriptions of each card will begin with the traditional meaning ascribed to the cards by the fortune tellers as part of the oral history surrounding the cards.

The Major Arcana are not described here in their numeric order: rather they are organized according to their positions and roles in the Tarot Spread. The Fool (0) is first, then the four rulers of the elements, then the baseline of the chart. Next the Wheel of Fortune (10) is described, then the High Cycle Spokes, then the Low Cycle Spokes. Finally, in the section on The Tarot Map, the Court card known as the Knight of Swords is shown, since this is the card that shows the Taro cave's location.

Once again, you will find it helpful to refer to the foldout at the back of the book, particularly when you wish to see the actual colors used in the individual cards.

THE FOOL (0)

"The wise mans eyes are in his head; but the fool walketh in darkness."
Old Testament, Proverbs, 26, 5.

Traditionally this card represents folly combined with virtually unlimited possibilities. See Diagram 9.

In the middle ages a fool was a professional traveling comedian sometimes remaining in service to the wealthy and powerful. Like the modern clown, the fool was often the butt of jokes played out in slapstick.

The Tarot's creators gave him only three fingers on each hand. This is not a mistake or an act of carelessness. Throughout the deck, missing fingers on one or another hand indicates a flaw in the deformed person's nature. A flaw in the right hand indicates a problem with watery characteristics. A flaw in the left indicates problems with earth. This poor fellow suffers from both.

The fool represents the living human soul wandering through the world harassed by its animal nature. When it is joined to the body, the spirit becomes subject to suffering and materialistic impulses.

Diagram 9: The Fool (0)

LE MAT
THE FOOL

The fool's staff and stick suggest the fiery will which guides him, because wood is fire in the form of earth.

At Eleusis near Athens the Greater and Lesser Mysteries were celebrated in honor of the earth Goddess Demeter and her daughter Persephone. This was one of the most famous mystery cults of ancient Greece. The Greater Eleusinian Mysteries began with a march from Athens several hours walk away. Prospective initiates brought supplies to the initiation process carried in a sack at the end of a knobbed stick. The fool is a candidate for initiation, though not yet initiated: this coincides with the traditional meaning of unlimited possibilities.

Dogs are a symbol of mortal nature in the Tarot and Greek myth, of death and the suffering a mortal body brings to the embodied soul.

The Fool (0) wanders through the Minor Arcana of the chart as indicated by the bells and knobs portrayed in this card. As described earlier, multiplying the circular objects displayed gives a total of forty, the number of lesser mysteries which lie in the chart. Adding the unseen circular objects adds up to 96, the number of positions on the wheel. He is like the two creatures in The Wheel Of Fortune (10) who travel around the rim of the wheel of fate.

Note that the ground on which he stands is nondescript. This is significant, for the ground depicted elsewhere is much more realistic. He is out of touch with reality.

The Chart's Four Rulers

THE PAPESS (2)

"I met a lady in the meads,
Full beautiful- a faery's child;
Her hair was long, her foot was light,
And her eyes were wild."

Keats, *La Belle Dame Sans Merci.*

As described earlier, The Papess (2) rules over the suit of cups and the element water in the chart. See Diagram 10.

Tradition maintains that she stands for wisdom, intuition and purity.

No female pope ever existed outside the realm of fable, and this one is the disguised ruler of the element of water. Water is the mysterious element: mists and haze obscure vision; the ocean deeps are dark and mysterious; eyes opened under water are unable to see without blurring. Water was viewed by the ancients as the gateway of souls into death, in part because water was believed to extinguish the fires of life. These characteristics are reflected in the veiling of her throne. The other important characteristic of water, that of union, is not reflected here.

Diagram 10: The Papess (2)

LA PAPESSE
THE HIGH PRIESTESS

Books are used for the transfer of knowledge. The book held by the Papess has eight lines of writing on each page. This is an indication that the book refers to the wheel's rim which has eight cards belonging to the male elements (air and fire), and eight belonging to the female elements (earth and water).

In light of the book and the shrouded throne, it is implied that the wheel is protected from improper revelation by obscurity, a characteristic of the element water: in other words, water guards the mysteries of the wheel. This is likely an aspect of the Goddess Persephone, daughter of Demeter, wife of Hades God of the dead.

THE EMPRESS (3)
"Her children rise and call her blessed"
Old Testament, *Proverbs*, 31, 28.

Ruler of coins and the element earth, tradition maintained that the empress stood for material wealth and motherhood. See Diagram 11.

Her throne represents a plowed furrow of earth, and there is what appears to be a palm branch protruding from beneath her. Some have imagined that the throne was actually wings, but that is nonsense: if you observe Temperance (14) you will see that the Tarot's creators were perfectly capable of drawing wings when they chose to do so. The empress is the Goddess Demeter, earth mother in the age of Zeus. Demeter slept with a mortal in a thrice plowed field. In myth she did not usually couple with Gods so much as with mortals, symbolic of plants that join with the earth, giving birth to the wealth of nature.

Diagram 11: The Empress (3)

L'IMPÉRATRICE
THE EMPRESS

THE EMPEROR (4)

"The pure sky longs passionately to pierce the earth,
and passion seizes the earth to win her marriage."

Aeschylus, *The Danaids.*

Tradition tells us that the emperor represents power, authority and leadership. He rules over the suit of swords and the restless element air. See Diagram 12.

The Emperor's throne does not actually touch the ground, and he is not sitting upon it. Instead he restlessly stands on feet the color of sky, and his crown is the shape of a wind-blown cloud. He is Zeus.

As with the other elemental rulers, the throne is a symbol of the kingdom he rules.

Diagram 12: The Emperor (4)

THE POPE (5)

"He drew a circle that shut me out-
Heretic, rebel, a thing to flout.
But Love and I had the wit to win.
We drew a circle that took him in."
Edwin Markham, *Outwitted.*

Tradition maintains that this card represents a spiritual leader, dogmatism, kindness and ritual. He rules the suit of sticks and the element fire. The columns are phallic, suggestive of masculine qualities and of temples (or churches). See Diagram 13.

Unlike the other elemental rulers, this card depicts followers. There are two people in the foreground. Both have the monk's shaved pate. The hair on one swirls clockwise and on the other, counter-clockwise. This distinction is not trivial, but its relevance will not be clear until Judgment (20) has been inspected closely. In the meantime it is indicated that one of the followers has a more elevated status than the other: The one on the left carries a hat and his bald pate is colored gold.

It is interesting that the pope gives a benediction with only two fingers, probably a reference to the two cycles of the wheel and chart. The cross on the pope's glove appears to indicate a Christian influence, but this symbol is found in a number of other traditions where it often represents the four directions (north, south, etc.), or the four elements, as it probably does here.

The Pope is Dionysos. It is strange that the connection of Christ to Dionysos is not better known in the modern world, although when Christianity was dominant it is to be expected that every effort was made to hide the connection. The issue isn't whether Christ was or was not Dionysian: what matters is that any intelligent Pagan would have little trouble making the connection.

Diagram 13: The Pope (5)

LE PAPE
THE POPE

The Chart's First Cycle

THE MAGICIAN (1)

"And the earth was without form and void; and the darkness
was on the face of the deep."

Old Testament, *Genesis*, 1, 2.

Traditionally, this card represented creativity and originality. See
Diagram 14.

The symbols of the four elements are shown in this card, with all save the
wand (the stick) laid out upon the table. The table has only three legs in view, one
each for the beginning, middle and end of all things. It could be thought of as a
"table of contents" for the entire spread. The dice represents the influence of
chance in nature.

It has often been observed that the brim of the magician's hat forms a
rough infinity sign (a figure of eight lying on its side). However, since the card
predates the invention of the symbol, this
detail doesn't seem too relevant.

Diagram 14: The Magician (1)

LE BATELEUR
THE MAGICIAN

Who comes at the beginning of
things, oversees the substances of which the
universe is made, works at the table of the
seasons? Obviously the creator of the
universe is the most natural candidate.

The magician appears youthful,
perhaps even pre-pubescent, which is to say
without defined sexuality; something to be
expected if sex-differentiation is a
characteristic associated with the elements
and does not exist before their creation. In
other words, sex results from the four
elements, owing its existence to them.

It is sometimes thought that the
magician holds a coin in his right hand, but
actually he holds a golden egg. The ancient
Greek tradition of Orpheus maintains that in
the beginning of the universe Eros was
hatched from a golden egg. Since the next
card, The Lover (6), depicts Eros, this card
obviously refers to the Orphic mysteries. By

Hellenic and Roman times, the ancient Pagans in religious centers like Delphi generally believed in a single over-God not at all different from that of the Christian sky-father. This was a development fueled by the speculations of their brethren, the philosophers.

The stick is held above the table, for it is the symbol of fire and the Tarot tradition reached back to a time when the special nature of fire was emphasized. Fire is the element of divinity, life and magic.

The laws of the universe come into being as follows: The Creator comes first and by drawing out the elements, establishes their rulers (Papess, Empress, Emperor and Pope). The nature of the elements and of their combinations cause events to develop in certain predictable ways guided by the Gods and referred to by the other Major Arcana of the chart's baseline.

THE LOVER (6)

"Be fruitful, and multiply, and replenish the earth...."

Old Testament, *Genesis* 1, 28.

The traditional interpretation of this card is love, choice and harmony. It is said that the young man must choose between the two women, his mother and his lover. See Diagram 15.

Eros, romantic love, is about to shoot the young man with one of his darts, and by so doing ensure that the lover wins out over the mother. In other words, any choice faced by the young man is more apparent than real. If a universal law is being inferred here, then it is that love sets the universe into motion, and starts the elements mingling. Sexual distinction comes from the elements, and sexual union comes from love.

In this context it might be best to think of love as being willful desire, rather than the more ideal divine love. This is, after all, still the first part of the lower cycle.

Behind Eros there is a porthole almost entirely surrounded by rays colored yellow, red, blue; yellow, red, blue,.... The young man's tunic happens to have the same order of colors. As the sky porthole surrounds Eros so the clothing surrounds the young man: this indicates that Eros and the young man are equivalent, that the young man is expressing the will of Eros on earth. Eros is a divine archetype, expressed by *arete* in our world.

The young man is missing a finger on his right hand suggestive of a nature that is flawed with respect to the qualities of water. Note that the magician in card (1) had all his fingers in tact.

As mentioned, the Orphics told that Eros was born from a golden egg such as that held by The Magician (1) who is located in the previous position on the chart baseline.

Diagram 15: The Lover (6)

L'AMOUREUX
THE LOVER

THE CHARIOT (7)

...he that hides a dark soul and foul thoughts
Benighted walks under the mid-day sun;
Himself his own dungeon.

Milton, *Comus.*

The traditional meaning of this card is control of the physical and mental aspects of human nature, overwhelming power, excessive order, triumph over life's obstacles, and trouble. See Diagram 16.

The young man wears a crown showing dominion and holds a scepter or stave which, as fire, represents willfulness.

In Plato's dialogue *The Phaedrus* an image much like this one is introduced. According to Plato both the light and dark horses (the good and bad inclinations) of our characters must be controlled so thoroughly that reins are no longer necessary. In this way the charioteer, the human soul, can rise up into heaven and take its place in the great train of the Gods, or as a Christian might say, pass through the gates of Heaven. But is this what is being shown here?

We must grow a little suspicious of the young man when we notice that the hand holding the stick, symbol of fire, is missing a finger.

When we look more closely we realize that the chariot is so stylized that the horses are intrinsic to it, and the wheels are of absolutely no use. What's more, the sides and bottom of the vehicle are in contact with the ground and movement is impossible. The result of the young man's firm control is immobility. This refers to the fact that a fixed will is unable to adapt to changing circumstances: Though at first it empowers, it soon becomes a millstone.

The shoulder-plates of the armor resemble old and new moons. Judging by the expressions on their faces they are miserable. The young man is between them in the position of the full moon. He is attempting to hold himself in the center position, the pinnacle of power and life. In

Diagram 16: The Chariot (7)

other words, the charioteer is resisting the natural flow of events. The initials S.M. on the chariot could mean anything, but a good guess is that they are a Latin acronym for "Senescent World". In any case, their inclusion is significant, for it demonstrates a knowledge of reading and writing in a largely illiterate age.

In this world we inhabit, everything has a period of growth and decline. Everything has its day and the end of its day. Yet we fight against the inevitability of decline and act as if such behavior was somehow virtuous. Wisdom does not arise through the conquest of nature: Nature and the natural order cannot be conquered. Wisdom is only possible if we become one with the natural order of things, a lesson the charioteer has not yet learned.

JUSTICE (8)

"'Tis with our judgments as with our watches, none
Go just alike, yet each believes his own."
Pope, *Essay on Criticism*, 1.

Tradition tells us that this card represents justice and well-meaning actions. In medieval times this was a familiar symbol for law: The scales weighed the evidence and the sword was an assurance that evil would be punished. Yet in the context of the Tarot it takes on a somewhat different meaning. This is the Goddess of Winter, Dike, who closely resembles her mother Themis, the older and more primal Goddess of Justice from which all the seasons came. See Diagram 17.

A sword represents air and hence action rather than punishment in the Tarot: the meaning here is assessment followed by action based on it. Notice that once again the hand holding the sword is missing a finger: the action taken is flawed.

There are two ways of looking at this card. On an individual level, past actions may be judged and new actions taken as a result. Retrospective vision is always blurred by prejudice to some extent, so new behavior will be imperfect. Then too, if we fight the natural order we are judged accordingly.

The charioteer's resistance of decline cannot continue unchecked forever. A violent and painful fall is inevitable for those who resist the changing seasons by the power of their will.

Diagram 17: Justice (8)

THE HERMIT (9)

"Nor deem the irrevocable Past
As wholly wasted, wholly vain,
If rising on its wrecks, at last
To something nobler we attain."

Longfellow, *The Ladder Of St Augustine.*

This card traditionally represents withdrawal from the world for a time of assessment, self-discovery and solitude. See Diagram 18.

It has been suggested that the hermit holds the lamp aloft to beckon the soul onwards, but in light of his position in the chart it is he himself who is in need of guidance. He faces back towards the path he came by to find out where he went wrong.

The hand holding the lamp is missing a finger so we know that hindsight is flawed.

It is not by coincidence that the lesser mysteries of the first cycle, the fifth card of each suit which lies above this card, have such painful traditional meanings as unemployment and sorrow. The consequences of resisting nature's flow have now made themselves felt, and the soul must learn from past mistakes if they are not to be repeated.

Diagram 18: The Hermit (9)

VIIII

L'HERMITE
THE HERMIT

In the beginning of the cycle things were drawn together. Now there is a tendency for pulling back.

First Cycle Summary

There are many levels to which the events of this cycle can be related, but for now an assessment at the personal level of the soul's experiences following birth will do.

After birth in The Magician (1), the soul leaves behind the mother and seeks self-expression and expansion in The Lover (6) through pursuit of the young woman. In The Chariot (7), the soul attempts to gain control over itself and its world but in doing so offends against the natural order, so that in Justice (8) the inevitable consequences of suffering begin to be felt. By the time the soul has advanced to the position of The Hermit (9) it realizes that something has gone badly astray and it seeks to discover why by looking back.

It might help to take a few moments and look at these five cards together, in order to fix the smooth progression of events in mind. Remember that they can also be looked at as follows:

Table 20: The Low Cycle Major Arcana Related to the Seasons

Spring	The Magician (1), The Lover (6)
Summer	The Charioteer (7)
Winter	Justice (8), The Hermit (9)

The Chart's Second Cycle

THE STAR (17)

"The morning stars sang together, and all the sons
of God shouted for joy."
Old Testament, Book of Job, 38, 7.

Tradition maintains that this card stands for great potential, hope and rebirth. See Diagram 19.

The new cycle begins with an offering being poured into water and onto earth. The left hand pours into earth, the right into water, showing the symbolic significance of flaws in these hands in the other cards. In any case, the two feminine elements are to play an important role in this cycle. Notice that the woman (representing the seeker's heart) has no missing fingers: She is perfect. Her nudity suggests freedom from all possessions and pretense.

The fact that this is the beginning of a cycle shows that the great star is the morning star, harbinger of the sun. The star is rising: by ancient tradition water is associated with the east and earth with the west. The woman pours into water with her right hand so this hand is on her eastern-most side. Rising just behind her shoulder, the great star must therefore be to the south east, rising with the new cycle.

Diagram 19: The Star (17)

XVII

L'ÉTOILE
THE STAR

Recall that the star has sixteen points and represents the wheel. Unlike the sun in card (19) the rays are of only two colors, so the order of the courts is not yet known. All of the stars combined represent the Tarot deck, which means that the general shape of the divine order, if not the details of it, has been made known to the aspiring heart. Because the stars are behind the woman, she has not yet seen them, though she intuits their presence. Given the atmosphere and details of this card, gentleness, peace and sacrifice were responsible for bringing this vision of Truth to the fore.

The masculine characteristic of willfulness is giving way to the feminine virtue of receptivity. Wisdom has become accessible.

There is a very striking reference to the Eleusinian Mysteries in this card. That a libation is being poured to East and West from the two plemochoi, sacred vessels used for this purpose in the mysteries at Eleusis, is one indication. The woodpecker on the tree behind is another. He is Picus, a woodland spirit who was harbinger to the rains which played an important role in the myths and rituals associated with that place, and was closely associated with the Greater Mysteries there. The pouring of the Plemochoi took place one day *after* the Greater Mysteries were revealed, though here we are looking at the beginning of a new cycle. This is because the Greater Mysteries were but a starting point for the millions who received initiation at Eleusis, though most would never go much further. The initiation referred to by the higher cycle in the Tarot deck goes far beyond that.

THE MOON (18)

"Oh, swear not by the moon, the inconsistent moon,
That monthly changes in her circled orb,
Lest thy love prove likewise variable."

Shakespeare, *Romeo and Juliet*, 2, 2.

Traditionally this card meant obscurity and deception. See Diagram 20.

The crescent of the new moon is featured (the face shown), once again evoking beginnings, but the moon's rays are of three colors to show that all three phases are involved: Beginning, middle and end all play their part. The phase of the moon is spring while the color is dark, wintry: death in the springtime.

There is rather more to it than this, however: the rays are evenly spaced around the moon's orb and this means the total number of rays can be deduced. There are ten dark blue, and ten white rays. The smaller red rays number twenty. This makes a total of forty rays, suggestive of the Minor Arcana of the Chart. The moon is feminine, so the bigger rays imply the female elements of water and earth. The male elements have been grouped together indiscriminately in the red rays. The three element system implied by the moon's three phases harks back to the

Diagram 20: The Moon (18)

LA LUNE
THE MOON

time when fire and air were not distinguished and that seems to be reflected here.

The pool of water in the foreground is a tomb. Its squared sides are similar to those of the tomb in Judgment (20). Crayfish are a symbol of immortality because they continue to live despite shedding their shells periodically as mortals shed their bodies.

In ancient times some philosophic and religious traditions believed that the dead went up to the moon, drawn, perhaps, by its dark light, and dwelt there while awaiting rebirth. The droplets rising in this card are the souls of the dead. Further, dogs, symbols of mortal nature, were thought to guard the gates of the land of the dead, and both dogs and gates are shown in this card.

The perspective of this card is very unusual: The crayfish is *rising* into the land of the dead. In other words, this card is drawn from the other side of the grave, from the perspective of the dead.

What is death and obscurity doing at the beginning of the higher cycle? Numerous religions from Christianity to Buddhism address the need to die to the flesh in order to be reborn into the spirit. Death is the ultimate sacrifice: When we die, we lose everything. To mystics the world over, when the material world is lost, the spiritual is gained.

Passing through Artemis' watery gate into the land of Persephone, the initiate is dying to everything, surrendering everything.

THE SUN (19)

"The glorious sun
Stays in his course and plays the alchemist,
Turning with the splendour of his precious eye
The meagre cloddy earth to glittering gold.
Shakespeare, *King John*, 3, 1.

The Sun (19) traditionally meant success, joy and friendship. See Diagram 21.

The figure on the left is missing a finger. It is not clear whether the other one is or not, but this seems doubtful.

These two boys are the Dioskouroi, the Gemini twins, one of whom was said to be mortal, the other immortal. So great was their love that when the mortal one died, the other shared his immortality with him and they spent alternate days in heaven and hell. That is why the hands of the boy on the right can be assumed to be properly formed.

The wall behind the two boys represents the wall separating the mortal from the immortal.

Diagram 21: The Sun (19)

LE SOLEIL
THE SUN

Just as the droplets in the Moon (18) were human souls on their path away from life, so those shown in this card are making the return journey. Where the moon is introverted and receptive, the sun is extroverted and penetrating.

This card is describing the mechanism by which the human soul perceives wisdom: Grace. It is selfless love (rather than the more profane variety) which overcomes the flaws of mortal souls and provides them with the Truth that makes them immortal.

Recall, in passing, that the rays of The Sun (19) are the key to understanding the order of the court cards, and hence of the Mysterion which is the physical personification of wisdom. It's appropriate that the sun should play so important a role in our enlightenment. The God Wheel was also conceptualized by the ancients as a sun wheel, sacred to Apollo.

There is one other aspect of this card that deserves attention, although it tells us of another card and God. The sun's rays are colored in an orderly way:

red, yellow, blue, red, white, green—
red, yellow, blue, red, white, green—
red, yellow, blue, *yellow.*

In other words, the same sequence is repeated 2 ½ times around the sun with only one card not fitting the pattern. This is the Queen of Cups, Persephone. She is keeper of the mysteries of the ancient religion, and thus keeper of the secrets relating to the sun wheel. The throne of the queen of cups is veiled, just like that of the Papess (2).

JUDGMENT (20)

O beloved Pan and all you other Gods of this place,
grant to me that I be made beautiful in my soul
within, and that all external possessions be in harmony
with my inner man...

Plato, Phaedrus, (Socrates' prayer to Pan).

Traditionally, this card means judgment, rebirth and development. See Diagram 22.

Clearly this image was intended to call to mind the last judgment in the Christian book of Revelations, but this is misleading.

As The Moon (18) depicts the soul's death, this card depicts its rebirth. It rises between a man and a woman. Note that the man is on the right and the woman is on the left, a reflection of the order of the elements around the wheel and an indication that the figure in the foreground is like the hanged man and the central figure in The World (21). The piously clasped hands of the man and woman indicate that the elements come together in peace in the reborn soul. The carnal Eros of the lower cycle now acts to create a more rarefied union.

Diagram 22: Judgment (20)

LE JUGEMENT
JUDGEMENT

The rays surrounding the heavenly figure are the same as those surrounding The Star (17), calling to mind its influence. Indeed, if the blue smoke is included as well, then the porthole shown here contains the same colors as that in The Lover (6) at the opposite end of the chart. Thus there is a deliberate similarity between beginning and end.

The cross shown in this card represents the dominion over the four corners of the earth and the four elements. The only other cross shown in the Tarot is the one on the Pope's glove. While on the subject of The Pope (5), it is worth comparing the hairstyles of the two followers of the pope with the reborn figure shown in Judgment (20). The latter's hair spirals inward in a clockwise fashion just like the left hand figure in the pope's card, a figure who appeared to have an elevated status on account of his hat and his golden pate. This connects the reborn soul with the influence of fire (The Pope (5)), not surprising since illumination is involved in the rebirth.

This is the rebirth of the soul in a manner reflecting the rebirth of Dionysos. At the Alcyonian lake at Lerna, the priests blew trumpets to herald the return of the murdered Dionysos back to life. He returned as a blending of male and female.

THE WORLD (21)
"Serene I fold my hands and wait,
Nor care for wind or tide nor sea;
I rave no more 'gainst time or fate,
For lo! my own shall come to me.
                    John Burroughs, *Waiting.*

The traditional meaning of this card is completion, synthesis and perfection. The central figure is said to be an hermaphrodite. Actually, his breasts are circles, quite different from those shown in The Star (17) and Judgment (20) so that they seem more like symbolic tattoos or drawings than breasts. They link him to the reborn Dionysos who took on feminine characteristics in his sojourn in the underworld. See Diagram 23.

The hermaphrodite's legs are in a mirror position of the hanged man's (but differ from those of The Emperor (4)), and he echoes both The Hanged Man (12) and the reborn soul in Judgment (20). He carries a wand like that of The Magician (1), suggesting that he has come full circle and returned to the indivisible source.

Notice that the symbols for the four elements on the outer edge of this card are combined symbolically: Aquarius and the eagle (water and air) are shown with clouds, while lion and cow (fire and earth) are shown with leaves (vegetation being a combination of the heat and light of the sun with traces of earthen ash). Note too, that it is water in the form of rain which initiates the growth of plants. Thus the elements are shown to be at peace with one another and in a creative, life sustaining form.

Diagram 23: The World (21)

XXI

LE MONDE
THE WORLD

The wreath has six divisions. If these represent Spring, Summer and Winter of the two cycles, then a new order has appeared between them in this card: The high cycle is no longer above the low cycle. This may suggest immortality. A new and perfect balance between time's three aspects could spell an end to death and decay.

This is the card of the fruition of wisdom, an event in which earth plays a pivotal role. The earth both creates materialism and provides us with the means of becoming free of it.

The central figure wears the sash given to initiates at the Samothracian mysteries. He carries two wands in his hands. At the Eleusinian Mysteries, initiates were given wands after their greater initiation. Two wands suggests a deeper level of initiation than most initiates receive. His tattooed chest indicates a return from the dead in the train of Dionysos. His legs are in the same basic configuration as the Emperor (4)—Zeus, Air—except that the leg crosses behind. The earthly reflection of Zeus' mysteries are not exactly the same as they would be in heaven. The only other Major Arcana with this leg position is the Hanged Man (12), who personifies the highest wisdom available to mortals. The wreath which surrounds the central figure refers also to the victor's laurel, worn by those who have expressed *arete* in the athletic and other contests. In short, he is the initiate of many, perhaps *all* mysteries.

Notice that three of the elemental symbols in the corners of the card have haloes, but the cow does not. The cow's head is turned in such a way that the wreath acts as her halo. Time's transformations are characteristics of earth. "The World" is another name for the earth. The earth Goddess of Justice, Themis, is the mother of the three Seasons: she is crowned by the wreath which contains them.

Earth is the womb from which all things in this world come. The wreath is not circular: it is shaped like vulva, surrounding the initiate. He is in a state of birth, fresh and new in every moment: sacred child of Mother Earth, transformed in the blissful mystery of Her creative center. He is beyond past and future, living only in the present, in the ecstasy of Her true nature where birth, life and death are one.

Second Cycle Summary

The journey of the soul through the first cycle is paralleled by its movement through this second one, except that where the first cycle deals with the consequence of embodiment, the second deals with the way of becoming free of it: Wisdom. See Diagram 24.

The second cycle is the cycle of the initiated soul. She begins in The Star (17) by honoring the female elements and restraining those impulses springing from the male elements such as fiery willfulness. As a result, a dim perception of the nature of Truth is made possible.

Next, the initiate begins her journey to the heart of Truth by renunciation: entering the realm of death through visionary experience, in The Moon (18).

In The Sun (19), she discovers love, a center point where mortal and immortal touch. At this self-less position she gains a full understanding of the laws and origin of her nature.

This leads to union of the hither-to conflicting aspects of character and hence to spiritual rebirth in Judgment (20).

Finally, in The World (21), the fully initiated and spiritually immortal soul stands balanced in the center point of the wheel of destiny, now and forever free.

Once again, these five cards can be viewed as beginning, middle, and end:

Table 21: The High Cycle Major Arcana and the Seasons

Spring	The Star (17), The Moon (18)
Summer	The Sun (19)
Winter	Judgment (20), The World (21)

There are two ways of comparing the cards making up the two cycles. Firstly, the parallel positions in the two cycles (e.g.: the fourth position consisting of Justice (8) and Judgment (20)) can be contrasted. Secondly, the two cycles can be viewed as a continuum, with the first cycle as "the way of outgoing" and the second as "the way of return". In this latter instance the first card in the sequence can be compared to the last, the second with the second-to-last, and so on. Look for parallels in the symbols and general composition of the cards.

The Minor Arcana Of The Chart

It might be worthwhile to consider the general trend of the positions as they move through the two cycles in the chart. Graph 1 (male elements) and Graph 2 (female elements) were made by subjectively assigning the traditional meaning of each chart position a positive or negative value between two and minus two. These values were based on the traditional meanings of the cards. Zero refers to a neutral value. For example, "encouraging travel but may be too rapid" (8 of Sticks) was given a value of 0, "inheritance and abundant good fortune" (10 of coins) received a value of positive 2, while "total destruction" (10 of swords) received a value of minus 2 in these graphs. While no two people are likely to agree in every instance, certain general trends will be obvious to every observer. Traditional meanings are listed at the end of this appendix.

Immediately you can see that all suits begin the first cycle on a very positive note and end it negatively. (At the fifth position on the horizontal axis.) The second cycle begins in a positive way, but by the end of it the male and female suits experience a very different trend: The male elements end negatively while the female elements end positively. See Graph 3.

Graph 1: Trends of Fire & Air in Chart

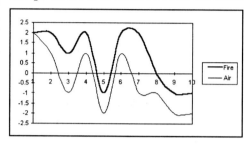

Graph 2: Trends of Earth & Water in Chart

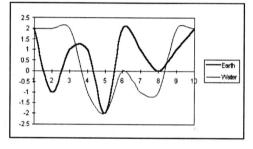

Graph 3: Trends of Male & Female Elements in Chart

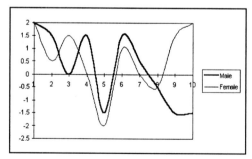

An Elemental Approach

You will recall the table below was given at the beginning of this chapter. If the trends of the chart are considered along with the associations given here, it becomes possible to make sense of the results of combining of the elements which took place in the beginning, under the influence of The Magician (1).

Table 22

AIR	FIRE	EARTH	WATER
Spirit	Life	Matter	Death
Action	Awareness	Immobility	Obscurity
Disunion	Seed	Womb	Union
Aggression	Willfulness	Passivity	Receptivity
Thought	Reason	Body	Emotion

The moment a living soul (fire and air) is embodied (placed in contact with earth and water), its male elements begin to quarrel with the female elements, chafing at the new restraint. As long as there is conflict, harmful interactions will occur and folly will result. For example, when willfulness (fire) dominates emotion (water) obsessions are born. When matter (earth) influences will (fire) the result is a grasping, selfish nature. Moderation, then, is the ultimate and healing virtue. The ideal is peace and harmony between the opposites. As the hands of the man and woman in Judgment (20) suggest, the male and female elements should be in reverent and peaceful composure. Dialogue must replace conflict and understanding must replace resistance. Looking back at the two cycles, they can now be summarized as follows:

1. Fire and air (living souls) enter the body and come into contact with earth and water, immediately beginning to conflict with them. That they are naturally combative is clear to anyone who has thrown water into a fire, or watched a furiously boiling pot. The struggle is not particularly violent in the body of a healthy person: it's more like an argument.

2. As with any conflict, both sides do harm, each according to his or her nature. Fiery willfulness in particular causes great problems, because it leads to materialism and resistance towards the natural order of things. The result, by the end of the first cycle, is misery.

3. If we, as souls (air), learn our lesson, we are able to discover humility and receptivity. Instead of battling with water and earth, we adopt their peaceful, receptive nature and wisdom begins to grow. The feminine transforms us.

4. By the end of the second cycle water and earth have given their gift of wisdom.

The relative difficulties experienced by swords and sticks in the second cycle indicates the probable fates of those who continue to feature the impulses of air and fire over those of earth and water. In other words, the predominance of an element in our character make-up will roughly determine which suit best defines our fate.

The Tarot's designers would argue that each step in this progression through the chart is not to be shunned: In time, unless the soul fails to learn its lessons, it will grow wise. Resistance and conflict will be replaced by harmony and wisdom.

The Wheel's Spokes

THE WHEEL OF FORTUNE (10)

"No man of woman born,
Coward or brave, can shun his destiny."
                    Homer, *Iliad*, 6. (Bryant's translation).

Traditionally, this card represents destiny and fate. See Diagram 25.

The spokes are symbolically grouped into high and low. The frame and wheel take the familiar shape of the Tarot spread. The crank at the center of the wheel is the thing which drives it. Find the center and freedom from the mechanism is possible. As mentioned previously, the characters on the rim are male and female, rough representations of the elements.

The figures on the wheel's rim are monkeys. In the middle ages these animals were thought to be associated with the lunar cycles, or in terms of life, with Spring (beginning), Summer (middle) and Winter (end). This shows the emphasis on aging or mortality in this card. Further, monkeys are not as bright as humans though similar in other respects: they are ignorant. The faces of those shown here express misery, indicating that bondage to the wheel of fate is a generally unpleasant experience.

Diagram 25: The Wheel of Fortune (10)

LA ROUE DE FORTUNE
THE WHEEL OF FORTUNE

One tradition accompanying the cards identifies the figure at the top of the wheel as a sphinx. Like the Sphinx of ancient Greek myth, he is a guardian of sorts. (In the Greek myth of Oedipus, a sphinx guarded the riddle which describes a man: "What goes on four legs in the morning, two at midday, and three in the afternoon?" Once again we find ourselves touching on the three divisions of time; beginning, middle and end, and on their role in human life.) The sphinx holds a sword, symbol of air, because he is overseeing the fate of souls. Solve the riddle posed by the action of time, and freedom results.

Perhaps there is a hint given here about the nature of the solution to that riddle. The sphinx is on a platform at the top of the wheel. If the wheel were to turn even a little, common sense suggests he would tumble from it. Even so, he seems comfortably settled in his spot. How can this be? Time does not move, but only appears to: the wheel appears to move, but for the one who solves its riddle, there is no motion. Change is an illusion, and the three seasons are also one.

This card was probably added as an afterthought, because it was needed to fine tune the relative difficulty of discovering the spread. Its location in the sequence was a vital clue to recognizing that the wheel's spokes were formed from cards drawn from the center of the sequence of Major Arcana.

The Low Cycle Of The Wheel

TEMPERANCE (14)
"Of all mortal things none has birth, nor any end in accursed death, but only mingling and interchange of what is mingled - birth is the name given to these by men."
Plutarch on *Empedocles.*

The traditional meaning of this card is moderation, temperance, and the mixing and bringing together in union. In the middle ages temperance commonly meant moderation or "mixing in right proportion". See Diagram 26.

The woman is an angel, a being who acts upon the urging of divine will.

The jugs shown in this card are similar to those in The Star (17), but the fluid in this instance is defying gravity, so it does not represent typical water. It has been suggested that this card refers to the mixing of spirit and matter, which is born out by its location at the beginning of the first cycle, the point where the creation of the universe or of life occurs.

Diagram 26: Temperance (19)

XIIII

TEMPÉRANCE
TEMPERANCE

THE DEVIL (15)

"There is some soul of goodness in things evil,
Would men observingly distil it out."
Shakespeare, *Henry V,* 4, 1.

The traditional meaning of this card is bondage, downfall, confusion and materialism. See Diagram 27.

As we've already noted, the devil shown here is not malevolent. Rather, he suffers from Downs syndrome (mongolism), and consequently from retardation.

The sword the devil holds has no handle, cutting the hand that wields it. In the Tarot deck, swords symbolize the element air or one of its characteristics. It is probable that action is being referred to here, so that the actions of the devil bring harm to him. Because the soul is associated with the element air, wings are often used to depict its status, as in the *Phaedrus* of Plato where wings were said to grow along with the soul's wisdom. The devil has bat's wings indicating that his soul is in darkness, the favored environment of the bat. On close inspection of the right-hand wing we can see that its bones are distorted where they come into contact with the tip of the sword. This tells us that the devil's actions damage his very soul.

The male and female in the foreground of this card are on the same sides as the male and female figures in the background of Judgment (20): That is, male on the right, female on the left. This is the same orientation of the sexes as exists in the elements of the court cards on the rim of the wheel. This is no coincidence. The initiated figure in the center of the wheel in The World (21) is symbolically connected with both the devil and the resurrected figure in the tomb of Judgment (20). This is the same soul in each of these cards, a soul whose situation varies depending on his cycle.

At first it may seem confusing that both the male and female imps are equally in bondage, given that the male attribute of willfulness has been singled out as predominant in the first cycle. However, both male and female elements suffer in the lower cycle and each are troubled by the close

Diagram 27: The Devil (15)

proximity to one another. Both might prefer freedom, if they could conceive of it. We should keep in mind that materialism is not a trait of earth alone: it is the result of fire coming into contact with earth. The devil's pedestal, to which the imps are tied, appears to be an anvil. That is, it is made of iron, an earthen substance.

Apart from the hands and the feet shown in this card, there is an unusual degree of realism in the drawing. If the hats of the two imps are looked at closely, it will be seen that the horns and the animal ears give every appearance of being stuck on, rather than being a natural part of the imp's physique. Why might this be? If the imps were purely symbolic of something, then the ears would likely be depicted as their own. The scene shown in this card represents an actual ritual.

The hat worn by the devil has confused many people over the years. A simple explanation, although on the surface a mundane one, is that it is a kerchief tied on with a string. Agricultural laborers throughout the ages have resorted to protection of this sort from the heat of the sun. The two "horns" are tree branches, as are those stuck in the imp's hats.

The two imps have rather coarse, foolish faces. They may represent local drunks in the area where the Tarot's makers lived. Alcohol dulls the mind giving it a mental handicap, not unlike mongolism.

As we already noticed, the devil's chest carries tattooed or painted breasts on it, one of which is incomplete.

Downs syndrome sufferers were sacred to Dionysos, for like drunks they suffered from the sort of darkness which occurs when the fire of life is dimmed and the initiate enters the underworld. Iron is indicated by the anvil. This requires a little explanation.

Iron contains fire that is released as sparks when it is struck. This fire was thought to come from the forge fire (and was a metaphor for life). Water causes iron to rust (turn bloody-colored, and lose its capacity to spark—i.e.: lose its "life"). Iron was called "the woe of mankind", a term also applied to delightful Pandora, who was sometimes depicted being shaped by Prometheus in a forge. Embodiment brings sorrow: we are the "iron race".

To summarize, we appear to be dealing with a ritual depicting the dark cycle of the soul when materialism has locked the spirit in darkness. The devil is not evil: he is ignorant. The Tarot is unimpressed by Christian nightmares, and in fact would believe Christians shared in the predicament of the devil shown here: bewilderment, confusion and ignorance.

In many respects, this card is representative of the entire low cycle.

THE TOWER (16)
"Man is born unto trouble, as the sparks fly upward."
Old Testament, *Job*, 5, 7.

The traditional meaning of this card is complete and sudden change, downfall, and the breakdown of old beliefs. See Diagram 28.

The phallic tower has no door so it is as much a prison as a stronghold. The toppling crown-shaped battlement suggests that a kind of sovereignty is being overthrown.

The dots in the sky might at first seem to be stars or sparks but they happen to be the same color as the rays of the moon. The tower has three windows, likewise indicating the three phases of the moon. (The longer and higher central window suggests that as in The Chariot (7), the tower represents an attempt to maintain the summer position perpetually.) The moon represents obscurity and the passage of the three divisions of time; beginning, middle and end. This suggests that the fall of the tower is the result of these things.

There are thirteen red and thirteen white dots. Not by coincidence, there are thirteen lunar months in a solar year (with one and a quarter days left over). There are only eleven blue dots, but this is the color of the dark, waning phase of the moon, exactly the position to represent the end of a cycle. The two falling men have the misfortune to be personifications of the dark phase: when they are added to the dark "sparks", the total number becomes thirteen. Thus an entire lunar year is represented here. As the point marking the start of the new year approaches, change cannot be put off any longer. The length of a particular season may vary from year to year, but the passage of the year does not vary. Change is inevitable.

Ignorance and the inexorable march of fate are the hallmarks of the lower cycle and the cause of the tower's fall.

The two falling figures are calm as they plummet earthward. They reach towards the blades of grass, a metaphor throughout the deck for wild untamed life. The men are temporarily whole, as

Diagram 28: The Tower (16)

evidenced by the completeness of their hands: the figure in the foreground has all of his fingers.

In our struggle to control the circumstances of our lives we strive to promote security. Security is inflexible; it is an attempt to hold the constantly changing universe at bay. Perhaps fortunately, in this world nothing is permanent, so no matter how hard we try to protect it, our security will inevitably be swept away—in death if not before.

Our failure to successfully resist change is bitter to the taste yet good for us. If we were to have our way, we would dwell in a tepid, stagnant, and lifeless world built by the dictates of our petty fears and desires. The whole grand, swirling, beauty of nature would be sacrificed to our security, and we would live in a fantasy world of our own invention. Life itself is the enemy of security.

When change forces down the protective walls we've built, we are anxious in our insecurity, but if we pay close attention, we notice there is also a sense of relief and of a more intense awareness of reality. It is at these moments that we often learn the most about ourselves, because at such times we perceive life as it is, rather than life as we think we want it to be.

Unfortunately, it does not take us long to begin constructing new walls, but these too will fall in their turn.

This is why the figure in the foreground has all of his fingers: the shattering of his dreams may have effected a cure, however temporary.

The High Cycle Of The Wheel

FORCE (11)
"All things in moderation"
The Temple of Apollo, Delphi.

Traditionally this card means strength and resolution. See Diagram 20.

In the middle ages this image often stood for spirituality overcoming materialism.

In the Tarot deck the lion is a symbol for the element fire. The woman is prying the lion's jaws apart, jaws whose nature it is to hold onto things. A gentle heart is loosening the grip of the grasping will which caused so much trouble in the first cycle. Under this woman's influence no new towers are going to be built and nature is free to take its allotted course. Even the longing for wisdom, a kind of spiritual materialism, falls away and the soul stands open to whatever comes its way.

Diagram 29: Force (11))

THE HANGED MAN (12)

"I know that I hung
in the windy tree
for nine full nights.
Wounded by the spear,
consecrated to Odin,
an offering to myself
on the tree
whose roots are unknown."

Snorri Sturluson, *Odin's Song.*

The traditional meaning of this card is transition, sacrifice, renunciation and rebirth. See Diagram 30.

Green is a rare color in the Tarot where it apparently means "life". The hanged man's gibbet has a green cross-piece and sprouts from two green clumps of earth. The man's head is beneath the surface of the earth, his hair resembles the roots of a plant, and we may suppose that he is listening to the wisdom of the earth, a wisdom reflected in The World (21) where the central wreath (the wheel's spokes) crowned the cow (earth). Likewise, the hanged man's legs are mirror reflections of the initiate in the center of the world card, suggesting Zeus' wisdom. Recall that the shape of the hanged man's gibbet shows that he is taking the place of the wheel: he is one with it. There are six cut branches on each tree supporting the hanged man's gibbet. Hidden in the clumps of soil are six blades of grass, three on each side. Six times four times two equals forty-eight, the number of alignments on the wheel, and hence the number of positions depicted in the chart (including epitomes).

Actually, since there are two charts, one inverse and one quintessential included in the overall chart, this card probably only represents one half of the overall chart: the high cycle portion. Being in the summer position, he epitomizes the high cycle.

Diagram 30: The Hanged Man (12)

LE PENDU
THE HANGED MAN

Just as The Devil (15) contained details which hinted that it depicted an actual ritual, so too, The Hanged Man (12) has one crucial detail that would be unlikely if its subject were purely symbolic: The hanged man's neck and face are swollen with blood as a result of his inverted position. Like The Devil (15), this card is at the center position in its cycle.

DEATH (13)

"Look at this world, glittering like a royal chariot; the foolish are immersed, but the discerning do not cling to it."

The Dhammapada, 13, 5.

By tradition, this card means transformation and the replacing of the old with the new. See Diagram 31.

The skeleton is still suffering from decay because here and there flesh continues to stick to the bone. It is in a process of transformation. This is why the skeleton's right foot is invisible: death stands with one foot in the present and one foot in the invisible past.

Death stands on the head of a girl and near that of a queen, showing that youth and high position will be harvested. The hands and feet lying about on the ground are all flawed in some way. Most have the wrong number of fingers or toes, and the only one that is perfect has the wrinkled appearance of old age. Death conquers all in this world. It cannot and should not be resisted. For the mystic, the present is all that exists and death is continuous, as is creation. We live in the illusory world of memory, of conditioning and thought, but truth only exists in the eternal present. To step outside the world of thought means to step outside the illusory world of continuity, and live in the ever-changing present.

Diagram 31: Death (13)

Black is a rare color in the Tarot. Both here and in The Devil (15), where it is used to represent the earth, it suggests "oblivion". The blue and yellow hue of the grass is unique to this card, indicating another perspective of reality is being adopted.

Lest it be imagined that death is perfect, he is missing a finger from his right hand. Only that which is changeless can be considered to be lacking in flaws. Death, too, is within time, though he stands at the bridge to timelessness.

The skull is not typical. A close inspection of it suggests that it may have been meant to indicate the phases of the moon, particularly the waning moon. Once again the relentless motion of time is indicated.

This card, lying at the end of the high cycle when the soul has been granted wisdom, depicts the central feature of life: Change. The essence of wisdom is to accept the turning of the wheel of fate without resistance. Wisdom is only possible when the transience of all things has been accepted, and death holds no fear.

Summary of the Progression Through The Seasons

Spirit and matter come together in Temperance (14) giving rise to materialism and confusion in The Devil (15). The essence of materialism is resistance to change and the inevitable result is that nature overpowers all our attempts to restrain it as shown in The Tower (16). Wisdom is born when the materialistic impulse is stilled in Force (11). The Hanged Man (12) is caught in the moment when wisdom is being revealed to the soul by the element earth. Like the central figure of The World (21), he is poised precariously in the present having left the past behind. When the higher cycle ends in Death (13), the soul is freed from its past obsessions and fears. It dwells in the eternal present, in harmony with the universe.

The Table (23) below summarizes the meaning of the positions of the chart's baseline and the wheel's spokes.

Interested readers may once again find it useful to look at the sequence of events in the two cycles by contrasting parallel and opposing positions in the high and low cycle. It would also be useful to once again compare the wheel and the chart cycles. See Diagram 32.

It would be possible to add to the list of clues and symbolic information provided by the Tarot, and to greatly expand the things it implies about their religion. However, enough is given here that a keen reader can begin to do the rest alone. There is a lot to digest, but once digested it continues offering insight after insight without apparent end. If some find themselves still curious and eager to get to the bottom of things, then this appendix will have served its purpose. Only one thing remains to be outlined here: the information leading to the cave.

Table 23: Summary of the Meanings of Major Arcana

Chart Baseline

Lo-Spr	Magician (1)	Creation
Lo-Spr	Lover (6)	Joining and mixing of elements
Lo-Sum	Chariot (7)	Overwhelming order, resistance to change
Lo-Win	Justice (8)	Inevitable judgment and results
Lo-Win	Hermit (9)	Reflection on past mistakes
Hi-Spr	Star (17)	Rebirth, fresh start
Hi-Spr	Moon (18)	Renunciation, restraint, surrender
Hi-Sum	Sun (19)	Grace, illumination
Hi-Win	Judgment (20)	Rebirth, transformation
Hi-Win	World (21)	Wisdom, timelessness

Wheel Spokes

Lo-Spr	Temperance (14)	Mixing of Spirit and Matter
Lo-Sum	Devil (15)	Materialism
Lo-Win	Tower (16)	Forced change
Hi-Spr	Force (11)	Restraint
Hi-Sum	Hanged Man (12)	Renunciation and enlightenment
Hi-Win	Death (13)	Acceptance of change, transformation

The Tarot Map

The court cards are the most confusing in the deck. If you take the time to get to know them well, you will discover that every pattern you have found is enigmatic, to say the least. Partly this is because they are concealing information about a subject that was only available to the fully initiated: the Gods are not revealed completely in the cards. However, there was another reason for their obscurity. The Tarot's creators knew that having got this far, we would be intent on greater information, and would attempt to make sense of the wheel by determining what the strange symbolic representations on the court cards mean. And while they were not intending to immediately satisfy our curiosity, they did expect us to discover the means of satisfying it by looking at these cards and wondering about them. In one of these cards they showed the location of the cave where we could discover the things they were still concealing.

As always, the clues are well-hidden and only accessible to someone who has perceived the greater pattern first. And while the full story is not given here, the proof required to verify the location is provided in the cards in a fashion which only makes complete sense when one is standing on the mountain in the proper place with the proper attitude: a mind that can see both the forest and the trees, and is open to the order of both cards and location.

Consider what the cards' creators would have known we would know, once the cards had been thoroughly digested. (These points were simply a matter of careful deduction based on the evidence we would have before us in the cards, coupled with a few books on matters related to the ancient religion and its myths. As a mystery writer once put it: *when you have eliminated all the possibilities, whatever remains—however improbable—is true.*) In any case, interested readers might enjoy trying to retrace the logical reasoning that lies behind these assumptions.

We were be expected to know or at least suspect:

•That the creators had a Mysterion and must have concealed it. (An obviously sacred object such as this wheel would never be destroyed.)

•That the cards were designed to carry the world view of their creators into the future, without anyone understanding them, until the time was right.

•That the creators were Pagan, and they considered themselves, with apparent justification, to be part of an ancient Greek tradition that existed thousands of years before the card's invention, and they were claiming direct knowledge of and connection to the greatest centers of religious knowledge in the ancient Greek mystery religion.

Sanctuary of the Gods: Appendix

•That the creators represented some sort of survival up to renaissance times, and this must have been accomplished in secret, and that they viewed themselves as preservers of the Western religious and philosophic tradition.

•They knew we would realize they had existed in isolation, almost certainly outside the urban centers, to have remained undetected for so long.

•We would realize that as incredible as it sounds, this meant they must have gone underground at the time of Rome's conversion to Christianity, and that they must have done this in an organized and well funded manner—otherwise they would have perished in the nine hundred years they were underground.

•They knew we would suspect they had something more than a Mysterion to offer in terms of material objects: that when they went underground they almost certainly had the means, the motive, and the opportunity to gather many things besides their own knowledge and the wheel.

So if we took the trouble to understand the cards well enough, we would know a cave probably existed. Confident that we would eventually arrive at that conclusion, they gave us a map.

First the Tarot's creators realized that they had to describe their location somehow, since we would not be keen to travel to all the mountains in Europe and the Middle East in search of theirs. They knew we would expect some geographic clue and be looking for one. They decided to use something so obvious that no one would ever think of it unless he was looking. They gave the cards the name of their valley: the Taro. (The cards are known variously as Tarot, Taro, and Tarocchi; the only geographical Taro in Europe is the Taro river, south of the Italian city of Parma.) Given an approximate location, we would be able to find the mountain. (As it happens, this river is not far from the earliest references to the cards, and the earliest surviving deck.)

In the Knight of Swords beneath the horse's feet, a mountain is shown. See Diagram 32. On it's side is a circle around a dot, symbol of the sun (and hence of the sun wheel, the Mysterion). No one would have imagined it was a diagram showing buried treasure without first understanding the Tarot's secrets, and looking for such a diagram in the knowledge that it must exist. And it was presumed that we would eventually realize the courtiers were Gods, and would know from Homer that Gods were gigantic compared to mortals. The ground beneath the courtiers, unusually rough if seen as clumps of earth beneath a normal person, makes better sense when viewed as mountains beneath the feet of Gods. So there was a mountain where something was hidden, and a circle and a dot marked the spot.

There was a problem with this. What if someone a century later was sitting in the resettled valley playing around with the cards, and he looked up at the mountain above him and saw it was the same as the picture on the cards? The circle and a dot would make him pretty curious. This could lead to the discovery of the cave prematurely. It was intended to be the very last step in understanding the cards, not the first one. Something had to be done. And they knew that we would realize this fact and be ready for it. They gave us another little trick that must be seen through.

Diagram 332: The Knight of Swords

CAVALIER D'ÉPÉE
THE KNIGHT OF SWORDS

There is, of course, more to the business of precisely locating the cave than this picture. This and the name Taro are only the first steps to locating it, and while it narrows the search it is not sufficient to arrive at the exact spot. Naturally the cards' creators were very cautious on a matter of such great importance. And their caution is necessarily echoed here.

A final observation: in legends dating back to the time of local conversion to Christianity, King Arthur and the twelve knights of the round table were said to be buried in a cave beneath a mountain in England, waiting for a time when they are once again needed and wanted. (The Knights of the Round Table are related, in all likelihood, to a British Pagan variation of a God Wheel.)

There are other myths of burial beneath mountains awaiting a time of rebirth, coming from other regions of Europe, and similarly showing pagan elements. Could the British and other legends have been references to the Taro cave, or to other pagan burials elsewhere in the European lands? Or are they are just stories, as we have been accustomed to view them?

The Traditional Interpretations of the Chart Cards

The traditional meanings of each card have undoubtedly been subject to gradual evolution over time, but on the whole they seem remarkably similar to those meanings the symbols in the cards indicate. The traditional meanings of the wheel's positions are included very briefly below. Those who are already familiar with the Tarot may find this useful only in so far as it shows how traditional meanings of individual cards can be related to Mysterion positions, something which is summarized in three charts at the end of the book. Readers in search of greater detail should seek out a traditional book on the subject—the descriptions offered here are intended as little more than a general introduction.

A little has been added to each listing, an extra paragraph *(in italics)* of concepts based on the philosophy the Tarot describes. They are one person's attempt to pull the ideas together and show how they might be reflected in a philosophy of daily living. These should not be given the same weight as the traditional interpretations that precede them: they are really included in a spirit of fun and ought, perhaps, to be ignored if one is in a more formal, investigative mood.

The relationship of the wheel and the chart is provided in three Tables at the end of this list. The first shows the God Wheel as it is currently presumed to be, the second shows the Elemental Wheel, and the third shows the Tarot Wheel.

The organization of the traditional interpretations given below is as follows. The suits are given in the order *Cups, Coins, Swords, Sticks.* Each suit is broken into four Courtiers that are given in order: *Page, King, Queen, Knight.* Each Courtier is broken into six Spokes that appear in order: *Temperance (14), Devil (15), Tower (16), Force (11), Hanged Man (12), Death (13).* This provides a total of 96 positions from the wheel. Thus the first in the list starting below is Cups, Page, Temperance; and the last (at the end of the list) is Sticks, Knight, Death.

Page Cups with Temperance - Love, friendship, and union. A joining together of opposites. (2 cups)

The one who is open to others and to life is not empty, for the world rushes in to fill the inner reaches of the heart. The one who is open is also the one who opens, for all those around tend to respond in kind. In the subtle joy of sharing, all are transformed in ways unseen, and all grow stronger in the secret reaches of their beings.

Page Cups with Devil - Happiness and fulfillment, perhaps as a result of healing. (3 cups).

We need the mysteries of night to prepare the coming of day's revelations, the pain of longing to take the full measure of unity's joy. Wisdom does not come before its portion of sorrow, nor truth before the bitter taste of lies. Embrace at once the whole of the night—already it is dawn.

Page Cups with Tower- Weariness and dissatisfaction with what has been achieved. (4 cups).

Nothing escapes the work of hidden hands. If a position is taken, an enemy materializes and mischief follows. Can you see the beauty in the crumbling stones? Can you smile at sorrow? None but you yourself has given it life.

Page Cups with Force - Energy wasted on daydreams and shortsighted whims when decisive action is called for. (7 cups).

It is not by restraint of longing nor its blind release that wisdom comes. The middle way has no place for dreaming or thoughtless gratification. As changeable and mysterious as the wind, the right pairing of actions and moments can only be found in unadorned simplicity. Hold by releasing, release by holding: let all things move freely, even yourself, as nature dictates. If this seems hard perhaps there is too much effort applied. If not too much, then too little. Play with it!

Page Cups with Hanged Man - Pointlessness and inaction in shifting circumstances. (8 cups).

The weather changes, the wind shifts, and the waters dip and rise as wave meets wave to scatter the jumbled crests and sea-green foam. For the swimmer treading water all is random bobbing, but to the sailor high up his mast and searching out a way to shore, the patterns are revealed. We all must sometimes work to stay afloat: best to have a sensible if flexible goal so the work is met with progress and the rhythms all around are clear.

Page Cups with Death - Wish is granted, goal is attained. (9 cups).

The rains plummet earthward to cover and seep into the welcoming soil. Sometimes nothing can stop the mingling waters: life itself draws them in so the seeds can quicken in the darkness and raise their tender shoots towards the sky. Be grateful and savor life's delight wherever you may find it.

King Of Cups with Temperance - A decline brought on by inconsistency. (ace cups inverted).

The undivided heart cannot be conquered. Yet it often seems as if life itself is a cause of inevitable division. But is it? Unity is found at the eye of the storm where the mind is at peace, setting aside its endless search for greater comfort, greater pleasure, less fear. The undivided heart perceives an undivided world where everything is suddenly open.

King Of Cups with Devil - Weakness threatens success but drive and vision may yet be restored. (low cycle cups epitome inverted).

The fire of vigor is sometimes dampened and the world grows darker, farther away. Struggle is the only hope: struggle for greater clarity, greater understanding, greater control of a mind that stumbles like a sleepwalker lost in the night, a sleeper who cannot find his waking world.

King Of Cups with Tower - A reunion or a return of happiness. (5 cups inverted).

We fight against the things we hate and cling to those we love. What foolishness! Time ends all things naturally, whether we are at war with the wheel or not. Fall when it is time to fall, rise when it is time to rise. If you learn this secret, fortune will favor you—though fools will not know why.

King Of Cups with Force - Thoughts, events, and feelings are oriented towards the future. (6 cups inverted).

There are moments when fate walks beside us, and all around we may sense the shape of things to be. Every action is steeped in significance because, like the seed at the moment when it falls from the tree, every shifting breeze will leave its mark in the days and years to come. If you can walk strong in the knowledge of your good intent you may know the power of a bright destiny, and the quality of greatness may follow in your wake.

King Of Cups with Hanged Man - Restraint proves difficult, but necessary for success. (high cycle cups epitome inverted). *Few things are more difficult than renunciation. The fool's heart in all of us aches for the things that cannot be had. Do you think you can possess? It is illusion. Things come into your hands and fall away again: they come and go. Why not let them? If you hold back your grasping gently and watch—discover the way to see rather than to possess, to be rather than to experience—little by little the effort may fade and watchfulness only remain. And then the bridge is near.*

King Of Cups with Death - Egoism creates strife. (10 cups inverted)
The fool lives his life at war. Grieving the past, fearing the future, restless in his efforts to escape the troublesome present: he lashes out at a world that seems to threaten. But the world is at peace. War is in the heart of the fool—reflecting back at him from a placid world, its calmness smooth as a mirror's face. Peaceful heart, peaceful world.

Queen Of Cups with Temperance - Great fertility of all sorts; spiritual, mental, or physical. (ace of cups).
What a joyous season is spring! From every unwatched corner, from every secret place, the seeds are quickening and the untamed creatures giving birth. Before long they will show their faces in the summer sunshine; the rich green leaves of the rising plants, and the tumbling animal young as they play together under a watchful mother's eye.

Queen Of Cups with Devil - Joyous beginnings which contain the seeds of future unhappiness. Self restraint and flexibility are called for. (low cycle cups epitome).

When the fool achieves his heart's desire he feels like singing: his joy seems unstoppable, his virtue assured. But things embraced often bring trouble. His pockets filled with gold, the fool's possessions may one day weigh him down if he cannot find a way to let them go. Walk lightly through this world: can you learn to enjoy whatever comes in a way that does not breed resistance to change?

Queen Of Cups with Tower - Sorrow or regret brought on by lack of completion or wholeness. (5 cups).

We often live as if we were simple fragments hurling in a straight line through space, but this is not life's way. We live our lives in cycles, spirals even, with every action balanced by another, curling back around ourselves, drawn into the orbit of our central being. Can you embrace the shape of life? It has already embraced you.

Queen Of Cups with Force - The present is strongly influenced by memories or past actions. (6 cups).

Memory is the friend of all sorrow, yesterday is the fool's most beloved source of wealth. Well then, should we flee the past? Time will carry it away for us, and anyway what we flee follows in our hearts. Instead, let us consider calmly the fragments the past has left behind, looking into them in a gentle, playful search for their meaning.

Queen Of Cups with Hanged Man - Longing for what has been lost brings sorrow but integrity can lead to its restoration. (high cycle cups epitome).

Success in life comes when hearts are set on mastering the demands of the present, and not on longing for the dreams that spring like wailing spirits from the past. Feel the splashings of your bubbling heart, follow them back to the single stream that pours pure and strong from the center of your being.

Queen Of Cups with Death - Lasting happiness through peace and virtue. (10 cups).

The heart that is free lives in paradise, in a place of peace that will long outlast the petty, flittering lives of fools. Of all the worlds our minds explore, none compares with the one beyond purposeful creation. The world that has been freed loves the people who have freed her, and like a tender mother guards them all their days.

Knight Of Cups with Temperance - Betrayal or conflicting interest results in separation or strife. (2 cups inverted).

*The selves of others have value equal to the self within. It is not that they **should** have this value: it is that they do. Where there is war, there is fear or miserable longing. Where there is fear or miserable longing, war will soon come. This is why war and strife are the pastimes of the weak, and peace the habit of the strong. Each heart has its reasons for the things it does: reach into others' hearts and feel their reasons from within so that conflict may have a chance to end.*

Knight Of Cups with Devil - Hedonism leading to eventual sorrow. (3 cups inverted).

Pleasure is fine, but it is fleeting. The fool lives to prolong and repeat his pleasures: he lives to fight the truth. Like water thrown on sand, pleasure soon drains away leaving the fool digging in the dust to try and bring it back. Let it go! Wanting and suffering are always found together.

Knight Of Cups with Tower - A new approach to changed goals or circumstance. (4 cups inverted).

When things change it often seems difficult to move with them. In truth, creativity is nothing more than letting go. Our lives are lived in countless little ruts laid down by thought, with all the mud and confinement ruts can bring. Unless we find the means to step out and move across our lives in freedom, we will never know what is possible. Life is a trackless wilderness to the wise: life is freedom.

Knight Of Cups with Force - Back on track through joining of forces. (5 cups inverted).

Water on fire explodes into steam: passion swept by anger will enrage. But if the forces can be brought together in constructive endeavor, the result will be energy. Energy is what drives life. It is the sole addiction of the wise. Make peace in the warring parts of your world: peace is the mother of energy.

Knight Of Cups with Hanged Man - The present is less important than future events which are fast approaching. (6 cups inverted).

Waiting is an art seldom mastered but often sorely needed. To wait means to open yourself to the moments as they move past. It involves neither rejection nor seeking. Most attempt to wait by leaning into the future or, if they anticipate trouble, dragging along in the past. Waiting is done best by letting past and future go free and watching what happens.

Knight Of Cups with Death - Energy is focused through powerful longing. (7 cups inverted).

Desire can be polished, stripped of its lesser manifestations. What is found at the root of all longing? It is emptiness and loneliness. To escape these two, the heart imagines their opposites and gives them the illusory shape of the things in our world that can be seized and held by struggle. Distracted, our energy is drained in the battle and we feel too dull to suffer. For a little while we are half dead, and then the fog of sorrow seeps back again. This is our lives: we chase the shapes and ignore their source so we are never satisfied. Can emptiness and loneliness end? Never by running!

Page Of Coins with Temperance - The beginning of wealth and comfort. (ace of coins).

There is great comfort in the warmth of the family hearth, in the foundation of a warm atmosphere in which to live. The earth can be bountiful for those who are fortunate, and to any if they can master the art of accepting gain and loss without resistance. To maintain what has been well started requires the ability to move and change one's thoughts as though they were gusts of wind through trees, while the heart holds steady as a mountain.

Page Of Coins with Devil - A fleeting taste of wealth and power. (low cycle coins epitome).

Any gain is seen by the wise as a temporary whim of fate since change is inherent in all things. Will you command the earth to hold fast, making her submit to your will? It may seem so to the fool, but have such victories any meaning? The earth does not resist foolishness: in the fullness of time all things revert to form and the dreams of the fool disperse like steam into the sky.

Page Of Coins with Tower - Material loss brought by forces beyond one's control. (5 coins).

The stones of even the greatest castle crumble in time. It is not that walls are too weak or the forces of dissolution are too strong: falling is in the nature of stone. You may spend your life resisting the nature of things, but can you accept, or better yet, can you submit to fate and fall with the stones? It lies within the nature of every earth born child to do so.

Page Of Coins with Force - Generosity and kindliness. (6 coins).

The line that divides us one from another is a false resistance, a cry of pain. The miser counts his money on the sands by the sea, but every time he begins, a new wave breaks and scatters his pretty gold: it sends him scrambling to once more take hold and so begin again while the moments of his life speed forever by. How much better to share the beauty all around, happy in the company of friends!

Page Of Coins with Hanged Man - Humility and patience are the key to future success. (high cycle coins epitome).

Beneath the conqueror's feet Earth lies quiet. He strides about, his footfalls heavy on the stones, and relishes his supremacy. She makes no sound, makes no move. When he is gone she will remain. It is wise to know one's limitations and the importance of waiting for the correct moment to act. Such a person will never inherit a fool's kingdom. Everything comes to the one who waits, steady in the knowledge he is just one among the multitude.

Page Of Coins with Death - Inheritance or abundant good fortune. (10 coins).

How comes the greatest wealth? Not by war but by the way of peace. It cannot be stopped, cannot be prevented. You can enjoy but never own it. It grows out of the shapes of mountains, it rises like a mist from the evening sea. It is in the stars at the moment of becoming and lies as far beyond our touch as the clouds that cross the summer sky. You can no more stop it than change the moments that have fallen away behind you.

King Of Coins with Temperance - Skill and dexterity bring new information. (2 of coins inverted).

How seamless is the union of spirit and flesh, how closely the two work together! Some say the spirit leads, some that it is the body, but in truth neither leads absolutely. They are like two good friends who travel together, the troubles of each shared by the other. Strengthen and hone the body, and you will enhance the mind; enhance the mind, and you will build the body's health.

King Of Coins with Devil - A low standard brings poor results. (3 coins inverted).

Excellence is the noblest goal. It may come to the one who observes to understand perfection in the various occupations of life—who observes to understand perfection, though he knows it can never be acquired. The fool does not know what perfection is. He thinks it is success or orderliness or pleasure, but it is much more subtle than that. Perfection is neither more nor less than taking an action that exactly fits the events of one unique moment in time, then leaving it forever behind. Excellence may come, but not by seeking.

King Of Coins with Tower - Some loss of position through failure to conserve. (4 coins inverted).

Reason must inform passion as passion must invigorate reason, or the result is inevitable confusion and dullness. The fool may be clever, he may be quick, but he cannot outrun the truth. There is no wisdom when proper balance has been lost: seek the subtle path of moderation.

King Of Coins with Force - Badly made choice causes concern. (7 coins inverted). *You cannot restrain the primal forces and expect to grow strong. Like the torrent of a mighty stream resisted, the forces will move and you will move with them, swept along in panic wherever they may dictate. In decision making cultivate peace and leave your petty hopes and fears behind.*

King Of Coins with Hanged Man - Dissipation, laziness and deceit. (8 coins inverted). *Misdirected energy rules the fool's life. First he goes this way, then he goes that: not in free interaction with the world but in fitful pursuit of his confused dreams. Pleasure rules him for he does not know its limitations. He thinks he is always on the verge of something better and cannot understand that his "better" is a dream. Poor thing, he will stop at nothing in his desperate struggle.*

King Of Coins with Death - Dissipation and strife may lead to the loss of something treasured. (9 coins inverted). *Energy is scattered and momentum is lost. If the fragments cannot be united again, there is little hope of return. When the parts of our existence are allowed to war too long, it is not just peace that is lost. There is, in the strife and suffering, the loss of promise too and this is a sign for the end of the fool.*

Queen Of Coins with Temperance - A rocky start to new undertakings leads to some anxious moments. (2 coins). *Life begins in painful struggle and every undertaking must expect the trials of difficult times, especially in its early moments. When the fledglings fall the question comes: will they rise or plummet earthward? The mother watches in love and worry to discover the will of fate, but she knows even so there is little she can do.*

Queen Of Coins with Devil - Skill and effort in a current profession leads to solid success in the future. (3 coins). *Hard work is often needed in this world of effort. To shirk is to lose. Better to cultivate the habit of earnest labor in constant pursuit of greater perfection. Laziness does not pay in any sense, while hard work always pays in some way or other.*

Queen Of Coins with Tower - Great success tainted by a lack of generosity. (4 coins). *he fool lives in a narrow world and cannot see the smallness of it. He does not know that all around and even within is giving and taking. And even when he gives, the fool imagines taking: he sees profit in the exchange. Giving without gaining, taking without gaining, these are the twin secrets of the wise.*

Queen Of Coins with Force - Hard work brings material profit. (7 coins).
The farmer works many days preparing the fields and planting. Even then he weeds and prunes, takes care of the life within his charge to see it growing healthy and strong. This is the time of his spiritual harvest. And when the seasons pass and reaping time comes, he takes rich provisions to see him through to next year's crop. Too often an easy profit gives a small return.

Queen Of Coins with Hanged Man - Openness and curiosity plays a role in achieving a goal. (8 coins).
The earth opens wide to welcome all that comes. She never denies what her children seek, no matter how foolish their desires. The wise are also open, with minds that turn always to the strangeness of each moment, their hearts wide with wonder, their souls forever trembling in the excitement of their surprise. It is a fool that knows anything or nothing: the wise never move beyond the moment of discovery.

Queen Of Coins with Death - Prudent foresight prevents loss. Be prepared for any eventuality. (9 coins).
There are, in the patterns that fill the world with order, the shapes of things to come. So complicated, so hidden from mortal eyes! Not for the wise the agony of fear about the future: their beings are turned instead towards the subtle patterns of the present. In these, each according to his lights, the world to come is sensed.

Knight Of Coins with Temperance - Wealth or security leads to corruption. (ace coins inverted).
The fool longs to be the greatest, the strongest, the best. And when fate grants him ascendancy he rises like a king, gleeful in his triumph, proud in his strength, poised to stay forever at the pinnacle of being. But in the end, like an ant beneath a busy man's foot, the fool lies broken and discarded. In every time and place the fool is maddened by success.

Knight Of Coins with Devil - Materialism brings hardship unless balanced by generosity. (low cycle coins inverted epitome).

The great stone of Sisyphus is made of purest gold. Forever he must push it up the hill, forever see it roll back down. But when others offer to share his burden he bellows with rage and sends them on their way: it is his stone, and he will never let it go. The gateway to freedom for any possessor is the secret of sharing and the secret of letting go.

Knight Of Coins with Tower - Situation improves through hard work and moderation. (5 coins inverted).

Moderation and hard work are never far apart. To measure effort in profit and loss is to cheapen and distort its meaning. Effort guided by wisdom is never misapplied: its value lies in the doing, not in any end result. Even if the result is good, do not confuse it with the doing.

Knight Of Coins with Force - Envy, selfishness and untrustworthiness. (6 coins inverted).

Pride in excessive possession is rooted in envy: the fool takes pleasure in the envy of others because he is never free of envy in himself. Pity the fool! He kicks the stone he tripped over and walks away triumphant. The burden of a petty self is far more terrible than any harm the petty man can do: there is no greater misfortune than the proud possession of one of these.

Knight Of Coins with Hanged Man - Weakness of character. (high cycle coins inverted epitome).

The strong character is undivided, its being sharp and calm. Sometimes weakness passes for strength when greed or fear rules the soul like a tyrant, stamping out the calmer voices. But this is not true strength, for that only comes in the harmony of the portions when the passions are so pure they have no name.

Knight Of Coins with Death - A bad gamble or excessive risk-taking. (10 coins inverted).

Fate is heartless and favors none consistently. Rely on fate and the fall is near. Your heart and mind were made for this task: to discern the patterns of the things to come while remaining in the present, calm and always ready. Deny your human traits their role, trusting in ignorance, and you should still expect the random dictates of events.

Page Of Swords with Temperance - Betrayal and deceit arising out of pettiness. (ace swords inverted)

He who resists the inevitable and rightful play of children is himself a child but does not know it. Set free the rightful child within, for then you will come of age and love will follow. To love is to live among a team of equals, to resist is to live and to die alone. Love can free you from the suffering of pettiness and show your heart a world at peace.

Page Of Swords with Devil - Immorality, especially dishonesty, brings its just rewards (and, perhaps, an improved character). (low cycle swords epitome inverted).

Where the child once lived on make-believe, the adult lives on faith. Children know the games they are playing, but adults rarely do. What is the preference of the fool? First the comfort of apparent truth, second to command others by its power, and third the pride of possessing wisdom. For each of these things the false serves the fool as well or better than what is true, and best of all demands no effort—in the beginning. And fools delight in following fools.

Page Of Swords with Tower - A need for caution and careful progress. Alternatives should be studied painstakingly. (5 swords inverted).

There is always the temptation to settle on an answer, to rest on it and only move on when another answer is offered in its place: stepping stones to keep us dry in the face of life's unending flood. Uncertainty is painful, but there is no other path to the truth. Do you see that the discomfort of not knowing is nothing compared to the misery that comfortable falsehoods bring? Wisdom begins with recognition of the ever-present lies.

Page Of Swords with Force - Change is impossible through inability or unwillingness. (6 swords inverted).

We do not change because it is right to change, nor because we want too, nor because love requires it. We change because we have no choice, because we have seen the truth and the false has therefore ceased to be. Formulas cannot save us: a method is a fence designed to steer us in the right direction, but can fences set us free? Let the fences crumble and look past them: you are already free.

Page Of Swords with Hanged Man - Refusal to address one's own inadequacies. (high cycle swords epitome inverted)

It is unpleasant to know one's weaknesses, so most prefer to avoid seeing them. When a petty fool truly discovers he is petty, his burdens are increased, but in a little while that pettiness is gone. When he denies his nature, the sharpness of the suffering is dulled, but never, not in a thousand lifetimes, could such a person grow in wisdom and be free.

Page Of Swords with Death - Shameful conduct causes misery. (10 swords inverted).

We often imagine that our darkest actions will hide forever from the light of day, but things buried in darkness have a way of pushing themselves back up into the light. Every action has its consequences. Only a fool imagines he can act in secret and thus be free of the seeds he has sown.

King Of Swords with Temperance - Harmonious and fruitful balance through the interaction of opposites. (2 swords).

Embrace the many beautiful sides of your being. Unite the male and female, the weak and strong, the introspective and outgoing, the pleasure loving and the self sacrificing, the thoughtful and the observant, the passionate and the calm. Choose among the qualities and your balance will be destroyed, accept their diversity and you cannot go far wrong. But refrain from doing harm.

King Of Swords with Devil - Strife and struggle are unavoidable. (3 swords).

Violence descends at times, for a season, and then is gone. It whirls around the spirit, scattering thoughts like autumn leaves, and pours out a great flood, sweeping the heart from its rest, to rage within the storm clouds and slashing rain. Lucky is the one who has made himself wise in the season of comfort.

King Of Swords with Tower - Much needed peace and rest after struggles. (4 swords).

Adversity comes, adversity goes. The pattern of change is never-ending and always repeating. There is wisdom in this: suffering shall pass, and happiness too. Can you find the balance between them? It includes them both; it is the cycle. Acceptance or rejection places you on the outer edge, now on this side, now on that, but if you go beyond choice altogether and live with the motions of fate, you will enter the center where the balance is unending.

King Of Swords with Force - Need for a new strategy to overcome difficulties. Deceit may play a role in the situation. (7 swords).

Except for the dying, there is always a way for the one who can find it. No-one will ever restrain the sky. It sends out winds, and the winds send breezes that let out their breaths as silent as mist: and so sky moves the airborne dust in the innermost room. To escape from a world of troubles, change and move as freely as that infinite host, the children of sky.

King Of Swords with Hanged Man - A fundamental conflict brings restraint and difficulties. (8 swords).

There is, in each of us and in all the things we love, a conflict we will meet from life's first moments to its very last. Death seizes the wise in the days of their youth and shakes and torments and never lets them go. It becomes their teacher: it shows them the truth for it alone will play no games. Even the fool must labor perpetually to hide it behind his web of lies. Yet always death will out: everything ends. What then will you do?

King Of Swords with Death - Great suffering and mental anxiety due to anticipated loss. (9 swords).

The fool learns nothing from the changing seasons. He walks in blindness before the light. In the lake he is thirsty, in the desert he drowns: he will not release his suffering for to him it is the source of all riches and power, and true wealth and freedom mean nothing at all. Poor thing! If he would just this once let it all go . . . .

Queen Of Swords with Temperance - Destructiveness and great loss through spite (2 swords inverted).

To hurt another is to hurt your own self: your fear and desire, your pain, may help you ignore the consequences, so too your pretense that the other deserves the harm, but what is done there is also done here. The cost of hurting is a warped mind and heart, and as through the mirror warped, all things you see will have lost their true shape. Dehumanize the victim in your words and feelings, and it is you who truly is debased. Your soul knows this well: a kindness there is a kindness here. Attend the quiet voice!

Queen Of Swords with Devil - Struggles brought on by immoral circumstances or actions. However, good will come of it. (3 swords inverted).

To be human is to invite failure—again and again and again. Things rarely come without a struggle. Best is to do as the situation demands without attachment to the consequences, next best to seek a worthy goal. Do not dwell on troubles, since this will only lend them strength. Instead take strength in doing what is needed. Never stop searching for balance in the face of trouble: the strength to go on is somewhere within.

Queen Of Swords with Tower - Immoral motivation brings defeat, perhaps even the loss of a person or opportunity. (4 swords inverted).

It is easy to lose sight of the urges that drive us, and in doing so, lose sight of the results they will bring. Don't fear the truth: fear its denial! Know why you act and what it means. A good heart works with its fate to build a good life, a bad heart rebels and makes things worse. What is the difference? Misunderstanding!

Queen Of Swords with Force - Things are shaky: constructive action is not possible at present. (7 swords inverted).

It is subtle, the difference between wise restraint and foolish resistance to life's flow. The fool always shouts at the top of his voice: how can he hear the wind in the trees? Calm yourself gently, for the sake of listening, not for profit but to discover. When heart and mind grow peaceful together, the fabric of life itself is subtly transformed.

Queen Of Swords with Hanged Man - Some success, but this is limited due to a failure to grasp favorable opportunities. (8 swords inverted).

For a mind in fragments, consistent effort is rare. Like gusts of wind, thoughts and emotions seize and sweep us about in useless and contradictory effort. How to be whole? Open the parts of yourself to one-another so balance is restored. Do you see the humor in your struggles?

Queen Of Swords with Death - Partial improvement, but this hides a further cause of difficulties. (9 swords inverted).

Even the fool has his moments of balance but his delight at this pleasure causes him to fasten on some false cause. He takes hold and won't let go, warping himself in his urge to prolong. For the fool even moderation is an invitation to excess. How much more so random success?

Knight Of Swords with Temperance - Great power, force, strength, and virility. May indicate fertility or activity. (Ace swords).

Pure energy lies at the core of our persons. The essence of life, it may lie hidden behind layers of resistance or be channeled towards destructive ends, but in the wise its light shines undimmed as alertness and clarity and love: wherever they look, they see.

Knight Of Swords with Devil - A tragic fall or loss of mobility. (low cycle swords epitome).

Energy is susceptible to diversion in each of us. A moment's inattention and our world can change, forced into unbalance by our resistance to nature. Life can be hard, but we must ride it: as the kestrel rides the storm, we must ride the gusts and squalls of life. But if lost for a time, don't give up: the way home is never so far as it seems.

Knight Of Swords with Tower - Near total defeat. Degradation, sorrow and loss. (5 swords).

It is in our natures to lose at times. We don't like that so we fight against our fates and follow the lies that promise us comfort. Defeat is not your enemy, nor suffering, nor death. Ignorance and lies are the things to fear, for they are true disasters. Nothing hurts the wise who see, everything in the end destroys the fool.

Knight Of Swords with Force - Necessary movement or journey. Though beneficial, it involves uncertainties. (6 swords).

Change is an unavoidable aspect of life. We often seek to hold life steady in those situations we prefer, but this is rarely possible for more than a short time, and is only accomplished by setting oneself at war with life itself. Yes, it can be done, but the fools who temporarily manage to achieve their dream of security are usually as near to dead as the living can be.

Knight Of Swords with Hanged Man - Failure to make good on a promise or promising situation through pursuit of self interest. (high cycle swords epitome).

Success comes to those who work, certainly, but the greatest success comes to the wise who do not seek it. Life itself, and nature, seem to take a personal interest in helping those who are free from care. Often the loudest impulse is the most foolish: don't be so quick to act that you fail to act soundly.

Knight Of Swords with Death - Total destruction, especially of a plan or alliance. Lawlessness. (10 swords).

Order and disorder alternate like all the other pairs of opposites. When disorder rules anything can happen, but given the presence of fools, some form of violence is often the result. While the fool thrashes about, hysterically seeking profit or safety or revenge, the wise sit calmly to one side and watch to see what good may be done.

Page Of Sticks with Temperance - Difficulties and a loss of trust, perhaps brought on by others. (2 sticks inverted).

Improbable unions can give rise to confusion but in the blending of opposites there is always great promise. Difference breeds fear among the weak where it gives pleasure to the strong, and so it is dangerous to emphasize difference when strife is in the air. Pity the fool: what seems strange at such moments is often very commonplace—a problem within, and not in the world outside.

Page Of Sticks with Devil - Dishonesty leads to disappointing setbacks. (3 sticks inverted).

You cannot stop the countless liars from distorting things but you can at least be truthful to yourself. A skillful deceiver is nowhere near as dangerous as the listener who prefers lies to the truth. Such people have the power to destroy themselves and others without pity or reason. Though he seems to lead, the deceiver also follows.

Page Of Sticks with Tower - Reality falls short of the ideal. (4 sticks inverted).

An ideal is born of thought and longing. Longing distorts and the ideal is therefore distorted. For this reason the wise have no time for ideals: they turn their attention to the world that is. The fool chases visions into the desert, the wise sit quietly by the river.

Page Of Sticks with Force - Indecision resulting in embarrassment or concern. (7 sticks inverted).

In every situation there are a thousand alternatives and more. How are we ever to choose the one which is best? Set ourselves aside, releasing any center and act as reason and love suggest—just act, and never hesitate. Was the choice wrong? It doesn't matter if we waste no energy in regrets and go on to act again with the changing circumstances. Do not relive your mistakes by ignoring them or failing to let them go. Balance!

Page Of Sticks with Hanged Man - Energy wasted on petty quarreling diminishes success. (8 sticks inverted).

The child plays with paints, dipping his brush in the water to clean it. At first the water is bright with color, but in time it dulls and becomes a murky gray. So it is with our minds and feelings. As children our thoughts are single and our emotions pure: but as we grow and add more and more, the purity is lost. Wisdom loves a quiet and harmonious mind: a mind as supple and fresh and clear as a child's.

Page Of Sticks with Death - Ill health or other obstacles can and must be overcome. (9 sticks inverted).

The body behaves like a projection of mind, and mind like a projection of body: the relationship between the two is seamless. A spirited mind is a spirited body: it cannot guarantee health in the face of life's adversities, but a greater chance of health. Seek harmony between mind and body: it will lend strength and grace to both.

King Of Sticks with Temperance - Creation. A person or enterprise is born. (ace sticks).

The moment of birth is a sacred time, equal in value only to death. The alpha and the omega: each a mirror image of the other and close, too close to be distinguished. The fool believes he has but one birth and one death, for the wise such moments are countless. For them every instant is both birth and death, and life consists of nothing else. To see this directly is to stand on the bridge between the worlds.

King Of Sticks with Devil - Creativity and will power give some success, but lack of balance creates problems. (low cycle sticks epitome).

How do you balance an unwavering will with the flickering flame of creation? The fool's will is based on knowing so it has no place for the uncertainty of creation. In the minds of the wise, will comes from the peace that follows on openness, so for them creation and will are one.

King Of Sticks with Tower - Unavoidable struggle demanding total application and boldness if victory is to be achieved. (5 sticks).

Boldness is another way of describing freedom from the consequences of actions. True freedom from consequence means actions that are pure, stemming from an undivided mind and heart. When you cannot move apart from chaos, at least it is best to take a wider view. Open yourself to the struggle, absorb the whole of it so that you are only one more part, and you may see the way to its end.

Sanctuary of the Gods: Appendix

King Of Sticks with Force - Triumph and/or good news through compromise. (6 sticks).

Good will balances all positions, for all positions have equal weight. Honor often brings the generosity of adversaries for they too may suspect the madness of all struggle. Rigidity and lack of due consideration is a recipe for tension as distance breeds fear and fear breeds war. Better to show good will while there is still the chance for sensible talk. Once a foe is crazed with fear or desire the time for talk is gone. Don't ever be like that yourself!

King Of Sticks with Hanged Man - Success brings corruption and dreams turned sour. (high cycle sticks epitome).

The fool who desires success and doubts his talents suffers. But such a fool is cursed indeed when success visits him: denying his doubts, he cannot be free of them, not being free he tries to fill himself with proofs and protestations of greatness. Warped by vanity and pride, rotted from within by doubt, the successful fool forever loses touch with the world. Only weakness embraced can be left behind.

King Of Sticks with Death - Overburdened by success or excessive dominance. Fighting just to hold on. (10 sticks).

The fool seeks power. And when he gets it he seeks to hold it. But holding power is resisting the flow: the more successful his hold, the more violent his fall. Power breeds rigidity and rigidity ends in destruction. Change is the law. The wise have no love of power, and will never actually accept it, though the fools who live for power will never comprehend restraint.

Queen Of Sticks with Temperance - Deflation: facade crumbles. (ace sticks inverted).

When appearances are at odds with reality, the world lacks balance and chaos will one day intrude. False beauty is lost in the bitter lines of age and events always show the nature of the fool eventually. What is genuine is rare, and lost behind the crowded frauds: it is quiet where they are loud, it is modest where they are brazen. It is beyond price.

Queen Of Sticks with Devil - All is not as it appears. (low cycle sticks epitome inverted).

The well raised dog has fewer brains than the fool, but far more sense. He knows the hearts of those around him by the simplicity of his vision. The fool is clever and complicated: he knows much and sees very little. He cannot tell brass from gold.

Queen Of Sticks with Tower - Intricate deception which can only be overcome by decisiveness and a cool head. (5 sticks inverted).

A subtle fraud can move the world and call the lambs to slaughter. He will pay the price of his work, but this will not preserve his victims. Such an one may only be known by the fool who has other interests, or by the wise who are free from all influence. Look to the source of easy victory, against the one who wants little and offers much.

Queen Of Sticks with Force - Delay and apprehension brought on by unfinished work or incomplete preparation. (6 sticks inverted).

Everything in its place and time can smooth much trouble from life. We put off things to avoid an unpleasant effort, but such things follow us around with every passing day, growing stronger all the time. In the end the pain of avoidance exceeds the pain of the work itself. Better to do a thing without granting yourself the freedom to delay: no choice, no pain.

Queen Of Sticks with Hanged Man - Energy squandered, opportunities missed. (high cycle sticks epitome inverted).

A good fate is almost indistinguishable from a bad one. Some ride the path of misfortune down to disaster, some mount the steps of good luck up to triumph. The difference lies in what is done more often than in what was offered. Better to live in a world of opportunities than one of dangers. A word of caution to the "lucky": avoid pride since it brings ignorance and distortion and these may compel an early fall.

Queen Of Sticks with Death - Intrigue and deception bring harm to the innocent. (10 sticks inverted).

Scoundrels do not win: they are losers from the first. To harm another for one's own profit is a sign of sickness. Human justice may never catch the deceiver, but there is a natural justice that operates behind the warped and empty mirrors of the liar's mind.

Knight Of Sticks with Temperance - Leadership and initiative bring success. (2 sticks).

True leaders take no great pleasure in their role, and they do not place themselves above even the lowest of the team. Leadership is a task like any other and involves no special license to entertain one's childish insecurities by asserting power over others. Only the weakling could think of doing such a thing. Pity him his life.

Knight Of Sticks with Devil - Application of creativity and initiative bring practical rewards. (3 sticks).

There is no harm in profit if it is not bought at a fool's price: do no harm or you will suffer the penalty. In the labors of this world the wise have some advantages. They do not need as much, they get things more easily, and they are not burdened by the nightmare of possession when things come into their hands and later leave them.

Knight Of Sticks with Tower - Prosperity arising from a balanced effort. A rich and peaceful interval. (4 sticks).

When the forces of the self come together in harmony the result is music that can charm the tender harvest from the soil. Moderation is like a dance with you the dancer and fate your partner: at first you stumble, awkward in the newness of the steps, but after mastery, form can be forgotten behind the subtlety of easy invention. Always enjoying, relaxed, engaged, the master dancer invents the moments of his life like the carefree child that plays a happy game.

Knight Of Sticks with Force - Success through a courageous battle against overwhelming odds. (7 sticks).

A virtue of the wise is that they cannot be beaten. Drowning, for example, and sinking beneath the sea, their eyes see the beauty in the trail of bubbles that rise toward the sunlight on the surface above. For the undefeatable, if victory is possible, it will come.

Knight Of Sticks with Hanged Man - Encouraging travel or communication. However, travel may be too rapid and information received may be exaggerated. Caution is essential. (8 sticks).

There is no benefit in hurry either in thought or in deed. For each person in every situation the proper pace is different, but in every case to go too fast or slow results in error and war against the true nature of events. For the wise there is no significant difference between great speed and slowness: all that matters is timing.

Knight Of Sticks with Death - Concern about the general flow of events and the integrity of one's forces. The calm before the storm. (9 sticks).

Sensitive to the patterns of the moment, you will know the likelihood of events soon to come. Prepare well in the moments of peace for violence and disorder will always return, and then, though wisdom is possible, it is far more difficult and arduous. Beware of delay: time is not a barrier as the fool believes. In truth, the moment of reckoning is now.

The Relationship of the Chart Cards With the Three Wheels

In order to associate the wheel's positions with the appropriate traditional meanings accompanying the cards, the following three Tables may be helpful. The first relates chart meanings to the God Wheel, the second to the Elemental Wheel, and the third to the Tarot Wheel. These can be used with the traditional meanings provided in the previous section.

Table 24: (Tentative) God Wheel Positions on the Chart—*Italicized positions are Inverse Chart cards*

Ares	Sw 1	Epitome	Sw 5	Sw 6	Epitome	Sw 10
Zeus	Sw 2	Sw 3	Sw 4	Sw 7	Sw 8	Sw 9
Herakles	*Sw 1*	*Epitome*	*Sw 5*	*Sw 6*	*Epitome*	*Sw 10*
Hera	*Sw 2*	*Sw 3*	*Sw 4*	*Sw 7*	*Sw 8*	*Sw 9*
Apollo	St 2	St 3	St 4	St 7	St 8	St 9
Dionysos	St 1	Epitome	St 5	St 6	Epitome	St 10
Hestia	*St 2*	*St 3*	*St 4*	*St 7*	*St 8*	*St 9*
Athena	*St 1*	*Epitome*	*St 5*	*St 6*	*Epitome*	*St 10*
Hermes	*Cn 1*	*Epitome*	*Cn 5*	*Cn 6*	*Epitome*	*Cn 10*
Hades	Cn 2	Cn 3	Cn 4	Cn 7	Cn 8	Cn 9
Hephestos	Cn 1	Epitome	Cn 5	Cn 6	Epitome	Cn 10
Demeter	Cn 2	Cn 3	Cn 4	Cn 7	Cn 8	Cn 9
Poseidon	*Cp 1*	*Epitome*	*Cp 5*	*Cp 6*	*Epitome*	*Cp 10*
Artemis	*Cp 2*	*Cp 3*	*Cp 4*	*Cp 7*	*Cp 8*	*Cp 9*
Aphrodite	Cp 2	Cp 3	Cp 4	Cp 7	Cp 8	Cp 9
Persephone	Cp 1	Epitome	Cp 5	Cp 6	Epitome	Cp 10
	Peace	Order	Justice	Peace	Order	Justice
	Material Cycle			Spiritual Cycle		

Table 25: Elemental Wheel Positions on the Chart—*Italicized positions are Inverse Chart cards.*

Air (Air)	Sw 1	Epitome	Sw 5	Sw 6	Epitome	Sw 10
Air (Fire)	Sw 2	Sw 3	Sw 4	Sw 7	Sw 8	Sw 9
Air (Earth)	*Sw 1*	*Epitome*	*Sw 5*	*Sw 6*	*Epitome*	*Sw 10*
Air (Water)	*Sw 2*	*Sw 3*	*Sw 4*	*Sw 7*	*Sw 8*	*Sw 9*
Fire (Air)	St 2	St 3	St 4	St 7	St 8	St 9
Fire (Fire)	St 1	Epitome	St 5	St 6	Epitome	St 10
Fire (Earth)	*St 2*	*St 3*	*St 4*	*St 7*	*St 8*	*St 9*
Fire (Water)	*St 1*	*Epitome*	*St 5*	*St 6*	*Epitome*	*St 10*
Earth (Air)	*Cn 1*	Epitome	*Cn 5*	*Cn 6*	Epitome	*Cn 10*
Earth (Fire)	*Cn 2*	*Cn 3*	*Cn 4*	*Cn 7*	*Cn 8*	*Cn 9*
Earth (Earth)	Cn 1	Epitome	Cn 5	Cn 6	Epitome	Cn 10
Earth (Water)	Cn 2	Cn 3	Cn 4	Cn 7	Cn 8	Cn 9
Water (Air)	*Cp 1*	*Epitome*	*Cp 5*	*Cp 6*	*Epitome*	*Cp 10*
Water (Fire)	*Cp 2*	*Cp 3*	*Cp 4*	*Cp 7*	*Cp 8*	*Cp 9*
Water (Earth)	Cp 2	Cp 3	Cp 4	Cp 7	Cp 8	Cp 9
Water (Water)	Cp 1	Epitome	Cp 5	Cp 6	Epitome	Cp 10
	Begin	Middle	End	Begin	Middle	End
		Low Cycle			High Cycle	

Note:

The order of the elemental influences in this and the two other charts is the same as the vertical order of the elements on the chart. Thus the elements progress (bottom to top) from water to earth to fire to air. The elemental influences have the same order within each element.

An interesting pattern shows itself: the epitomes for each cycle on the quintessential chart are surrounded on three sides by the other cards of the quintessential chart. The inverse epitomes are surrounded on three sides by the other cards of the inverse chart. This calls to mind the gibbet of the Hanged Man (12), which takes the same configuration, surrounding him on 3 sides; of the stars in The Star (17); and of the apparatus in The Wheel (10). In each case the central component is surrounded on three sides by the other components of the spread.

Table 26: **Tarot Wheel Positions on the Chart**— *Italicized positions are Inverse Chart cards.*

Sw, Knight	Sw 1	Epitome	Sw 5	Sw 6	Epitome	Sw 10
Sw, King	Sw 2	Sw 3	Sw 4	Sw 7	Sw 8	Sw 9
Sw, Page	*Sw 1*	*Epitome*	*Sw 5*	*Sw 6*	*Epitome*	*Sw 10*
Sw, Queen	*Sw 2*	*Sw 3*	*Sw 4*	*Sw 7*	*Sw 8*	*Sw 9*
St, Knight	St 2	St 3	St 4	St 7	St 8	St 9
St, King	St 1	Epitome	St 5	St 6	Epitome	St 10
St, Page	*St 2*	*St 3*	*St 4*	*St 7*	*St 8*	*St 9*
St, Queen	*St 1*	*Epitome*	*St 5*	*St 6*	*Epitome*	*St 10*
Cn, Knight	*Cn 1*	*Epitome*	*Cn 5*	*Cn 6*	*Epitome*	*Cn 10*
Cn, King	*Cn 2*	*Cn 3*	*Cn 4*	*Cn 7*	*Cn 8*	*Cn 9*
Cn, Page	Cn 1	Epitome	Cn 5	Cn 6	Epitome	Cn 10
Cn, Queen	Cn 2	Cn 3	Cn 4	Cn 7	Cn 8	Cn 9
Cp, King	*Cp 1*	*Epitome*	*Cp 5*	*Cp 6*	*Epitome*	*Cp 10*
Cp, Knight	*Cp 2*	*Cp 3*	*Cp 4*	*Cp 7*	*Cp 8*	*Cp 9*
Cp, Page	Cp 2	Cp 3	Cp 4	Cp 7	Cp 8	Cp 9
Cp, Queen	Cp 1	Epitome	Cp 5	Cp 6	Epitome	Cp 10
	Temp	Devil	Tower	Force	H-Man	Death
	Low Spokes			High Spokes		

Index

Author's Note:

Interested readers of this edition who have access to the Net are invited to write to me with any comments or questions they might have. I will try to answer each letter personally. The address is:
- **nathancate@icqmail.com**

There is also a web page with comments, links and additional information. If readers are interested a forum may be added in the future.
- **http://nathancate.tripod.com**

I look forward to hearing from you.

Nathan Cate

Aknowledgements:
Cover art by Paul Chatenay. My thanks to France Cartes for permission to use their facsimile of the original deck. Fonts: Times New Roman; Felix Titling; Cobleigh Titling Caps; Chaucer; Caesar Open.

ISBN 1552124479

9 781552 124475